Emerson's Daughters

EMERSON'S DAUGHTERS

ELLEN TUCKER EMERSON, EDITH EMERSON FORBES, AND THEIR FAMILY LEGACY

KATE CULKIN

University of Massachusetts Press
AMHERST AND BOSTON

Copyright © 2025 by University of Massachusetts Press
All rights reserved

ISBN 978-1-62534-876-0 (paper); 877-7 (hardcover)

Designed by Deste Relyea
Set in Adobe Jenson Pro
Printed and bound by Books International, Inc.

Cover design by adam b. bohannon
Cover photo, unknown photographer,
Seated Portrait of Edith Emerson Forbes and Ellen Tucker Emerson c. 1858.
Courtesy Houghton Library Repository, Harvard.

Library of Congress Cataloging-in-Publication Data
A catalog record for this book is available from the Library of Congress.

British Library Cataloguing-in-Publication Data
A catalog record for this book is available from the British Library.

TO ANDERS AND SONJA

"I no longer canter along the ground as in old days, but skip from tree-top to tree-top, and everyone says, 'we understand it: she has a nephew & a niece.'"

—Ellen Tucker Emerson

CONTENTS

List of Illustrations ix
Acknowledgments xi
Preface xiii
Abbreviations xix

CHAPTER ONE
"Our Beautiful Poem Edith, and Our Excellent Prose Ellen"
(1839–1851)   1

CHAPTER TWO
"We Each Have Something Good and Both Want All"
(1852–1860)   21

CHAPTER THREE
"I Was Never So Carried Away by Anything Before"
(1861–1865)   41

CHAPTER FOUR
"I Wrote for Myself as Well as for You"
(1865–1872)   62

CHAPTER FIVE
"What a Mercy It Is That There are Women in the World to Arrange for Men"
(1872–1875)   88

CHAPTER SIX
"The Power of Our Life Has Been Very Kind"
(1876–1882)   107

CHAPTER SEVEN
"In Reading a Biography I Always Like Best the Personal Parts"
(1882–1892)   126

CHAPTER EIGHT
"Be Content to Remain a Dove and Let Me Remain a Cat"
(1882–1892)   158

CHAPTER NINE
"Thank You Over and Over for Helping Me Out"
(1898–1903)   170

CHAPTER TEN
"I Am So Glad We Had So Much Time Together"
(1904–1909)   190

CHAPTER ELEVEN
"Wherever She Went, She Planted a Garden"
(1909–1929)   206

Notes   225
Frequently Cited Sources   275
Index   277

Illustrations follow page 148

LIST OF ILLUSTRATIONS

Figure 1. Sketch of Ellen and Edith, c. 1847.
Figure 2. Ellen and Edith, c. 1858.
Figure 3. Edith and Will Forbes, 1865.
Figure 4. Edith with her first five children, c. 1876.
Figure 5. Ellen and Edith with Ellen's donkey, 1876 or after.
Figure 6. The Emerson and Forbes families in front of Bush, 1879.
Figure 7. Ellen with Edward's family in Antibes, France, 1893 or 1894.
Figure 8. Edith in a garden, c. 1910.
Figure 9. Ellen standing with a crutch, c. 1900.
Figure 10. Edith on the SS *Kleist*, 1910.

ACKNOWLEDGMENTS

This book has taken a long time, but it would have taken even longer without the support of the many people and institutions who made my work possible. I am grateful for this opportunity to thank them.

I found homes in the Society for the Study of American Women Writers and the Women Writing Women's Lives seminar near the beginning of this project. These communities of writers and scholars committed to feminist life-writing projects have kept me going when I felt myself losing faith. More recently the Oxford Life-Writing Centre and the Biography and Memoir Masters program at the CUNY Graduate Center have given me two more communities of writers that have stretched the way I think about telling someone's story. Special thanks to Phyllis Cole, Christopher Hanlon, Megan Marshall, and Sandra Harbert Petrulionis, who have been so generous in their encouragement and advice, and Sydney Stern and Sarah Covington, for their leadership of WWWL and BAM, respectively.

Friends from college, graduate school, my jobs at Bronx Community College and the CUNY Graduate Center, and other stops along the way have been invaluable for their companionship, advice, hospitality, and humor. Thank you to Chad Anderson, Patricia Auspos, Michelle Bergland, Maks Bondarenko, Jeremy Braddock, John Dahl, Ladi Dell'aira, Stephen Duncan, Chris Duva, Carol Faulkner, Jordi Getman Eraso, Jennifer Hart, Linda Grasso, Susan Goodier, Ben Judson, Prithi Kanakamedala, Mara Lazda, Emily Locke, Patti Loughlin, Cielo Lutino, Etta Madden, Kari Miller, Jenny Mondesir, Marnie Mueller, Victoria Olsen, Julia Paulk, Andy Peach, Kristen Perreault, James Polchin, Ursula Pontieri, Tammy Rose, Tamar Rothenberg, Julia Rodas, Katherine Stebbins, Andy Sturm, John Thomas, Greg Tulonen, Patricia Valenti, and Tiffany Wayne.

This project originated in a workshop in Concord sponsored by the National Endowment for the Humanities and the Community College Humanities

Association. Funding from the Houghton Library, the Massachusetts Historical Society, the Robert and Ina Caro Travel Award from BIO, the CUNY Chancellor's Research Award, and the Professional Staff Congress-City University of New York Research Award has been invaluable.

This book could not exist without the archivists at the Houghton Library and the Massachusetts Historical Society. Anke Voss and Jessie Hopper at the Concord Free Public Library William Monroe Special Collections created a welcoming space and shared their extraordinary collections and knowledge of the town and its people, as did their revered predecessor Leslie Wilson.

I thank the team at the University of Massachusetts Press for allowing this book to move from my computer to the world. Thank you to Matt Becker, Mary Dougherty, Chelsey Harris, Ben Kimball, Kellye McBride, and Sally Nichols, as well as the anonymous reviewers who made this work stronger.

At the beginning of the pandemic, both sides of my sprawling family started text chains which continue to this day. They are twenty-first century versions of the Emersons' journal letters, binding us together across states and countries and lifting us all up. Frank and Trish Culkin, my parents, passed on their love of history and biography to me, leading to this book. I thank them, as well as my own sister Sarah Mengshol, and my brother-in-law, Andy Mengshol.

Neilson Abeel Jr. has been by my side throughout this project, whether we were in pandemic isolation, tracing Ellen's path in the Azores, or exploring Oxford pubs. His patience and optimism have been critical. I thank Audrey, Dugan, Josephine, Bagheera, Shorty, Gavin, and Veronica for their company when I was unfit for human companionship.

One of my favorite things about Ellen and Edith is the seriousness with which they took the job of aunt. I take it seriously too. This book is dedicated to my nephew and niece, Anders and Sonja. They make it easy to be a proud aunt.

PREFACE

This is a biography of a sisterhood. Ellen Tucker Emerson (1839–1909) and Edith Emerson Forbes (1841–1929) were born in Concord, Massachusetts two-and-a-half years apart to Lidian Jackson and the famous philosopher Ralph Waldo Emerson. Their lives took very different shapes. Ellen remained in the family home and took on the day-to-day tasks of serving as her father's secretary and caring for their aging parents, while also being deeply involved in the Unitarian Church. Edith married William Hathaway Forbes, of the wealthy Forbes family, moved to Milton, Massachusetts, and had eight children. Beneath those surface differences, however, was a deep connection that lasted until Ellen's death. They first forged a partnership in their adolescence, as their father called on them to run the house as their mother withdrew from the task. This book traces the evolution of that partnership, as they responded to the demands and opportunities created by their father's career and fame; their loving, intellectual, and at times difficult mother; historic developments, such as the Civil War, suffrage, and American imperialism; personal ones, including the births of Edith's children and opportunities to travel and study abroad; and inevitable ones, brought on by the aging process of their parents and themselves. In doing so, it not only highlights this particular set of sisters' relationship but also the importance of sisterhood in the nineteenth century more generally, as well as the role of single women in families and the ways in which older women negotiated their lives.

This is a biography of a correspondence. Phyllis Cole and Jana Argersinger have argued, when examining female contributions to transcendentalism, that "writing originally intended for private audiences merits consideration equally with public writing."[1] Ellen and Edith's letters to one another formed a bedrock of their connection. In a time and a community that took letter writing seriously, the Emerson sisters were celebrated as correspondents. Their younger brother Edward praised Ellen's ability to create "instantaneous domestic pictures, verisimilitudinous memory-tales"; Elizabeth Hoar described Edith's letters as "a perfect store house of the lovely stories."[2] When they travelled, friends and family back home waited for their letters to arrive as if they were a serialized novel. The sisters wrote two types of letters. Their "journal letters," often sent when one was traveling, consist of detailed logs of their day, including what they did, who they saw, what they ate and wore, what they read, and their reactions to it all. Their "business" letters address everything from their father's work and their parent's health to renovations on Bush, the Emerson family home, and suggestions for Christmas gifts. The letters evidence the workings of their partnership, as well as the tensions brought on by fundamental differences in their personalities and the adjustments required through major life events, such as Edith's marriage and their parents' deaths. These documents had practical purposes, but they also served as a creative and intellectual outlet for both sisters, who strove to improve their letter-writing. They critiqued one another's missives, praising a good turn of phrase and lively tale or demanding more information or context. These letters are invaluable for the social and cultural history they contain, and the biographical details they reveal, but they are more than primary sources. They are the glue of a sisterhood and, taken together, an impressive body of written work.

This is not a book about self-reliance. Ralph Waldo Emerson famously stressed the importance of the independent mind, writing "the great man is he who in the midst of the crowd keeps with perfect sweetness the independence of solitude."[3] Laurence Buell notes, even as his ideas evolved, "he remained convinced that the key to reform of any sort lay in the activation of the individual person first, not the group first."[4] Waldo's ability to express such ideas in print and tour the country to deliver them in person was dependent on his daughters' labor as housekeepers, secretaries, accountants, and hostesses to the streams of visitors who came to speak to the "great man." Later, as his memory failed, they took on the role as editors for his final publications. By saying this is not a book about self-reliance, I do not mean only to point out that irony (or hypocrisy). Ellen and Edith thrived on lives intentionally built on connection and community. They not only supported their father and mother, but each other. Ellen's dedication to her role as aunt was critical to Edith's children; Edith intervened when she saw the work at Bush was overwhelming Ellen. They also committed themselves to community in other parts of their lives. Ellen valued opportunities to serve on committees for the Concord school board and Unitarian organizations, cherishing the "delight of the common work."⁵ Edith, even with eight children, found ways to forge bonds with and assist a wide circle of young people. They also fed their intellectual lives through communal activities, such as reading Dante and *The Odyssey* with Elizabeth Hoar, along with the exchange of ideas in their correspondence with one another and with other friends and relatives. In this, they were like many of their female peers. As James Perrin Warren notes, "for most women in nineteenth century America, eloquence develops from the give-and-take of conversation, not from the oracular utterances of a divinely inspired speaker."⁶

This is a family history of two women who understood the importance of preserving family history, including the lives of their female ancestors, and shaping the legacy of their family. Ellen inherited the mantel of historian of the Emersons from her great-aunt Mary Moody Emerson, who gave her a cache of family documents and some of her almanacs. She not only preserved that material, but wrote the short manuscripts "What I Can Remember of Stories of Our Ancestors Told Me by Aunt Mary Moody Emerson" and "What I Can Remember About Father," as well as the longer *The Life of Lidian Jackson Emerson*, a biography of her mother.⁷ Edith ensured her father's correspondence with Thomas Carlyle was collected and preserved.⁸ She paid equal attention to her sister's letters, editing them to produce a seventeen-volume typescript, as well as typescripts of her own letters from the two "round-the-world" trips she took in the early twentieth century.⁹ Both sisters, and their brother Edward, encouraged James Elliot Cabot to include more emphasis on Waldo's family in his *A Memoir of Ralph Waldo Emerson*. They succeeded to some extent, but Edith felt the book did not go far enough. If it were ever to be revised, she hoped Lidian would be featured more, as it "would be only justice to her to stop hiding her."¹⁰

This is a book about imperfect women who, along with the good they did, held racist and sexist opinions. While they were certainly not alone in the 1800s, it is far from enough to say they were products of their time. This is particularly true of the Emerson sisters, who were introduced early to transcendentalists and reformers who challenged prevailing ideas about white supremacy and women's roles. Ellen refused to support women's suffrage, even as she was elected to the Concord school committee; Edith distained Irish immigrants, expressed racist ideas about Black Americans, and supported American imperialism in the Philippines. Examining how Ellen and Edith arrived at their beliefs and maintained them makes up part of the ongoing project of understanding how the limited goals of privileged white female reformers help shore up existing racist, sexist power structures even as they fought to make room for themselves. As Kyla Schuller argues, "White feminist objectives work to liberate privileged women while keeping other structures of injustice intact."[11]

This is a work of recovery that builds on critical scholarship about Ralph Waldo Emerson and women's contributions to Concord and transcendentalism. It is perhaps surprising that the sisters need "recovering" as, unlike many nineteenth-century women, there is an abundance of material by and about them in major archives and in published material, including Ralph Waldo Emerson's letters and journals. Despite this documentary evidence, until recently Ellen and Edith have made only infrequent appearances in works on Emerson, although Carlos Baker does provide an insightful portrait of Ellen's role in taking care of the house and her parents.[12] The one major, and still relatively recent, exception is scholarship on Ellen's relationship with Waldo as his memory failed in the last two decades of his life. Nancy Simmons, Joseph Thomas, Ronald Bosco, Joel Myerson, and Christopher Hanlon explore the workings of what Simmons named the "Emerson factory," focusing on Ellen's collaboration with James Elliot Cabot to edit and publish Waldo's lectures in the 1870s and 1880s.[13] Ellen is so critical to the understanding of this period that Bosco notes "the narrative of Emerson's later life in this Historical Introduction" to the 2010 edition of *Letters and Social Aims* "is nearly as much about Ellen as it is about her father."[14] While providing valuable biographical context, Bosco, along with Myerson, ultimately casts Ellen's and Cabot's contributions in a negative light, the reason the editors have decided to exclude the majority of Waldo's publications from 1870 forward from the Emerson canon.[15] Hanlon, alternatively, sees Ellen's contributions as leading to a "more communitarian, cooperative account of intellectual life than Emerson previously emphasized in his published work."[16] Rather than depicting her contributions as a challenge to Emerson scholarship, in other words, Hanlon sees Ellen as a writer and editor whose efforts should be respected on their own terms.

The scholarship on Ellen's collaboration is invaluable, particularly in its detailed analysis of the different hands involved in editing the lecture manuscripts and the influence of the collaboration, but it is only part of the story. While Bosco and Myerson do address Edith's work on the poetry anthology *Parnassus*, and Robert Habich notes the collective work of all three Emerson siblings with Cabot to stress the importance of family in his biography, the depth of Ellen's partnership with Edith is not considered.[17] This work, moreover and understandably, also only depicts Ellen's and to a small extent Edith's contributions within the context of their father's work. That is a critical story, but the significance of Ellen's and Edith's lives goes beyond the support they gave their famous father.

During the same period in which the sisters have become more prominent in Emerson scholarship, there has also been a flowering of work on the contributions of women to the transcendentalist circle. Scholars including Phyllis Cole, Sandra Harbert Petrulionis, Noelle Baker, Tiffany Wayne, Jana L. Argersinger, John Matteson, Megan Marshall, Kathleen Lawrence, Patricia Valenti, and Sarah Wider have expanded the understanding of women's roles among the transcendentalists. They have recovered and analyzed these women's contributions as authors, correspondents, editors, and publishers, as well as the influence of female family members on the thinking, careers, and activism of male transcendentalists.[18] Critical contributions to an understanding of Ellen's life appear in this work. Cole provides insight into Ellen's inheriting the family documents from Mary Moody Emerson, and Petrulionis examines her commitment to abolition. Delores Bird Carpenter's *Selected Letters of Lidian Jackson Emerson* and her introduction to and annotation of Ellen's biography of her mother are a major contribution to understanding the significance of the Emerson women.[19] Beyond specific information about Ellen and Edith, this body of scholarship, with its careful attention to the ways in which women participated in transcendentalism and the communities of intellectual exchange and support women created beyond university classrooms, lecture podiums, and pulpits, has been central to my ability to understand the significance of Ellen's and Edith's lives both in terms of their work for their father and beyond that labor.

This biography is possible because of the care the Emerson and Forbes families took in preserving and making available Ellen and Edith's correspondence. The descendants of Edith and her brother Edward carried the mantle of family history forward. Raymond Emerson and Edward Waldo Forbes, in particular, ensured the survival of these documents, with Edward keeping many in his office safe at the Fogg Museum at Harvard. The J. M. Forbes Family Archives Committee donated the materials that make up Edith Emerson Forbes and William Hathaway Forbes Papers to the Massachusetts Historical Society beginning in 1995. Edith E. W. Gregg, Edward Emerson's granddaughter, published the two-volume *The Letters of Ellen Tucker Emerson* in 1983; this edition was included in the digital *North American Women's Letters and Diaries* in 2001.[20] Gregg's family donated her collection of Ellen's letters to the Houghton Library at Harvard University in 2003. The Ellen Tucker Emerson Collection, it is important to note, includes a significant number of unpublished letters, and the original of some of the letters Gregg included are significantly longer than the published version. The Houghton also holds the majority of Ralph Waldo Emerson's correspondence and the rest of the family's archival material, donated primarily by the Ralph Waldo Emerson Memorial Association; the holdings include two sets of the typescripts of Ellen's correspondence. The American Antiquarian Society holds the Ellen Tucker Emerson Letters, one hundred letters written by Ellen between 1863 and 1865; these are available as a digital edition through Alexander Street Press.[21] Edward's great-granddaughter, also Ellen Emerson, donated the Edward Waldo Emerson and Emerson Family Papers to the Concord Free Public Library in 2019; the library also holds a set of the typescripts of Ellen's letters. Together, these collections make up an extraordinarily rich set of materials, which allow the story of Ellen and Edith's partnership to be told.

ABBREVIATIONS

Names of People

JEC—James Elliot Cabot
ETE—Ellen Tucker Emerson
EWE—Edward Waldo Emerson
LJE—Lidian Jackson Emerson
RWE—Ralph Waldo Emerson
EEF—Edith Emerson Forbes
WHF—William Hathaway Forbes

Emerson's Daughters

CHAPTER ONE

"Our Beautiful Poem Edith, and Our Excellent Prose Ellen"

(1839–1851)

"A daughter was born to us this morning at eight o'clock," Ralph Waldo Emerson wrote to family intimate Elizabeth Hoar on February 24, 1839. Lidian, his wife, "did not expect it quite yet: but the little soul was impatient for light and action... she seems to be a fair round perfect child & very well contented with her new estate."[1] Lidian had named her Ellen, he added. The mother soon shooed everyone out of the room, wrapped the little girl in an eiderdown, laid her in front of the fire, and listened to the "cunning little baby-noises" from her bed.[2]

Ellen, whose full name was Ellen Tucker Emerson, was born into a loving, intelligent, complex family. She joined a two-year old brother. Her parents, by the time Ellen arrived, had already lived rich lives and were entering their second—or even third—acts. Her very name reflected an earlier stage. Her father, who since college had gone by Waldo, first married Ellen Louisa Tucker. She died of tuberculosis less than two years after their 1829 wedding. He mourned her so deeply that fourteen months after she was buried, he opened her coffin to convince himself she was really gone.[3] Now, "Lidian, who magnanimously makes my gods her gods, calls the babe Ellen," Waldo wrote in his journal.[4] Lidian later told her daughter that she had chosen the name so the first Ellen Tucker Emerson would be her "guardian angel," as reading her letters had convinced Lidian that her predecessor was "a holy creature, truly religious."[5] If a ghost is going to haunt your marriage, perhaps she thought, it is wise to give her a seat at the table.

By the time Lidian wrapped Ellen in the eiderdown, many of the iconic moments in Waldo's biography had passed. He had been born in Boston on May 25, 1803, to Ruth Haskins and William Emerson, a minister. William had died in 1811, leaving Ruth with an infant daughter, who died in 1814, and five sons and plunging the family into economic instability. To support her children, Ruth took in boarders, moving frequently, and sold her husband's possessions, including his books.[6] Waldo had graduated from Harvard at the age of eighteen with a middling academic record, been a schoolteacher, returned to Harvard to train for the ministry, and been appointed minister at the Second Church in Boston. He had married and mourned the first Ellen Tucker Emerson and opened her coffin. He had delivered his Lord's Supper sermon, in which he rejected communion, left his post as a minister, and traveled to Europe, where he met Thomas Carlyle. He had published his first book, *Nature*, in 1836, the same year the Transcendental Club began to meet; rather than a formal organization, it, in James Elliot Cabot's words, consisted of the "occasional meetings of a changing body of liberal thinkers, agreeing in nothing but their liberalism," who defined themselves against the conservative thinkers in Harvard University and the Unitarian church.[7] He had delivered the American Scholar address in 1837 and the Divinity School address, which led to his estrangement from Harvard for decades, in 1838. His beloved brothers Edward and Charles had died, in 1834 and 1836, respectively, and he had befriended Margaret Fuller, Bronson Alcott, and Henry David Thoreau. In 1834, he had moved to Concord, Massachusetts, boarding with his step-grandfather Ezra Ripley in the Old Manse. He had written the "Concord Hymn"; its famous opening—"By the rude bridge that arched the flood / Their flag to April's breeze unfurled"—was sung at the dedication of a monument commemorating the Battle of Concord in 1837.[8] Waldo was only thirty-six, but he had already started on one life and then charted a different course.[9]

Lidian's life also had taken a dramatic shift of direction. In an era when the average age of marriage for a white woman was approximately twenty-two, she was about to turn thirty-three when she wed Waldo.[10] Born on September 20, 1802, to Lucy Cotton and Charles Jackson, a merchant, she was a proud daughter of Plymouth, Massachusetts, where her ancestors had arrived in 1620. Her name was then Lydia. Her parents died within two months of one another in 1818, and she and her older sister Lucy and younger brother Charles shuttled between family members, with the sisters attending Mrs. McKeige's school in Jamaica Plain for a year. Lydia, intelligent and intense, developed strict habits, resolving to "go to bed at 1:00 and to rise at 5:00, to read only religious material until 11:00 each morning, to augment practicing her dancing steps with jumping rope and jumping over a low stool, to always leave the table hungry, to take cold baths, to wear loose clothing, and to sleep with the windows of her room open."[11] She lived a life of the mind, forming a Reading Society with her friends, attending lectures, and studying German.

Lydia was both deeply religious and deeply skeptical of organized religion. As a girl, the "church seemed to her anything but good and attractive" and useless in answering the question "What is Truth," which haunted her. She knew, according to Ellen, "what the Church undertook to be, and seeing it so false, she could not hope for any help in that direction and never, all her life long, entertained for a moment the thought of joining it."[12] While she never felt compelled to join the church, her faith underwent a transformation around 1826. "Christ was shown to me," she later told her children. "Life was henceforth transfigured for her. The Bible was a new book. Its words now expressed what she felt and what she knew at first hand," Ellen recalled in the biography she wrote of her mother.[13]

In 1832, Lydia believed she had settled into what would be her life. She moved into her Aunt Sarah Squire Cotton's house, where she set up her room just as she wanted, purchasing furniture, wallpaper, and a rug. Her life "was exactly to her taste, she loved perfection and exquisite order and with her small space of one room to care for and her command of her own time she was able to have it," Ellen concluded.[14] Lydia told her brother she had established herself "in the character I have always intended formally to assume in due time—that of an Old Maid."[15]

Lydia Jackson's encounter with Ralph Waldo Emerson knocked her plan to be an old maid in Plymouth off course. She first heard him preach at Boston's Twelfth Congregation Church on Chambers Street around 1833, so rapt that her body ached from straining forward to take in every word.[16] In 1834, Waldo preached and lectured in Plymouth. After his first sermon, one of Lydia's friends asked her, "I wanted to know how you felt to hear your very own ideas preached. What Mr. Emerson said was just what you always say."[17] Lydia herself was "so lifted to higher thoughts by the sermon that she hurried out of church as soon as it was over and home lest anyone should speak to her."[18] Soon after they were introduced, Lydia was shocked to have a vision of herself dressed as a bride moving towards Waldo. On January 26, 1835, another vision of Waldo's face appeared before her. The following day, his proposal arrived by mail. "I have immense desire that you should love me, and that I might live with you always . . . I am persuaded that I address one so in love with what I love, so conscious with me of the everlasting principles, and seeking the presence of the common Father through means so like, that no remoteness of condition could much separate us, and that an affection founded on such a basis, cannot alter," he wrote.[19] Lydia, despite her qualms about leaving the life which so suited her and after explaining to Waldo that she did not know if she would be a good housewife, said yes.

Waldo and Lydia married on September 14, 1835, in the Winslow House. Two days earlier, Waldo had delivered a "Historical Discourse" on Concord at the town's bicentennial celebration, then left for Plymouth on the thirteenth.[20] It was not the first nor the last time the history of the Emersons and the history of Concord would be entwined. The couple returned to Concord, to the two-story white house Waldo had purchased on Lexington Road, sitting on two and a half acres of land just outside the town center.[21] Called Bush, it would be their home for the rest of their lives. Lydia had lobbied to stay in Plymouth, where she already owned a house and was deeply enmeshed in the community where her family had lived for over two hundred years. But Waldo would not live there.

Waldo had resided in Concord for less than a year, but it already felt like home. Like Lydia to Plymouth, he had historic connections to his chosen town. Waldo's ancestor Peter Bulkeley established Concord in 1635 as the first inland Puritan settlement, becoming the founding minister of First Parish the following year.[22] William Emerson, Bulkeley's great grandson and Waldo's grandfather, was also the minister at First Parish and built the Old Manse, from which he watched the Battle of Concord on April 19, 1775. He was appointed chaplain of the Minuteman and died of dysentery in 1776 in Vermont; Ezra Ripley, his replacement at the First Parish, married his widow, Phebe Bliss Emerson.[23] By the time Waldo proposed to Lidian, his mother and brother Charles were also living in Concord. The landscape, moreover, called to him. "Plymouth is streets," Waldo argued, and he needed a "sunset, a forest, a snow storm, a certain river view" to be inspired.[24] Lydia acquiesced and arrived in her new town with a new name as well as a new address. Waldo had re-christened her Lidian.[25]

The Concord in which the newlyweds settled had a population of a little over 2,000 people and fewer than 400 households.[26] Located at the confluence of the Concord, Assabet, and Sudbury Rivers, the Algonquian name for the area was Musketaquid, meaning "grassy plain." By 1835, the Industrial Revolution had reached Concord, which came to be known for the pencils produced there, including those made by the Thoreaus.[27] There was still a great deal of agriculture, however, and with Walden Pond and its woods near Bush, Waldo could easily find the sunsets, forest walks, and river views he craved. Boston was eighteen miles and a four-hour coach ride away. Concord was not yet famed for its nineteenth-century literary community, just starting to assemble with Waldo's purchase of Bush. The Battle of Concord was also not the claim to fame it came to be; the town skirmished with nearby Lexington over which could take credit for the first battle in the American Revolution and thus take supremacy in the historical narrative beginning to gel sixty years after the conflict. Waldo's "Concord Hymn" had been part of his town's campaign. As the county seat of Middlesex County, it had more political activity and influence than many other small communities, but it was still a quiet town.

As Waldo and Lidian built their life in Concord, the intellectual spark that drew these two brilliant, unconventional people together remained. An intellectual spark, however, cannot run or fund a household. As Lidian had suspected, she did not love being a housewife, even if she loved being Waldo's spouse. It was much harder to achieve the perfect order she craved in a big drafty home, with small children and visitors streaming through to pay homage to her increasingly famous husband, than in one room. "Her house must be handsome, and her children must be well dressed, these were necessities to Mother's mind," Ellen remembered.[28] She despaired when she could not achieve her perfect standards, such as the day she spent "moaning on the sofa" after failing in her "housekeeperly ambition" to clean the house from top to bottom.[29]

Lidian, moreover, was living with her mother-in-law. Waldo built an addition for his brother Charles and his fiancé Elizabeth Hoar to live in once they married, turning the L-shaped house into a square. When Charles died in 1836 while visiting his brother William in New York, before his marriage could take place, Waldo's mother Ruth moved in instead; Waldo informed Lidian of the decision in a letter written the day after Charles' funeral.[30] Elizabeth Hoar remained in the family circle, with the Emerson children calling her "Aunt Lizzy." Ruth and Elizabeth offered companionship and helping hands to Lidian, and Lidian and Elizabeth became friends. Lidian and Ruth, however, at times butted heads over differences about child rearing and religion. And Elizabeth's close relationships with Ruth, whom she called Mama, and Waldo's aunt Mary Moody Emerson could make Lidian feel left out in her own home.[31]

There were financial tensions as well. Lidian received $600 a year from her inheritance, and Waldo received $1,200 annually from his first wife's share of her family estate, but family commitments ate up much of the money. Waldo helped support his mother, his brother Charles until his death, his developmentally-delayed brother Bulkeley, and Mary Moody Emerson, and he lent money to his brother William. Lidian, before her engagement, had pledged much of her income to her sister Lucy and her children, after Lucy's husband abandoned them amidst a business scandal.[32] Waldo and Lidian agreed about supporting loved ones, but they squabbled over how to spend the remaining money. Waldo wanted to scrimp and save, while Lidian aimed to purchase the best they could afford and thought "it absurd to go without important conveniences," even as a financial panic in 1837 made them "poorer than before."[33]

Despite these tensions, Bush was a happy place as the family expanded and Waldo's career climbed to new heights. The deaths of parents had upended Lidian's and Waldo's childhoods, and they valued a stable home. They both, moreover, adored children. Lidian gave birth to their son Waldo on October 30, 1836. "I know not which grows—improves—most rapidly—his physical or spiritual nature. We are never weary of watching the beautiful phenomenon," Lidian wrote to Elizabeth Peabody, the writer and educator, when he was two months old."[34] When Ellen arrived two years later, the parents enjoyed watching the relationship between the siblings grow, as well as tracking their intellectual, moral, and physical development. "I think you can help little Ellen a great deal, by bringing her playthings & playing with her," Waldo advised his namesake in 1840.[35] On November 22, 1841, he arrived home to find Lidian had given birth to their second daughter, three weeks earlier than expected. Young Waldo was fascinated by the new baby, but Ellen had "retired to bed without knowing what riches the day had brought her."[36] It was an inauspicious start to a sisterhood that would be central to Edith's and Ellen's lives.

Edith went unnamed for over a month. Waldo began to refer to her as Lidian, but the adult Lidian resisted. Even once they decided on Edith, Lidian wrote to her sister, "I shall not let the Lidian be added to her name it spoils it."[37] Her resistance suggests, while she complied with Waldo's change of her name, she resented it. She took a stand for her daughter that she did not take for herself.

While the family grew, so did Waldo's reputation as a writer and lecturer. New England's expanding lyceum circuit became his main public speaking outlet and an important source of income. Speaking engagements were important to his writing process; Emerson depended "on the 'congenial' responses from his lecture audiences to his continuing work on a lecture which might bring it to the level of polish required of a printed essay."[38] In 1840, he extended his reach, lecturing in New York for the first time. The Transcendental Club stopped meeting, but *The Dial*, a journal founded in 1840, became an outlet for the loose band of thinkers and writers; first edited by Fuller, Waldo took over beginning in 1842. The month after Edith's birth, Waldo published *Essays: First Series*, which included "Self-Reliance," "Circles," and "History." While receiving mixed reviews, the volume helped establish Waldo's international reputation; in essays that offer "an exploration ... of finding the universal meaning in our individual (yet common) experiences and a rejection of materialism that see no connection, no meaning, no trace of humanity in our individual experiences," Waldo was laying out the ideas that he would revisit throughout his writing life.[39]

These developments were important milestones in Waldo's career. They also marked what Lidian witheringly named "Transcendental Times."[40] Lidian herself thrived on intellectually stimulating conversation. "While she talks, she thinks; and you see it ... she is a soaring transcendentalist," the painter Sarah Freeman Clarke wrote to her brother James Freeman Clarke, a theologian and a member of the Transcendental Club.[41] Lidian, however, resented the work required to entertain the people who trooped through Bush to meet with her husband. Ellen later remembered her mother's recipe book from that time was a "confirmation to the impression I received from her that she had a goodly family to cook for. All the receipts begin 'take 3 pts. sour milk,' or 'beat 2 doz. eggs.'"[42] Lidian complained to her children, "Poor Grandma and I were never half through eating our meat before the whole company of Grahamites, having bolted their potatoes and squash and beans, were sitting looking hungrily for the pudding."[43] Ellen, familiar with her mother's dramatic tendencies, as an adult wondered if she had exaggerated. Elizabeth Hoar, however, confirmed Lidian's view, labeling the visitors "Waldo's menagerie" and recalling "a feeling of horror" when she saw him in the parlor surrounded by a circle of "men with long beards—men with bare feet."[44] It is both touching and telling that Ellen, writing five decades later, felt compelled to offer evidence, in the form of the recipe book and Elizabeth Hoar's testimony, that backed up her mother's memories.

Lidian did not just grumble about the visitors to her children years later. At the height of "Transcendental Times," she took a "sheet of square paper" and wrote "Transcendental Bible," a piercing parody, while visiting her brother. She then came home and "read it to the circle in the parlour."[45] After a series of biting aphorisms, the "Bible" concludes, "If you have refused all sympathy, to the sorrowful, all pity and aid to the sick, all toleration to the infirm of character, if you have condemned the unintellectual and loathed such sinners as have discovered want of intellect by their sin, then you are a perfect specimen of Humanity!"[46] She had no more tolerance for hypocrisy and sanctimonious pontificating in the transcendentalist circle than she did in the church. Ellen claimed her father always laughed when he remembered the screed, calling it a "good squib."[47] But Lidian's anger is palpable, even as the "squib" also provides evidence of her humor and intelligence.

There were other reasons for Lidian's anger. When Waldo gave up "family prayers" soon after their marriage, it became "clear to her that he was not a Christian in her sense of the word, and it was a most bitter discovery," Ellen recorded.[48] In 1841, Lidian herself underwent another religious metamorphosis. She "waked to a sense that she had been losing—had lost—that blessed nearness to God in which she had lived so long.... Her religion was still the foundation of her life, but its fulnes [sic] was gone."[49] As she cared for three young children and an avalanche of guests, she had neither the husband nor the God she thought were hers when she moved to Bush.

Waldo's intense friendships with other women, particularly Margaret Fuller and the poet Caroline Sturgis, were another source of tension. "It is not too much to say that in the early 1840s Emerson was living emotionally, though not physically, in what would now be called an open marriage," Waldo's biographer Robert Richardson explains.[50] Waldo drew boundaries with Fuller when she pushed for an even closer connection in 1840.[51] His deep relationship with Sturgis continued for years, however. Kathy Lawrence argues, even though their intense correspondence declined after she married William Tappan in 1847, "Sturgis remained a constant in Emerson's life as an example of human possibility" who provided him "with an alternative source of emotional support" and "enabled him to believe in the real existence of a new kind of American individual that he believed was essential to the spiritual health of the Republic."[52] Making matters more complicated, Lidian valued these women for intellectual companionship herself, including attending some of Fuller's Conversations, the courses for women she ran in Boston beginning in 1839.[53] Her responsibilities meant, however, that Lidian only had so much time to foster the intellectual connection Waldo had found in her and now sought elsewhere.

Amid this marital tension, a bomb exploded. "My boy, my boy is gone," Waldo wailed to Mary Moody Emerson on January 28, 1842. Young Waldo had died of scarlet fever the day before. "My darling & the world's wonderful child, for never in my own or another family have I seen anything comparable, has fled out of my arms like a dream," the heartbroken father continued.[54] Ellen also had scarlet fever, and that night Lidian had both her daughters in her bed. "I was left alone with the baby—and Ellen (who was to take her father's place in my bed that I might take care of her), grief desolating grief came over me like a flood—and I feared that the charm of earthly life was forever destroyed."[55] As three-month old Edith peered around the bedstead, Lidian hoped she saw "the angel Waldo smiling to his innocent little sister still able to see him."[56]

The heartbroken family stuttered along. Within weeks, Waldo was off lecturing in Providence and New York, driven to fill the family coffers as City Bank had failed to yield a dividend in October.[57] "How art thou, Sad wifey? Have the clouds yet broken and let in the sunlight?" he wrote from Rhode Island in February. "Edith and Ellen shall love you well & fill your time, and the remembrances of the Angel shall drive you to sublime thoughts," he suggested.[58] In Concord, Elizabeth Hoar helped Lidian, who did take comfort in her girls even as she struggled to find meaning in her son's death. Ellen was "very pleasant and very wise."[59] Edith was a "bright little lamb," who was "wise enough for four months though she has seen but three."[60]

Waldo died just weeks before Ellen's third birthday. Unlike Edith, she was old enough to feel the loss and remember how the family changed. She searched for her missing sibling out the window and envisioned him "picking flowers" in "the Angels' garden."[61] Through his own desolation, her father recognized her pain, even as she acted out and tried "papa's patience." "Poor little affectionate Ellen.... Babes need babes to quiet each other & and keep them from tormenting the Universe and she has lost as much as we in her irreparable Brother," Waldo wrote to his own brother William.[62]

For Ellen, the framing of young Waldo as the incomparable, irreplaceable "world's wonderful child" sent to uplift humanity was as devastating as the loss of his companionship. In the biography she wrote of her mother in the 1890s, Ellen cast a stone at one mourner. "Miss Margaret Fuller had felt like Father that this child had been born to lift higher his fellow men. She could not get over it that he had died and I was left," Ellen remembered.[63] In a carefully crafted narrative that stresses how the community gathered around the Emersons in their grief, her decision to include it, over five decades later, suggests the depth of her pain. By pointing her finger at Fuller, however, she deflects blame from others. Her father's words and actions sent a similar message, if more subtly; there is no record of his saying he regretted Ellen's survival, but he repeatedly depicted his lost son as a child like no other in private and published writings. Almost a year after the death, Lidian wrote her husband of "the sayings & performances of that 'small mercy' Ellen—for which you sometimes pray to be thankful," suggesting they "may seem marvelous in the distance."[64] In a culture that valued eldest children over younger ones and sons over daughters, Ellen absorbed the message that her survival was cold comfort to the adults who mourned her brother. Smart and observant, she listened to what people in Bush said; as an adult, she read her parents' letters and saw the message anew. Ellen's complex emotions around young Waldo's death, combined with the nineteenth-century conflation of ideas about femininity, nurturing, and sacrifice, primed her to commit herself to caregiving and prove her worth to her family throughout her life.

"The miseries" is how the "small mercy" later referred to the years between young Waldo's death and Edith's third birthday, when her younger sister grew "big enough to play with."[65] Lidian also saw that period as a dark time, lamenting in 1845 that she had "lost Ellen's most important years." The parents' grief did haunt the household. In the same letter Lidian worried that she had lost Ellen's critical years, she described a dream in which she found her son alive in his tomb and carried him home.[66] Waldo denied the depth of his feelings in his essay "Experience," claiming, "The only thing grief has taught me, is to know how shallow it is."[67] But he did in fact mourn deeply, pouring his feelings into the poem "Threnody." He writes of "The gracious boy, who did adorn / The world whereinto he was born" and staggers under the knowledge that the child "has disappeared from the Day's eye."[68]

Waldo and Lidian's mourning put even more strain on their tense union. Margaret Fuller's visit at the end of the summer of 1842, less than a year after their son died, marked a low point. Lidian, caring for a toddler and an infant, had a fever and swollen face from a dental crisis. Waldo and Margaret went on long walks, where he spelled out a dismal view of marriage. As Fuller remembered it, he said, "Ask any woman whether her aim in this union is to further the genius of her husband; and she will say yes, but her conduct will always be to claim a devotion day by day that will be injurious to him, if he yields."[69] Lidian frequently burst into tears and confessed to Fuller the challenges of being the wife in an imperfect marriage, rather than a muse and intellectual companion.[70] Edith, at nineteen months, may have sensed her mother's distress; keen-eyed Ellen, three-and-a-half years old, certainly noticed her mother's tears.

Differing ideas about sickness also caused tension. Waldo, according to Richardson, "hated sickness, talk of sickness, and letters about sickness."[71] On the other hand, "the sick were to Mother's mind rather enthroned," Ellen explained.[72] The difference was not just philosophical. Lidian was often ill, with the border between anxiety and depression and physical frailty porous. In July 1843, for instance, after being a "miserable dyspeptic" all summer, she went to Plymouth alone to "mend her strength and spirt" for three weeks; Ruth Emerson and Elizabeth Hoar cared for the girls.[73] Waldo worried about Lidian but found her illnesses frustrating and inconvenient. He was opposed to the idea of servants, but when his wife was exhausted he had to hire housekeepers and at one point a governess; in 1846, all the Emersons squeezed into a few rooms in Bush so a housekeeper and her four children could occupy the rest of the house.[74]

Lidian and Waldo's correspondence during these difficult years, however, provides a more complex picture than mere misery. There is ample evidence of them engaged with and cherishing, in Lidian's words, "our beautiful poem Edith, and our excellent prose Ellen."[75] The girls visited their father's study to show off the bugs they captured, doted on the "red bird" Lidian gave Edith, ate corn popped by Thoreau over their fire, and loved when their cousins visited.[76] Lidian conceded to Ellen's wish for a birthday party when she turned four, inviting over twenty children. She "set a long table, with a big vase of Ever greens in the centre and the sugar-plum—& currant cakes, ginger-bread-cakes, soda-biscuit, figs, sliced apple & oranges" which "made a great show that pleased the babies well." Lilian's stress that "*We all* had a fine time" was an attempt to ease her husband's concerns about her state of mind.[77] That year Ellen, Lidian reported with pride, came "forward fast in reading," and memorized the letter Waldo sent her while on tour.[78] She, in turn, dictated letters to her mother to send to "Papa." "I am a good girl—sometimes I am naughty and sometimes I am good," she declared. She added, "Edie is a good girl, I want you should come home," the last sentence a frequent refrain in her missives to her father.[79]

1844 was a significant year for the residents of Bush, and not just because that was the year Edith grew "big enough to play with." Lidian gave birth to Edward Waldo Emerson on July 10, 1844. Lidian was almost forty-two and with Edward's arrival the family was complete. She hoped that, while she had lost a critical portion of Ellen's childhood, she could be there for Edith and Edward. "The other children are of softer material as well as of more tender years. Perhaps I can yet take care of them," she wrote.[80] Edith later remembered "the comfort of Edward's birth" as part of the "returning cheerfulness after Waldo's death."[81] 1844 also brought milestones in Waldo's career. He published *Essays: Second Series*, which met with wide praise and "can be seen as a turning point for Emerson toward applying his philosophical tenants to the political."[82] *The Dial*, meanwhile, came to an end; during his two years as editor, the journal had consumed precious time and energy, and Waldo was happy to bid the responsibility goodbye.[83] Just a month before Edward's birth, the Fitchburg railroad began running four trains a day from Concord and Charlestown, which cut the trip from Boston from four hours to one, at two-thirds the cost, and integrated Concord into the larger world in a new way. This change boosted Concord's economic prospects and made it easier for Waldo to travel for lectures.[84] In April, Waldo delivered his first major anti-slavery speech, trailing after Lidian who had joined the Concord Female Anti-Slavery Society in 1837 and, along with other female abolitionists, pressured him to use his influence for the cause.[85] Finally, Waldo purchased fourteen acres of land on Walden Pond, where in 1845 Thoreau would build his cabin and go to live for over two years.[86]

Ellen was only two-and-a-half years older than Edith, but young Waldo's death and their parents' subsequent despair exaggerated the age gap. Ellen took on a maternal attitude toward her younger sister and brother that never fully disappeared, addressing them as her children in letters well into adulthood. Once Edward moved from his mother's bed to the crib, all three children slept in the nursery until Ellen was ten, with Edith and Ellen sharing a trundle bed. "It is beautiful to see how happy these children are—how they entertain, teach, and love one another," Lidian wrote to Waldo in 1848.[87] Decades later, Edward reminisced to Edith about how "delightfully" Ellen's "imagination and spirits invented amusements, while drawing ours out of doors," when they were young.[88] At times, however, Ellen's influence over her younger siblings could unsettle them. When Edith was seven, she worriedly asked her mother if she would go to "Heaven or to a place full of fire and chains." Her vision of the afterlife came from Ellen, who had informed her that some people were "in chains and fire" in hell; Lidian assured her that "a little girl who wished to be good as much as she did, might expect something very different of her Heavenly Father—from fire and chains."[89]

Waldo and Lidian veered apart on religious matters, but they were perhaps surprisingly in concert on the religious education of their children. They agreed on keeping of the sabbath, though "not with the old severity."[90] As Waldo mused in his journal, "The Sabbath is my best debt to the Past and binds me to some gratitude still."[91] Beyond that, Lidian was in charge. She took the children to First Parish and had them learn a hymn each Sunday, gathered in her or their grandmother's room. As they grew older, they had to learn two, then three hymns, and were eventually given "the task of writing out the idea of the hymn."[92] Lidian read them "interesting Bible stories" with an emphasis on the

Old Testament, which she felt was "the children's part of the Bible."[93] Their father, Edward remembered, "was glad to have us go to church. His own attitude in the matter was, that it was only a question for each person where the best church was—in the solitary wood, the chamber, the talk with a serious friend, or in hearing the preacher."[94]

The hymns learned, Waldo took over at four o'clock on Sundays, escorting the children on a walk. This was the spiritual education the author of "Nature" wanted to share with his children—his version of the "best church." They might head toward Walden Pond, or the nearby cliffs, or "old clearings, cellar-holes, and wild-apple orchards of the Estabook country."[95] After their little legs made the five-mile round trip to Baker Farm, a proud Waldo pronounced, "you will deserve to have an entrance into the sacred order of Professors of Walking. Very few belong to it." He told Ellen, Edith, and Edward "the name of every flower" and showed them "how the ferns came up crozier-shaped, and how their seeds were on their leaves, how pretty the milk-weed seeds . . . were with the silver fish inside, & how the gold finches surrounded the thistles."[96] He pointed out rare plants to which Thoreau or the poet Ellery Channing had introduced him and recited poetry to his small companions as they rambled. The three Emerson children each wrote reminiscences in which these walks feature prominently. "We all remember . . . when we ran down the hills with him it was a fearful delight it seemed as if we shouldn't be able to keep our feet but we always did and the speed was something glorious," Ellen wrote.[97] She grew up to be deeply religious and deeply curious about the faith of others, while remaining a Unitarian, Edith attended Unitarian churches throughout her life, and Edward rejected organized religion. But their connection to nature, and particularly the Concord landscape, fostered on these Sabbath tromps remained with them all.

The Emersons took great interest in their children's intellectual as well as spiritual development. Their early education took place with tutors and family members in Bush and at small schools often run by friends of the family. Ruth Emerson taught her grandchildren to read, sitting with them by the fire in her room. Ellen was always a step ahead of Edith, of course. In 1843, she attended a school run by Ellen Fuller Channing, Margaret Fuller's sister who had married Ellery Channing in 1841. Waldo reported, "Ellen learns very well at Mrs. Channing's school, and Edie very well at Nature's."[98] When Ellen attended a school led by Abba Prescott, a member of a local abolitionist family, at age five, her father pronounced, "it is time for you to begin Latin," and gave her *Cleveland's Latin Grammar*.[99] In 1846 and 1847, all three Emersons joined the Alcott sisters and the Channing children in the Emersons' barn to be taught by Sophia Foord (sometimes known as Ford), who had earlier worked as first the Alcotts' and then the Emersons' governess. Louisa May Alcott remembered, "Many a wise lesson she gave us there, though kindergartens were as yet unknown; many a flower-hunt with Thoreau for our guide, many a Sunday service where my father acted as chaplain, and endless revels where young and old played together, while illustrious faces smiled on."[100] Anna Alcott, Louisa's older sister, took over in the summer of 1847; the following summer Louisa, then fifteen, served as the teacher, delighting Ellen with fairy stories.[101] Jane Whiting, another Concord abolitionist, was the Emerson children's teacher from November 1848 through February 1850 at a school Waldo helped organize. Ellen later remembered, "Miss Whiting's scholars thought she was a perfect teacher."[102] Helen Maynard, a Concord native who had graduated from the State Normal School in West Newton, Massachusetts replaced her in August 1850.[103]

The Emerson children's education, as the range of teachers indicates, took place in the context of the community Waldo helped to build in Concord. While ideas about communal work and labor reform intrigued him intellectually, Waldo's vision of community centered around the warm hearth of Bush and the streets of Concord. Turning down the invitation to join Brook Farm, the utopian farming community founded in 1841, he explained his "present position has even greater advantages than yours would offer me for testing my improvements in those small private parties into which men are all set off already throughout the world." He also argued, "surely I need not sell my house & remove my family to Newton in order to make the experiment of labor and self help."[104] He would run his experiments from his home.

Waldo's growing reputation, and sometimes financial support, attracted writers and intellectuals. Henry David Thoreau, born and raised in Concord, met Waldo after graduating from Harvard in 1837. Part of Waldo's plans for creating a domestic utopia included "ameliorating or abolishing in my house the condition of hired menial service"; to this end, in April 1841, Thoreau agreed to serve as Bush's live-in handyman, for which he received board and access to the library, and was seen as more of a family member than a servant.[105] Margaret Fuller considered moving to Concord, and, although that plan did not come to pass, she made several extended visits. The Alcott family moved to the area in 1840; they lived in Hillside, just up Lexington Road from Bush, from 1845 through 1852, and purchased Orchard House, even closer to Bush, in 1857. Unlike Thoreau, they turned down Waldo's invitation to live with them, but the families were close.[106] The Hawthornes, who had started their marriage in the Old Manse in 1842, purchased Hillside from the Alcotts in 1852, rechristening it Wayside. They left for England in 1853, but were again in Wayside by 1860; the family owned the home until 1869, although Nathaniel died in 1864.[107] Una, Rose, and Julian Hawthorne and Anna, Elizabeth, May, and Louisa Alcott were Ellen, Edith, and Edward's friends, with stories of apple bobbing at Orchard House and dancing with Julian dotting the Emerson siblings' letters. The community Waldo helped create was not just one of intellectual conversation and philosophical publications, but also of raucous childhood games and lessons in the barn.

While life in Bush stabilized after Edward's birth, 1847 brought another disruption. Waldo, feeling frustrated and uninspired, accepted an invitation to lecture in England. When he sailed on October 5, he planned to be abroad for up to a year, an unfathomable length of time for his three young children—now eight, five (almost six), and three. Lidian was not left to care for Ellen, Edith, and Edward by herself. While Ruth Emerson went to live with her son William in New York, Lidian's sister Lucy moved in, joining two servants, Abby and Almira Stevens. One more person would be in residence. Lidian asked Thoreau—a favorite of hers and the children and familiar with the household from his earlier stay—to live with them while Waldo was away. He packed up his cabin on Walden Pond in September, settling into the house the day Waldo sailed.[108]

"Either he had great tact and skill in managing us and keeping our spirits and play within bounds, or else he became a child in sympathy with us, for I do not remember a check or reproof from him, no matter how noisy we were," Edith wrote in her remembrance of Thoreau.[109] He saw each child for who they were. "Ellen and I have a good understanding—I appreciate her genuineness," he reported to Waldo. Edith, already envisioning her adult life, told him, "after her fashion: 'By & by, I shall grow up to be a woman, and then I shall remember how you exercised me.'" Of Edward, he said, "He is a good companion for me." His final conclusion regarding the children was one Waldo would cherish: "I am glad that we are all natives of Concord."[110] Waldo may have been less happy with Thoreau's report that Edward had asked, "Mr. Thoreau—will you be my father?"[111]

Thoreau was responsible for more than child's play. In Waldo's absence, he was the landscaper and gardener, handyman, tutor to Edward while the girls went to Abby Alcott's school, and, coordinating with Lidian, Waldo's secretary and accountant. The last was a trying job given the family's tight budget, requiring regular meetings with Abel Adams, Waldo's financial advisor.[112] For all its challenges, Waldo and Thoreau himself were somewhat surprised by how quickly he adjusted from his quiet existence at Walden to life in a busy household. "It is a little like joining a community, this life, to a hermit such as I... it is good for society, and I don't regret my transient nor my permanent share in it," Thoreau wrote in December.[113] This sense of community was what Waldo envisioned in his utopian ideas about the home, but he was not there to participate. And he likely had not included his children replacing him with another father figure as part of that vision.

In November, Lidian snuggled Edward on her lap with Edith and Ellen sitting next to her at her "worktable." Thus ensconced, she transcribed her children's thoughts for their father. Edward requested, "Write to Father I am a good Boy." Edith wanted to make sure her father knew "I know how to read, almost. I can read off fast—all but a few words." Ellen contributed, "I want to know if he thinks I'd better keep a journal & write it out of school."[114] There were also reports of Edith's birthday gifts and requests for toys, but Edith's and Ellen's emphasis on reading and writing suggest they had internalized the importance of these activities to their family. For the rest of his time abroad, Waldo received updates on the children's intellectual growth from Lidian, Thoreau, and Edith and Ellen themselves, as they wrote or dictated letters to their father to bridge the distance. Ellen composed poems and did begin her journal, while Edith memorized three nursery rhymes by Jane Taylor "of her own choosing" and taught one to Edward.[115]

It is significant that the Emersons recorded these developments in letters. Ellen, Edith, and Edward grew up in a family, a community, and a culture that increasingly valued correspondence. The Emerson siblings' childhoods coincided with an explosion of American letter writing. In 1840, the year after Ellen's birth, Americans sent 27 million letters through the post office; by 1860, the number was close to 161 million.[116] Just as postal services became more reliable and postage rates dropped, developments including industrialization, urbanization, immigration, and a growing population led to family separations. Americans, in turn, began to conceive "of themselves as correspondents who could maintain regular, not occasional, relations with people they could not see" and the ability to write letters emerged as a critical social skill.[117] Correspondence became a way to bind together families and friends across growing geographical distance, as "the letter was the primary form of communication for individuals separated by the nation's extensive geography, a primacy grounded in mass literacy and the building of a vast postal network."[118] Letters were passed among friends and family eager for news; reading letters aloud to friends and families was often a social activity.[119] Authors, moreover, used their correspondence to shape their ideas and their public personas, with the transcendentalist circle, in particular, focusing its intellectual energy on correspondence. As Robert Hudspeth explains, "The Transcendentalists distinguished themselves in the genre because their letters were often an art, one that explored their most abiding concern: to know the nature of the human self that was individual and yet part of a larger, divine reality."[120]

Their father's long absence immersed the Emerson children into this world of letters and thus into the epic Emerson family correspondence, astonishing—even in an era so focused on letters—for its breadth and quality. While Ellen had dictated earlier letters to Waldo, the trip drew Edith and even little Edward into the activity. Waldo appreciated their efforts, deeming his daughters "matchless writers."[121] Edith's "printed letter" was a "treasure," but of course the "short pert good notes" of Ellen, almost three years older, were more sophisticated.[122] Waldo bid Thoreau to give his praise to Ellen "who by speech, and now by letter, I find old enough to be companionable" and joked she "must be my own secretary directly."[123] The jest proved prophetic.

It was letter writing, or the inability to write letters, that forced Thoreau to spill a secret. Lidian collapsed in January, spending much of the next two months confined to her room. She and Thoreau entered a conspiracy of silence, not wanting to worry Waldo. Exhausted, she propped herself up in bed to make sure her correspondence with her husband continued; he would know something was amiss if her letters stopped. Six weeks into her siege, Thoreau broke the news. Lidian was plagued with "jaundice, accompanied with *constant nausea*, which makes life intolerable to her," he reported to Waldo.[124] He had to send the news because Lidian could not. Her doctor threatened to withhold treatment if she continued to tax herself by writing letters. Thoreau assured Waldo the children "were quite well and full of spirits."[125] He read to them each night and did his best to keep anxiety at bay for his young charges. But having one parent out of the country and the other confined to her bed was unsettling, and likely contributed to the sense of responsibility Ellen, as the older sister and elder daughter, felt to care for her family throughout her life.

Lidian had never dismissed Thoreau as one of her Transcendental Bible's hypocrites. Ten months of running a home together brought them closer. Thoreau's biographer Laura Dassow Walls explains, "Henry's own love for Lidian was certainly the deepest he ever knew for a woman to whom he was not related."[126] Their choice not to inform Waldo of Lidian's illness immediately indicates how close they had grown, along with Lidian's sense that her illnesses were a burden to her husband. While Thoreau reported to Waldo "Lidian and I make very good housekeepers," however, they were in some ways just playing house.[127] They could have daily interaction and emotional intimacy, without the long-term pressures of a marriage, raising children, and running and funding a household. As Waldo could harbor a love for Caroline Sturgis outside the work of a marriage, Thoreau and Lidian could cherish one another in an idealized way. "When I love you I feel as if I were annexing another world to mine. We splice the heavens," Thoreau wrote of Lidian in his journal.[128]

Lidian's connection with Thoreau, like Waldo's with Sturgis, suggests a marriage in crisis. But perhaps in the confines of nineteenth-century gender roles and a marriage rife with love, admiration, disappointment, and anger, the Emersons carved out a partnership that gave them room to seek affirmation elsewhere. Marriage reform was in the air, as an "array of activists viewed the legal, social, and cultural institution of marriage as an obstacle to a more equitable society," advocating for changes ranging from liberalizing divorce laws to calls for "free love" and open marriage.[129] The conversations worked their way into Waldo's subconscious. In 1840, he had a dream in which a congregation debated "the Institution of Marriage" with some speakers raising "grave and alarming objections"; the dream concludes when he awakes "well convinced that the Institution of Marriage was safe for tonight."[130] Waldo was also intrigued by the ideas of the French socialist philosopher Charles Fourier, whose utopian plans included organizing humanity into "communes called phalanxes" and who aimed "to create a world in which no desire went unmet," which included the end of monogamous marriage.[131] Some marriage reformers were Fourier acolytes who "developed a secular justification for the abolition of marriage."[132] Waldo, in an essay on Fourierism in *The Dial*, expressed admiration for Fourier's goals, but ultimately, as he had with Brook Farm, rejected the idea of living in such conditions as unrealistic.[133] For all his grumbling and musings about wedlock, the Emersons certainly never joined public efforts for marriage reform. The public conversation around the possibilities, however, may have encouraged Waldo and Lidian to seek flexibility in their private partnership, even as their extramarital relationships also caused pain.[134]

"Ellen is already thinking what will be done when you come home; but then she thinks it will be some loss when I shall go away," Thoreau reported to Waldo in late March.[135] It would be four months until Waldo sailed into Boston Harbor, on July 27, 1848. The trip had boosted his reputation. He had given sixty-nine lectures, often to large crowds, been feted at dinners and receptions, renewed his acquaintance with Thomas Carlyle and William Wordsworth and met Charles Dickens, George Elliot, and William Thackery. It was less successful financially, and he mourned the time lost with his children and his absence during Lidian's long illness. "I can hardly regret my journey, on the whole, & yet it seems in every way to have cost too much," he reflected to Lidian in March.[136] But now he was back, his children taller and older and happy to see him, even if they missed Thoreau.

In June 1849, Ellen made her own extended trip away from home, staying on Staten Island with her uncle William's family for almost three months. She had turned ten in February, and this opportunity was an exciting step into the world. Ellen took with her the first Ellen Tucker Emerson's Bible, with the command from Lidian to read "a dozen verses in the Psalms everyday." Ellen later remembered, "I did, but I wasn't old enough; it was a ceremony."[137] William and his wife Susan had three sons—William Jr., born in 1835; Haven, born in 1840; and Charles, born in 1841. On this trip and throughout their lives, the New York and the Concord Emerson cousins got along famously. Meanwhile, William and Susan's less-fraught marriage made their home a calm oasis, and Susan, with no daughters, doted on her niece.

Distance equaled correspondence in the Emerson family. Letters flew between Concord and Staten Island. Lidian sent advice which illuminates her moral, gendered ideas about child rearing. Ellen, she cautioned, should "try to *refrain from doing* anything that is not pleasant or beautiful" while a guest. "Should not the presence of a *young lady*! Or rather the manners of a young lady, make the boys' play *quieter?*" she asked.[138] In addition to admonitions to behave, Lidian raised complex ideas about memory and experience for her ten-year-old daughter to ponder. Noting that Ellen would always remember the trip, she added, "The minutest circumstance word and action are recorded forever in your mind, and can and may, & perhaps *will*, be some time all brought back as fresh as at the hour of their occurrence."[139] Edith dictated letters to her mother to keep her sister apprised of events in Concord, reporting, "I have discovered another wild-cherry tree—up on the grove by the garden."[140] Everyone cherished the reports Ellen sent back, although none appear in the family archive. After praising one missive, Lidian added, "We hope you will often 'have something to say' and will fill many pages to be sent home."[141] Ellen took the instructions to heart, as would her sister when she grew old enough to travel. Throughout their lives, the Emerson sisters were renowned for their delightful, detailed correspondence, with family and friends anxiously waiting to read the latest installment when they wrote from a trip.

"It was a very happy home," Edith declared in her remembrance of her father in 1922.[142] This was a regular refrain of the three siblings as they looked back at their childhood. "Didn't we have a happy home and the best of chances in our childhood and youth?," Edward wrote to Ellen in 1906.[143] Ellen expressed a similar sentiment when writing Edith in 1894: "I think ours was a capital home to grow up in."[144] As adults, Ellen and Edward did not deny the difficulties. It was in the letter in which she described their "capital home" that Ellen named the three years after young Waldo's death "the miseries." Edward, meanwhile, called out "Mother's sensitive organization and body" as the only mar on their youth.[145] Edith, relentlessly optimistic, downplayed the challenges, particularly of their mother's emotional health.[146] But taken together, their letters during their childhoods and their later memories of that time paint a portrait of a home in which affection and laughter played a more significant role than their parents' reputations as a stern, emotionally remote philosopher and his depressive, sickly wife suggest. As Ellen and Edith grew up and ventured beyond Bush, that family bond would stay central to their understanding of themselves and the world.

CHAPTER TWO

"We Each Have Something Good and Both Want All"

(1852–1860)

"I am not quite contented with Ellen's school, at this moment," Waldo wrote to Caroline Sturgis Tappan in August 1852. "All her schoolmates persist in not being of the right age, or the right turn of mind, for her," he noted. He concluded, "The teaching is of something less importance in Ellen's case, that she is a good scholar & will learn easily and well anywhere. But I wish she should have a good, reasonable & well-behaved set of schoolmates."[1] For the next decade, a complex matrix of familial, social, and professional demands drove the choices the family made about Ellen's and Edith's education, as they balanced the girls' schooling with the demands of running Bush and Waldo's career. Through stops and starts, the Emerson daughters received some of the best educations available to girls in that era, but it was still a process circumscribed and interrupted by caregiving and family responsibilities. As they balanced the demands of school and family, the girls hammered out the partnership that would serve them throughout their lives.

The Emersons' choices about Ellen and Edith's education took place in a society with growing educational options for the daughters of the emerging white middle class. Over three hundred female academies and seminaries opened between 1790 and 1850, a development driven through a confluence of social and economic changes. Industrialization and urbanization meant that women's work was less in demand on family farms, while also creating a gap in women's lives between childhood and marriage; as men moved west and postponed marriage to start careers, a cohort of single women who needed a way to support themselves emerged; and religious revivals often advocated for the education of women as a way to strengthen their spiritual authority in their families. Middle-class parents also saw educating their daughters, particularly at single-sex schools, as a mark of status. Although these schools prepared some women for careers as schoolteachers, writers, editors, and reformers, female education advocates often justified them in the language of separate spheres and female duty, arguing that educated women would be better mothers, wives, and citizens for the Republic.[2] While the Emersons lived in a circle of intellectual, ambitious women, they, too, viewed education as a path to life in the home, not beyond it.

"The family fortunes mended early in the fifties & Ellen went to Lenox to school," Edith later remembered.[3] Lenox meant the Sedgwick School, which Lidian favored because it encouraged "healthiness," and Ellen preferred because her friend Ida Wheeler might attend.[4] Waldo's priorities included ensuring his daughter study arithmetic, Latin, and French. Waldo likely factored in the fact, since Caroline Sturgis Tappan now lived in Lenox with her family, having Ellen in school there would make it easier to see her. Waldo expressed some qualms, writing, "I hate to lose the girl too. Ellen chatters with her mates; with me she is so quiet and intelligent, as no one else is." He envisioned her experience at the school at as ultimately beneficial to him, explaining to Sturgis Tappan he could sacrifice a "year of quiet reason" to ensure that "she shall chatter well."[5] One of his primary goals in sending Ellen to school, thus, was to mold her into a better companion for him.

Ellen arrived in Lenox in June 1853, four months after her fourteenth birthday. Elizabeth Sedgwick, who founded the institution in 1828, stressed the importance of "forming" in her students the "habits of patient, careful study, of a concentration of their powers, bearing upon a single point, as the sun's rays are collected in a focus, and in inspiring them with a love of knowledge for its own sake."[6] The author Catharine Sedgwick, the sister of Elizabeth's husband Charles, was often in residence at the Hive, the Sedgwicks' home.[7] The Sedgwick girls had a rigid schedule. Ellen reported to Edith, "We go to school at eight in the morning and are dismissed at one. Mrs. Sedgwick wishes us to study an hour at home every afternoon and we go to the schoolroom at four in the afternoon to sew an hour while Mrs. Sedgwick reads. After that we must take our walk."[8] Ellen, anxious among strangers, found much to worry about in her first term. She fretted over her rooms in the Clifford Street house run by Jennie and Francis Farley, the latter a member of Brook Farm.[9] Elizabeth Sedgwick had promised Ellen and Ida their own space, but two other girls were assigned to share it. Ellen complained, "We can never be alone a minute and we don't like either of them," and begged her mother to have her father intervene; Sedgwick finally moved the other students.[10] Ellen was initially so homesick that anything that reminded her of Bush, even her copy of Virgil, made her want to cry.[11] She soon made friends, however, particularly with Sally Gibbons, whose mother was the abolitionist and prison reformer Abigail Hopper Gibbons, and Addy Manning, the daughter of a New York merchant.[12]

Ellen detailed her academic anxieties in letters to her father. She complained the thirty minutes devoted to arithmetic were not sufficient. In Latin, she struggled with a "puzzling part of Virgil" and complained that Elizabeth Sedgwick did "not teach scanning"; in French they learned grammar but had stopped speaking the language after Grace Sedgwick, Elizabeth's daughter and the French instructor, felt the students were laughing at her.[13] Waldo promised, "if you keep your own eye on the books you value most, they will, in the course of a year, take their right place." He concluded, "Keep up a brave heart, my dear child, as true persons always may!"[14] He later felt stronger about her speaking French, commanding Ellen to tell Grace, "that it is a principal point with you to learn to speak French; & at all events, that papa, who knows that no French man or woman ever set foot in Concord, was on the verge of sending you to a convent in Montreal, for no other purpose."[15]

Lidian's support was more ambivalent. When Ellen reported she was settling in, Lidian replied, "I do not know whether I feel most glad or sorry to know that for all you do not call yourself homesick but happy."[16] After Ellen noted she had not had time to read a daily Bible verse, as her mother had requested, Lidian suggested that she ask Sedgwick to give her shorter lessons in arithmetic or French, two of the subjects important to Waldo.[17] But mother and daughter, and sometimes Edith, also kept up a lively correspondence about literature. They discussed *The Pilgrim's Progress*; Elizabeth Gaskell's *Cranford*; Charles Dickens' *Bleak House*, serialized from spring 1852 through fall 1853; Catharine Sedgwick's *The Linwoods*; and *The Lamplighter*, whose author, Maria Susanna Cummins, had been a Sedgwick student.[18] Ellen explained to her mother, "I have never read any [novels] that I am not sure you would be willing to have me." She continued, "I consider however that Miss Sedgwick, Miss Edgeworth, Grace Aguilar, the author of *Ruth* and *Mary Barton* and the Waverley Novels are not forbidden."[19]

Ellen experienced religious life beyond Concord's Unitarians for the first time, as Sedgwick had the students rotate among the churches in the area. The exposure to other forms of worship, even as she held firm to her own beliefs, sparked of a lifelong curiosity for Ellen. She complained of one minister, "being a Presbyterian, his doctrines are so different from what I have always been taught to believe, that I dislike him still more, and, feeling so, will it do me good to try to listen to him?"[20] She was fascinated, however, when she visited the Shakers near Lenox with the Wheelers; "a little old lady with her arms spread far out on each side and her eyes shut whirled from one end of the room to the other many times," she reported to Lidian.[21] Sermons by the visiting Henry Ward Beecher thrilled her the most. Ellen raved to her mother that Beecher "preached differently from any one I ever heard before, just as he ought to, as if he was talking to one and not to a church" and noted "I couldn't take my eyes off him, he grew so handsome to me."[22] As with the novels, Ellen's reflections on her religious outings were a source of intellectual connection with Lidian. In response to Ellen's letter on Beecher, her mother replied, "How much I should like to hear him. I have always thought him just the person that would 'speak to my condition.'"[23]

The Emerson sisters continued the correspondence that would connect them throughout their lives. Ellen maintained the role of elder relative, addressing her sister as "my dear babe" and signing off "Aunty."[24] She lectured Edith on the importance of practicing the piano, even as she begged her father to let her stop piano lessons herself, and corrected Edith's grammar.[25] Edith wrote chatty, detailed notes that kept her sister updated on life in Bush. She reported, for instance, "Father has bought Eddy two packs of crackers, a bunch of grasshoppers, two doubleheaders, and a bunch of Chinese rockets. I go into water every night, and am learning to swim."[26] While her tone was cheerful, she also documented the churn of domestic help and was beginning to serve as her mother's secretary at the age of eleven.[27] The sister's personalities shine through these letters, with Ellen maternal and worried and Edith breezy and trying to amuse her family. Their relationship would evolve, but certain lifelong patterns were set.

On the last day of 1853, Ellen wrote to her mother, "Oh how I wish I were at home. It seems now as if I was old and home and school and time when I was young were gone."[28] Ellen was worried that life at Bush would never be the same after the death of her grandmother, Ruth Emerson, in November. Waldo's and Lidian's responses illuminate their different approaches to their children's emotional lives. An alarmed Waldo, on a lecture tour, asked Lidian, "What business have fourteen years to be melancholy?"[29] As someone whose home-life was shaped by Lidian's moods and whose brother Edward suffered a nervous breakdown in 1828, he likely feared signs of depression manifesting in his daughter.[30] His reaction mirrors his denial of grief after his son died. Lidian, however, saw her own vulnerable emotional state as evidence of an enlightened sensitivity and interpreted Ellen's sentiments as evidence of a similar enlightenment. She wrote to her daughter, "I do rejoice that you have reflection and feeling enough to look pensively at the dark side"; she did, however, encourage her to "look on the bright side too" and count all the blessings the Sedgwick School had brought.[31] She defended Ellen in stronger language to her husband, proclaiming, "The coming Soul must bring pensiveness at least, and I should be sorry if Ellen did not, at this age, give signs of its approach."[32]

While they differed on the response to Ellen's melancholy, the Emersons presented a united front when they felt Elizabeth Sedgwick treated her unfairly. Ellen shared the nuts and raisins her mother had sent her for her fifteenth birthday with her classmates, keeping back the chocolate which Sedgwick forbid. Sedgwick scolded her, saying those foods were also forbidden. A distraught Ellen explained to Lidian, "I got so confused that I couldn't make her understand and she thinks still that I did very wrong, when I am sure I meant to do quite right."[33] Her parents found Sedgwick's attitude outrageous, particularly when she told Ellen her family could not send ripe fruit the following summer as punishment.[34] Waldo, according to Lidian, was "disgusted and provoked" and declared he wished to send Ellen a case of nuts and figs immediately.[35] The image of the esteemed author fuming about Sedgwick's food rules, which amused Ellen's classmates, runs counter to what Kathleen Lawrence has described as the "myth of Emerson as a sterile philosopher living on an ideal plane."[36] Still, it was Lidian who led the charge. Sedgwick eventually backed off, perhaps to ensure Ellen re-enrolled; in a letter acknowledging the rules were confusing, she asked if Ellen would continue the next term.[37] Having Waldo's daughter in the school was a feather in her cap.

While she did stay after the testy exchange, family obligations soon ended Ellen's time in Lenox. In early 1854, Waldo was away on a lecture tour for weeks. Lidian's difficulties maintaining the household, and retaining servants, sharpened without the support of her husband and elder daughter, and her periodic exhaustion returned. While the family discussed Ellen taking over housekeeping as early as January, Waldo decided, "I think you are learning & enjoying & in a state to do both and do not wish waste your time in new beginnings."[38] But by July, the plan was set for Ellen to come home in the fall. Ellen thought her education would continue in Concord as she oversaw the house.³⁹ Waldo declared, however, "Your mother is very feeble; & I doubt much if in October I can spare you to go to school anywhere. I think we shall have to instal you as housekeeper for a time sole & sovereign.... Meanwhile your Mother will be relieved, which she needs."⁴⁰ The decision made, Waldo confessed to Abel Adams, "if Ellen were not coming home in October, with ambition to keep house for us, I should be seriously tempted to sell mine, so feeble is Lidian, & such is the trial of bad domestics."⁴¹

Many middle-class families voiced concerns about both female "feebleness" and "bad domestics," but these issues took on dramatic dimensions in Bush. The exact nature of Lidian's of health problems in 1854 is unclear, as it had been in the 1840s and would be throughout her life. Her children suspected that a case of scarlet fever when she was nineteen had "made the invalidism of the rest of her life."⁴² The siblings also felt their mother's high-strung nature contributed to her frequent exhaustion, as evidenced by Edward's statement about "Mother's sensitive organization and body."⁴³ Waldo often defaulted to "feeble" to describe her when she was unwell. In 1848 her sister-in-law Susan Emerson was so concerned she offered to have Edith and Ellen come live with her for months, but only referred vaguely to Lidian's "illness."⁴⁴ Depression at times accompanied her physical symptoms; she once described enduring both "acute pain" and "no hope in my heart, no aspiration in my soul."⁴⁵ Her symptoms often included a fever, insomnia, and lack of appetite, and she refused to eat or walk outside. While exhausted, her drive to perfect her house led to periods of frenetic activity that weakened her further. As Ellen reported in March 1855, "She always says, 'All I want is to work work work work' and I can't persuade her anyway to rest till she gets sick so she can't get off the bed and the sicker she is the more she wants to work."⁴⁶

Similarly vague health concerns were rife among white, middle-class women.⁴⁷ In 1856, the author and educator Catharine Beecher declared, "there is a delicacy of constitution and increase of disease, both among mature women and young girls, that is most alarming."⁴⁸ Jennifer Luden has described the phenomena as "a mysterious epidemic" beginning in the mid-nineteenth century, the "hallmark" of which was "an inexplicable, incapacitating fatigue" along with "headaches, insomnia, digestive problems, chronic pain, anxiety, inability to concentrate, and vertigo."⁴⁹ In 1868, Dr. George Beard grouped the symptoms under the name neurasthenia.⁵⁰ Historians and biographers struggle with how to interpret these symptoms, wary of repeating a still-common pattern of dismissing women's complaints as psychological while also acknowledging how resentment of the constraints on women's lives could contribute to ill health. Easier to document are the treatments women received, including leeching of sexual organs and, beginning in the 1870s, the extreme "rest cure," which involved complete isolation from family and overfeeding for weeks.[51]

Lidian consulted with doctors but avoided the worst of the treatments. She harbored the same skepticism toward the medical profession and alternative treatments that she did toward the church hierarchy and the transcendentalists who occupied her living room. When suggesting a tonic, her brother-in-law Charles Brown acknowledged her "great antipathy to Quacks and Quackery"; in the 1860s, she would council Edith to reject a doctor's advice if she disagreed with it.[52] Lidian, moreover, had read her uncle's medical books as a teenager, and acquired her own copies when her children were small, along with a chest full of homeopathic remedies; henceforth she was "diligent in consulting" the medical texts and "selecting remedies for her own ailments and those of all her large clientele of dependents and semi-dependents."[53] One of Lidian's preferred cures was bed rest while someone, often a daughter, read to her.[54] In this way she took some control over her health and created a circle of female conversation that kept her intellectually engaged. In the process, however, she shifted the burden of housework to Edith and Ellen.

Waldo's reference to "the trial of bad domestics" was another common refrain that took on an exaggerated importance in Bush. "Domestics" referred to employees who were strangers, often immigrants hired through employment agencies called intelligence offices; by the mid-nineteenth century this arrangement had largely replaced "help," who were considered like family (and sometimes were) in the North. Domestics, understandably, routinely left positions for better opportunities or in protest of poor treatment. Employers saw this mobility as betrayal, continuing to cast their relationship with their workers in personal terms even as the "service relation" was increasingly part of an "impersonal cash nexus."[55] Lidian, with exacting standards even she could not meet, was especially demanding as an employer. Her anxiety about servants ran so deep it manifested in a dream in which she rose from her coffin to scold the maids who were not cleaning the parlor quickly enough for her funeral.[56] Waldo's desire to "ameliorate or abolish" hired labor also complicated the issue.[57] While he had accepted the reality of hiring servants, his preferences also likely shaped the plan to bring Ellen home from school rather than hiring a housekeeper.

One person stood up for Ellen as her parents decided that the needs of Bush would trump her education. Caroline Sturgis Tappan had kept an eye on Ellen during her time in Lenox. They already knew one another from Sturgis Tappan's visit to Bush in 1845, when she had sketched the young girl and helped her learn to draw; in Lenox, she invited Ellen and her friends to her home, teaching her to row a boat and giving her small gifts.[58] Now Sturgis Tappan took Waldo to task for privileging his domestic trials over his daughter's education. She advised him to send Ellen "still to school—especially to French & dancing & to keep her with girls." He reported his blunt response to his brother: "Ah, thought I, & where is my house to be in the meantime."[59] Although Sturgis Tappan's campaign failed, Ellen always remembered her advocate warmly, as she did Thoreau. Their relationships with Lidian and Waldo may have been a strain on the Emerson marriage, but Sturgis Tappan and Thoreau's presence was a boon to the children.

Ellen claimed to her parents to be excited about taking over housekeeping, but she expressed qualms elsewhere. She took the new duty seriously, preparing by reading Catharine Beecher's *A Treatise on Domestic Economy*; the most popular American housekeeping manual in the 1850s, the volume combined practical knowledge with an emphasis on women's roles in the moral development of their family and their nation.[60] Ellen enthused to her mother, "I am still gladder that I may not go to school this winter, but stay at home and keep house. I am going to try very hard to learn soon, that I may be a wonder of a housewife for you."[61] Ellen acknowledged more complex emotions to her cousin Charlotte Haskins Cleveland. "I am so glad I have known it beforehand, for now I am ready to begin, but if it had been suddenly decided after I got home, alas poor me what should I do!" she admitted.[62]

Despite the decision to bring Ellen home, Lidian's exacting standards made it difficult for her to cede control. "I haven't fairly begun my housekeeping yet for of course Mother can't at first give up all power," Ellen reported at the end of September.[63] Lidian, according to Ellen, felt her daughter was forgetful and did things too slowly.[64] Eventually, however, days of reading to Lidian and monitoring the ripening of the pears did give way to duties including cleaning; supervising servants; and acting as Waldo's hostess, secretary, and accountant. A new duty fell on her in February 1855, after Helen Maynard left the Concord school to get married and her replacement quit abruptly. Ellen added tutoring Edith and Edward to her schedule for several weeks. She made time to educate herself as well, rising early to study Greek before breakfast.[65] Still, "Mother is no better than she has always been," Ellen confessed to her cousin Charlotte. She continued, "Oh if there was only any way to make her well."[66]

In this frustrating moment, a gesture from an old friend cheered Ellen. In December 1854, Louisa May Alcott sent Ellen a copy of her first published book, *Flower Fables*. Ellen went into a "swoon" on seeing the dedication. "To Ellen Emerson, for whom they were fancied, these flower fables are inscribed, by her friend, the Author," it reads.[67] Ellen explained to Emma Stinson, "When the Alcotts lived here Louisa used to read her stories to me and I used to go wild about them, and made her write them for me. She says that 'twas I who made her publish them for I showed the written ones to Mother who liked them so much she advised Louisa to print a book."[68] The dedication may have been more than a remembrance of a childhood connection. Alcott, so responsible for her family fortunes, perhaps sought to lift the spirits of another young woman who had family responsibilities falling disproportionately on her shoulders.

The arrival of Franklin Sanborn transformed Concord's educational offerings and gave Ellen a path back to school. Sanborn was a Harvard student and Emerson acolyte whom Waldo recruited to take over the Sudbury Road school in March 1855. His sister Sarah, an experienced teacher, joined him.[69] Bronson Alcott, as well as Alcott's own inspiration, the Swedish educational reformer Johann Heinrich Pestalozzi shaped Sanborn's pedagogical approach; Pestalozzi argued that education, rather than emphasizing rote learning and discipline, should seek to emphasize students' innate intelligence in a familial atmosphere. Sanborn also positioned himself as the heir of the school run by the Thoreau brothers in the 1830s and 1840s, stressing his commitment to co-education and outdoor activities.[70]

The first Sanborn class of seventeen students included Ellen, Edith, and Edward.[71] A frustrated Ellen complained, "I have to study out of school now which I don't like and to make me still more miserable Mr. Sanborn has told me that I may write a composition on History." Cautious about criticizing a man whom her father endorsed, she added incongruously, "I think Mr. Sanborn is a very good teacher and everybody likes him."[72] While she did give more positive reports about reading Milton and learning algebra, in June she wailed, "Oh dear I'm so glad that vacation is so near, for I am so tired of studying all the time."[73] Edith, not writing letters to her sister now that she was home, left little record of her early days under Sanborn, but her later reluctance to leave the school suggests she was happier there than Ellen.

The Emersons enrolled Ellen in the first class at the Agassiz School for Young Ladies in Cambridge the following fall. Waldo's plan to travel less while completing *English Traits* helped make the move possible.[74] His burgeoning friendship with Louis Agassiz, the Swiss naturalist and Harvard professor, also influenced the decision. Elizabeth Cabot Cary Agassiz, Louis' wife, founded the school to supplement her husband's university salary, thus relieving him from the pressure of lecture tours.[75] Elizabeth, who later helped found Radcliffe College, advertised the institution as a chance for young women to be educated by Harvard professors, including Louis. Enrolling Ellen allowed Waldo to contribute to his friend's finances and lend his endorsement not only to the school but to Agassiz himself. In a letter welcoming Ellen as a pupil, Louis concluded he and Waldo would now have a "personal acquaintance."[76] The men had recently become part of a group which held regular dinners in Boston; in 1856, the ritual was formalized as the Saturday Club, meeting each month at the Parker House, of which Waldo declared, "Agassiz is my chief gain from it."[77] Ellen spent the next two years studying at the Agassiz School, but each term Waldo weighed the importance of Ellen's education against the needs of the family and his work.

Waldo's limited commitment to his daughters' education mirrored his limited commitment to women's rights, an issue on his mind as Ellen prepared to move to Cambridge. Six days before the Agassiz term began, Waldo delivered his first lecture on women's rights at a Boston convention. In it, he supports women's property rights and endorses women's suffrage, but wonders to what degree women desire the vote and roots women's value within the nineteenth-century ideology of separate spheres. He praises women for their "sentiment" and intuition and envisions women primarily within the domestic sphere and as those who can "civilize" and spread beauty in the world.[78] The reformer Caroline Healey Dall commended the speech, but reported to him, "some of the papers thought it doubtful whether you were for us or against us."[79] Twenty and twenty-first century scholars have also debated that question.[80]

Putting the speech in the context of Waldo's choices regarding Ellen illuminates the shallowness of his commitment to women's rights. The lecture celebrates a path for women that mirrors Ellen's experience. Waldo suggests, "The part which women play in education, in the care of the young, and the tuition of older children is their organic office in the world. So much sympathy as they have makes them inestimable as mediators between those who have knowledge, and those who want it."[81] Ellen was not a teacher, but she did serve as a "mediator" of knowledge as her father's secretary, fulfilling what her father defined as a woman's "organic office in the world." Waldo's gift to Ellen of Coventry Patmore's *Angel in the House* while she attended the Agassiz School makes clear he conveyed this vision directly to his daughter as well as to the suffrage convention. Ellen later remembered her father told her it "was a good book for me to read."[82] In the poem, published in four parts beginning in 1854, Patmore idealizes his wife as a docile, devoted woman whose purpose is to serve him. Waldo also quoted the poem in his address to the women's rights gathering, to illustrate the sentiment that women "should magnify their ritual of manners. Society, conversation, decorum, music, flowers, dances, colours, forms, are her homes and attendants."[83] Ellen cherished the gift and returned to the poem throughout her life, as she internalized the message that her value came from her ability to care for her family.

Although her father had a limited agenda for her education, and she accepted those limits, Ellen's love of her Agassiz experience should not be diminished. Within a week, she declared, "I rejoice in the school, everything about it is so pleasant," and she flourished socially and intellectually.[84] She developed a strong connection with Ida Agassiz. One of Louis Agassiz's children from his first marriage, Ida taught French and German at the school. Ellen experienced the relationship as a serious crush. While describing their friends in language that sounds romantic and even sexual to modern ears was common among nineteenth-century girls, Ellen's feelings for Ida go beyond friendship, as the teacher became a central figure in Ellen's emotional life.[85] Ellen never had a romance with a man, and she seems to have rejected the idea of courting and marriage at a young age. She dreaded co-ed dances and at first had difficulty bonding with the other Agassiz students, "for their interest and conversation is apt to be gentleman and of course I cannot join."[86] She did not explain why joining was impossible, but, perhaps significantly, Ellen was writing to Addy Manning, who would enter a long-term partnership with the sculptor Anne Whitney a few years later.[87] The connection with Ida was the first of several intense friendships Ellen would have with women throughout her life, at least one of which she discussed in terms of a romance.

Ellen's emotional and intellectual interests reinforced one another. She was gifted at languages, but studying German with Ida spurred her interest and helped her overcome her shyness; she explained, "Of course I always liked it you know that but now since I study it with Miss Ida and above all since my tongue was untied I love it beyond all my other studies."[88] When Ida was not available to teach, Ellen's motivation flagged. Lidian and Waldo encouraged the friendship, perhaps in part because it addressed Waldo's desire for his daughter to master French and German. For her New Year's gift in 1858, they gave Ellen a daguerreotype of Ida. She cherished it, carrying it with her when visiting friends in Concord and Boston and asking them to comment on Ida's beauty.[89]

Ellen boarded with George and Susan Hillard at 62 Pinckney Street in Boston, where she found a supportive community.[90] Her Concord friend Birdy Cheney also enrolled at the Agassiz School and boarded with the Hillards.[91] Harriet Beecher Stowe was often a guest, and Ellen found, "I like her ever so much, and am glad enough always to find her here."[92] As with Sturgis Tappan in Lenox, moving to the Agassiz School put Ellen in contact with many of her father's friends, including Anna Barker and Samuel Ward, whose daughter, also Anna, was her classmate, and Anna Lowell, whose readings she attended. Anna Ward told her, "when I didn't know what to do about anything or if I was sick or when I wanted to go anywhere, to come over and tell her and she would arrange it for me."[93] After months of being the caretaker, it was comforting to have an adult take on the role for her.

While Ellen settled in Cambridge, Edith thrived in Concord. More extroverted than her sister, she enjoyed the social as well as the academic life of Sanborn's school. Edith was thrilled in November, the month of her fourteenth birthday, when her father gave her permission to appear in a tableau as Titania from *A Midsummer's Night Dream*. Her biggest concern was her costume, and she craved sisterly advice, as Lidian did not like the costume the girls at school had proposed. "I wish you would tell me what you think would be best," she wrote.[94] Edith, who shared her mother's deep connection to animals, sent her sister detailed reports on the family cat Goethe, including information about the tissue paper dress she made the pet.[95] Ellen resented valuable space in a letter being dedicated to an animal, complaining "nothing makes me so angry as to hear that cat adored."[96] For all the fun, Edith bore the burden of care in January when Lidian again had a bad spell while Waldo was away lecturing. "I am afraid you are beginning to think about your fate again, how you have been sick all the time since Father went," Ellen wrote to her mother, still worried about Bush while in Cambridge.[97]

Ellen was right to be concerned, as Lidian's troubles again put her education into play. In January Ellen speculated, "next year will probably be an apprentice-ship in house-keeping and after that I hope to begin my career as superintendent of the house."[98] Ellen's use of terms such as apprenticeship, career, and superintendent indicate the seriousness with which she accepted the mission and that she understood the value of her work to the family and to her father's career. That gift of Patmore's *Angel in the House*, and Ellen's reading of Catherine Beecher's advice manual, however, suggest that Waldo and Ellen framed her role within the ideology of separate spheres. In this vision, Ellen's housekeeping was not a career demanding intelligence and organization but a demonstration and fulfillment of her feminine nature.

Ellen received a stay from returning to Bush. In February, Ellen reported to Edith, that Anna Barker Ward "had persuaded" Waldo that "I had better stay another year at school ... Mrs. Ward seemed very glad."[99] Barker Ward thus succeeded where Sturgis Tappan had failed, convincing Waldo to put Ellen's education above his convenience. The women's history with Waldo makes their advocacy for Ellen striking. In August 1840, before either married, they joined Margaret Fuller on a visit to Concord, during which Waldo thought the women had pledged their devotion to him. He expressed bewilderment and annoyance when Anna announced her engagement to Samuel Ward soon after, despite his own marriage and children and his friendship with Samuel. He wrote to Sturgis Tappan, "I thought the whole spirit of our intercourse at Concord implied another solution," and worried Sturgis Tappan would marry soon as well.[100] As Eleanor Titlon explains, "Emerson could entertain a 'mere imagination' and an absurd one: that his four friends Miss Fuller, Miss Sturgis, Miss Barker, and Mr. Ward would remain forever celibate."[101] Knowing Waldo's self-involvement firsthand, Sturgis Tappan and Barker Ward pressured him to put his daughter's education above his own needs. Ellen always felt close to Anna Barker Ward in the years that followed. While she did not connect it directly to Ward's fight for her, two decades later Ellen declared, "nothing can ever change the fact that such a home as yours has always been open to me, or the consciousness of the blessing and happy relations that I owe to it."[102]

Barker Ward's victory was not complete. While Ellen continued at the Agassiz School, the compromise was that she would commute from Concord, shouldering household duties as well as school work.[103] Illness kept Ida away from teaching, dulling Ellen's interest in languages. By October, Ellen was ill herself. She complained to Sally Gibbons that "everyone in the world has tried not only to baby me to death but to tell what Herculean labors I have been undergoing ... preached to me on the necessity of prudence, husbanding my strength etc., etc., and also frightened my poor papa and mamma into the belief that I am falling a victim to I don't know what."[104] While Ellen did drive herself to exhaustion at times, her depiction willfully ignores the fact that her parents also created the circumstances that caused her to work so hard.

Events far beyond Concord soon captivated Ellen. Growing up with their mother's fierce commitment to abolition, Ellen and Edith had been "mortified" when she draped their front gate with black cambric to protest the country's complicity with slavery one Fourth of July.[105] Now, as national events inspired local action, Ellen embraced her mother's passion. The 1854 Kansas-Nebraska Act dictated that these territories' settlers would decide if they would enter the Union as free or slave states. "Great is little Concord," Ellen raved of its citizen's contributions to Massachusetts State Kansas Aid Committee, which raised money to help abolitionists settle in Kansas.[106] She joined a sewing circle, in which women made flannel underclothes to send to the settlers, and she loved listening to Sanborn and her father discussing the issues. Ellen went so far as to say, "what pleases me most is to hear from any quarter that the North will be bold and leave the South."[107] Ellen had likely heard disunion discussed, as it was popular with some Concord reformers, including the Thoreau women.[108] Edith was quieter on the issues, although she contributed a doll for a fair held in Salem to raise money for Kansas.[109]

"I shan't go to school for a year I think and I don't want to, which I am very glad of," Ellen wrote to Haven in September 1857.[110] The return of the Alcott family, who settled up the road in Orchard House, helped ease her transition. Due to the Alcotts' "great love and talent for Theatricals," that winter Concord saw a "Series of Dramatic Entertainments" put on on a stage built in the "vestry of the Unitarian church." In one, Edith played the "Peg Woffington part of sitting in a picture frame to be showed to critics," while Edward opened the show with a prologue written by Franklin Sanborn.[111] Edith and Ellen rejoiced when their cousin William Emerson announced his engagement to Sally Gibbons, Ellen's Sedgwick friend.[112]

Waldo framed Ellen as the angel in the house, and she accepted it, but she was willing to criticize her father. In the summer of 1858, Waldo traveled to Newport and the Adirondacks, frustrating Ellen with his lack of communication.[113] She scolded, "We were all indignant enough before at your not writing a word, but now the word has come, you don't tell us anything, and I don't think that's pretty. Neither does Mother." She added, "I send you Edie's letters which are models for you. She begins at the beginning and tells us everything that happened to her, and you say 'I have had good luck and you may write to me.'"[114] She wrote sharply in regards to the household accounts, which she managed when her father traveled. While Waldo called her "the best accountant in the house," the job was stressful.[115] The Emersons were far from poor, but money felt tight at times; anxiety from the economic vulnerability of his childhood, moreover, stayed with Waldo, and he passed that anxiety to Ellen.[116] When to pay which bills and how much was owned to various parties often dominated their letters, with Ellen pleading for him to provide her with more money as she stretched each dollar.

"Edith goes down to school every day at Cambridge ... Ellen goes back as quietly to Mr. Sanborn, as if she had never left the village," Waldo reported to his brother William in October 1858.[117] Edith eventually boarded with Anna Cabot and Charles Russell Lowell in Cambridge; in addition to her classes, she studied German independently with Ida, who was not teaching at the school. "You envy me for being here, but you know you have Miss Ida and the Lowells there; we each have something good & both want all," Ellen wrote to Edith in early December.[118] While each sister did find things to enjoy in the arrangement, they each would have preferred to be at the other school, a concern their father dismissed. Edith did honor Ellen's request to report on "Miss Ida," and one of Ida's confidences regarding Ellen must have thrilled her: "I miss her dreadfully, I hate to go into school now, it seems so strange without her," Ida confessed.[119]

Edith, at ease socially, quickly made herself at home with the Lowells and among the Agassiz students. She spent evenings reading in the Lowell parlor with their adult children "Miss Hatty," age twenty-three, and "Mr. James," twenty-two; she was enchanted by their dogs Snap and Fleance. Ellen noted, "Edith adores each one of the family separately and all collectively, and they are all as careful of her as possible, so that the child is in kind of a Paradise."[120] At school, Edith had playful foot fights beneath the desk with Clover Hooper, who would later marry Henry Adams.[121] She loved Harriet and Anna Lowell's Shakespeare Club; readings included *A Midsummer's Night's Dream*, in which she was assigned Mustard Seed, and *Merchant of Venice*, in which she was Jessica.[122] More comfortable than her sister in co-ed groups, she filled her letters with tales of walks, conversations, dances, and skating parties on Fresh Pond with a large cohort of young women and men. For all the social whirl, Edith still lived for letters from her family, rushing home to check if one had arrived and scolding her siblings and parents when they did not write often—or long—enough.

Although not as intellectual as her older sister, Edith was a quick and able student. Latin was her favorite subject, and she mentioned Ovid frequently in her letters home; she wrote to Edward of how "lovely" she found the story of Phaethon's sisters mourning him and turning into trees, which resonated with her connection to her siblings.[123] She found a nemesis in Henriette LeClere, the

French teacher, complaining about the "disagreeable French time" and reporting she felt the teacher was petty in her interactions with students. LeClere's request that she "coax" Waldo into giving her an autograph did amuse Edith, however.[124] Befuddled and annoyed by Louis Agassiz's lectures, Edith used the time to sketch portraits of her classmates; she praised herself for not feeling "hopeless" when she did follow his thinking.[125]

Life in Bush kept Ellen busy. Alice Jackson, the daughter of Lidian's brother Charles, had moved into Bush and attended Sanborn's school.[126] Ellen worked on assignments in her father's study, and she turned to him for help, particularly with recitations.[127] Notably, Ellen, Edith, and Edward all portrayed the study as a place where they bonded with their father in their memoirs. Edith wrote, for instance, "Many hours I spent in his study, for he loved to teach us how to learn the poetry and to recite it, hearing it over and over with inexhaustible patience."[128] The room was not just the place for his work and his meetings with notable men and women of letters, but a place of family connection through the written word.

The morning of Ellen's twentieth birthday, Waldo opened his toast with "Baby" but then "corrected himself saying that I was now too reverend a personage for that title."[129] While still a student, she also took on duties as a substitute teacher at Sanborn's school, earning praise for her ability to control the classroom.[130] It was clear Ellen was no longer a child as she entered a new decade with new responsibilities. While her friends began to marry, she continued to direct her emotional energy toward women. She was thrilled to reunite in a "joyful time" with Ida in April. "I was so afraid that Ida and I might have grown apart. But it was all the same and better. I couldn't see her enough she was so beautiful I couldn't have enough of her," she wrote to Edith.[131] Ellen also found a new friend in Louisa Leavitt, Sanborn's cousin who was teaching at the school. Ellen cast their connection as a shared commitment to the students, noting "I want someone who likes to talk about them, and she is the only person."[132] However, Ellen clearly worried that others would find something odd about their friendship. She promised Edith, "Don't think that Miss Leavitt has run away with me as those two have. That is the reason I don't like to have her see me drawn to her, for fear she may think so."[133] It is unclear to whom "those two" referred, although one is likely Ida.

Ellen's caution suggests she understood the need to be circumspect in her affection with women. Lisa Merrill explains, "Despite the predominant ideology of women's passionlessness that allowed women's love for each other to be generally accepted—often likened to the sentimental attachment of sisters or close friends," nineteenth-century women attracted to other women were "keenly aware of the disapproval such feelings between women might engender."[134] Franklin Sanborn and Ellery Channing, in fact, gossiped cruelly about Ellen that spring. While they praised her as talented and admirable, Channing suggested such a "superfluity of talent has its misfortunes and is so apt to be unattractive in a woman." He added, "Unmarried women are so odious; yet there must be such cast-away persons doubtless, who have the misery of associating with similar neutrals of their own sex."[135] Ellen would not have read this exchange, and Channing's disastrous marriage to and treatment of Ellen Fuller would have undermined any credibility his opinions had in their circle.[136] But the existence of such an exchange, combined with her caution around Leavitt, indicate Ellen likely understood the need for the "keen awareness" Merrill describes. Her commitment to caring for her parents, in this context, helped camouflage her rejection of marriage to a man and attraction to women. Her life as a caregiver did require sacrifice, but it also provided Ellen some freedom from the pressure to enter a traditional relationship under the guise of feminine devotion.

Over the summer of 1859, the Emersons dismissed their servants and Ellen and Edith took on all the housekeeping duties. The arrangement was a return to Waldo's interest in running the house as a communal, family endeavor, although it was his daughters who shouldered the burden. Ellen at first tackled the cooking, while Edith served as the "chambermaid"; they switched responsibilities after several weeks. Ellen framed it as a learning experience, explaining, "I believed it necessary to know something about the management of such affairs," even though she feared the family might starve as she learned to roast mutton and bake cottage-loaf.[137] By late August they prepared a tea so pleasurable, including Edith's first pies and Ellen's ginger-cakes, that their father "made us several speeches about it."[138] Edith was less enamored with the arrangement, finding it a "degrading life." She resented how the work "shut out everything else" and felt "very sorry" to have to devote all her time "to getting ready something to eat." Both sisters were proud of the "sense of power" they developed from the experience, but their different attitudes toward domestic labor were set.[139]

Edith was rewarded at the end of the summer by a trip to Naushon, the island in Buzzard's Bay owned by the Forbes family. Lidian accompanied her. It was their second trip—the summer before the entire family had gone, with Edith visiting with Edward and Ellen accompanying Lidian and Waldo later.[140] John Forbes was a wealthy railroad magnate whose fortune originated from his family's business in the China trade, including opium smuggling.[141] Waldo was a great admirer of Forbes, and the Emerson siblings got along famously with the six Forbes children. Edith loved Naushon. "The establishment reminds one of English story books, for the family have no society except their guests of whom there are usually six for each week... everything is arranged for pleasure," she wrote.[142] Ellen, meanwhile, stayed in Concord tending a festering wound on her father's ankle.[143]

Ellen's reward came in the fall. The partnership the sisters had formed took a new shape, as Edith, now seventeen, took a year off from school to take on the role of housekeeper and Ellen returned to Sanborn's school. Unlike the summer, Edith had servants to help her, but she was still less than thrilled with the arrangement. Noting she "found enough to do in running after the cook and chambermaid," she complained, "housekeeping did not sharpen my intellect, and I was too stupid to write any letters... all the exercise which my handwriting got was in writing business notes, notes of invitation, thanks, and answers to invitations."[144] Making it more frustrating was the fact that, like Lidian, Edith's "heart" was "entirely set on perfect order and neatness," a level never achieved.[145]

While Edith struggled with housework, political events swept into Concord. On October 16, 1859, John Brown led the raid on the federal arsenal at Harper's Ferry. Thoreau was one of the first people to defend Brown publicly after the attack. Waldo soon followed; at Boston's Music Hall on November 8, he depicted Brown as "the new saint awaiting his martyrdom... who, if he shall suffer, will make the gallows glorious like the cross."[146] Sanborn had been one of the "Secret Six," a group which helped support Brown, and officials found letters from Sanborn in Brown's Maryland headquarters. Fearing arrest, Sanborn destroyed papers in his possession and fled Concord repeatedly from October through February.[147] These flights made Waldo "uneasy"; he urged Sanborn, "By all means return at the first hour wheels or steam will permit."[148]

Sanborn's departures tossed the school into chaos, with the women left behind forced to pick up the pieces. Ellen had hoped to return to the Agassiz School in January 1860; it would be her last chance to study with Ida, who planned to quit teaching. Sanborn's absence made it difficult for Ellen to leave his school for practical and symbolic reasons. Part of Sarah Sanborn's plan when her brother left in October was to have Ellen teach, and Ellen took on the role again in January. "Mr. Sanborn was constantly disappearing, the other teachers overworking in consequence," Ellen later explained; she noted, as "the oldest scholar, I was often called upon for one thing and another, and had my hands full sometimes."[149] Ellen and Edward's presence, in addition, visibly embodied Waldo's backing of Sanborn, whatever his private qualms. While Ellen pitched in, she wrote her father, again on a lecture tour, anguished letters making it clear how much she wanted to return to the Agassiz School. When he didn't reply to two missives, she scolded, "you haven't noticed or answered them and I asked you to talk about my going to Cambridge."[150] She also took up her case with Sanborn one of the times he returned to Concord, asking "whether I should take this term or the next in Cambridge"; he, unsurprisingly, answered, "Next."[151] Waldo agreed. On February 18, he wrote to Ellen, "If your staying gives, as it must, a certain feeling of stability, girls & boys will stay, who will otherwise grow restless & go. I think you had better wait till my return, which will be on Thursday or Friday."[152]

By the time Waldo did return, Ellen had resigned her hope of returning to the Agassiz school before late spring, perhaps due to guests at Bush. John Brown's daughters Annie, age sixteen, and Sarah, age thirteen, enrolled in Sanborn's school in late February. They lived with the Emersons for their first weeks in town. Ellen reported, "They are very willing to talk and it is very interesting to hear them," adding that Annie "kept house for her father at Harper's Ferry all summer, and knows all about it."[153] While Ellen quizzed the girls about their father and their upbringing, which struck her as so old-fashioned that they seemed almost out of time, Edith and Alice Jackson were "occupied for the last week in dressing them in Boston fashion, that they should look like the rest of the world when they go to school on Monday."[154] Meanwhile, Edward came down with typhoid fever, creating more worry and more work. Edith noted she "gave up all other business and spent two months in nursing him."[155]

There was one last gasp of drama. When authorities came to arrest Sanborn on April 3, Concord flew to his aid. Grace Mitchell, a Sanborn student, ran through town to rouse help. Anne Whiting, a local abolitionist, clambered into the marshals' carriage, "put herself in the way, and fought with a cane, and so prevented them from getting Mr. Sanborn in, and gave the people time to collect."[156] This spectacle delayed the proceedings until Judge Ebenezer Hoar appeared with a writ of habeas corpus, and the marshals had to free Sanborn. Ellen stayed by Edward's bedside, but she was delighted to report, "The town is in a high state of self-complacency, it flatters itself that this is the spirit of '76."[157]

When Ellen finally returned to the Agassiz School in April, she commuted and still bore a heavy burden of housework.[158] Edith's frustrating experiment in housekeeping over, she re-enrolled in Sanborn's school in the fall for her final year. But Ellen, at age twenty-one, knew her formal education had come to an end in October. As she packed away her school notebooks, she "felt as if nothing could be so good as to go straight back and continue such a charming life till age made it ridiculous, which it is already perhaps."[159]

Abraham Lincoln was elected the month after Ellen packed up her notebooks. Within six weeks, South Carolina seceded from the Union. The beginning of the Civil War coinciding with the end of the Emerson sisters' formal schooling dramatically marked a new era in their lives. For all the interruptions, Ellen and Edith's education exceeded the opportunities available for most young women in the mid-nineteenth century. Going forward, they would remain intellectually engaged, in reading groups and Bible study. They would use their training to serve their communities and family, eventually aiding their father with his work as he aged, a twist on his vision of educated women as helpmates. But those developments were over a decade away, a decade in which Ellen and Edith strengthened their partnership as the country broke apart.

CHAPTER THREE

"I Was Never So Carried Away by Anything Before"

(1861–1865)

"Alas! That Fort Sumter should be lost so easily," Ellen wrote to her mother on April 15, 1861.[1] The outbreak of the Civil War electrified her. Visiting the educator Increase Smith and his family in Dorchester, Massachusetts, she consumed newspaper reports, found comfort in attending church, and concluded her cousin Charley Emerson was the only man in her family built to be a soldier. After witnessing the Eighth Regiment marching in Boston a few days later, she reported to Edward, "the cloaks the Governor has given them are very handsome and imposing, I think, and it looked very real and revolutionary to see how many of them had no other uniform."[2] She and Edward took pride in the fact that Concord had raised $4,000 for the war effort and drew parallels between the current April conflict and the Battle of Concord. The Concord Regiment set off exactly eighty-six years after that event in which the town took such pride, causing Lidian to declare, "Is it not a wonderful and most auspicious omen that our Soldiers went forth to fight for liberty and right on the Nineteenth of April."[3] Edith was more subdued in her response, as she would be throughout the war. She was also away from home, visiting Cousin Mary Watson in Plymouth, Massachusetts, and her letters only briefly comment on the conflict. For the next four years, the war would at times zoom to the center of the sisters' attention, especially when death and injury in their circle forced them to confront its cost, while at others it faded into the distant background, behind the busy work of caring for their parents and household duties. Americans turned to Waldo to articulate their emotions during the brutal years, and Ellen and Edith continued to do work that made his writing, publishing, and lecturing possible. They were nineteen and twenty-two years old when the war broke out, and the conflict was the last sustained period of time the sisters would live together. This pivotal era in American history would prove pivotal in the Emerson family as well.

On April 23, Waldo delivered "Civilization at a Pinch" as part of his "Life and Literature" series in Boston. He had composed the lecture quickly in response to the outbreak of the war, writing, "The nation which Secessionists hoped to shatter has to thank them for a more sudden and hearty union than the history of parties ever showed."[4] Despite this endorsement, Waldo and Lidian balked when Edward expressed his desire to enlist. Despite Waldo's vocal support of the war, neither he nor Lidian endorsed the idea. The overt reasons were that, so far, only saving the Union—not ending slavery—was the goal of the war and that, at just seventeen, Edward was too young. "I will never consent to it till the War is avowedly for Universal Freedom," Lidian declared.[5]

Edward, instead of enlisting, started at Harvard in July.[6] Waldo and Lidian teased one another over who missed him more. Waldo "began to jeer at her for being homesick for her son, and she laughed at him for making a cat's paw of her, by which to hide his loneliness."[7] Edward's sisters descended on his room in Cambridge and fretted over how he arranged his clothes. By the end of October, however, Edward "found he had no strength for College and is at home again trying to get well," Ellen explained to the New York Emersons; she added "his papa is brokenhearted that College is lost."[8] With Waldo's intervention, the Harvard president agreed Edward could withdraw and begin again the following July.[9]

"We are all knitting socks & mittens for soldiers, writing patriotic lectures, & economizing with all our mights," Waldo wrote his brother.[10] The war circled closer. William Forbes, the son of Waldo's friend John Forbes and a favorite of all the Emerson children, enlisted. The thought worried Edith, who asked her brother, "is he glad to go—or is it a sense of duty that sends him?"[11] Casualties among their circle—including the death of William Putnam and the injuries of James Lowell and Wendell Holmes—forced Ellen to "understand something of the horror."[12]

While taking in the history unfolding around her, Ellen focused on documenting the family history. She had inherited the mantel of family historian from Mary Moody Emerson when she and her father had visited her in Brooklyn in January 1861. Mary, along with Cousin Hannah Haskins Parsons, told Ellen "story after story, all new, about the Ancestors," then gave her precious family documents, including the almanacs of Mary's which Waldo had not already claimed and the letters of Waldo's grandmother Phoebe Emerson.[13] As Mary

Moody Emerson's biographer Phyllis Cole explains, history was women's work in the Emerson family: "these manuscripts had survived in the keeping of daughters and granddaughters... before now returning with Ellen to Concord. They were coming to Waldo's branch of the family, but for Ellen's continued custodianship and delectation more than her father's."[14] Ellen wrote "What I Remember of Stories of Our Ancestors Told Me by Aunt Mary Ellen Moody," to record what she learned.[15] She also unearthed letters from Mary to Ruth Emerson dated from 1811 through 1820 when going through family papers. As Mary, now age sixty-seven, was declining in physical and mental health, Waldo took joy in reading the old missives, "which reinforce all ones respect and tenderness for her."[16]

In different ways, the Emersons contributed to the war effort as 1861 rolled into 1862. In January, Waldo traveled to Washington, D.C. to speak at the Smithsonian and meet Abraham Lincoln, while Edith and Ellen joined the relief work of the women of Concord. Ellen encouraged her father to meet John C. Fremont, whom Lincoln had removed of his command in November 1861 after Fremont, as commander of the Army of the West, issued a proclamation that freed the slaves of Missouri.[17] She was more excited to report, however, "there is to be a mass-meeting of sewers here on Thursday to make clothes for the negroes at Port Royal," referring to the South Carolina islands where freedpeople were being paid by the Union Army for their work on the cotton plantations that had been liberated from Confederate forces.[18]

May 1862 was a month of transition for the Emerson family. On May 6, Henry David Thoreau died from tuberculosis. When he had first fallen ill, the Emerson children felt it best not to disturb him. His sister told Lidian he watched them from the window and asked, "Why don't they come see me? I love them as if they were my own."[19] Ellen, Edith, and Edward began to make regular pilgrimages to see him. Edith later remembered, "he always made us so welcome that we liked to go. I remember our last meetings with as much pleasure as the old play-days."[20] Waldo delivered his eulogy on May 9 at First Parish, and published a revised version in *The Atlantic* and an obituary in the *Boston Daily Advertiser*. In these remembrances, Waldo praised Thoreau but also painted him as a "hermit" and "a stoic."[21] But for the Emerson children, Thoreau had not been a hermit but a beloved and crucial source of frivolity and affection throughout their childhoods. Waldo's eulogy did account for this, stating Thoreau "threw himself heartily and childlike into the company of young people whom he loved, and whom he delighted to entertain, as he only could, with the varied and endless anecdotes of his experiences by field and river."[22]

Two decades later, Edith provided Franklin Sanborn with a loving tribute for his biography of Thoreau. She stressed his patience—how he never tired of playing with them or scolded them for making noise. She remembered, "He was always most kind to me and made it his especial care to establish me in the 'thickest places,' as we used to call them."[23]

On May 12, Edward set forth on a cross-country trip to California in the hopes the voyage would shore up his still-ailing constitution. He traveled with Cabot Jackson Russell, a Harvard classmate whose family hoped the excursion would keep him from enlisting.[24] Ellen wished "a huge bear" would return in the place of "that willowy boy."[25] His family lived vicariously through his letters. When one arrived from Omaha, Edith "flew to the east door and screamed 'Father! Ellen!'" She reported the treasured document was shared with "a relieved, joyful and admiring audience."[26] Edith took Ellen to task for not writing Edward more regularly, but Lidian defended her elder daughter. "Poor Ellen—she shall not be scolded at. Surely she works hard from morn to eve, and has to keep house for mother, and write all her business letters. Assuredly she would write you if she could," Lidian explained.[27] Both her parents expected this work of Ellen, and created the conditions in which Ellen accepted it as her due, but Lidian at times illustrated her lucid understanding of what Ellen shouldered. Of course, clarity about Ellen's burden did not lead Lidian to relieve her of it.

That spring, it was Edith that Lidian defended. The previous March Franklin Sanborn had proposed to Edith and reacted unchivalrously to her rejection. Edith and Ellen are silent about the events in their existing correspondence. In her diary, Edith only notes that she walked to Walden Pond with Sanborn on the day of the proposal; she then quotes lines from the hymn "Jesus, Lover of My Soul," perhaps a sign of her distress at the situation.[28] Sanborn and Lidian's exchange provides the evidence of the conflict. On March 9, 1862, Sanborn responded to what must have been a blistering letter. "I still believe you to be my friend, in spite of certain expressions in this note and that of Sept. 12th '61, where you speak of me as 'angry without a cause,' making an 'extraordinary assumption,' cherishing 'an unjust resentment,' 'till time shall bring you to your better self' etc.," he wrote. He then outlined in excruciating detail every slight he felt Edith had dealt him, concluding, "I have lost confidence entirely in Edith's capacity for friendship, as I understand the word. I long ago gave up the hope of obtaining her love, but I did rely on her friendship."[29] He blamed Edith for the fiasco and suggested that Lidian overcome her prejudice towards her daughter to sympathize with him. Lidian did apparently discuss the matter with Edith, who answered each of Sanborn's charges with reasonable explanations.

As with the fruit and nuts incident at the Sedgwick School, Lidian took the lead in defending her daughter. Waldo tried to distance himself from the affair, but he eventually sent his own withering missive. In July, he wrote, "If a character as pure & gentle as Edith's has failed to make its due impression on one who at one time fancied himself her lover, & if her friendly attempts to soften his supposed suffering are regarded with squint suspicion, & he presumes to indulge in applying to her name a string of dishonoring phrases, it is plain that he was from the first out of place in her society."[30] By this time Sanborn was engaged to his cousin Louisa Leavitt, the teacher with whom Ellen felt such a connection. Still, he wrote another obsessive letter stating his grievances. Waldo took himself out of the brawl, but Lidian answered with another furious response. Her postscript read, "I have asked Edith if she wants to read your letter and my reply—she declines to see either."[31] Sanborn sent one more letter, then the exchange seemed to have been dropped. Edith and Ellen remained friends with Louisa, whom the entire family liked and for whom, after this ugly exchange, they likely felt sorry; Sanborn remained in their circle. Edward never forgot his anger, however. In 1917, he refused to write a biography of Sanborn for the Massachusetts Historical Society, even as he chronicled much of the Concord scene of his youth.[32]

On July 8, Ellen and Edith decamped to Newport, Rhode Island. They visited with Sarah Freeman Clarke, a landscape painter who had attended Margaret Fuller's Conversations and taught in Bronson Alcott's Temple School.[33] Edith and Ellen traveled with Clarke's niece Lilian, the daughter of the abolitionist and author James Freeman Clarke. As he often did with his female friends, Waldo hoped Clarke would inspire his daughters, even as he discouraged their ambitions to secure their support for his work and home. Waldo advised Ellen to "make what acquaintance you can with her character & her love of art & her skill with it."[34] Ellen praised Clarke's home as "the prettiest possible combination of a very nice old-fashioned and a lordly new one."[35] Clarke sent Waldo a letter "thanking him for the loss of his daughters" and praising Ellen as a "copy of her mother." It was a compliment from the woman who had described Lidian as "a soaring Transcendentalist" when she first met her. Lidian teased that she had to "console" Waldo, who liked to take full credit for "Ellen's excellence."[36]

A visit to the nearby Portsmouth Grove Hospital for wounded soldiers interrupted the summer pleasures. Waldo noted, "tis a strange tragic interlude in a Newport summer. But it being there, I am glad you should meet it."[37] Ellen was anxious before their first excursion on July 10, writing to her mother, "I am terribly frightened at the idea of going and asking men what we shall do for them, and, most of all, offering to write letters for them." She added, "But as people say they wish it, perhaps we shall." She also asked her mother to send a piece of linen "to make lint of," meaning bandages, because the hospital was undersupplied for its 1,800 patients.[38] After handing out buttered bread, Ellen, despite her anxiety, spent the afternoon speaking with men about the horrors of war, the Union's prospects, their frustrations with some military commanders, their admiration of General George McClellan, their patriotism, and the sad state of army food. She concluded the men "narrate their suffering as their common lot, and the terrible neglect and oppression of chaplains, surgeons and officers comes out quietly and shows that they have learned to consider it natural." Her revelations that "I didn't know their lot was quite so hard," led Ellen to wish that more "gentlemen" would enlist as privates, so those in the infantry would be treated better.[39] The exchanges were evidence of the deep curiosity Ellen had towards the experiences of others; she noted, "I was left alone with a hundred convalescent soldiers for two or three hours and asked every question that I had long been wishing to have answered."[40] Edith engaged less with the soldiers. After passing out food, she sat, emotionally exhausted, and wrote a birthday letter to Edward while waiting for the ferry.[41]

For their second week in Newport, Edith and Ellen moved to the home of Henry James Sr., where they joined his children William, Henry, Robertson, Wilkie, and Alice. They had "the best time in the world, laughing continually, of course, what with Mr. James and all the four boys, and taking walks on the cliffs, drives on the Avenue, baths on the beach, and going to parties in the evening," as well as sailing.[42] Ellen underscored the sense of joy in the house, telling her cousin Haven, "the funniest thing in the world is to see this delectable family together all talking at once."[43] When the Wards invited them to extend their visit and stay with them a few days, the sisters agreed, even though they knew it would inconvenience their parents; it was a rare moment of putting themselves and their chance for pleasure in front of Waldo and Lidian's desires.

The biggest news of the fall was Lincoln's declaration on September 22 that he would free the slaves in Confederate states on January 1, 1863. Ellen wrote to Haven, "Emancipation gives this family great pleasure, though Father and Mother complain that it is slow, and the January may just counteract the good of it. Still, Mrs. Emerson rejoices often and aloud, and is surprised that the sky doesn't look different."[44] With emancipation now overtly part of the war, Edward returned to Concord on October 6 insisting he must enlist. The trip home from California, which involved sailing south, traveling across Panama, then sailing up to Boston, had exhausted him, however, and he agreed to return to Harvard.[45] He roomed with Thomas Ward, Samuel and Anna Barker Ward's son, and, to regain his strength, attended classes but did not take exams.

Ellen and Edith took on their own intellectual challenges, while maintaining their war efforts. Edith continued to study Italian and read Virgil with Louisa Sanborn.[46] Ellen formed a Bible class with Louisa, Una Hawthorne, and Lizzy Leonard, which was "pure delight from beginning to end."[47] She agreed to teach Sunday School and serve as an observer for the Concord schools' annual oral examinations, which occupied much of her time in October. She found her observation duties engaging, describing recitations she found particularly charming to her family.[48] Both sisters continued their efforts for the war, working for the Soldier's Aid Society, making clothes for formally enslaved people, and participating in lint parties to make bandages. Ellen, however, lamented that dancing "isn't patriotic" so "apple-bees and contraband sewing" made up their social lives.[49]

The composition of the household changed in November, when a ten-year-old girl named Edith Davidson came to live at Bush. Edie, as she was called, was the daughter of Isabella Hale and Francis Davidson, a Boston merchant. Edie was originally to live with the Emersons for six months and attend Sanborn's school, with the Davidsons paying board. Ellen was the motivating force behind the arrangements, finalizing them with Isabella.[50] It is unclear what promoted this development. The Davidsons, who had older boys, may have fallen on hard times or there may have been a rift in the marriage. Francis' Boston business disappears from city directories and newspaper advertisements after 1861; the family disappears from the census in Massachusetts after 1860, although Isabella, at least, continued to live in Boston. Francis may have had to travel to make money. He lives until 1874, but Ellen only refers to Edie staying with her mother, not her parents, when she is away from Bush.[51] Isabella moved to Concord in the 1890s, dying there in 1896.[52]

Whatever the Davidsons' motivations, Ellen immediately began to refer to Edie as "my daughter" and embraced the opportunity to help raise a child. She was about to turn twenty-four and many of her friends were married and having children. While she had committed herself to staying in the family home, and had no interest in marrying a man, she found a way to fulfill her desire to mother. Ellen explained to her Aunt Susan, "It is a great comfort to have such a round warm little creature to sleep with me, and I delight to strut around Concord's streets leading her, and to hold her in my lap."[53] The transition was harder for Edie, who was at times desperately homesick in her first months at Bush, falling against Ellen in tears.[54] There was no move on either side, however, for her to return home, and she eventually settled in happily.[55] While Ellen took on primary responsibility for Edie, the family embraced her, with Lidian taking joy in giving her the "Mother's Blessing" before bed and Edward and Edith doting on her.[56] The arrangement lasted much more than six months, with Edie living on and off with the Emersons for several years. Throughout, Ellen paid careful attention to Edie's moral development and behavior and often worried she was too willful and wild.

There was other drama as 1862 gave way to 1863. The Emersons fretted about Louisa May Alcott as she slowly recovered from typhoid fever, acquired during her six-week stint as a nurse in Washington, D.C. "I do what I can for the . . . comfort of the family," Edith told Edward.[57] Edith's and Ellen's social calls, war efforts, and care of Edie, meanwhile, left Lidian feeling neglected. In February 1863, Ellen planned a "visit" to her. As she explained to Haven, "I forsook the housekeeping and gave up two or three regular engagements, and just as I would visit any one else I am staying with her."[58] Of course the housework was not really forsaken—during the "visit" Ellen rose early to tend to it, then devoted the rest of the day to her mother. One of their main activities was going through Lidian's papers and burning some of them. In March, Ellen went to visit William and Susan Emerson in New York, leaving Edie in the care of her "Aunt Edith." Ellen called on Mary Moody Emerson, who eventually recognized Ellen despite her dementia, saw friends, and went sightseeing with Haven. But there was a melancholy aspect, as Aunt Susan suffered from headaches and worried about Charles, now in the army, and William Jr. struggled to recover from tuberculosis.[59]

Mary Moody Emerson died on May 1, less than two months after Ellen saw her in New York. During her final years, Mary's focus on death was so pronounced that, when his brother William sent word that Mary was dying, Waldo noted in his journal, "now that her release seems to be really at hand, the event of her death has really something so comic in the eyes of everybody that her friends fear they shall laugh at the funeral."[60] Ellen, for her part, was "very thankful that I saw Aunt just when I did, when she was so like herself."[61] Mary's niece Hannah Haskins Parsons accompanied Mary's body from New York City on the train, so Mary could be buried in the family plot. Afterwards, family and friends gathered at Bush.⁶² Listening to Cousin Hannah's stories of caring for Mary caused Ellen to reflect, "Oh dear what a hard life she has had with Aunt."⁶³ Rather than connecting her lot to Helen's, she wished Helen would stay so she could care for her for the summer. Ellen, Edith, Waldo, and Helen decided to honor Mary, the family historian, by visiting the graves of Waldo's great grandparents Joseph and Mary Emerson in Malden, Massachusetts, where Ellen copied the information from their tombstones.⁶⁴

The summer of 1863 was an odd combination of social pleasures and distressing news from the war. Edie Davidson was spending the summer with her mother, leaving Ellen free to travel. In early July, Ellen, Edith, and Edward, along with Una Hawthorne, visited the Wards in Canton, Massachusetts. They passed the days reading and laughing with the Ward's children Tom, Lily, and Bessie, spending at least an hour with Anna each afternoon. One thing weighed on Ellen. Anna Ward had converted to Catholicism in 1858, and Ellen wrote to her mother, "I wish all the time that we were all either Catholics or Protestants, the difference is such a constant discomfort, never forgotten for one minute."⁶⁵

The party went to Camp Meigs in nearby Readville to see the Dress Parade for the 55th Massachusetts Infantry, a unit for African American soldiers established after the first African American unit—the Massachusetts 54th—filled quickly to capacity. Robertson James was an officer, and he struggled to keep a straight face as he marched by his friends.⁶⁶ Later in the month, the entire crew—the Emerson and Ward siblings and Una Hawthorne—moved to Newport; the Emersons, Lily, and Una stayed with Lotty Hemenway, and Tom and Bessie with the James family. One day, Ellen boasted, "Lotty, Una and I went out to our shoulders and rode the waves in triumph," noting they were out past all the men in the water.⁶⁷ The trip was not altogether successful, however. The exhaustion that had plagued Edith for months continued, and Ellen fretted about money to the point that her father wrote to her, "Please do not fill your letters with distresses about dollars or I shall be dramatized in all private theatricals as the Screwing or Suffering papa."⁶⁸

Terrible news from the war brought it close. On July 13, a riot sparked by frustration over the recently implemented draft broke out in New York City, fueled by class and racial tensions. The rioters first attacked government buildings, then turned their violence towards African Americans and abolitionists, including looting and burning the Colored Orphan Asylum. The home of Sally Gibbons—Ellen's friend from the Sedgwick School who was engaged to William Emerson Jr.—was ransacked and set on fire, targeted because of her family's long commitment to abolition.[69] Ellen hoped the New York Emersons would leave and worried that riots would break out in Boston and even Concord.[70] The news of the riots was quickly followed by the report that Robert Gould Shaw, commander of the 54th Massachusetts Infantry, had been killed on July 18 in Charleston, South Carolina, at the Second Battle of Fort Wagner. Ellen declared his death "the greatest loss perhaps that Massachusetts has sustained during the war."[71] Wilkie James, an officer in the unit, was shot in the foot and the side. Cabot Russell, the father of Edward's companion on the trip west, found Wilkie in a Sanitary Commission hospital while searching for his son, also in the unit, and accompanied him back to Newport.[72] Young Cabot's body was never identified.

Shaw's death helped inspire Waldo to write the poem "Voluntaries," an ode to Union soldiers who gave their lives in the war, which was published in *The Atlantic* in October 1863. The final lines of the fourth stanza—"So nigh is grandeur to our dust / So near is God to man / When duty whispers low *Thou must* / The youth replies, *I can*"—often appear on memorials to veterans.[73] Lines earlier in the poem, which emphasize the carefree lives the young men have willingly abandoned to serve, might have been inspired by the full social lives of his own children, who brought the youth of Concord to Bush. Edith and Ellen took a decided interest in the poem. When Waldo sent it to Robert's father Francis, he noted he had already submitted the "verses" to *The Atlantic* but added "my daughters have made it a point that I should copy them for you." He concluded, "I could heartily wish that it were in my power to send you any just expression of the feeling which all the members of my family have, with the country, of the public debt to your house & its hero."[74]

In September, Edith accepted an invitation from the Forbes family to Naushon. Josephine "Effie" Shaw, Robert Gould Shaw's sister, was also a guest. As Edith was writing Ellen, Effie "danced in" with the news that Ida Agassiz was engaged to Henry Lee Higginson. Higginson, a merchant, had been badly injured in the Battle of Aldie in June 1863; he had known Ida since childhood.[75] Edith understood the enormous role Ida played in Ellen's emotional universe, but encouraged her to embrace the engagement as good news. She wrote, "I hope it will suit you, Ellen. It ought to."[76] Whatever private pain it caused, Ellen did celebrate the engagement. She wrote to Mary Higginson, Henry's sister, to congratulate her. Describing Mary as "O Enviable Girl," Ellen noted, "How happy you are in a second sister, and such a sister!"[77] Ellen did seem genuinely to like Henry. After the December 5 wedding, she explained, "I am an admirer of Major Higginson and for the first time discovered that a Bridegroom is interesting," praising, "this good soldier, with his scarred face, and the splendor of his uniform." She found Ida, of course, lovely, in her "full bridal array" and deemed the wedding "beautiful and satisfactory."[78]

In the fall, Edward was at Harvard, with the rest of the family reunited at Bush. Edith had taken on a Sunday school class and spent "hours at a time whenever she is in Boston in the bookstores, getting books for it."[79] On November 26, the country observed the first national Thanksgiving holiday. It had long been celebrated in New England, where it was often, as was the case with the Emersons, more important than Christmas, but each state had set its own date.[80] Waldo reflected hopefully, "Mr. Lincoln, in fixing the day, has in some sort bound himself to furnish good news & victories for it."[81]

On December 13, Edith set out for an extended visit with Susan and William Emerson, who had relocated from Staten Island to Manhattan's 22nd Street. Haven warned her, "I hope you will find us amiable enough to be endurable. So much sickness does not sweeten the temper of a family."[82] Charles Emerson was home from his military duties on sick leave. William Jr., who had married Sally Gibbons the day before Thanksgiving, was growing ever-weaker from tuberculosis, and Susan suffered from excruciating headaches. Edith brought her own health concerns. She went to New York for treatment of what her father described as a "weak back" that had plagued her for several years and the exhaustion that had stalked her throughout 1863, another example of the vague health concerns that haunted nineteenth-century women.[83]

Waldo accompanied Ellen, checking into the St. Denis Hotel on Eleventh Street and Broadway, while Edith settled in with her uncle's family. When Waldo gave the lecture "Fortune of the Republic" in Brooklyn, Edith chose to stay home mending her father's and Charley's gloves, which she deemed a "pleasure."[84] Waldo and Edith visited the bookstores Appleton's, Miller's, and Scribner's and chose a cake basket at Tiffany & Co. for Sally and William's wedding present. The arrival of the Concord Emersons coincided with the end of Charley's leave. Edith described him as, "pale, peaked, and blue, taking opium, which makes him fractious."[85] While he "was like our old Charley" on the night before his departure, his parents were deeply worried.[86]

Waldo and Edith met Dr. Charles Schieferdecker on December 18. Schieferdecker was a practitioner of hygeiotherapy, a "water cure" popular in the United States from the 1840s through the 1870s. Based on the idea that water was purifying, patients consumed large amounts of cold water and took baths and wrapped themselves in wet sheets throughout the day; robust exercise, particularly walking, and a strict diet, were also prescribed.[87] Edith was skeptical, particularly of the long list of food Schieferdecker considered harmful. She reported, "the man knows a good deal, but he carries his hobbies too far." Edith worried he would "spring trap after trap on me, 'till he has (if it is a possible thing) made me a perfect Betty afraid of everything but bread and meat."[88] Her fears that her doctor would "trap" her and his refusal to take her concerns seriously were an inauspicious start to the treatment. They also may have been well-founded. In 1874, a coroner's jury found Schieferdecker guilty of criminal neglect when a patient died under his care.[89] Sally's report that she had heard Dr. Schieferdecker was a Confederate sympathizer did nothing to shore up Edith's confidence. Her experimental bath at his Institute, at 68 West Fourteenth Street, was also not promising. Edith's revulsion is palpable in her description of "three cot bedsteads with dirty mattresses & pillows without sheets or cases, wet sheets hanging round the walls"; she also took note of the "unpainted wooden sitz baths and long, large bath tubs."[90] Edith wondered if she could stand submersing herself in the tubs and if she would have to lie on unwashed sheets.

Once Edith started the treatments, her distaste only grew. She resented the doctor's food restrictions, particularly his objections to ice cream, and felt they made it difficult to socialize. The rigid schedule, including two baths a day each followed by a mile walk and drinking a quart of very cold water, disrupted the long hours of sleep she required, leaving her more exhausted than ever.[91] While enjoying the actual baths, she despised lying on the bed under a blanket used by someone else. Edith filled letters with descriptions of her hatred of the doctor, her sense that he was out to get her, and the absurdity of his claims. A month into her treatment, she complained, "my back is weak again, and often aches, and I am just getting well of a bad cough which has bothered me for a week or two, and worried Haven still more, besides that I am troubled as I was at Newport, and have the same objection to morning, and my cheeks are hot and spotty, and not the cool red they were a month ago."[92] A concerned Lidian instructed her, "see if he will not let you use your own judgement in all things where you feel his rules are *hurting* you."[93] Waldo was concerned, but irritated too, comparing Edith's resistance to her complaints about going to the Agassiz school.[94] Their responses reflect the ongoing debates in the family about illness, but also suggest Lidian taught her daughters to stand up to male physicians and make their own judgements about their health. Ultimately Edith continued the treatment for over two months, making the modifications she felt critical.

In Concord, Bush was busy, with the Civil War shaping their lives far from the battlefield. There was a dinner for General Francis Barlow, who had grown up in Concord and who was recovering from injuries suffered at Gettysburg. Wilkie James, also recuperating, visited in January. Even though puss oozed from the wound in his foot, he looked "natural and very fat."[95] Mary Peabody Mann, the reformer who was the wife of Horace Mann and the sister of Elizabeth Peabody and Sophia Peabody Hawthorne, organized a Sanitary Commission Fair on February 22. Ellen worried people would not come from Boston and found no passion for Mann's suggestions about what she might contribute; eventually she agreed to "receive and protect the spoons" people contributed, sell food, and, beforehand, promote the fair and "exhort every age and condition to be there."[96] Ellen's fears proved unfounded, as the fair raised $500.[97]

The family controversy around Edward enlisting roared back, resulting in an angry exchange between the sisters. In January, Ellen reported she had told Ellery Channing that her brother felt "his time coming," and he would be leaving college for the military the following summer.[98] Edith was apocalyptic, shocked that, if true, her brother had made the decision without consulting her and, if not, wondering why Ellen was "telling your fictions around the town." Worried that Ellen and Edward had made a private pact, she extorted, "that's no excuse at all, if you have, it's treason and disrespect to Father and Mother." She concluded, "I think you are very cool and impertinent about it."[99] Things had cooled down by January 26. "I am glad that you have agreed to say no more about Edward's going away, I thought you would *push* him into the army next," Edith wrote. She regretted her earlier tone, however, adding, "But my dearest sister, you shouldn't be so humble to this little chit, when she presumes to scold her betters, she ought to be boxed on the ear!"[100]

The flareup was about Edward, but it was also part of a broader readjustment in the sisters' relationship as they became peers. Ellen had always taken a maternal attitude toward her younger sister. Now that Edith was in her twenties and out of school, it was clearer the sisters were only two years apart in age. As their relationship shifted to that of partners and friends, there were some rough patches. Ellen joked about their shifting roles when she packed a trunk to send to her sister, noting that it was "so much like old times" and that now that she was "old" the roles were usually reversed and Edith was more likely to care for her.[101] The dustup about Edward's enlistment ended with Edith apologizing for being a "little chit," but part of the motivation for it was her insistence on being seen as more than the little sister.

When Edith had arrived in New York, her cousin William's wasted appearance shocked her.[102] By February, Edith despaired that he looked "as Mr. Thoreau did the last week."[103] Edward was in New York when William took a turn for the worse at the end of the month. Edith sat with her aunt, suffering from another headache, while Edward joined his cousin and uncle at William's bedside. In the middle of the night Edith heard Haven "slowly and heavily dragging himself up the stairs."[104] William had died at three in the morning on February 29, fourteen weeks after his marriage. Susan felt too frail for the trip to Concord for the funeral, so Edith remained with her in New York. When William was buried in the family plot in Sleepy Hollow, Sally declared, "I have his name."[105]

Edith remained in New York for another month, continuing the water cure and aiding her family in their grief. She served as a liaison between the Emersons and Sally, offering to accompany the young widow to her in-laws' home when she felt ready. Edith begged Ellen to come to New York, feeling unequal to the task of comforting her aunt and Sally, but Ellen remained in Concord.[106] Her animosity towards the doctor did not decline, and she missed her parents and siblings. On March 18, the doctor agreed she could finish her treatment, as long as she continued to bathe at home. The doctor was more interested in the letter Waldo sent him ending the treatment—which he praised for its combination of "logic and emotions"—than in giving his patient instructions. Edith eventually made him promise to give them to her in writing by the following week, reporting to her mother that her "practical question seemed to amuse him."[107]

Reunited, the sisters fell back into their routines, socializing with the Alcotts and Hawthornes, reading Dante with Elizabeth Hoar, and going to their gymnasium class.[108] They welcomed Haven for a short visit, after which he headed to Washington, D.C. and Virginia to work for the Sanitary Commission as an acting assistant surgeon for a month. Reporting on his experience in Fredericksburg, he wrote, "Every part of the human body which a minnie ball can find and not cause immediate death seemed to have its illustration among the thousands that thronged that hospital city," noting the wounded lay in every nook and cranny of the town, including churches and the city hall.[109]

Edward made two more bids to join the army. In May, his father agreed to write a letter to the President of Harvard endorsing Edward's petition to be released from school to enlist. The university, however, turned down all the petitions submitted by students at that time.[110] In July, as the Confederate Army closed in on Washington, D.C., Edward declared he was dropping out to join the military. Edith, who had been relieved when Harvard rejected the

May petition, pulled out the biggest weapon she had to stop him—their father's cultural importance. "Which seems to you of most value to your country—the services of one private for a month or so or Father's life and work?" she asked him. She continued, "For it is plain to us all that Father must break down, his public life must cease with your going for he has neither heart nor health for work."[111] Ellen, in her biography of Lidian, credits John Forbes with making the argument to Edward. The conversation, if it happened, likely occurred the day Forbes accompanied him to the Massachusetts Statehouse to see if Edward could be assured garrison, not active, duty if he enlisted. Finding even the powerful Mr. Forbes could not get the guarantee, Edward wrote his father, invoking Edith's logic, "I have concluded that I have no right to destroy perhaps your usefulness and comfort for the summer for the sake of something which might not prove the good I hope it might."[112] Years later, Ellen wrote in Lidian's biography, "How grateful were Father & Mother to Mr. Forbes" for persuading Edward to change his mind.[113] It is notable that Ellen obscures Edith's role in her account. Edward was haunted by his choice; in his obituary, Bliss Perry declared, "he carried the regret of being unable to go to the Civil War to the end of his days."[114] Ellen, as she shaped the family history, may have wanted to paper over Edith's role in this painful part of his life.

After the Hawthornes had returned to Concord in 1859, the Hawthorne, Alcott, and Emerson offspring were close. As Julian Hawthorne later remembered, "Our place and the Alcotts' adjoined ... we naturally fraternized with our neighbors, and my two sisters and myself and the Alcott girls were in and out of one another's houses all the time, almost forming one family." He added, "And the three Emerson children, Ellen, Edith, and Edward, being but ten minutes' distance in space and even nearer in amity, were not long in getting into the game—nine of us in all, while our elders looked on approvingly. It was a fine nucleus for good society."[115] Una appreciated that community when Nathaniel Hawthorne died on May 19, 1864, while on a trip to New Hampshire. She declared to Edith in September, "I think sometimes that I can never feel as if I had a home on earth again. Papa was my house and my rest beyond all others, and I think nothing can ever make up to me for his absence."[116] She confided that Edith was the only person to whom she had confessed the depth of her grief, begging her friend to tell no one, particularly Sophia Hawthorne.[117] Una would continue to lean on the Emerson sisters, particularly Edith, for years.

An outdoor adventure in August brought the young Concordians together in happier circumstances. Ellen, Edward, and Una, along with Tom Ward, Lizzy

Simmons, David Loring, Sam Hoar, and George Mann camped for almost a week on Mount Monadnock. Waldo had memorialized the New Hampshire mountain in a poem, and it was "a point of attraction to all the Transcendentalists."[118] There was a hut, but the group often slept outside; they cooked large meals over a fire and scrambled up paths and over rocks. The trip became an annual event for several years, with a rotating cast of characters, including Edith and May Alcott; Waldo and Ellery Channing joined briefly in 1866, although it rained so hard that day Channing scurried away and the rest retreated to the hotel at the bottom of the mountain for the night.[119] After the 1865 excursion, Ellen raved, "we saw sunrises and sunsets, the mountain shadow on the sky, rose-coloured cloud at the door of our hut, pouring rain, and deafening wind."[120]

These co-ed, unchaperoned trips of young, unmarried people run counter to images of nineteenth-century middle-class culture cleaving to a Victorian sense of propriety that also, as Tiya Miles explains, "assigned the playroom and parlor to girls and the field and stream to boys."[121] Miles argues that exploring and experiencing the outdoors gave nineteenth-century girls a way to challenge gender and racial stereotypes. Ellen, at twenty-six, was no longer a child when these camping trips began, but she found a sense of freedom on them that made her feel like one. "It is a little patch of youth let in to my old age, and prized accordingly," she confessed.[122] But she also took over much of the cooking and cleaning of the camp, bringing her domestic duties and sense of gendered responsibility to these outdoor adventures.

The mood in Bush alternated between optimism at the chance for a Union victory and sorrow as the loss of life continued to pile up at the end of 1864. Their circle mourned Charles Lowell, who had been killed in October, shortly after he married Effie Shaw. Ellen reported to Mary Waterman details not included in Lowell's obituaries, including that he was already bleeding internally by the time he "mounted for his last charge."[123] On a happier note, William Forbes, John Forbes' son who had been taken a prisoner of war in July, had been released in December and was home on leave. At a square-dancing party at the Wards, he went out of his way to reserve Edith for the quadrille.[124]

As March 1865 rolled in, there was hope the traumatic conflict of the past four years would soon end in victory for the North. The month also marked the beginning of a new era for the Emerson sisters on a personal level. On March 3, William Forbes traveled to Concord to propose to Edith, and she immediately said yes. "How proud I am to have a Colonel," she declared to Will. She dreamed of the day she could "do everything for" him and be a "good wife for the hero";

she told Will she looked forward to the time when she "might have the joy of watching you and stroking your hair."[125] From the beginning, she envisioned herself in a very different marriage than the tense one of her parents, marked by her dedication to caring for her husband and open displays of physical affection. It would not be a marriage that challenged gender roles, although Will and Edith formed a strong partnership.

"After an acquaintance of four or five years the parties had come to a perfect understanding," Waldo reported.[126] Will's affection for Edith had often been noted, with Ellen claiming, "Will has loved Edith from first sight."[127] They met in 1858, when the Emersons visited Naushon. Waldo's respect for John Murray Forbes was mirrored by Edward's for Will; Edward cast him as an older brother years before marriage made the relationship official. Despite the affection between the families and Will's interest in Edith, a series of crises had kept him from courting her. In January 1860, he was expelled from Harvard after a prank for the secret society Med. Fac. went dreadfully awry. Will snuck into the college chapel, where the security guard John Hilton confronted him; while the order of events is unclear, Will hit Hilton with a billy club and Hilton shot at Will with a pistol and handcuffed him until sunrise. Will was arrested and eventually expelled, with the incident covered in papers across the country because of Will's famous father.[128] The Emersons sided with the Forbes; his mother Sarah Forbes wrote to Ellen, "all of you—you have been so kind to W., I shall never forget it."[129] Still, he despaired, according to his biographer, "I can never have any hope of Edith Emerson now."[130] That October his sister Ellen committed suicide, devastating the family.[131] Will joined the army in December 1861 and was taken prisoner of war in July 1864. He was released in December of the same year.

Perhaps this final trauma compelled Will to action, taking even their closest friends and family by happy surprise. Sarah Forbes stated, "It does not seem strange at all because I thought of it all so long ago" but added, "it has come suddenly just now, we are all happy about it."[132] Una Hawthorne scolded, "Oh Edith, what a perfect Machiavelli you are! I think you should be just at the head of the most secret state department."[133] Letters of congratulations poured in as news spread of the union between the Emersons and Forbes families, each powerful in its own way. Ellen declared, "Never was an engagement so pure a pleasure to all people nearly interested and at the same time so lovely a spectacle to all the world."[134]

Ellen immediately embraced Will as her sibling. She wrote to Haven, "I am sure you rejoice with Edith in her entire happiness and Edward and me in receiving such a brother."[135] But the engagement did mean a major change in her life, not all for the better. She had come to see Edith not just as her baby sister but as a partner. She would now face the day-to-day challenges of housekeeping and caregiving alone. Her anxiety was apparent when she worried the engaged couple might wall themselves off as an exclusive pair for the five days they stayed in Concord after the engagement. She was pleased and relieved, then, to report "my joyful surprise and my gratitude when the two continued to talk, to walk, and to sit with us and were so merry and talkative that they were the source of pleasure all the time."[136] Their circumstances might be changing, but Ellen was not losing her sister to marriage.

Waldo was thrilled with the turn of events. He saw in Will the character he admired in John Forbes, and he took pride in announcing the engagement. As he explained to Caroline Sturgis Tappan, "Although the friendship is an old one, this covenant is only since Saturday. He begins with his heroic looks & he mends on acquaintance day by day."[137] He praised Will and the match to John Forbes, stating, "I am rejoiced to give my little country girl into the hands of this brave protector."[138] Lidian, while happy, was concerned with how the marriage would influence her life. She suggested the couple put off the wedding for three years; she then offered a date at some point after the end of the war, but not at least for eighteen months. Ellen and Edward came to their sister's defense. "No indeed! They shall be married as soon as they please! It's the only way!" they cried.[139] The demands of caring for Lidian had shaped many elements of her children's lives, but the siblings stood together to ensure the start of Edith's marriage would not be one of them.

The Forbes welcomed Edith. Sarah Forbes stressed that the war changed normal social rules, writing to Edith, "Now my dear come over to us & do not let us be separated more than this war separates us all—It is no time for formal etiquette, & I hope you will come here at once."[140] Will and Edith thus traveled to Washington, D.C. to spend a month at 264 I Street, where his parents had settled for the winter. These precious weeks allowed Will and Edith to learn more about each other and plan their new life. In a heartbreaking gesture, Sarah Forbes gave Edith her deceased daughter Ellen's ring engraved with an "E," confessing Ellen had longed for the marriage and would have wanted Edith to have it. The Forbes introduced her into their circle, where their warm embrace of her, her father's fame, and her own charm made social acceptance easy. Her position in the influential Forbes household gave Edith access to the latest gossip about the war, such as the evening Charles Sumner discussed a secret report which suggested Lee could not mount another campaign unless he used "negro troops."[141] She passed on each detail to her family. John Forbes purchased a carriage for the young couple, causing Lidian to exclaim to her sister, "Our little girl's life is like a fairy tale right now." But the fact that Will would likely soon be called back to his regiment, and into harm's way, hovered over the social whirl and excitement. "She needs to have some pleasant things to lay up when Will goes to the War again," Lidian believed.[142]

On March 31, Will accompanied Edith back to Concord, then left immediately to rejoin his unit, the Third Battalion of the Second Massachusetts Cavalry, in Virginia. He hoped to make it in time to experience the final throes of the conflict. In the dramatic two weeks which followed, the couple exchanged a flurry of letters, describing their love for one another, their hopes for the future, and their experiences of the last days of the war. Their correspondence often went astray, causing anxiety and dismay. They interpreted their relationship through the lens of the war, particularly when it came to their shared commitment to happiness. Both expressed gratitude for the month they had spent with one another, even if that should be the sum total of their time together. Edith pondered, "Shall we have another such? Yes, we may hope for even happier days, when we have peace and no anxieties or dread of parting."[143] She reflected on finding bliss amidst the death and destruction that so many had met during the war. "It makes our own happiness almost—I cannot find the word—but it seems a responsibility, a boon too great and undeserved," she wrote to Will.[144] They often referred to their responsibility to treasure the blessing they had found in one another as a way to honor those who had suffered. This emphasis was a response to the war, but their shared experiences of coping with depressed family members also strengthened their determination to be happy. The burden of Lidian's depression may have fallen most heavily on Ellen, but Edith certainly felt its weight and toiled to find ways to cheer her mother; the burden may have been at the root of her relentless optimism. And Ellen Forbes' suicide had devastated Will's family. They wanted to ensure those dark legacies did not haunt their new home.

As Will fell back in with his regiment, the Emersons experienced the final days of the war on the home front. On April 3, when bells tolled in Concord to celebrate the fall of Richmond, Edith and Ellen ran to hear the cannon salute, Ellen "fairly prancing and screaming" on the way. They then paraded to the Hawthornes, where they gathered with their neighbors around the piano to sing "The Battle Hymn of the Republic," "The Star-Spangled Banner," "Hail

Columbia," and "My Country 'Tis of Thee."[145] That evening, Waldo and Edith scoured his study to find the right victory hymn for Edith to bring to her Sunday school class. On April 10, the bells rang again, this time signifying Robert E. Lee's surrender the day before. Edith pinned on an eagle broach, Ellen grabbed a small paper flag, and they joined the crowd, including their father, at the Concord post office. Ellen reported to Edward, "We have had the salute and the bells, have promenaded the town, each with a little flag, have called on Aunt Lizzy, and spent the rest of the morning devouring the newspaper."[146] Edith, though, lamented at her "small capacity for joy," as she waited anxiously for word from Will.[147] She had received just one of the many letters he had written since he left ten days earlier. Only after John Forbes telegraphed to inform her that a "jubilant letter" from Will had arrived could she rejoice, even more so when she learned Will had been present at Lee's surrender.[148]

The news of Abraham Lincoln's death on April 15 shattered the personal and national joy. "This day is hard to bear—So dark and sad for the country that the gloom is heavy over all," Edith wrote to Will, noting that her anxiety about him made it even harder to tolerate.[149] Will's brother Malcolm was in Ford's Theater when the shots rang out, and Will reported on April 16 that the troops had heard rumors of Lincoln's death, but they had not yet been confirmed.[150] That same day, the Emersons joined an overflowing crowd at First Parish, with even Waldo in attendance. Edith had her Sunday school students recite Luke 12:48, "For unto whomsoever much is given, of him shall be much required," to encourage them to count their blessings. She and Will strove to cherish their good fortune in the face of tragedy, and Edith hoped to encourage others to do so as well.

The nineteenth of April was usually a day of celebration in Concord. But on April 19, 1865, like communities around the country, Concord held a service for Lincoln. Ellen reported, "today we have kept the funeral of our dear, our good President, with more real grief than would have seemed possible for a people to feel at a President's loss."[151] Edith decorated the church's altar with white hyacinths and a garland of English violets, her favorite flowers.[152] Waldo delivered the address, striving to honor the martyred president and comfort his mourning neighbors. He praised Lincoln above all as an American, representing the best of American values, including common sense and courage. "In four years,—four years of battle-days,—his endurance, his fertility of resources, his magnanimity, were sorely tried and never found wanting," Waldo declared, in front of the bouquets carefully arranged by his daughter. "There, by his courage, his justice, his even temper, his fertile counsel, his humanity," Waldo continued, "he stood a heroic figure in the centre of a heroic epoch. He is the true history of the American people in his time."[153] Edith was rapt. She reported to Will, "I never sat still for so long in my life—I did not move a finger, and only dreaded the end. I was never so carried away by anything before."[154] Ellen and Lidian agreed with Edith's estimation, and the speech was printed in newspapers around the country. Waldo dismissed any praise. People were moved not by his words, he claimed, but by the emotion the dramatic events of the past week had brought about.

With that sobering sentiment, the Emersons gathered at home. Within weeks, they would launch into the frenzy of planning the wedding and outfitting Edith's new house in Milton. In the next months, Edith's marriage, followed quickly by a child, would reshape their family. But on this night, those changes lay ahead. As the Emersons so often did, they sat together contemplating the intertwined fates of their family and the nation, expressing thanks for Edith's upcoming union and the victory of the Union, even as they mourned Lincoln and those lost in the war.

CHAPTER FOUR

"I Wrote for Myself as Well as for You"

(1865–1872)

On October 3, 1865, in the Bush parlor decked with greenery and autumnal leaves and filled with family and friends, Edith married William Forbes. Wearing a pearl cross pin given to her by Sarah and John Forbes and a white muslin dress, she spoke her vows clearly and with confidence; nerves caused Will to stumble over his. The house burst with joy. It was a union of two people deeply in love and of two families who cared for and respected one another in a time of peace after the calamitous years of war. After a quick costume change, "down the walk went Edith Emerson in her brown hat and dress, away from her father's house for evermore, and gave her hand to her bridegroom at the gate and he put her into her seat, tucked the shawls around her, walked round and got in the other side, and they whirled away," Ellen reported.[1] Children threw shoes after the buggy, and then, at Waldo's command, the remaining party went in to a feast of oysters and pudding.

The months before the wedding had been a whirlwind of planning. Edith, however, was so calm it was if "she had been married a half a dozen times at least," according to Elizabeth Hoar.[2] She was confident in her choice of husband and loved to organize events, so few jitters tripped her up. Gifts poured into Bush, from silver butter dishes to a full set of Hawthorne's works, sent by the publisher Ticknor and Fields.[3]

Edith and Will took the buggy to Higginson's House in Pigeon's Cove, a lovely town on the Massachusetts coast. "The first letter I sign with the new name must be to you," Edith wrote to her mother; Will wrote Ellen, underscoring she had gained a brother, not lost a sister.[4] Even as they took care to remember her family and thank them for their beautiful wedding, Ellen and Will began to build their own world, planning their home as they gathered "very bright scarlet woodbine leaves," rosehips, and "bluish bayberries" on their walks.[5] They moved to Naushon after a week. By the end of October, Edith was pregnant.

Ellen and her parents, while thrilled with the match, struggled with their new reality. "I never knew before what real missing was," Ellen thought the day after the wedding, crying uncontrollably. It was more than simply missing her sister, closest friend, and partner in caregiving. Her younger sibling, who had always followed behind her, was entering a life beyond Ellen's experience. As she explained, "where Edith was I could not imagine to myself. I had never seen her there."[6] While Lidian wished she could have just one more week with Edith as a little girl back in her bed, Waldo proclaimed, "There are several very agreeable circumstances about that child's going away, but there is one sad one and that is that she is gone."[7]

Edith and Will moved into a "cottage" next to his parents' house in Milton, Massachusetts, with an apple orchard on one side, a grove of pine and spruce trees on the other, and a wisteria branch over the front door.[8] Milton is thirty-two miles from Concord. In 1865, the distance made Edith seem quite far away, and yet trains made a day trip possible. While Edith's marriage changed the sisters' relationship and altered the family dynamic, it quickly became clear that Edith would remain tied to life in Bush. Edward and Ellen had their own rooms in Milton, and there was a constant stream of visits and correspondence between the homes. Edith was now a Forbes, but she would always be an Emerson.

Edith settled easily into her new life, taking great interest in each element of her home. "Everything matches, down to the purple soap," Una Hawthorne raved, wondering "at such absolute perfection."[9] While she had found housekeeping at Bush frustrating, Edith, with the Forbes money, had more help, and her daily life no longer included caring for her mother. She described the people she hired as "fairies" who magically took care of the house and grounds. She was strict with the fairies, however, wary of the chaotic churn of servants at Bush; she told her mother, "But I very much fear that people in Concord will never have the best girls—they spoil them so—and are too submissive."[10] Edith would become increasingly critical of her servants in the years to come, as she grew comfortable wielding the power that came with the Forbes money.

As she adjusted to her life without Edith nearby, Ellen took on another caregiving duty. Alicia Keyes, known as Lily, moved into the house in November, and Ellen began to refer to her as "daughter." Unlike Edie Davidson, there is no mystery around the arrangement. Lily was the ten-year-old child of Martha Prescott and John Keyes, a Concord lawyer who was serving as U.S. Marshall for Massachusetts. The Keyes planned to live in Boston for several months, but "Lily wanted to spend the winter at the Emersons with Miss Ellen," her father remembered in his autobiography.[11] Unlike Edie's seemingly unstable domestic situation, Lily was from a prominent family and actively sought time at Bush. Ellen and Lily would remain close, but Ellen never felt the moral and financial responsibility she did for Edie. Still, her presence consoled Ellen "a measure for the loss of my Ediths," she reported to her sister.[12] Ellen was being dramatic—even as Ellen bonded with Lily, Edie Davidson continued to spend long stretches of time at Bush.

Ralph Emerson Forbes was born on July 10, 1866, sharing his birthday with Edward. Edith wrote to her brother, "I only hope he will prove as great a joy and comfort to his mother and father as his uncle has always been to his."[13] Ellen, in residence for the birth, reported, "Edith was a little heroine, tranquil & cheery all day, she did not appear to lose her consciousness."[14] Edith was confined to bed for weeks. Mrs. Rounsville, the baby nurse, according to Ellen, "does more things I should have supposed the human mind could have invented, seeming to know all about everything, and succeeding invariably in returning Edith to comfort."[15] Lidian, from afar, however, was horrified that the nurse told Edith not to breastfeed for three days, remembering "my babies nursed immediately or they would have killed themselves and their mother."[16] Will had whooping cough and could not hold the baby for over a month, but his bedside visits always cheered Edith.[17] "The birth of your babe touches this old house & its people & its neighbors with unusual joy," Waldo wrote to Edith, hoping young Ralph would "be worthy of these great days of his country."[18]

The day after Ralph's birth, Edward, finished with his studies at Harvard, set off to Burlington, Iowa. He was to work for Charles Elliott Perkins, Will's cousin who was the superintendent of the Chicago, Burlington, and Quincy Railroad.[19] Ellen hoped he would find satisfaction and independence. "You have been born thrall to us, to an uncommon degree, and though I know how delightful it is to be one, I consider it easier and happier for a girl than for a boy, and regret very much having sometimes so clogged your good times," she wrote.[20] Ellen was the family member most sympathetic to the pressure Edward felt as the only surviving son of the great Ralph Waldo Emerson. But her letter also dismisses her own sacrifices as something natural for a "girl," part of her ongoing demotion of her own desires below that of her family members.

When Edith was a child, Lidian had predicted that "Edie was born to be a mother."[21] Her vision proved correct, as Edith found motherhood enchanting. Ralph, according to her, was one of the "model babies," who slept soundly, ate easily, and flourished on the attention of a large circle of family and their friends.[22] Edith's letters document in detail his development and the physical reality of recovery from childbirth. On Naushon, Edith found she could not produce enough milk to keep up with his appetite, so her mother-in-law arranged for milk from "one cow" to be sent to the house, which Edith mixed with two glasses of hot water and a little sugar to supplement Ralph's diet. Edith was "jealous of that old bottle," from which Ralph drank.[23] She swam, hoping it would cure the headaches, tiredness, and back aches that plagued her. Will, recovered from whooping cough, had a large boil and swollen arm, and Edith worried he worked too much. These complaints paled next to their happiness.

Despite the joy Ralph brought, the strain of the new family dynamics and Edward's absence were visible over the holidays. At Thanksgiving at Bush, Ellen did find talking late into the night with Edith an "oasis" from the labor of making pies and planning the dinner.[24] Edith, however, complained to Edward of "the torment of Ellen being such a one-idead creature," continuing, "if her own health, Mother's and mine all depended on her care—Sunday Scholars & Bible study would still reign preeminent over all her days and hours . . . It makes me so mad!"[25] Concern for Ellen, who did exhaust herself, motivated some of her outrage. Her own exhaustion brought on by new motherhood may have made Edith crave extra attention, but her declaration echoed her rebuke of Edward's desire to enlist. Family duties should trump all else. In that construction, Edith seemed blind to the intellectual and emotional satisfaction Ellen received from teaching Sunday school. Even as she stepped out into the world as a wife and mother, Edith wanted to be cared for her by the elder sibling who had babied her so often.

Rather than back away from Sunday school, in January Ellen decided to join the church formally, which would allow her to take communion.[26] "It may help me," she explained to Haven, adding, "If it does, then indeed, I shall have reason to rejoice that I have entered." Only after she was able to frame the choice as part of the process of becoming a Christian, rather than the culmination of that process did she make her choice. Her parents were bemused. Waldo was "surprised," and told her, "he should feel as if he abridged his boundless freedom if it were himself, but if I feel no difficulty then there is none." Lidian was "glad to hear it, though she never could see her own clear way to doing it."[27] While women's piousness often is associated with submissiveness, for Ellen joining the church allowed her to assert her own identity as her sister became a wife and a mother.[28] Given the that rejection of communion was central to Waldo's decision to step away from the ministry, Ellen's emphasis on "access" to the "Communion table" as a benefit underscores how this choice was a declaration of independence. Through the church, she could carve a space for herself, and participate in activities that did not serve her family, as well as challenge herself intellectually. She was an active participant in debates about the direction of the Sunday school classes, for instance, believing the teachers should teach more doctrine but concerned she herself had not learned enough to take on the task.[29] In the coming years, she became even more engaged, attending Unitarian conventions as a delegate, which brought her a "flood of joy."[30]

It is notable that Ellen announced her decision to join the church in a letter to Haven Emerson.[31] She was often philosophical in her correspondence to her cousin; freed from the demands of recounting household and budgetary information and the tradition of the journal letter, her letters to Haven offer a glimpse of the intellectual she might have been under other circumstances. In the same January letter, her thoughts on how to raise children, newly on her mind due to Ralph, and the role of prayer spilled out. Responding to a letter from Haven, she wrote, "Yes, I believe you are right that nobody can, directly, help us much after we have grown up, and that we must decide everything for ourselves then, though I think children can be, and are, very much helped by people in whom they confide." After ceding that point, she stressed how helpful prayer was to her, hinting that it pained her that her cousins did not have such succor. "That prayer is our access to God and that nothing is too small to be asked about, and that all those promises to prayer are always kept. It seems as if the great reach and the minute adaptation to our needs of this wonderful intercourse between the creature and the Creator was not half believed in anywhere, and those who like you were brought up outside of the Christian faith were less likely to have been taught it except in the most general outline," she explained.[32] She believed that Haven would not become misanthropic despite his lack of faith, but still wished he could find the comfort she found in the church.

Edward had returned from his westward journey in time for Christmas and Ralph's christening in Milton.[33] Eye problems cut short his job with the railroad. Ellen was thrilled to have him home, claiming "he takes half my care, does three quarters of my work, and does everything with me."[34] His aid and company were particularly welcome, as Waldo was off on a two-month lecture tour. Edward began to teach a Sunday School class and help Ellen raise money for the Freedmen's Bureau.[35] He also helped Will establish a vineyard in Milton, a scheme Will set up in part to help Edward find a sense of purpose and earn money.[36]

Edith was pregnant again by the end of February but did not slow down. She regularly visited Concord, with Waldo musing, "Ralph in one month had so changed that in April it was an angel's visit, in May a diabolical interruption."[37] In her gardens at Milton, she and Will "could almost weep with joy when we gaze upon the blooming carrots & strawberries, pears & peaches; the straight clean walks, the bushed peas, the splendid rhubarb & asparagus, and all the other wonders, including my hop vine."[38] Four days before she gave birth, Edith was, "in the thick of business, carpeting, preserving, sewing both by seamstresses in and out of house and my own hand, gardening, farming, housekeeping, etc."[39] She tended to her family, her home, and her gardens, and they all thrived.

Edith Forbes, known as Violet, was born on October 28, 1867, with her mother reporting she had no "after pain or trouble."[40] Violet was as amiable as Ralph, although her doting parents worried she was "limp" and did not "have half the backbone" older brother had as an infant.[41] Ellen was in Milton, ecstatic to be an aunt once again. "I no longer canter along the ground as in old days, but skip from tree-top to tree-top, and everyone says, 'we understand it: she has a NEPHEW & a NIECE,'" she declared.[42] When she returned home two days after Violet's birth, Waldo insisted on going to meet the baby himself, whereupon he found "her little rosebud mouth was beyond praise."[43]

Edith took care to document her experience as a mother in her letters. While noting she was "sometimes ashamed" to write at such length about her children, her purposes were twofold. "I think I can make my pictures more clear for you to see if I put all in and because, when some time in the future I want to recall my babies, these little unimportant details will bring back more vividly the dear little two shows at play, and I wrote for myself as well as you," she explained to Lidian.[44] The letters thus helped maintain her bonds with her family in Concord, while also giving her a path to remember the fleeting time with young children.

Now a married twenty-seven-year-old woman and mother of two, Edith became more vocal about her opinions—and her frustrations. During an August 1868 stay, Lidian fell into her pattern of obsessing, worrying about when to take her walks and write her letters to the point that she could do neither. Edith urged Lidian to take a lesson from her own experience with the water cure, which she only enjoyed after refusing to do the "odious walk" each day.[45] When that same summer Ellen and Lidian journeyed to Mountain House in

Princeton, Massachusetts, with the hope the fresh air would build up both of their constitutions, Edith brought her family to Concord to care for Waldo. The patriarch sensed his younger daughter's stay was not entirely voluntary, joking, "Edith has been held here against her will, and I fear much to the prejudice of her comfort to take care of her dear lonely sour papa."[46] Whether by nature or by family dynamics, Edith rarely demonstrated Ellen's and Lidian's tendency towards martyrdom, choosing plans that made her happy and complaining when she did not like the way things played out.

Edith also grew more opinionated about Ellen's choices, especially when they put her sister at risk. Ellen could not shake a cold over the winter and spring, even as she cared for her ailing aunts Susan Emerson and Lucy Brown, both in Concord, and looked in on Sophia Hawthorne, also sick.[47] The infection worried Edith and Edward, who had enrolled at Harvard Medical School. But Ellen's difficulty taking a break also infuriated Edith. When her elder sister returned home early from a trip to Newport, Edith deemed her a "provoking creature," explaining, "To come trotting home when she was gaining so much pleasure and future health as I believe, and there was no decent reason why she should leave it. I have no patience with her. I want to shake her."[48]

Edith wanted Ellen to be happy, but on the terms she set. Edith begged Ellen to accompany Lidian for an extended stay in the summer of 1868, promising Ellen she could spend her days reading novels. When Ellen declined, Edith framed Ellen's refusal as a choice between her Sunday school students and Ralph and Violet.[49] "You prefer seeing them to seeing my chicks," she complained, again blind to the importance of the role the church played in Ellen's life.[50] That same summer, Ellen was fascinated when she attended the "Templar Festival," a gathering of the lodge of the Good Templars, a temperance organization. Ellen explained to Edith she was "sometimes very much attracted, sometimes repelled by what I saw," but she was at least considering joining.[51] Edith replied, "Your letter of yesterday struck a chill to my soul—*Don't* for the love of your sister, don't disgrace us by joining a secret society." She added, "It seems as if it would be a bar between us" and noted the thought of Ellen as a Templar made her feel as ill as the time she dreamed that Ellen had converted to Catholicism.[52] Edith's intense reaction indicates how important the bond with her sister was, but also her sense that it might be fragile. She had left home and forged a new life, but at least part of her wanted Ellen's life to remain the same, with the sisters' connection at the center of it. Ellen, at home with her parents, however, needed to create a community for herself and follow her own interests.

While Ellen asserted her independence in some areas, changes in Waldo's health drew her even closer to him. Their trip to New York in April 1868, when Packer Institute in Brooklyn Heights invited Waldo to lecture, highlighted the early stages of this change. For once, Ellen's desires shaped their agenda, and they headed straight to Henry Ward Beecher's Brooklyn church from their overnight ferry. She was pleased her father seemed to enjoy the sermon, so "there could be no doubt that he had come willingly, for I from the beginning had made such a point of coming that I had given him no smallest chance to be recusant, and had feared secretly it was wholly 'self-sacrifice' for my benefit." After the sermon ended, the crowd leaving the church spotted Ulysses S. Grant on the street and took chase. "Father and I joined madly in this pursuit, and ran along, now in the street, now out, like little boys beside the trainers, and one way and another succeeded in seeing his head and shoulders and now and then an uninterrupted glimpse of his face," Ellen reported.[53] (Grant eventually made it to the ferry and took refuge in the lady's cabin.)

Ellen's description of the trip is marked by a new sense of father-daughter adventure, particularly the charming, if bizarre, chase of Grant. More ominously, Ellen also records her surprise that Waldo did not know the way from the ferry to the church. This passing mention of Waldo's confusion marks the beginning of regular references to his memory loss, disorientation, and difficulty working and eventually communicating in the Emerson's children correspondence; Emerson scholars as usually define it as a type of aphasia.[54] Even the "mad pursuit" of Grant may have been a sign of this decline, evidence of the lowering of inhibitions that can accompany memory loss. Waldo and Ellen's trip to Middlebury College in Vermont later in the summer was also notable for entertaining jaunts along with hints at Waldo's deterioration.[55]

In 1868, the deaths of Susan Emerson, on February 6, and William Emerson, on September 13, also reshaped the family. Their aunt and uncle had been a critical source of love and support for Ellen, Edith, and Edward, and Susan had provided the children with a different model of maternal love than Lidian's devoted but exhausting one. Waldo was with William, his last living sibling, when he died in New York City, grateful he was "intelligent to his last moment."[56] The Forbes and Edward were on Naushon, and they, oddly, learned of their uncle's passing by seeing his obituary.[57] Ellen never addresses the omission in her correspondence, although she writes at length about the funeral. While she found the minister's description of her uncle comforting, she was disturbed that he included the religious service, for "it jarred very much on all the minds that knew that neither Uncle William, nor Father, nor Haven nor Charles believed in it."[58] Ellen's faith was at the center of her life, but she respected the choices of others. Her cousins did consult with Ellen about what to include on the tombstones, and she urged them to include the names of their parents' parents, and even their parents' grandparents, along with their mother's maiden name "in brackets," as "gravestones are often genealogically important and useful."[59] Even in grief, Ellen had her eye on documenting the Emersons' historical legacy.

Soon, the Emersons faced another disruption. "This Saturday morning a bolt fell from a clear sky, and tore me up by the roots," Ellen declared on October 24th. Her family had ordered her "to pack my trunks, settle my affairs, make my will, and go to Fayal Wed. 28 to stay till June."[60] While she had been worn down all year, her strength completely gave out in early October. Edward and Edith came up with the plan, first convincing Waldo and Lidian of its feasibility, then "conspiring" with them to convince Ellen.[61] "Our enemies have fallen," Edward crowed to Edith after their sister and parents agreed.[62] As part of her campaign, Edith assured Ellen that she, Edward, and Will would care for their parents, visiting and writing often and making sure Lidian was not "neglected or worried."[63] Still, given how much her parents depended on her, Ralph and Lidian must have felt the situation was dire in order to spare their daughter.

"Its snow white houses nestle cosily in a sea of fresh green vegetation, and no village could look prettier or more attractive," Mark Twain wrote of Fayal in the *Innocents Abroad*.[64] The Portuguese island, part of the Azores, had been a popular destination for Americans seeking rest and recovery since the 1840s. The family of Charles Dabney, the United States Consul to the Azores and a friend of John Forbes, was at the center Fayal's American visitors. The Dabneys were "liberal Unitarians" who made sure that "vacationers had access to most of the luxuries they had left behind in New England and had hosts with whom they shared similar religious convictions" on the Catholic island.[65] While trying to convince Ellen to go, Edith leaned on this point, promising, "it must be a wonderful place, and the Dabneys are all so good and kind that you wouldn't be a stranger to them for a moment."[66]

Ellen set sail on the *Fredonia* on November 4, 1868.[67] Charles Dabney and his daughter Clara were on the boat; so was Mary Watson, a woman who lived in Milton and was three years older than Ellen.[68] Ellen, on her first trip abroad, had been excited to gaze at the horizon from the deck but was so sea sick that she spent nine days in her cabin.[69] Once on dry land, Ellen found Fayal, despite the constant rain, a "beautiful and interesting place," covered with fascinating flora.⁷⁰ She also praised the residents of the island, but in condescending terms that infantilized them. "I delight in the Portuguese people as a spectacle, their manners sure to be pretty when you meet them, but out in the country not only pretty but innocent," she reported.⁷¹

Ellen's departure made clear just how many tasks—small and large—normally fell on her shoulders. Edith worked with Edward to organize Waldo's readings and mitigate the tension that arose between her parents without Ellen to care for their needs on demand. Waldo leaned on Edith to negotiate Thanksgiving invitations and organize packages of mail for Ellen.⁷² By January, he was arguing Edith should keep an ill Lidian in Milton because the doctor "thinks so highly of your nursing"; at the same time, he urged Edith to come to Concord to host a dinner, as Elizabeth Hoar was out of town.⁷³ From abroad, Ellen worried that Edith was going to exhaust herself, but Edith worried she was not doing enough.

Will Forbes thrilled Waldo by asking him to offer a series of private classes for "young men, his friends or acquaintances" consisting of "readings of poetry and prose, and conversations." The author relished the chance as an "old scholar" to share his favorite readings.⁷⁴ After some debate, women were also invited. Will was intellectually interested in the readings and happy to invite his circle to see and talk with his famous father-in-law. The lectures, in addition, allowed Will to funnel money to his wife's family, as each "Reading" cost ten dollars; Waldo was gratified to receive a six-hundred-dollar advance, and he eventually earned $1,100. Waldo suspected Will's motivations, telling him it was "a fine piece of knightly courtesy & daring, that you should invent & create this little college of yours for my exclusive benefit and pleasure."⁷⁵ Taking place on Saturdays from January through March 1869 at Chickering Hall, Waldo found the format, in which he read another author's work, critiqued the texts, and had a conversation with the audience, easier than a lecture as he began to struggle with public speaking. "By opening with a statement of critical opinion on a particular writer followed by an illustration of that position through a judicious selection of passages drawn from the author's poetry or prose, he relieved himself of the pressure he always felt to prepare and then follow a formal lecture text," Ronald Bosco explains.⁷⁶ At a party following the February 11 event, an anxious Edith quizzed people about their response; to her great relief, some wanted more lecture, some wanted more reading, but overall everyone enjoyed the event.⁷⁷

On Fayal, for the first time since she was fourteen and took over as Bush's housekeeper, Ellen controlled her time. While she later told Elizabeth Hoar that life there looked "empty," she thrived on the leisure.⁷⁸ She and Mary boarded at a hotel, often in the company of sea captains waiting out bad weather, but the Dabneys were central to her experience. Making "every day amusing and happy," they welcomed her for Thanksgiving and New Year's, as well as into their day-to-day lives.[79] Clara had cared for Ellen while she was seasick, an experience which bonded them and made it easier for Ellen to ask for support and help stave off homesickness. In a revealing statement, Ellen declared she was confident in Clara's affection, because "taking care of people makes you love them."[80] Like Ellen, Clara was the eldest, well-educated daughter of a prominent, tight-knit family who shouldered a great deal of familial responsibility. They recognized one another as kindred souls, but Ellen did not harbor the intense emotions for Clara that she did for Ida Agassiz. Ellen initially found Mary Watson and Clara's younger sister Roxanne Dabney, both outspoken and rambunctious, off-putting, but she also came to cherish their friendships.[81]

Ellen's days revolved around walking, reading, writing letters, and visiting her new friends when their health allowed, as the Dabneys all caught the measles and the flu in February.[82] The arrival of the just-published *Little Women* caused Ellen to reflect on the Alcotts, although she loaned her copy to the Dabney grandchildren before reading it herself. "Louisa has always been the most lively and original girl, and her three sisters were bright and able to help her in all her schemes, and their childhood and youth were full of the most amazing and interesting works and plays," she remembered.[83] The only reliable source of mail was the *Fredonia*, which arrived every two months, an eternity for her to wait for letters. It was easier to send mail, as ships regularly took refuge from storms at Fayal, allowing Ellen to sneak in a few more missives home, accompanied by boxes of oranges.[84] As the end of her stay neared, Ellen knew she would be happy to be home, "but I hold on here pretty fast too, and grudge to see the days slipping away from me."[85]

The Emersons tried to ensure Ellen did not exhaust herself after she arrived home on May 27, 1869.[86] As she blocked out her summer travel on a chart, hoping to coordinate coverage at Bush with Edith, she thought, "It is a terrible sight when all marked out in black and white how few useful days I allow to my family."[87] In reality, she still took on a great deal of caregiving, including tending to the boil on her father's foot, packing up 132 boxes of strawberries from the Bush grounds, cleaning the "garret," and caring for Lidian. In one letter, she plaintively asks Edith if she could ask Waldo to change his own poultice.[88] Edie Davidson came for much of the summer, a joyous reunion. Sixteen years old, she was no longer an emotional child, but a young woman eager to help Ellen, and Ellen reveled in their discussions about religion and the proper conduct of life.[89] Edie's presence also helped ease the wistfulness that threatened to overwhelm her when Ellen thought of her good friends and charming life on Fayal.

In their own ways, Edith and Ellen had developed some perspective on Lidian's moods. In July, Lidian complained she had "no heart and no feeling left." Although she quickly added, "I love my children, my grandchildren," Ellen noted it was "in a tone that as if she would correct the first statement by the last."[90] This story was not included in the version of letter that was published in the two-volume set of Ellen's correspondence, and, while relatively mild, it is one of the most open expressions of frustration or resentment on Ellen's part towards her mother.[91] Perhaps the months on Fayal had given her the distance to see that Lidian was ultimately impossible to please, no matter how hard Ellen tried. Edith had long been able to take a firmer hand with her mother. Ellen admired Edith's approach, expressing relief that her mother was in her sister's "fierce and faithful talons" when Lidian visited Milton in August.[92] The talons helped, at least temporarily. When Lidian returned to Concord, Ellen was shocked and relieved that instead of being "worried, collapsed, and everything dreadful," she was "acting quite like other people, and with her mind quite free to hear stories."[93]

Edith's success with her mother was all the more impressive as she balanced with it with care of her children and, by the beginning of August, a third pregnancy. Even as they fretted over Violet's bowlegs, Will and Edith's overt commitment to having a happy home showed in their approach to childrearing.[94] The children spent their days having tea parties and romping with tin horses, sledding in the winter and splashing in the ocean in the summer. Will sang and read to his son and daughter, while Edith wrote letters in their names to her family. At the center of family life, Ralph and Violet often fell asleep in the parlor as the grownups gathered for family chats.[95] To preserve their memory of Violet at this age, the Forbes hired Edmonia Lewis to create a portrait—likely a medallion—of Violet. Lewis, a Black and Ojibwe sculptor, had recently returned from Rome, but she had received her initial artistic training in Boston; the Forbes likely knew of her bust of Robert Gould Shaw, which sold one-hundred copies beginning in 1864.[96]

The preparations for Thanksgiving just as her trusted maid Brigid left to get married caused Ellen to relapse in November.[97] In response, Edith and Edward tried to persuade Ellen, Waldo, and Lidian to board at the Old Manse with Elizabeth Ripley for the winter. Ellen promised her concerned siblings, "I find I am quite able to keep house and keenly enjoy it" and that even on worst days now she was not as "shaky" as when she left for Fayal. She thanked Edith and Edward deeply for their concern, but concluded, "We are so comfortable, so prosperous, so thankful to be at home, we can see no reason for recklessly throwing away our blessings."[98] Even if the Bush trio turned down the plan, the fact that Edith and Edward paired up to try and convince them is significant. The two "babies" were now adults, one with a family of her own, the other in medical school. With some distance from Bush they were able to identify the problems within the house, and they were willing to take action.

1870 proved to be a year of health crises for the Emersons. Edith and Edward's concerns turned out to be well-founded, and in January Ellen's doctor recommended she take a two-month rest in Milton. While she claimed the doctor made the recommendation to avoid "car journeying," the advice indicates he saw a dynamic in Concord harmful to Ellen's health.[99] Waldo and Lidian, despite their dependence on Ellen, accepted the solution, suggesting the severity of her decline. On her thirty-first birthday, Waldo asked Lidian to "Tell her we rejoice in her existence and wish her to do her best to prolong it." He also suggested she could "banish (or vanquish) her ails by taking ale" and wished he had thought to send her "the choicest brand" as a gift.[100]

In Milton, Ellen found "it very interesting to see Edith run her large and complicated life so different in every particular from mine." The differences manifested "most of all in the way it is managed, and the points made prominent, which usually are the very ones I should choose to sink." She admired how Edith handled it all, particularly the constant swirl of family, with her children, husband, and regular visits with her nearby in-laws. "I watch and admire," she explained to Haven, and "sometimes wish Edith was a talkative creature and would lecture on the why and wherefore."[101]

The sisters' differences could lead to conflict. When a visitor expressed surprise that Ellen had a signed a temperance pledge, Edith burst out, "She went and signed it three years ago and she's been running downhill ever since." Edith was taken aback by the virulence of her own reaction, even as the whole table "laughed and shook for a long time."[102] While quickly papered over, Edith's outburst is understandable. Not only had Ellen ignored her sister's suggestion about the Old Manse, but now she regularly reported Ralph's antics and tantrums to Lidian; Lidian, in turn, sent Edith advice. Edith's approach to mothering differed from Lidian's and she likely did not appreciate Ellen telling tales on her. And with Ellen sentenced to Milton, Edith needed to care for her while also picking up the slack at Bush. Even with her loving husband and her well-ordered household staff, Edith was exhausted—and worried about saying so, as it would make Ellen feel guilty and try to rush home.[103]

While Edith kept two households on track, Ellen, relieved of her own caregiving work, re-engaged with her intellectual side. With Mary Watson, her Fayal companion, she read *Eckermann's Conversations of Goethe*, critiqued Charles Dickens' account of his trip to the United States as "exaggerated," and debated "the woman question." Ellen also examined sunspots through Sarah Forbes' telescope, attended readings of both Goethe and Marlow's Dr. Faustus and Elizabeth Peabody's talk on kindergartens, and, at a dinner party, jumped into a "discourse" on "the Lowell Institute and the Technological School."[104] She eagerly reported these developments in letters to her parents, her enjoyment unmistakable.

By early April, Ellen's doctor allowed her to return to Bush, on the condition she "be quiet at first" and take regular rest days at Milton.[105] Despite that warning, Ellen accepted an important, and groundbreaking, responsibility, when she became the first woman elected onto the Concord school committee. Ellen took to it "naturally," and, despite her plans to "hold her tongue as a novice should," spoke her mind.[106] She justified this public role, like many other women, through the belief that the welfare of children fell within women's purview even if the work was outside of the home.[107] But even as she went happily about her duties, Ellen was slowed by a persistent cough. In mid-May, she was diagnosed with whooping cough, and soon Lidian had it as well. Ellen cancelled her plans to help Edith after the birth of her baby.[108]

Throughout the year, as Edith cared for her sister and prepared for her third child, she took up two projects with her father. One was *Parnassus*, an anthology of poems Waldo admired with which Edith had helped him since she was a teenager.[109] Sensing his productive years were drawing to a close, she tried to strike the impossible balance between pushing the stalled book forward and not overwhelming her aging father. Edith had hoped to get the volume out before Christmas 1870, to maximize profits, but realized by March that deadline was impossible.[110] In May, less than two weeks before her due date, she reported to Ellen, "I have corrected all the copying that came home & then managed to collect a little more to be done, but the rest Edward must get from Father while I am getting well," meaning recovering from giving birth.[111] She pleaded with Ellen to "try to make Papa feel that this is not hurrying it" noting, after deliberation, he usually agreed with the choices he had made over a decade earlier.[112] Edith also lobbied her father to gather his correspondence from Thomas Carlyle and have it copied.[113] These projects appealed to Edith, who liked categorizing information and arranging material, be it books, linens, flowers, letters, or poems. Still, *Parnassus* was a Sisyphean task and even the smaller job of the Carlyle letters caused administrative headaches.

William Cameron Forbes, known as Cam or Cameron, arrived on May 21, 1870. Edith, according to Will, had "an easy time" and their new son was a "good screamer."[114] Ralph and Violet "sufficiently accustomed their minds to his existence" and asked "where he came from."[115] In Concord, meanwhile, the ailing family was cheered by the arrival, with Waldo repeating "Cameron Forbes" multiple times and deeming it "a very handsome name."[116] Ellen took a flying one-day visit, confirming Edith was doing as well as Will had reported and that Cam "had a spacious rubicund face" even if he "quacked like a duck."[117]

Edith's initial easy recovery stalled, and she was confined to bed for over a month, with a "very long and tedious getting well."[118] Eventually Elizabeth Hoar went to help. Ellen confined herself to short daytime visits, keeping away from the children, due to her whooping cough. Ellen's request on one of these trips that the two sisters strategize about their mother's health must have been unwelcome to the postpartum, bed-bound Edith, who likely longed to shift her elder sister's attention from their mother to herself on these brief visits.[119] Even less welcome must have been Waldo's request that Edith find someone to copy the seventy-seven letters from Carlyle he had finally gathered together and sent her in June.[120] While one can only hope he made the request before her relapse, Waldo was reluctant to acknowledge any problem with Edith's health. When a throat abscess prolonged her recovery, he urged her to "not to give the least countenance to any hobgoblins of the sick sort, but live out of doors & in the sea bath, & the sail boat, & the saddle, & the wagon, & best of all in your shoes, so soon as they will obey you for a mile." He noted, "I expect so much of you" so that he refused to believe reports of her illness, although he did offer to help arrange for a nurse.[121]

Waldo's own struggles, along with his long-term philosophical aversion to illness, may have led to his denial of Edith's weakness. The effort of arranging and presenting his "Natural History of Intellect" course in June as part of Harvard's University Lecture series had exhausted him. He was physically drained and intellectually frustrated "by what he took as his failure to make a coherent case for a form of 'intellectual science.'"[122] He was also struggling to write an introduction to an edition *Plutarch's Morals*, translated by William W. Goodwin, a professor of Greek at Harvard. He had forgotten this commitment until a letter in February from Little, Brown and Company expressed the publisher's eagerness to receive it, as the book was almost ready for publication.[123] By August he had not "yet begun to write and doesn't feel quite able to" Ellen warned her sister.[124] To pile on, over the summer he learned Moncure D. Conway, an abolitionist minister he had known since the 1850s, had signed a contract with the British publisher James Camden Hotten to produce a volume of Waldo's unpublished essays. Waldo agreed to provide his own revisions, "an act of desperation to retain some degree of control over the publication of his writings."[125] Adding another project when he was unable to complete those on his plate alarmed him. The difficulties with concentration and memory lapses were growing harder to ignore.

While Waldo declined, by autumn Edith had regained her strength and Ellen and Lidian had banished whooping cough. On September 4, the Forbes rolled into Concord, suntanned, healthy, and bringing the news of Napoleon III's surrender. For the first time, the doting aunt and grandmother could cuddle little Cam.[126] Edith found comfort in her childhood home after her long recovery. For once she liked, at least in the short term, not being the person in charge; she explained to Ellen that in Concord, "My work was cut out for me & I knew just what to do-it all seemed very simple." Meanwhile the endless list of tasks she had in Milton "towered in my imagination mountain high & scared me."[127]

Certainly, one of the scary tasks was *Parnassus*, but Edith was soon back at it, with help from her sister. Ellen usually answered her Edith's questions to Waldo about the book, an indication of his struggles. When Edith took a "penitent" tone in a letter after Waldo had responded poorly to her suggestions, Ellen wrote, "Don't be too much frightened at a little recalcitration on his part, he beholds your work with joy and amaze."[128] By the end of December Edith was pregnant, but continued to plow ahead, with Ellen's urging. In February, Ellen umped the ante, writing to Edith that for Waldo's "peace of mind the sooner you get through Parnassus, and the sharper you drive it up the better," as he was overwhelmed by the lectures and other work.[129]

Even while her father struggled, Ellen built up her life outside of Bush. "My birthday comes on this year in a blaze of glory," she declared to Clara Dabney. She added, "And it does seem to me no one ever was so happy, so filled up on every side with accumulated blessings as I am."[130] She busied herself with the Bible Society's annual meeting, school examinations, and the endless rounds of visits and visitors.[131] She continued to forge intense relationships with women; in this period, she documented her physical, emotional, and intellectual responses to, among others, Georgina Lowell Putnam; Nina Lowell, the great granddaughter of Francis Cabot Lowell who founded the Lowell Mills; and Georgina Schuyler, Alexander Hamilton's great, great granddaughter. Ellen referred to Schuyler "one of my romantic friends," comparing that category to "hard-won friends."[132] The distinction seemed to be between those with whom she felt an immediate spark and those she struggled to get to know and understand.

Edith was equally busy, her fourth pregnancy not slowing her down as she took on new tasks as well as forging ahead with *Parnassus*. She and Will decided to build their own "moderate" wooden vacation home on Naushon, rather than continuing to squeeze their growing family into the Mansion House, as Will's parent's home was known.[133] They celebrated when Harvard conferred the bachelor's degree on Will that he would have earned if he had not been expelled.[134] In March the couple traveled to Florida, with their three children staying at Bush. That excursion, including the childcare arrangements, served as a trial run for a more ambitious Forbes adventure.

At the end of March, John Forbes invited Waldo to join a party including Edith and Will traveling to Northern California. The plan was likely cooked up by the Emerson children and John Forbes in response to Waldo's alarming mental and physical decline, exacerbated by work on the second "Natural History of Intellect" course at Harvard in spring 1871.[135] The invitation "at first shocked more than allured" Waldo, but he was soon "persuaded by my family and my physician to accept it," even cancelling the last natural history lecture to go.[136] Everyone hoped the voyage would help him recover his strength and address his troubling memory lapses and difficulty concentrating. In addition to Edith, Will, and John Forbes, the party of twelve included Will's sisters Alice and Sarah, Wilkie James, and the lawyer James Bradley Thayer, who wrote a memoir about the trip.[137]

The conversation around the voyage focused on Waldo's health—not around any concern for Edith or her pregnancy. Undertaking a long, voluntary trip while pregnant, however, was unusual for a woman in 1871. As Shannon Withycombe explains, "While domestic health advice continued to recommend fresh air and moderate exercise throughout pregnancy, by the 1870s this medical information also frequently cautioned against a multitude of public activities that could endanger a pregnant woman or her future offspring."[138] The Forbes' wealth, of course, ensured Edith would travel in comfort, including a private Pullman car for the party on the stretch from Chicago to California. Edith's willingness to embark on this trip is still notable, and it may have a response to growing up in the shadow of Lidian's endless illnesses. While she often had long recoveries from her pregnancies, Edith refused to withdraw from the world.

The Massachusetts-based members of the trip left Boston on April 11. After more of the party gathered in Chicago, George Pullman himself visited to make sure all was in order in their car, named the *Huron*. Elegant Pullman cars, launched just six years earlier, allowed passengers to sit in luxury during the day, among walnut paneled walls, brass fixtures, and plush seating; at night, their berths turned into beds separated by partitions for privacy. Cooks prepared meals in a three-foot kitchen, with Pullman promising John Forbes that "we could have as good a dinner as we could get at Parker's," Boston's famous hotel.[139] Edith saw the train trip as an opportunity to get Waldo to focus on their work, and Thayer remembered that Waldo brought the "manuscript sheets of his 'Parnassus,' on which he worked more or less with his daughter."[140] While the "more or less" suggests not that much got done, Waldo did discuss poetry with his fellow travelers. After a brief detour to Salt Lake City, where most of the men, including Waldo, met with Brigham Young on April 19, the group arrived in San Francisco on April 21 and checked into the Occidental Hotel.

The travelers quickly launched into sightseeing. The day after their arrival, the Unitarian minister Horatio Stebbins escorted Waldo and Ellen to the Cliff House, a hotel perched north of Orchard Beach famed for its view of the Pacific Ocean. Edith's children were on her mind. She asked Waldo to write Ralph about the sea lions they spotted from the balcony; they were "as large as bears, and much longer than bears," he reported to his grandson, noting the pups caused Edith and himself to talk of Ralph, Violet, and Cameron.[141] The excursion came with a price. Stebbins asked Waldo to speak at his church on Geary Street, leading Waldo to deliver "Immortality" on Sunday.[142] Similar invitations bombarded Waldo throughout the trip, to Edith's alarm, as she had hoped the voyage would be a time of rest and restoration.

Back in Concord, the responsibility for caring for the children for almost two months weighed on Ellen. Even though two staff members from the Forbes household—Jane and Maggie—accompanied them, Ellen worried that Ralph and Violet were now old enough "to have morals and manners and faculties to be looked after."[143] Things did not get off to a great start when Violet and Ralph spat in Jane's face and made such a racket that Lidian wondered if Ellen was "aunt to a lion."[144] After they settled in, Ellen focused on their education, making sure Ralph and Violet practiced reading, writing, and arithmetic; Cameron's task was learning to crawl. While at times overwhelmed, Ellen still gushed about her "astonishing pride that they call me Aunt."[145]

Soon Bush faced a more serious problem than rambunctious children. Edward, visiting from Cambridge, fell ill on April 17. Originally, he and Ellen thought it was "dumb ague," a type of malarial fever. But when his condition declined despite his treatment with quinine and he became "spotted," the doctor diagnosed varioloid, a mild form of smallpox. Maggie, Jane, the Emersons' servant Sarah and the cook Mrs. Kay reported they had all been vaccinated or had had smallpox, but Ellen quickly made arrangements for vaccinations for Lidian, Ralph, Violet, and herself.[146] Unfortunately, Sarah, who had helped clean Edward's room before the second diagnosis, soon came down with a more serious case of varioloid, after which Maggie and Jane agreed to re-vaccination. Sarah quarantined in a room in Bush, with Ellen caring for her. Meanwhile, Edward was struck with rheumatism, and spent almost three weeks in bed, eventually giving up the Harvard summer term. Concordians who had had smallpox themselves offered to help, but Ellen noted there was also fear of the "smallpox house."[147]

Through telegrams and letters, Ellen apprised Waldo, Edith, and Will of the evolving situation. She stressed the children were safe and healthy; Edward joked, "Sad to think how many hard-earned dollars are spent in sending word that those children are well—when a bull couldn't kill them."[148] Despite the reassurances, Edith was understandably alarmed. One of her concessions to pregnancy was to stay with her cousins Susan Jackson and William Barber in San Rafael while Will, Waldo, and others in the party travelled to north to Yosemite. There when she got the news, Edith implored Will to hurry back so they could decide whether they should return east. Fearing that Ellen would get sick with her "twice doubled cares," the Forbes also considered sending the children to their cousin Elizabeth Ripley in the Old Manse.[149] Ellen resented the implication that she did not have the situation under control. She snapped, "Shall I write my sister a little dissertation on small-pox & kindred subjects? I know something about it."[150]

Edith decided to see the California trip out. When the party reunited in San Francisco on May 15, she turned to worrying again about the constant stream of visitors who exhausted her father with their requests. Less-than rave reviews for his later appearances made it worse; the San Francisco *Examiner* wrote his final "effort in San Francisco was tame and uninteresting, by no means sustaining the claims to position which he is thought to occupy in the lecture room."[151] But father and daughter had a fine time picking out pictures at the gallery of Carleton Watkins, known for his stereographs of Yosemite and San Francisco. Waldo was delighted when Watkins, recognizing him, encouraged him to select large photographs as a gift; "There are advantages in being old," he confided happily.[152] Much of the party started east May 19, taking a private car first to Lake Tahoe so they could "spread ourselves out."[153] Once there, while rowing with Will and Alice, Ellen raved about the "Prussian Blue" water that was "clear as crystal and cold as a spring."[154] The entire party was reunited in the *Huron* to head east; after a stop in Niagara Falls, the Forbes and Emersons arrived in Boston on May 30.

Edward, finally recovered, announced he was going to Germany to continue his medical studies. A financial gift from Will helped make the decision possible; Edward was embarrassed and only accepted half of Will's offer, but knew it would relieve his father's worries about money.[155] The financial security also gave him confidence to propose to Annie Keyes, the elder sister of Ellen's "daughter" Lily, before he left.[156] While Annie and Edward had long been friends, and Annie had hinted at her feelings for Edward to Ellen, there had been no open courting. But if the engagement was the "greatest possible surprise" to the Emersons, they rejoiced in it.[157] Annie was serious, helpful, head-over-heels in love with their Edward, and a member of their beloved Concord community, all of which made Ellen and Edith happy to welcome her into their family. Edith congratulated Edward on not offering her "any of the Bessys of this world for a sister, for I *might* not have concealed my feelings!"[158] Ellen wrestled with more complex emotions, as she, Edward, Annie, and Lizzy Simmons had formed a "quartette" in recent years, and, as with Edith's engagement, she feared being left out. She was grateful that she and Annie were already "in the habit of trusting each other and talking about Edward" so she was "not an outsider entirely."[159]

John Murray Forbes, called Don, arrived on August 27 at 9:30 p.m. in the new house on Naushon. Ellen, Edward, and Annie were there for the birth. The indefatigable baby nurse Mrs. Rounsville declared Don was the most "cunning" of all the Forbes children. By October 3, her sixth wedding anniversary, Edith felt well enough for a buggy ride around the island with Will, who gave her a diamond and sapphire ring, and to entertain Ralph and Violet with tales of mermaids and mermen as they looked the whitecaps. "Oh what a good time we did have!" Edith reported. "Will was so glad to have me with him again, and the air was so fresh and sweet."[160] Four children in six years had not dimmed the love between Edith and Will, who continued to take joy in one another and their ever-growing family.

The Emerson family debate over women's suffrage intensified as the movement regained momentum after the Civil War. While Lidian and Edith supported the campaign, Ellen was stalwart in her opposition. She felt "terror" at the thought of female political participation, believing women had more power using their influence on men than they would voting themselves and fearing women would exhaust themselves if they became "part of political machinery."[161] Ellen held firm to this position even as she occupied an elected office on the school committee.

While out of step with her family, Ellen's views aligned with organized female anti-suffragists—or remonstrants—who "sought to preserve what they perceived as the special and unique place of women in the polity."[162] Ellen agreed, she told Edward, with the anti-suffragists featured in a debate published in the July 1871 *Old & New*; one praises "how infinitely subtle and pervading is the power exercised by women," adding, "They supply the principles of government, and need not assume its functions."[163] It was a position she maintained for the rest of her life.

Ellen shared not just the views but the background of many northern female anti-suffragists, who were largely white, economically advantaged, and well-educated, often with a family relation to a prominent man. The founders of the Boston Committee of Remonstrants, for instance, came overwhelmingly from powerful "Boston Brahmin" families whom the Emersons knew.[164] These women had already amassed social influence through their work in benevolent organizations and their connections to influential husbands, fathers, and brothers, and believed suffrage would put that influence at risk. To argue women should only have power through their influence on men, however, was to ignore the fact that not all women had similar connections, and, therefore, needed access to explicit political power promised by the vote. And it was to put aside the commitment to the ideals that Ellen celebrated as the legacy of the Battle of Concord each April 19.

Waldo's position in American society ensured that the tension over suffrage was not merely a private family debate. Tempers flared in 1871. When Ellen dismissed the requests for aid from a suffragist who visited Bush in October, Lidian wondered how her daughter could "express such selfish, blind, and cruel views."[165] A few weeks later, Ellen spoke out against suffrage at a Freedmen's Aid Society meeting at the house. Edith snapped "that the least those inferior & selfish minds that cannot see the benefit & privilege of voting can do is hold their idle tongues."[166] The timing was significant. That year marked the start of "women's antisuffrage mobilization," when *Godey's Ladies Book* published an anti-suffrage petition to the United States Congress signed by nineteen women in its editorial pages and encouraged readers to copy and circulate the document for more signatures.[167] Meanwhile, despite his weak support of women's rights, suffragists began to invoke Waldo in their arguments. In the same debate Ellen cited to Edward, a suffragist claimed the vote would allow women to "come to her domestic duties from higher ground, a condition upon which Emerson wisely insists when our best effort is demanded."[168] Suffragists also employed Waldo's "Concord Hymn" memorializing the Battle of Concord to "characterize suffrage agitation as a self-evident extension of the principles guiding the minutemen and to censure those who refused to recognize it as such."[169] Some activists took pilgrimages to Concord, to pay homage to the transcendentalists and shore up their connection to the Revolutionary spirit, documenting them in publications such as the *Woman's Journal*. These trips often included a stop at Bush.

Edith's comment about anti-suffragists "holding their tongues" highlights her awareness of the visibility their position as Ralph Waldo Emerson's family gave them. Ellen speaking out against suffrage from Bush's parlor had the potential to broadcast her message far beyond Concord. Ellen did seem to "hold her tongue" in the short term, as several *Woman's Journal* articles in the 1870s referred to Ellen in a positive light; they subtlety, and inaccurately, indicated her support for suffrage.[170] Decades later, however, the journal reported that Ellen had hosted a talk by anti-suffragist Alice George at Bush. The author speculated it would be "a grief" to the "departed spirits" of Lidian and Waldo to know their daughter would hold such an event in their home, confirming Edith's fears.[171]

While Ellen had much in common with other anti-suffragists, her stance is still striking given the position of her sister, mother, Louisa May Alcott—who bemoaned the lack of suffrage activity in Concord—and, however tenuously, her father. Why did she feel so strongly about the issue? What made her feel "terror"? The pressure on her to leave her education and take up housekeeping—even if her education did eventually continue—primed her to internalize the importance of feminine caretaking. Waldo underscored this message with his gift of the *Angel in the House*, a work Ellen cherished throughout her life. But Edith also had her education interrupted, and she supported suffrage. The family response to the death of young Waldo, where Ellen received the message that the wrong child had survived, offers another clue. A desire to prove her worth to her family through her care of them encouraged a belief that such care was the primary source of her value. Suffrage, in her view, threatened to disrupt the place of honor such caregiving held in American society. As with her decision to join the church, her anti-suffrage commitment in the face of opposition from

Lidian and Ellen also carries a hint of demure rebellion. She often deferred to the demands of her mother and sister, but rejecting suffrage in the name of feminine influence gave her a socially sanctioned way to assert herself.

The trip to California set the stage for an even more grand Forbes adventure in 1872. In January, they set sail for a seven-month tour of Europe with the four children. Jane—the nurse who had been in Concord for the smallpox episode— and their governess Caroline Leavitt, Louisa Sanborn's sister, accompanied them.[172] Edith initially expressed some qualms. The trip, she told Edward, would be more for education than "unalloyed pleasure," stressing the promise of seeing her brother was "the magnet that settled me in my wish to go."[173] The timing of the trip is odd, given Edith's hesitancy, Waldo's steady decline, and Ellen's health struggles. Edith may have felt her father's trajectory would only go down, so it was best to set sail while they could, or perhaps Edith believed the trip to California, combined with nursing Ellen in 1870, had earned her a reprieve from familial care. Ellen's report to Clara Dabney that "we are so pleased with Will & her that they had the energy & wisdom to go, and go while they are young," suggests a sense of "carpe diem" did inspire the adventure.[174]

Edith's customary optimism soon resurfaced. She reported from the ship, "My happy fortunes still follow me. I want to get home to tell the faint-hearted that a voyage with four children is no trouble."[175] The Forbes kept up a quick pace during the seven months abroad, with Will handling the logistics like "the best of generals."[176] In Paris, "I enjoyed the city a great deal as I walked and drove about," Edith reported, finding the Louvre "delightful" but the shopping "odious."[177] For much of March, the children stayed with Jane and Caroline in Montreux on Lake Geneva, while Edith and Will toured Italy.[178] Edward joined them for part of the Italian tour, sponsored by the Forbes. "You know it would double Will's and my pleasure to have you with us," Edith wrote to convince him to accept the offer.[179] His presence was all they could have hoped for. "He is so full of knowledge, quotations, similes of most comical kinds, and jokes of all kinds—besides it is delightful to see his extreme enjoyment in seeing the originals of all the pictures & statues he has studied all his life," Edith reported to his mother. Still, while she found Rome "perfectly enchanting," in Napoli "even in our nice hotel the noises through our open windows were distracting" and she was disturbed by the beggars constantly asking for money.[180]

The final leg of the trip took them back to England and up to Scotland. Both Will and Edith felt more comfortable in Britain, with Edith explaining of London, "very stately it is, much more so and more interesting than Paris, for it looks old and as if it had grown gradually and naturally, while Paris looks like a magnificent city made to order by one hand at one time."[181] It helped that in London "everybody that is famous & pleasant" welcomed the family.[182] Thomas Carlyle, in particular, "received Edith like a daughter," a feeling perhaps boosted by her commitment to preserving his correspondence with Waldo.[183] Will's parents joined them in Scotland, where sailing past the ruins of the Castle Urquart on Loch Ness, the ancestral home of the Forbes, was a highlight.[184] Edward had decided to relocate his medical studies to London, and Will and Edith were thrilled when he also joined them in Scotland.[185] Edward fell ill soon after they returned to London, however, plagued again by an abscess on his shoulder. Will and Edith devoted themselves to caring for him, "acting a part, always easy and natural to them, that of good angels," Edward reported to Waldo.[186]

Ellen, with both her siblings abroad, felt "a little solitary."[187] She took to writing Edward long, philosophical letters. As in her letters to Haven, she used her correspondence with her brother to think through her ideas about the world and her place in it. Edward's medical studies prompted her to use him as a sounding board for her thoughts on women's health; she feared women called to do public service would always suffer for it, but wondered why their Puritan ancestors had not similarly suffered, despite their hard work.[188] Her correspondence with Clara Dabney also took philosophical turns, as she speculated on growing old and wondered, "how much one can do beforehand to help oneself through."[189] Certainly her own health woes, combined with her concern for her aging parents, pushed these ideas to the forefront of her mind.

Waldo's memory loss was the issue that made Ellen most miss her siblings. When Waldo's lectured on "Books" on April 15, Ellen sat anxiously in the audience, "in about as great fear as I was able to bear, lest there be some terrific crash, for I hadn't heard it beforehand as I ought, and his memory is entirely gone." Her fears came to pass when Waldo read the same page twice through without noticing. Describing the incident to Edward, Ellen noted, "I mourn for you more than I can tell, for you are the only person in creation who could lay out the course for him and help him through."[190] While Ellen was upset, Waldo himself took it stride, and was happy the lecture series had brought in $1,300. Waldo also had begun to struggle to find words, often leading to nonsense sentences that Ellen claimed to find funny, but likely added to her anxiety about her father.[191] Years later, while providing anecdotes to James Elliot Cabot for his biography of Waldo, she depicted herself as deeply upset by these incidents, much more so than she did in her contemporaneous letters; for the time being, she noted the lapses in her correspondence, but did not dwell on them.[192] Soon there would be something more immediate to worry about.

"Ellen, something has happened at your house, but your Mother & Father are safe." Ida Agassiz Higginson rushed to deliver these words early on the morning of July 24, when Ellen was staying with her in Beverly, Massachusetts. The "something" was a major fire. Within a half an hour Ellen was headed back to Concord. All the way home, Ellen believed the blaze had leveled Bush, "so when I saw the house I had supposed forever lost, standing safely in its old shape among the healthy untouched trees, I was very thankful." While the study and the walls of the first story were intact, however, much of the upper story was destroyed and the floor was "a pond." Waldo greeted her as "houseless child" when she found him at the Old Manse.[193]

In the following week, as she and her parents settled into the Old Manse, Ellen learned more about the fire. The blaze broke out in the garret early in the morning, and "crackling inside the plastering" woke Waldo.[194] Concord answered Waldo's cries for help. In an extraordinary community effort, men ran into the burning house to save what they could, throwing the Emersons' possessions from the widows. Ephraim Bull Jr. pulled a hose to the roof, but it was ultimately the fact that the slate roof caved in and smothered the fire that saved any of the house. Annie Keyes, who sprinted to scene, covered Lidian with her waterproof. May and Louisa May Alcott helped secure the papers and furniture that littered the yard. Louisa acted as "sort of policeman & saved quantities of things" and May "ordered every body right & left and soon got things in good shape."[195] Waldo, according to Louisa, "looked pathetically funny that morning, wandering about in his night gown, pants, coat, and no hose" with "an old pair of rubbers wobbling on his Platonic feet."[196] Less amusing was his throwing the letters from his first wife and his son Waldo into the fire.[197] Meanwhile Lidian had on her "best bonnet," perhaps having found it on the lawn, and was "saying cheerfully, 'Oh well we shall have better house now.'"[198]

The citizens of Concord parceled out the Emersons' possessions to houses throughout the town, and Ellen spent much of her first days back finding out who had what and what had been lost forever. Ellen's feelings were complicated. She admitted she both loved the house and associated it with "dirt, waste, bottomless abyss of expense to no profit, deceit, ill-temper & shirking."[199] Said in the wake of the fire, her statement is one of Ellen's most forthright expressions of frustration. As she dealt with her shell-shocked parents and the aftermath of the disaster without her siblings, she must have felt particularly put-upon.

Ellen took days to write Edward about the fire, saying she "had to write letters to anxious friends & relations here," and she knew Annie had written to him.[200] The Forbes, who set sail before Annie's letter arrived in England, did not learn of the fire until they docked in Boston on August 14. John and Malcolm Forbes "went down to the harbor to meet them and told them of the fire, and so I didn't have it to tell," Ellen reported to Haven.[201] Ellen's reluctance to tell her sister the news suggests just how hard the fire hit her. The reality must have been overwhelming to process and describing it to Edith may have too painful.

The Emersons soon learned their community's generosity went beyond the night of the fire. Within days, John and Sarah Forbes sent Ellen $500 to buy a new wardrobe, as most of her clothes had burned.[202] That amount paled compared to the $5,000 dollar check Frank Lowell delivered, raised by "some of Father's intimate friends to enable him to rebuild his house more as he would like or for him to use for another other purpose he preferred."[203] This was a relief, as the house had only been insured for about half of the $5,000 it would take to repair it. Waldo was "perfectly astonished" by the gesture, but ultimately agreed to accept it. Soon there another gift, as the physician LeBaron Russell created a "Fund for The Rebuilding of Mr. Emerson's House," which eventually grew to $11,620, with contributors including Caroline Sturgis Tappan and James Elliot Cabot.[204] Combined with the insurance money, these gifts were more than enough to rebuild the house, including taking on projects long ignored.

For Ellen, always anxious about the family finances, the money was a godsend. She told Edward, "I think it was the loveliest thing I ever knew. It will really lengthen Father's life I believe. It will remove anxiety & overwork."[205] The reality was grimmer, as the shock of fire accelerated Waldo's existing memory and health issues, despite Ellen's insistence that in the immediate aftermath that he seemed fine. By the time the Forbes arrived, coming to stay in the Old Manse directly from the ship, Waldo was so "unwell" that Will and Edith were "thoroughly frightened."[206] But even in the face of that reality, the money inspired, and underwrote, Ellen and Waldo's grandest father-daughter adventure.

The Emerson family had undergone dramatic transformations in the seven years since Edith and Will had said their vows in Bush. Edith's marriage and first four children brought joy to the family. Ellen and Edith had taken their first trips abroad, moving far beyond Massachusetts. But there was also the growing awareness of Waldo's decline and the shock of the house fire. Going forward, Ellen and Edith would find their care for their aging parents taking on new forms and dominating their conversation, even as Edith's family continued to grow.

CHAPTER FIVE

"What a Mercy It Is That There Are Women in the World to Arrange for Men"

(1872–1875)

"We hope to send Father and Ellen off before winter, though I fear it will distress Ellen to leave the delights of arranging the house," Edith wrote to Edward in September 1872.[1] Plans for Ellen and Waldo to travel to Europe started brewing almost as soon as the Forbes arrived home. As with the trip to California, the family hoped the excursion would restore Waldo's physical and mental health. Edith pushed for the plan, as did Waldo's friends. Judge Ebenezer Hoar informed Waldo that an association had been set up, with money deposited in the Concord bank, and "its objects would be accomplished when you have spent its funds especially if you use a part in going to Europe." When Waldo resisted, Hoar retorted, "I should like to know what you are going to do about it."[2] The plan hinged on Edith's overseeing the restoration of Bush and caring for Lidian, which she swore to do. She kept her promise, even though by the end of October she was pregnant.

While fussing over the trip, the family took immediate measures to help Waldo recover from the fire, which had compounded his existing memory problems and left him unable to work. Ellen accompanied him to Maine, then they joined Lidian and Edith's family on Naushon. Will and Edward informed his publishers that Waldo could not be held to any schedule. Edward told Hotten, "he was killing father & told him that he must empower me to telegraph that there was no hurry." Will wrote to Fields & Osgood, who were to issue the book in the United States, that they better say "Do not hurry!"[3] Seaside days and removal of the publishing deadline helped Waldo recuperate, although the family understood there would not be a full recovery.

Reuniting with Edward was, of course, a draw of Europe. Edward, however, was still recovering from his summer siege and considering drawing his European medical training to a close. Edith urged him to put his health, and his desire to see Annie, ahead of other concerns.[4] While the trip would be easier if Edward accompanied his father and sister, Waldo's fame and literary connections, along with the number of their friends touring Europe, meant they could always find a helping hand. Edith also compiled "a book of maxims addresses &c" based on her travel experiences for Ellen to consult while abroad.[5] Edward decided to greet his father and sister in England, then sail home as they ventured to France. Once committed, Ellen looked forward to the adventure with more enthusiasm than her departure to Fayal. "This time she goes for Father's sake and feels easy about you because I! am to take care of you, and she is going to see Edward & enjoy everything & does not dread the voyage," Edith ensured Lidian.[6]

Waldo and Ellen set sail on the *Wyoming* from New York on October 23, 1872. Will ushered them on board, showering Ellen with grapes and flowers and entrusting a box of pears to Waldo. As the ship slid past Fire Island, they thought of Margaret Fuller, who drowned on that spot. Back in Concord, Lidian worried. "I don't like the thought of you and Ellen on the water this evening," she wrote to her husband.[7] Edith praised her mother for being "unselfish and lovely" in supporting the trip. She promised, "If I can make it up to you a little I shall be too happy. I will do my very best darling Mamma & we have so much to do—you and I—in getting ready for the return that the time will fly."[8]

While the first shipboard dinner was a stilted affair, soon Ellen's curiosity about human nature helped break down barriers. The differences in the religious practices among her fellow travelers fascinated her. The passenger list included Methodist, Baptist, and Presbyterian missionaries headed to India, a Quaker missionary heading to the south of France, an editor of *The Congregationalist* who planned to trace Paul's voyage in Greece, a Presbyterian minister sent by the "Congregationalist Board of Foreign Ministers" to "establish Protestantism in Italy," and a "young Mormon woman from Utah, going home to England for a visit."[9] Ellen discussed Hindu hymns with Mrs. Brown, one of the missionaries. After encouraging her new friend to sing, Ellen noted, "I liked best the one I heard first with its perpetual refrain of Koi Kani nahin, which she says means 'There is no other way.'" She also had a long talk with "Mrs. Rogers, the Quaker," after which she and Waldo wondered how someone who only spoke

English could convert anyone in France.[10] Lidian and Edith laughed at the thought of Waldo and Ellen surrounded by this group. Edith wrote, "How desperately funny was your ship's company—evidently convened for your sole benefit, for who else in the world would not have been daunted by such a set? You upholding the Unitarian, Father the Radical; we trust your German was Lutheran and the Austrian Catholic—that no church should be neglected."[11] Lidian teased Waldo, "I think you must have your heresies in such peril from all those religious people—from the missionaries to say nothing of the Quaker and the Mormons—that you are glad to have escaped with your philosophy (Transcendental—is it?) unharmed."[12]

"Never till just these circumstances made it manifest had I imagined what a revealing power there was in acts of worship," Ellen wrote to Lidian after a non-denominational onboard service. Ellen's curiosity, however, never led her to question her own beliefs or their superiority. "The differences in theology also appeared, and I got the first chance I ever had of well comparing ours with others, and I felt sure that we are nearer the truth in our whole swing than they are," she wrote. But she did concede, "they may touch in nearer in some one point."[13] It is unclear on what point she thought them superior, but she did praise Dr. Warren's sermon for assuming they were all Christians, and thus he did not need to instruct them. The following Sunday, tossed by the rough Irish Sea, Ellen and Waldo agreed that the morning Episcopalian service was "heathen," but enjoyed a Congregationalist service in the evening.[14]

The ship docked at Liverpool on November 3.[15] Any sadness at parting with her fellow passengers paled next to the joy at seeing Edward, who joined them in Chester. The next day included breakfast with the Bishop of Chester. Ellen spent the morning shopping for goods such as stockings and sponges that might be cheaper in Liverpool than Boston, one of the hints in Edith's book of "maxims." Edward and Waldo attended the meeting of the Archeological Society, where Waldo was asked to speak as the meeting drew to a close. He spoke "so well" and "showed such power that he (Edward) threw off the anxiety" that Ellen had raised through her descriptions of Waldo's failing memory.[16] The trip was off to a smashing start.

Ellen's lengthy description of the sea voyage did not arrive in Concord until November 18, but Lidian and Edith tracked it as best they could. Will Forbes contacted the "news office" to confirm the *Wyoming* had arrived, and Edith immediately wrote to her anxious mother. "So they are safe with Edward now Mamma dear, and I congratulate you that they are on dry land & will now be petted to death—and what a blessing it is that Father feels so much stronger so he will really enjoy seeing his friends."[17] In Milton, Edith focused on settling back into her home, which had been rented during the Forbes' long trip abroad and summer in Concord and Naushon. She was frustrated that it was filled with "rubbish" and tried to banish the tenants' ghosts, noting "the sensation is unpleasant . . . trying to make it home again."[18] Finding places for all their European purchases did add some pleasure to the task.

The Emersons had hoped to keep Waldo's trip abroad quiet so he could rest and not be overwhelmed with social obligations. The publisher Charles Norton, in London himself, however, "told everyone that could be interested," before the *Wyoming* even sailed.[19] "People are beginning to throng Father's doors and invitations whiz by hourly," Edward reported to Lidian soon after the trio arrived in London on November 6.[20] Waldo met with Thomas Carlyle, the sculptor William Wetmore Story, and Norton, among others, while Ellen and Edward spent time with Una Hawthorne. Waldo and Ellen also visited St. Thomas Hospital, where Edward trained. Waldo "was properly pleased and especially delighted with the children's ward."[21] Despite the frenetic social pace, Waldo slept eleven hours a night and praised the idle life. Waldo and Ellen said goodbye to Edward at the end of the week as he set sail for the United States, then made their way to Canterbury on November 13, arriving in Paris on November 15. The social whirl continued, as Charles and Anna Lowell helped them negotiate the city and made "each meal a festivity."[22] Paris also brought visits with Charles Emerson and his wife Therchi, a Hungarian woman he had married in Germany the previous year, and Henry James, who escorted Waldo to the Louvre.[23] While she worried about her father becoming exhausted, these visitors gave Ellen support and, at times, a break from caregiving.

Ellen fretted about expenses throughout their journey. They spent $198 in the first nine days after making landfall, despite penny-pitching tactics such as taking the cheapest rooms on the highest floor. Ellen confessed her financial concerns to her brother-in-law, but not to her father, noting "it seemed needless to trouble him, as I keep the accounts & do the deciding."[24] In those words were the familiar combination of martyrdom and pride that so often drove Ellen. Edith played her part of the optimistic cheerleader. She repeatedly told her sister not to worry about money, noting that Ellen and Waldo would never have another chance to travel in Europe together. "The money will be well spent if it gives you & Father health and pleasure," she reminded Ellen.[25] Seven years living as a Forbes had made her comfortable with spending. Edith also stressed that there was money enough. She explained that, according to Will, "Father's property will certainly yield for 3500 to 4000 a year & that will be enough to keep you all from poverty (not counting books, lectures or farm property as well.)"[26]

Even as she worried about money, Ellen built confidence as a traveler. While in London, hobbled by a sprained ankle, she was just grateful to return to her rooms "alive, without offending my driver."[27] The trip from Dover to Paris made her realize she spoke French quite well; she gave thanks for the grammar drills of her schooldays and acknowledged, "My courage after yesterday's experience is doubled."[28] By the time they made their way to Florence, she declared, "I entered Italy as bold as if I had been here twenty times, knowing exactly where and when I was going."[29] Despite her ongoing concerns about the expense and her developing confidence, Ellen was happy to hire a servant in Paris to escort them for the rest of the trip. Curnex, whom Lady Augusta Stanley recommended, was another source of support for Ellen, well worth the expenditure.[30]

The fact that Italy reminded her of Fayal helped Ellen feel at home when they arrived in late November, as did the friendly faces they encountered. As they wended through Marseille and Nice on their way, father and daughter bonded over the landscape's beauty; Waldo declared, "if you want to do the greatest kindness possible to anyone, send him from Lyons to Marseille."[31] In Florence, nestled in the Hotel du Nord, they reunited with Elizabeth and Caroline Hoar, which to Ellen was "the greatest event of Florence."[32] They were with the Hoars on Thanksgiving, when they decided "to keep the day" by going to church.[33] The American Consul, J. Lorimer Graham, "showered attentions" on Waldo and Ellen, sending flowers, inviting them to dinner, and taking them for a drive in a "lordly chariot."[34] They moved to Rome on November 30. Lily Ward lived there with her husband Baron Richard von Hoffman, a German aristocrat she had married in 1870, and she convinced the Emersons to stay with them for a week at Villa Celimontana. Ellen and Waldo lived in "great glory" with the von Hoffmans, who catered to their needs and whose windows offered them views Ellen "unwillingly" acknowledged were "more beautiful than America can be."[35] After weeks on the go, she was relieved to hand the daily planning over to her hosts.

Ellen's response to religious structures and experiences takes up much of her correspondence. In London, Thomas Hughes, a British politician and author of *Tom Brown's School Days*, took them to the Temple Church, built by the Knights Templar in the twelfth century. Ellen "didn't understand a word" of the "chanted" service, but sat next to a "saint" who "really loved the service, and faithfully and affectionately took care of me from beginning to end."[36] She loved Chapelle Evangelique de l'Etoile in Paris, finding Le Pasteur Eugène Bersier's sermon on the life of Jeremiah's servant Baruch "a revelation to me of a Bible history I hadn't understood before."[37] Bersier, Ellen felt, "is quite as broad as a Unitarian, always prays for and speaks of the great Church universal embracing all sects." She only wished she spoke French well enough to go to his Bible class and quiz him on his ideas.[38] In Florence, the interior of the city's famous cathedral underwhelmed her, but she found the exterior "so handsome" and noted "even Mark Twain and I could discern its beauty unassisted."[39] While in Rome, Ellen and Lily talked "quite freely in spite of the bugbear" of Lily's Catholicism, but it could be a source of tension. Lily gave Ellen a "ring, with many prayers for my conversion I know, poor child." Ellen explained it went to "my heart to see her tremble and her hands go cold when she talked to me, and I meanwhile sitting motionless under my shield, in an attitude that seemed heartless," at Lily's hopes for Ellen's conversion.[40] As on the ship, Ellen harbored a genuine curiosity about other forms of faith, but her "shield" prevented any deep questioning of her own beliefs.

In Massachusetts, Lidian and Edith worked on Bush, while Ellen weighed in via letter and shopped in Europe. Lidian and Edith promised to be economical, including taking advantage of prices reduced after Boston suffered an enormous fire in November. Ellen tried to stave off Edith. Asking her not to write to preserve her strength, she added, "And give up Bush. Your own work is enough for you. Leave mine for me."[41] Ellen was concerned about her sister, but she also wanted to maintain control over her domain. Despite her request, long exchanges about paint colors, rugs, and fabrics flew across the Atlantic. Edith, several months pregnant, found debating choices on shopping trips with her mother exhausting; she landed on a plan of alternating between sending Lidian on errands to Boston and going herself, with each bringing back samples and patterns. The strategy worked. "I consider it wonderful and astonishing that Bush is likely to turn out pleasing both to me & Mother, for our tastes seem about diametrically opposite, our judgement also," she explained.[42] Edith was, however, frustrated with the pace of the Concord labor, claiming they were, "very slow & hard to drum up."[43]

Edward arrived in Milton on November 26, having sailed to Boston on the SS *Batavia*. There had been some excitement on the crossing—not only was Mark Twain a fellow passenger, but the crew had rescued nine people from a shipwreck.[44] Annie was at Edith's house for the arrival, and she and her future in-laws gave him a joyous greeting.[45] He began training at Massachusetts General Hospital, where he promoted the practice of taking patients' temperatures, which he had learned in Germany.[46]

Edith and Ellen squabbled via letter about the feasibility of the travelers going to Egypt. "This racing on to Egypt uncured will make a cripple out of you. You are wildly imprudent all the time & we anxious in proportion," Edith warned, worried about Ellen's ankle as well as her father.[47] She added, "If this journey is to cure either of you, you must take it more gently—and in short stages & not always make Father move on."[48] Ellen forged ahead, however, making a plan to travel with a group consisting of the Americas William and Mary Whitwell, their daughters May and Bessy, and "the Scotch lady Miss Farquahr."[49] William Whitwell was a civil engineer from New Hampshire, whose son had attended Harvard Medical School with Edward.[50] All seven set off from Rome to Naples, from which they visited Pompeii, and where Elizabeth Hoar surprised them with a visit. They hit rough weather once they set sail on the *Nil*. "It is fatiguing to be darted against the headboard of your bed, and the next moment to begin a process of slipping the other way which lasts till you are all in a heap by the footboard," Ellen reported. To calm herself, she read the Bible story "of St. Paul's atrocious voyage in a ship of Alexandria sailing into Italy with deep sympathy."[51] Safely on shore, they spent Christmas at the Grand Hotel Abbat in Alexandria.

"Oh Edward, how shall I express my joy in Africa?" Ellen wrote from Shepheard's Hotel in Cairo.[52] Egypt was a revelation for Ellen, well worth the tension with her sister and rough crossing. She gloried in each person, each fruit, each bazaar. She was curious to learn about the people she encountered and blinded by prejudice, fixated on the men's dark skin. "I see so many kinds of dresses every day that I can't guess which is the prevalent kind, but a plain white nightgown is very common, and very striking and handsome too, only it takes a beautiful brown man to wear it," she wrote to Edward. She continued, "The foreignness and delightfulness of the Turkish bazaar and the Tunis Bazaar no words can tell," but added, "the moment you look at them as human creatures, it is dreadful to think how far they are from any hope of what we should call happy and comfortable life."[53] Her shield was down, her curiosity and empathy unable to envision that a life so far from her own could be satisfying.

"On Tuesday 7 January we sailed from Cairo for Philea in the Darbeeah *Aurora*, with Mahmoud Bedowa, Dragoman, a Reis or Captain & his mate, ten oarsmen, 2 cooks, a *factotum* boy, a head waiter named Marzook, & 2d waiter Hassan—in all 18; O the Company in the cabin were Mr. & Mrs. Whitwell, Miss

Whitwell & Miss Whitwell. Miss Farquhar; Ellen & I, the seven passengers," Waldo recorded in his journal.[54] The group "elected" Ellen "mistress," and she took on the familiar role of organizer. "I say now read, now stop, now go ashore, this you do yourselves and that you must let the servant do, you may have butter at this meal and at that you mustn't ask for it, you must dress for dinner, and so on," she reported.[55] The group completed a "general reading on Egypt" each day, and every other day Ellen and Miss Farquhar read "C. & Hansen's *Life of Paul*." Her ankle healed, she rejoiced in "the privilege of walking to and fro in Egypt" and learning Arabic from the waiters. At night, as the temperatures dipped, the group wrapped themselves in blankets and chatted under the moonlight. Ellen loved seeing the stars from her bed in her "little white and yellow room with its two windows."[56] It was a blow when they just missed the Wards and Clover Hooper and her new husband Henry Adams at Philae, the island marking the edge of ancient Egypt. Still, Waldo got to fulfil the "the wild desire to see 'him who lies buried at Philae,'" a reference to the myth of the location of Osiris' tomb.[57] Two Englishman who visited for dinner while they were at Assouan entertained Waldo and freed Ellen to explore. Waldo often rode a donkey when he did leave the boat, and Ellen was sure the "donkestrain exercise" benefited him.[58]

Egypt inspired lovely writing from Ellen. Always dedicated to documenting what she encountered, her response to the physical landscape combined with being freed from housework moved her closer to transcendental philosophizing than any other time in her writing life. Laying out her experience in the third person to Edith, she wrote, "Imagine seeing through vistas of columns a patch of greenest green grass, then smooth water, then mountains of fabulous pink and violet and every colour that belongs only in pictures, then this sky." She asked her sister to envision seeing from the room of a temple "the Nile smooth enough to take the sky and be blue shining water, mountains whose colours I have named but not their shapes, which make me keep looking again to see if it wasn't a mistake, if they were really so interesting and lovely, ruins to set off all the rest . . . and this sun all round you comforting and warming you to the heart's core, and this endless blue sky, so you feel distinctly that you are breathing the sun and sky and all in it." Of entering a pyramid, she wrote that you "ride through the green and up to a mountain which is so polite as to have a door, and you walk in expecting a deathly chill. No indeed, that mountain is as warm inside as out, so you are happy, and a candle being lighted, the mountain shows you the manners and customs of the ancient inhabitants." At the end of this rapturous letter, Ellen concluded, "You see I am happy."[59]

The *Aurora* sailed into Assouan on January 28, and they soon were headed back down the Nile. Ellen continued to collect adventures. As she, Bessy, and Mary cooled their feet in the river at Silsileh, "the old gods heard a few Sunday school tunes."[60] She gathered sand to take home, mourning that it was as close as she would get to the Sahara. At Denderah, Ellen "crawled into holes so small I could hardly get my hat through," filled with "suffocating and detestable" air.[61] Back in Luxor, they "fell in" with four boats full of American and English travelers, who quickly bonded and began hosting dinner parties on the different vessels. One of the families was the "Roosevelts of N.Y.," including their twelve-year-old son Theodore; Ellen found all three Roosevelt children "healthy, natural, well-brought-up, and with beautiful manners." When the Emersons and the Roosevelts decided to visit Beni Hassen together, Theodore rowed Waldo and Ellen, "talking to us as I hope Ralph will talk when he is three years older."[62] Edith and Miss Farquhar attended a service at the Coptic Church in Luxor. She reported to Edith, "I came away very much puzzled—of course disagreeably impressed by a part of it—but delighted with the prominent share of the children in the service and knowing very well that I had been in church—that was good—and most of all curious to know something about it all."[63]

Ellen's letters overflow with joy and energy as they made their way through Egypt and back to Italy. Waldo and Ellen returned to Cairo on February 13, having taken a train from Kolosna with Miss Farquhar. Although she had loved her tiny room on the boat, the "luxury of large rooms and beds" in Shepheard's Hotel was not lost on her; meanwhile Waldo "felt very gay" that they "had accomplished a good day's journey towards Concord."[64] They were at sea on at the steamer *Egitto* by Ellen's birthday on February 24. Father and daughter discussed mythology as they viewed Greece in the distance. Ellen was glad to report that the other six passengers, all from Pennsylvania, "knew how to make the most of Father and we had readings and much talk." On Sunday a concert of hymns went on for two hours. "I'm the happiest girl in the world, and whether I look at past, present, or future can only exclaim, how broad how bright how full my life is," Ellen wrote to her mother as she celebrated turning 34.[65] After a brief stay in Naples to avoid the crushing crowds of Carnival, the Emersons returned to Rome. On the Campagna, Ellen "galloped as I never believed before that horses could" on a ride with the author Alice Bartlett and Sarah Butler Wister, the actress Fanny Kemble's daughter.[66] Meanwhile Henry James kept Waldo company, easing Ellen's way with his solicitude towards the older writer.[67] In Florence, while at a dinner party, there was a small earthquake, which Ellen "enjoyed the whole from beginning to end."[68] A joyous dinner with the author Herman Grimm and his wife Gisela von Arnim gave Ellen the opportunity to use her German, leading her to think of Ida. Finding Waldo working on his "green book of poems" also cheered Ellen, as it was the first work her father attempted during their travels.[69]

By the time they returned to Paris in mid-March and said goodbye to Curnex, Waldo and Ellen were homesick. Not even the delights of the Louvre and a brilliant production of Molière's *Malade Imaginaire* could convince them there was any place better than their New England town. "The advantage of living in Concord seems to be so very great that I think there is no place to be compared to it," Ellen and Elizabeth Hoar had agreed in Florence, and now Concord called to them.[70] The unsettled state of Bush, however, gave them pause. "Your representations of the woes of house-cleaning and furnishing have been working in Father's mind ever since he read them in Rome and have dampened his ardour for going straight home," Ellen reported to Edith.[71] Edith pushed for them to stay as long as possible, even as Ellen reminded her that someone needed to do Ellen's work, and, if she was abroad, it would fall to Edith or Lidian.

The final leg of the trip was a return to Great Britain. London was a blur of social engagements and errands. Ellen rushed to get through Edith's shopping list, which included crockery, soaps, books, and, for Waldo's birthday, a monocle.[72] She and Waldo went to Westminster Abbey for Easter, which solidified her growing dislike of the Anglican Church. "Curious indeed is the effect of the Church of England on the minds of its clergy. I know it by heart now—I have seen it so long in so many places—but cannot in the least express it or even define it to myself. I pity them, is the upshot of it," she reported to Lidian.[73] A jaunt to Oxford was exhilarating. She "thought of Tom Brown and Mary and of Norman" as they circled Christ-Church meadow, a reference to Thomas Hughes' novel *Tom Brown at Oxford*, and attended lectures by the professor of religion Max Müller, their host, and the art critic John Ruskin, "whom" Ellen reported "I fell in love with."[74]

Ellen's birthday had been spent at sea, and so was Waldo's. After a swing through Edinburgh, they boarded the SS *Olympus* in Liverpool on May 16. Waldo turned seventy on May 25. The following day, Boston Harbor greeted them with the "best" sunset Ellen had "seen since we were in Egypt."[75] It was too late to disembark, so they walked off the boat the following morning, their adventure at a close.

"Oh! What a sight! What a sight! My whole dear town all assembled." Ellen and Waldo were overcome as they arrived in the Concord train station. Not only their family, or even just close friends, but the whole town assembled, a gathering arranged by Judge Hoar. Teachers ushered their classes to the celebration and wagons filled with Concordians filed by to greet the Emersons. The crowd accompanied them to Bush, as "the aged and lame and feeble people" who could not join waved their handkerchiefs from their windows. At the corner of their yard, a vine-covered arch bore the greeting "Welcome" and was surrounded by flower-pots; the school children sang "Home Sweet Home." Ellen was reminded that it was the second time in a year the town had gathered at Bush. "Ten months ago they had all been here to help us save what they could ... and now they had all come once more to see us into the house again." Ellen welcomed the "shining new magnificence of the house," in which things were largely the same but "everything is new and fresh and handsome."[76]

Edith gave birth to Edward Waldo Forbes on July 16, 1873, on Naushon. Her brother, who had just passed his final exams and graduated from Harvard Medical School, demurred that he was not worthy of a namesake; Edith replied, "You are a foolish boy not to know that whatever your fortunes may be you can never be any thing but your self—the best patron saint we could choose over our boy."[77] Ellen was summoned by telegraph and arrived when her newest nephew was "twelve hours old."[78] For the next week, Ellen and Will took turns sitting with Edith. Caroline Leavitt was again the Forbes' governess, and Edie Davidson had been hired to provide an extra hand with the older children. Edith longed for Waldo to join them, but instead he tried to work, putting off a visit until September. He did send effusive thanks for her efforts in restoring his beloved home. Of the new cabinets in his study, he wrote, "no carpenter's plane or chisel or hammer could design or finish or smooth them, nothing but beautiful love could work the miracle." He added, "A joy & comfort & reminder of you they are, every hour of every day."[79] When he did finally visit, he proclaimed of his fifth grandchild, "He's not misshapen at all—he is a very nice baby!"[80]

The financial panic of 1873 sent the American economy into a tailspin. A series of issues—including the over-expansion of the railroad and the failure of the bank Jay Cooke and Company—caused an economic crisis. On September 20, as panic spread, the New York Stock Exchange closed for ten days. Fifty-five railroads failed by November, followed by another sixty in the following year.[81] Will spent long days in the office, where the Forbes scrambled to secure the family's financial position and those of people who had invested in Forbes and Co.[82] The Forbes lost money, but not enough for them to put off plans for a new house in Milton.[83] The combination of Will's long hours, overseeing the final details on their new home, a rheumatic knee, and a fifth child in eight years did overwhelm Edith, however. She explained her "household lay heavy on my mind" while turning down Ellen's invitation to attend the dedication of the new Concord Free Public Library, a major event for the town and the family.[84] Edith interpreted the national financial crisis in only the most personal of terms.

"I was proud of Father's voice, proud of his skill, and more thankful for it than can be told," Ellen declared after Waldo spoke at the library dedication on a brilliant, crisp October day. Waldo's decision to give the dedication had worried Ellen, especially after she saw the "fragmentary nature" of a draft, which drew from existing texts on Thoreau, Hawthorne, and the benefits of reading.[85] Even though Ellen sewed the pages together to keep them in order, Waldo accidentally omitted the conclusion. However, he managed to "cover it up" and stirred the crowd. Waldo praised the donation that made the library possible, which came from William Monroe, a wealthy dry-good merchant originally from Concord. He also sang the benefits it would bring to all Concordians. "In the details of this munificence," Waldo intoned, "we may all anticipate a sudden and lasting prosperity to this ancient town, in the benefit of a noble Library, which adds by the beauty of the building, and its skillful arrangement, a quite new attraction,—making readers of those who were not readers,—making scholars of those who only read newspapers or novels until now."[86] Ellen understood the limitations under which her father now worked, but on this beautiful day she was happy and relieved to see him shine.

"Will and I are sitting in our library—at our new table in new chairs, admiring our fire and our red curtains," Edith reported on March 15, 1874.[87] As the "chaos" of last minute fixes by the workmen came to an end, Edith noted, "To me it looks like an old friend—the home I knew I was coming to."[88] Leading up to the move, Ellen had arranged to be in Milton from Tuesday through Friday for several weeks to help Edith transition from her "cot[tage] to her palace," while also occasionally taking some of the children back to Bush to ease Edith's load.[89] In Concord, the Emersons were equally content with the rebuilt Bush. "It is just like a novel, the burning and restoration of the house, and we always feel it so, and survey every day our rooms and our possessions with a feeling of romantic interest," Ellen explained to Sally Emerson.[90]

Edith paid tribute to her family as she planted her new gardens, literally bringing a little of Concord to Milton. She solicited honeysuckle, red lavender, monkshood, and lilies of the valley from Lidian; white anemones and Solomon's seal from Elizabeth Hoar; and a lace plant from Annie. She wanted Waldo to plant an elm tree on her property, to represent the "E" in Emerson, and a linden tree, both because the name reminded her of Lidian and Lidian had liked the linden trees at her childhood home. The transplanted flora provided her a way to solidify her connection to her birth family even as her roots in Milton grew deeper.[91]

Ellen, meanwhile, seemed re-energized through a combination of the trip, Waldo's relative stability, and the refurbished house. Her exposure to different religious traditions had made her more committed than ever to Unitarianism. As she travelled to the Unitarian Conference in Arlington that spring, there were "screams and embraces at the depot, accompanied by much laughing, dancing for joy, and crazy marchings up and down the platform." She added, "I don't believe any other thing throws people into such a state of wild delight . . . this going to a Conference when you're old."[92]

Ellen's Christian spirit and deep interest in children inspired her to consider adopting a young girl named Sarah Aurelio to remove her from a difficult domestic situation rife with "violence, injustice, and coarsening influences."[93] While Edith had welcomed Edie Davidson and Lily Keyes, both of whom Ellen called "daughter" but never planned formally to adopt, she now made a forceful objection. The girl would be "a drain on your own powers and purse," Edith argued. She drafted a detailed list of expenses Ellen might expect from a child and claimed that Will "says it would be very wrong for you to undertake either the care or expense." Edith also had non-financial objections. "I do not think it would be right for you to go out of your way to pick up a claim on you that would alter your present way of life & fasten you down to one child to the exclusion of your friends and relations to whom you are a great blessing—and we will none of us consent to give you up to her," she declared.[94] As with her earlier complaints about Sunday school, Edith wanted first claim on Ellen's time. There was also a racist component to the concerns. Sarah was of Portuguese descent, and Edith, Will, and Edward worried that she was of, in Edith's words, "possible bad blood."[95] Ellen herself had been condescending to the Portuguese in the Azores, but her ideas had evolved, at least enough that she considered welcoming the girl. But she put aside the plan, replying that she recognized Edith's wisdom. She poignantly added, however, "I always have a vague general expectation of adopting children."[96] Even if adopting a child as her father declined was not the right decision, the lack of sympathy for someone always so ready to care for her family and the prejudice towards a vulnerable young girl is striking. Edith cared for her sister, but she failed to understand fundamental elements of what drove her, including her desire to have a child. She, moreover, was generous in donating money to causes that advanced social justice, but racism and personal interest often drove her when the object of charity came too close to home.

The Forbes wealth warped Edith's experience of the world in problematic ways. But it is undeniable that Will's financial knowledge and comfort in using power helped his in-laws, as his efforts changed the Emersons' financial fortunes. First, he identified a scam. Lidian, her sister Lucy, and her brother Charles had inherited a commercial property on Court Street in Boston, the leasing of which was overseen by their cousin Abraham Jackson. Digging around to see why the property brought in so little money, Will uncovered not only that Jackson was pocketing a large percentage of the profits, but also that he rented himself the second floor of the building well below market rates. Will confronted Jackson and determined the best way forward was to sell the property, eventually getting Lidian $16,000 for her share and investing it in railroad stock. It took years for the events to play out, but the saga concluded in early 1875.[97] Will also examined Waldo's publishing contacts, with his father-in-law's reluctant permission. He found errors and perhaps deliberate mistakes, such as Waldo only being paid twenty cents a copy for royalties, instead of the promised thirty cents. Going forward, Will acted as Waldo's agent, combing over contracts and payments and sending brusk letters to get Waldo the best deal. Under Will's supervision, the publishers paid Waldo four times more than they had earlier.[98] "Though Father was no longer able to give lectures and earn, we were now rich, we had more money than we needed," Ellen declared of these changes.[99] Her work as household accountant was suddenly much less fraught.

The new house settled and her youngest child a year old, Edith returned to *Parnassus* in the summer of 1874 when Waldo, Lidian, and Ellen all joined her on Naushon. While Edith soon realized a "fortnight more will hardly finish it," the family worked "steadily" on that stay.[100] It was all hands on deck, with "every guest" pitching in.[101] Ida Agassiz Higginson provided critical aid. Edith and Waldo trusted her taste in poetry, and she "made herself especially useful" when her "classifying skill" came into play as they decided "under which heads the poems should go."[102] Edith continued to consult Ida on all decisions until the book went to press. Back in Concord, Waldo struggled with the introduction, but, likely with assistance from Edward and perhaps Ellen on this final step, the end was in sight.[103] When a check for $1,000 arrived from the Court Street property in September, Ellen wrote to Edith, "Court St. and Parnassus are great presents on their 39th anniversary from you and Will, and I think this is a momentous month."[104]

November was a rush of final decisions. "Correcting these proofs is work that pays well. Selections made long ago, and forgotten, keep rising, each as fresh as a star," Waldo joked.[105] The publisher James Osgood, significantly, corresponded with Edith, not Waldo, about whether he or the Emersons would shoulder the cost of the publication; Will decided Waldo should pay for the plates and retain the copyright.[106] Choices about the physical appearance of the book fell to Edith as well, although she gave in to Osgood's request that they produce red and dark brown covers, along with her preferred blue. Lizzy Simmons drew the laurel wreath that appears on the cover of the first edition, with the Emersons, the Forbes, Elizabeth Hoar, Ida Agassiz Higginson, and Ida's sister Pauline Agassiz Shaw voting on the final design.[107]

"This is a triumphant day for me, dear Ellen, for Will came home proud as a peacock bearing the first copy of Parnassus, blue and handsome," Edith crowed on December 18, 1874.[108] Edith's sense of personal victory makes it clear she realized how much credit she deserved for the book. The volume did meet criticism for mistakes in transcription and attribution, as well as the fact that it did not include an index of authors' names. The family began to identify corrections immediately. Waldo kept a list of needed revisions in a notebook, and Ellen and Edith made corrections in the copies they sent to friends.[109] Meanwhile, the book sold so well that a second edition was ordered almost immediately, giving the team an opportunity to make the changes quickly. The second edition appeared within six weeks of the first and was advertised as having "numerous corrections and revisions" and the requested author index.[110]

Edith's dedication to the manuscript is all the more noteworthy given the pain she had endured throughout the summer and fall. Her knee continued to plague her, to the point that she needed crutches or a "wheeled chair" to move about. Holding little Edward in the chair made her nervous, so he spent more time apart from her than the older children had; according to Ellen, this made him wild.[111] Then, in October she hurt her back when she rolled the beach wagon on Naushon. At a Sunday School convention in Greenfield, Massachusetts, Ellen missed a letter from Will explaining the gravity of the situation. "If I could have been of use I should be inconsolable that you didn't telegraph me at once that might I have come to you instead of going to Greenfield," Ellen wrote in apology.[112] Edith instead relied on Violet, now seven. "She is a remarkably capable and knowing little creature and under the discipline of a lame mother is fast learning the use of her sense," Edith boasted.[113]

Amid the *Parnassus* chaos, Edward married Annie Keyes on September 19, 1874. Annie, having often cared for the Forbes children and Waldo and Lidian during her long engagement, was already integrated into and loved by the family. Edward, the frail baby brother, was coming into his own, having joined the medical practice of Dr. Josiah Barlett in Concord.[114] The combination of Annie's helping hands and Edward's medical knowledge was a comfort to Ellen and Edith as they dealt with their aging parents.

In 1875, plans to celebrate the centennial of the Battle of Concord dominated the town. The Emersons, connected to the 1775 battle and Concord's nineteenth-century literary fame, were deeply involved. Edward joined the committee on Decorations and Dinner, while Waldo served on the Monument, General Invitations, and Reception of Guests committees. By April, the town was in a frenzy, as Concordians posted histories of their houses near their front doors and cleaned up private homes and public spaces. Twenty-thousand people poured in, including President Ulysses S. Grant. Fourteen guests squeezed into Bush, including Edith, Ralph, Violet, Edie Davidson, Effie Lowell, and the Jackson cousins; Edward and Annie put up five more.[115] The day took on national importance, not just for the significance of the battle, but as the kickoff for the centennial celebrations of the Declaration of Independence that would roll out the next year.

April 19 was chilly and dark, but the rain held off. The dedication of Daniel Chester French's *The Minute Man*, a sculpture made from the metal of ten melted cannons, was a highlight of the day. It was the first commission for French, who lived in Concord and went on to design the Lincoln Memorial; May Alcott, who had been his art teacher, recommended him to the committee. French's statue sat atop a rough rectangle of granite inscribed with the famous first stanza of Waldo's "The Concord Hymn"—"By the rude bridge that arched the flood / their flag to April's breeze unfurled / Here once the embattled Farmers stood / And fired the shot heard round the world."[116] As the 1775 bridge was long gone, the town also marked the anniversary by building a more elaborate one.[117] Waldo delivered a short address as part of the statue's dedication, despite his growing struggles with public speaking and writing. Ellen later described the centennial address and speech at the library as "all the writing he did after 1872."[118] His children did not express any anxiety about the speech either before or afterwards, however, with Ellen declaring the day a "brilliant festivity."[119]

Not everyone shared Ellen's opinion. Louisa May Alcott wrote a cutting description of the events for *Woman's Journal*, explaining that none of Concord's women had been invited to participate in the procession or sit on the podium. Told to wait outside the tent until an official escorted them inside, Alcott and a group of women eventually stormed in as "the spirit of '75 blazed up in the bosoms" of the "long suffering women." The event, she argued, was a lost opportunity to honor Concord's Revolutionary mothers. "It was impossible to help thinking that there should have been a place for the great granddaughters of Prescott, of William Emerson, John Hancock and Dr. Ripley.... It seemed to me their presence on that platform would have had a deeper significance than the gold lace which adorned one side... the men of Concord had missed a grand opportunity of imitating those whose memory they had met to honor."[120] She found it gratifying when a portion of the platform collapsed.

Ellen, who was of course William Emerson's great granddaughter, mentions none of the events Alcott describes. (Edith does not describe the event at all in extant correspondence.) Ellen was likely worried about Waldo's speech, and perhaps his dependence on her allowed her to enter the tent with him. Boston papers describe a chaotic scene and fail to mention Alcott's protest, although they do mention the platform collapse.[121] Given the crowds, it is possible Ellen did not see the women entering the tent. Still, it is a curious absence, suggesting the extreme tunnel vision on Ellen's part when it came to any fight for women's equality.

July took a devastating turn when, just days after his birth, Edward and Annie's first child died. They posthumously named him William. "All of us are thankful he lived, and that we had real comfort of him for those days," Ellen explained to Sally Emerson.[122] For a family haunted by the death of the young Waldo, however, the loss was a terrible blow. Annie was bed-bound for over a month, while Edward threw himself back into his medical and civic duties, his sisters fretting over his haggard appearance. Edith wrote Annie a series of letters to comfort her, a testament to the family commitment to the power of correspondence.[123] "Thank you for your letters to cheer her up," Edward replied.[124]

As the family mourned William, the volume of essays due to Hotten reared its head. The Emersons had hoped, upon Hotten's death in June 1873, that the book was dead too. The publishers Chatto and Windus, however, had purchased the firm from Hotten's widow and threatened legal action if Waldo did not fulfill his contract.[125] Waldo leaned heavily on Ellen in his attempt to finish the project, trying to cede the entire production to her. "The book no longer seems a great difficulty. Father feels the relief of having given it over to me, he chooses to believe I can do everything, and in the belief is happy," Ellen wrote to

Edith.[126] Transforming Waldo's lectures into publishable essays included much more than transcribing and light editing. Rather than coherent, polished talks, Waldo's lecture notes, particularly from more recent years, were "collections of Emerson's thoughts on particular topics," often lacking an introduction or conclusion; many passages had been used in multiple lectures over the years, leading to complicated page numbering. As Nancy Simmons explains, the "method of repeatedly retooling his material to new uses had served Emerson well during his long lecture career; for Ellen, however, the shufflings were a nightmare."[127] Ellen did find the work easier than three years earlier, as she was now "better acquainted" with the material and thus felt less "blind and helpless." She also felt less compunction about making his diminished faculties clear to him. "I have now not the least scruple about showing Father things, while then I couldn't bear to because it was the beginning and I hated to shock him with the sense his memory was failing him," she explained to Edith.[128] The project was ultimately "interesting and painful like most work," but Ellen knew she needed reinforcements.[129]

Help came in the form of James Elliot Cabot. A transcendentalist philosopher and editor, Cabot was already one of the family's top choices to serve as Waldo's literary executor, and he had helped on *Parnassus* while visiting Naushon the summer before.[130] Cabot had been reluctant to involve himself with Waldo's work, however, and Waldo was reluctant to call on him now. Ellen had a plan to overcome their mutual trepidation. She broached the subject with Elizabeth Dwight Cabot, Cabot's wife, and the women successfully conspired to convince the men to give the partnership a try. "Mr. Cabot is coming on Friday to spend the night and begin his task. Our spirits are high," Ellen announced in late August.[131] He returned in September and again in October. By October 15 they had sent much of the manuscript to James Osgood, who was to publish the volume in the United States. Describing the success after the men's initial hesitation, Elizabeth Cabot declared, "What a mercy it is that there are women in the world to arrange for men!"[132]

Even with Cabot on board, Ellen still worked tirelessly—transcribing, compiling, and organizing material, going over proofs, and prodding her father. She lost visits to Milton and Naushon and ignored her school committee work; she barely had time to mourn the death of Ida Agassiz Higginson's young daughter Cécile in August.[133] Ellen was proud of her contributions, while also wanting them kept under wraps to protect her father's reputation. In September, she wrote to Edith that she "bragged at dinner time of some of the neat corrections 'we have made.'" She noted, however, "I have been careful, ridiculously so for me" to not let her work be known outside the family circle.[134] She hoped Edith had been as circumspect. On November 13, having called on Cabot for one last marathon stretch of editing, Ellen declared "the book was ended."[135] *Letters and Social Aims* was published in the United States on December 15, and it appeared in Britain the following January.[136]

CHAPTER SIX

"The Power of Our Life Has Been Very Kind"

(1876–1882)

The collaboration on *Letters and Social Aims* marked the beginning of what scholars refer to as the "Emerson factory," meaning the process by which Waldo, Ellen, and James Elliot Cabot, in consultation with others in their circle, published work under the name Ralph Waldo Emerson.[1] The factory did not close shop with the appearance of that volume. The day that Ellen declared *Letters and Social Aims* "ended," she was already plotting what they would do next. She asked Cabot "at breakfast if he would go straight on as soon as I could get the book together, and we planned two more books which I hope we can do this next year." While "Father was aghast at my audacity," he was also "amazed and consoled to see the eagerness even which Mr. Cabot felt to do it," she told Edith. Ellen added, "It lifts a weight off all three of us. We had rather do it, and Father have it done, in his life-time than wait."[2] For the next six years, the factory production took up much of the family's time and energy, even as they negotiated dramatic changes.

By early 1876, the team had moved on to a volume of selected poems.[3] Waldo, better able to handle editing poetry than prose at this point in his decline, made the majority of selections and revisions himself.[4] Ellen reported to Edith in September 1876, "Father is still at work on the new poems, and I am not helping."[5] While Waldo was able to work, "not helping" was an exaggeration. Ellen solicited and conveyed advice from her siblings, Cabot, Elizabeth Hoar, James Russell Lowell, and Franklin Sanborn, among others.[6] She did, moreover, intervene actively with "May-Day," the title piece of Waldo's 1867 poetry volume. He had never been happy with the work's structure and now, overwhelmed with the revision process, decided to omit it. Ellen disagreed with leaving out such a prominent piece, and she asked Edith to study the poem "for rearrangement."[7] Ellen likely made most of the final decisions about the poem, including paring six verses and reshuffling what remained.[8] Years later Edward told Cabot that his father had "sanctioned" these changes.[9] *Selected Poems* was issued on October 30, 1876, another pressure removed.

While Waldo could work on the poems, an opportunity to lecture far from Concord brought his limitations into stark relief. The Washington and Jefferson Literary Societies of the University of Virginia invited him to deliver an address in June 1876, as part of commencement week. Waldo had recently given talks at the Massachusetts Historical Society, the Concord Lyceum, and a convention of Sunday school teachers in Concord, along with a few in private homes, each one "an enjoyable occasion to him and his listeners."[10] At those events, however, he was among friends, neighbors, and admirers, all of whom wished him to succeed. Waldo had never set foot in Virginia and had not lectured away from the Boston area in years. He was determined to go, though, as he saw the invitation as a step toward healing the wounds the country still suffered a decade after the Civil War.[11] Ellen, of course, would accompany him.

As they prepared for the trip, Ellen took primary responsibility for compiling the speech by excerpting Waldo's 1863 lectures at Dartmouth and Waterville colleges.[12] The oration occupied much of her time that spring. On their way to Virginia, she and Waldo stopped in Philadelphia to see the Centennial Exposition, where Waldo was "electrified at the first sight of the Main Building."[13] The train trip from Philadelphia to Virginia was less exhilarating; it was hot and Ellen and Waldo felt ill, even as they scrambled to polish the lecture. Only a serving of ice cream offered relief. Once in Charlottesville, their host Professor Frederick Holmes and his family warmly welcomed them. The night took a tense turn, however, when Holmes showed off a portrait of Robert E. Lee and a Confederate flag and praised "the chivalrous character and exploits of the Confederate Generals, and the brutal conduct of the Union Army."[14]

The talk, "The Natural and Permanent Functions of the Scholar," did not go well. The rowdy crowd could barely hear Waldo in the large Public Hall. Some clustered close to the stage, but more chose to ignore the lecture and socialize. In the immediate aftermath, Ellen emphasized to her mother that Waldo had spoken beautifully, but that the hall's size, the weakness of his voice, and the audience's behavior made the situation impossible.[15] Years later, she remembered it in more dire terms, claiming Waldo had been confused and exhausted the entire trip, while also wondering if the audience's behavior was "intentional hostility to a Northern man."[16] Waldo's celebrity offered a cushion and provided a target. At a reception following the speech "there were many many people who had read Father's books and really cared about him, and he was made much of by them to a degree not surpassed anywhere."[17] An article in the *Richmond Enquirer* by students to whom Waldo refused to give a copy of the lecture pilloried his performance, however, using it as "an occasion for reviving, rather than setting aside, the still deeply felt animosities that had driven the North and the South to war."[18] One author of the article later regretted the incident, which drew the censure of the university faculty, but for Ellen the message was clear.[19] This type of commitment was now beyond her father.

The declining health of Edie Davidson, plagued by a persistent cough, cast another shadow over the summer. She was under the care of Dr. Samuel Cabot, Jr., James Elliot's brother. By September, Ellen was convinced she would not recover, even though Dr. Cabot said Edie had "a good chance."[20] While they did not use the word tuberculosis, Ellen and Edith discussed the possibility of sending her to California, Colorado, or even Egypt to recover in a dry climate. They settled on Menton, on the French Riviera, and Edie sailed on October 3. Pauline Agassiz Shaw, three of Edie's "young friends," and her uncle joined Ellen and likely Edith in underwriting the trip.[21] Edward broke his leg in October when his horse fell as he rode to visit a patient at night, giving the Emersons another worry.[22]

The second half of 1876 did, thankfully, bring some delights. When Ellen and Waldo returned from Virginia, they met Charles Lowell Emerson, to whom Annie had given birth on July 3. The same month a donkey named Miss Graciosa arrived for Ellen from the Azores, exciting her almost as much as her new nephew. She had the "prettiest soft gray coat, white legs, and neat little black boots, and such a pretty face as no donkey ever had before," according to Ellen.[23] She took "Ciosa" on an expedition to the cliffs near Walden, offered rides to her Sunday school students, and rode her down Concord's Main Street, where "everyone was at door and windows" to watch.[24]

The poet Emma Lazarus visited Bush in August. She and Waldo had met in 1868 and started a friendly correspondence. When he did not include her poems in *Parnassus*, however, Lazarus demanded an explanation. The task fell to Ellen. In February 1875, she drafted two responses; neither has been found, but Ellen reported that she sent the blunter version which told "the whole truth," with the justification that while it "may grieve her at first" the truth "has healing power."[25]

Learning through the Wards of Waldo's decline, in 1876 Lazarus put bad feelings aside and invited Waldo to visit; he asked her to Concord instead. To Lazarus's disappointment, when she arrived, she found herself treated as the guest of Ellen and Lidian, an inevitability given Waldo's increasing difficulty communicating. While Lazarus resisted Ellen's insistence that everyone retire at 8 p.m. and pressed for time with Waldo, the visit went well. Lazarus gave advice on *Selected Poems*, and Ellen loved overhearing Lazarus' talks with Lidian. She reported the poet's "ardent persistent questions" eventually "got at many a corner of Mother's mind never before visited."[26] Ellen had her own questions, not surprisingly about religion. "Then think of what nuts it was to me, old S[unday]. S[chool]. teacher [*sic*] that I am, to get at a real unconverted Jew (who had no objection to calling herself one, and talked freely about 'Our Church' and 'We Jews') and hear how Old Testament sounds to her, & find she has been brought up to keep the Law and the Feast of the Passover, and the Day of Atonement," Ellen reported with delight.[27] Lazarus' biographer Esther Schor suggests, "Had Ellen not engaged this 'real unconverted Jew' with genuine warmth and empathy, we would not have the sole comment Emma Lazarus left behind about the Jewish life of her family."[28] Ellen, Lidian, and Lazarus kept up a correspondence after the visit, with Ellen visiting Lazarus at least once in New York City.[29]

"Did I tell you my family made me sign a pledge of abstinence from all public life for a certain time, except they allow me to keep my S.S. class. I am to do this next year as much of the neglected domestic business instead as I possibly can," Ellen reported to Clara Dabney in January 1877.[30] She made light of it, but giving up the school committee and her Unitarian and Sunday School conventions was a blow to the independent life Ellen had created beyond Bush. She mourned the sense of community she found through these activities. Ellen confided to Clara, "Few relations are more delightful than the relations of a committee among themselves, they are so intimate and full of the delight of the common work. Yet they fall to pieces in a moment when you leave the committee. You are at once an outsider and no matter what the disposition of your old associates may be they no longer have a right to open their minds freely to you as of old."[31]

By "domestic business" Ellen did not just mean the expected housekeeping and caregiving. As her collaboration with Cabot eased Waldo's anxiety, helped secure his legacy, and brought in money, Ellen's editorial responsibilities were part of her "domestic business." Even before her "abstinence pledge," she could see the results of this work in her father's more relaxed state. The combination of Cabot's editorial assistance and Will's help on financial matters were a potent medicine. "All his worries being lifted off once for all has made a difference in his health as well as his happiness," Ellen explained to Haven in April 1876. "Father considers himself now a truly happy man," she added.[32] So even though Ellen felt that "it makes a great difference both in the kind and degree of pleasure one has in the world whether there is a little public element in it," she sacrificed her public work to keep the domestic business in Bush on track.[33]

Edie Davidson died in Menton on April 15, 1877. Her brother William arrived in time to see her, as did James Elliot Cabot's son Arthur who had developed a strong friendship and perhaps a romance with her.[34] She was buried in France, her brother's wish. "She was a sweet and faithful sister to me," Edith wrote Ellen in a note of condolence, honored that Edie remembered the Forbes children in her last letter.[35] Ellen, for her part, claimed not to feel sad, echoing her father's denial of his grief after Waldo died, instead cherishing her memories. She did dream that Edie hugged her, adding "Now I would rather have had that than any other kind of dream."[36]

With all of her children beyond toddlerhood for the first time in eleven years, Edith returned to her habit of detailing her brood's exploits and development in extensive detail. "It is like a photograph of them all. Does she always write such letters?" William H. Channing asked after hearing one read at Bush. Elizabeth Hoar responded, "yes, and there are such beautiful stories about the children in them! They are a perfect store house of these lovely stories."[37] Edith's sense of their developing personalities comes to vivid light in her missives. She was concerned about Ralph's progress in school, but proud of the attention he paid his younger siblings as he taught them to swim and sail.[38] Don was "so calm, so merry, so sweet, so good, so picturesque," but could also be stubborn.[39] Cameron was a "gentlemanly little fellow," but "dreamy" and struggled academically.[40] Edward, still referred to as "Baby" at aged four, was rambunctious and loved above all to be with his father.[41] She adored her sole daughter Violet, so serious and helpful, confessing to Ellen "I could hardly take my eyes off her the other day she looked so lovely."[42]

Edith brought the same energy and organizational fervor she had applied to *Parnassus* to her children's lives. With other Milton women, she helped establish a kindergarten in 1875 and organized a dancing school. She read constantly to her children and taught them—the boys as well as Violet—to cook, sew, and garden. She threw herself into making valentines and decorating for Christmas to ensure each holiday was a delight.[43] By the end of the summer of 1877, however, Edith collapsed.[44] She stayed on Naushon to recover when the family left in October, with Ellen dropping her Concord responsibilities to fly to her side.[45]

Edith took the advice of both Edward and Dr. Lucy Sewall, one of the first female doctors on the staff of the New England Hospital for Women and Children, as she recuperated.[46]

Edith's collapse proved to be a prelude to a long siege of bad health and bad news for the Emersons. Annie's cherished sister Florence died in December, when Annie was heavily pregnant. The death of his sister-in-law and patient sent Edward reeling. He begged Annie to leave Concord to give birth, as "the poor boy has decided it is safer not to take care of her himself."[47] Annie reluctantly acquiesced, moving in with Edith. Edward thanked the Forbes for the "blessed kindness you have shown me in opening this city of refuge to my Annie"; he also sent instructions for spraying linens with carbolic acid solution and a request to remind the doctor to dip his hands in the same before any exam.[48] The baby, a boy named John, arrived on January 6. The ordeal bonded Ellen and Edith closer to Annie, underscoring that they saw her as a sister, not just the wife of their brother. Their own bond, of course, made them understand how devastating the loss of Florence was.

Edward rushed Annie back to Concord when Will and Ralph came down with scarlet fever in February. The disease was terrifying in the age before antibiotics. Will, Ralph, and Edith quarantined in their home, while the rest of the children spread out among Forbes relatives. Edith tried to remain positive, noting how precious the time was for father and son to spend together.[49] She was heartbroken, however, to be isolated from her other children, particularly when she could only wave at little Edward through a window.[50] Once her patients were no longer contagious, Edith and her servants had to disinfect the house—washing furniture and spraying books with carbolic water, swabbing down shelves and floors, filling in the cracks in the floor with turpentine, and sending rugs, bedding, and curtains out for cleaning.[51] When "Baby" Edward came down with a temperature at the home of Alice Forbes, Edith flew to his bed, embracing him for the first time in four weeks.[52]

"Siege no. two" began in April, when Cameron's sore throat proved to be scarlet fever.[53] Cameron, who Edith thought of as having a delicate constitution, had been the child Edith most feared getting sick, so this time Will and Edith kept their offspring at home. Edith and Ellen mourned the five additional weeks of school the Forbes children lost.[54] In Concord, meanwhile, Edward's two young sons had mild cases of scarlet fever themselves.[55]

In the midst of the siege, Elizabeth Hoar died on April 7, at the age of sixty-three. The woman the Emerson siblings called Aunt Lizzy had been a constant in their lives, caring for them when they were little and reading Dante and the *Odyssey* with them as adults.[56] As Hoar took ether on one of her final days, she told Ellen her epitaph should read, "the great joy of her life was in her nephews and nieces, among whom she numbered also the children of William and Waldo Emerson."[57] She left Waldo, Edith, Ellen, and Edward each one-hundred dollars, "for some remembrance of my love for them."[58] Edith spent hers on a set of encyclopedias, as it was something the family would use "constantly" and thus keep Aunt Lizzy in their thoughts.[59]

Throughout the scarlet fever crisis none of the Forbes children were sent to Concord, where Ellen was hard at work with James Elliot Cabot. The Emerson factory had put aside their initial plans for another volume to focus on preparing individual essays for publication. "Demonology" and "Perpetual Forces" had appeared in the *North American Review* in 1877; now the preparation of "Sovereignty of Ethics" for the same publication was Cabot and Ellen's "principle business."[60] They were also preparing a pamphlet of "Fortune of the Republic," a lecture Waldo had delivered the previous year, and editing "The Superlative," which would appear in *Century Magazine* in 1882. So while in late April, Ellen purported to wish she could take the children when they were pulled from school, she begged off. Work on "Superlative" and correcting the "Sovereignty of Ethics" proofs "must absorb me 'till Tuesday," she explained, and then Elizabeth Cabot was visiting.[61]

Ellen's willingness to put off helping Edith to focus on the editing work underscores how important it was to her. While she had forfeited the satisfaction of committee work, her partnership with Cabot gave her the pleasure of another shared endeavor. Ellen took pride in the collaboration. She noted in February 1878, for instance, "Mr. Cabot and I have been hard at work all day on three lectures each of which I flatter myself will be very good."[62] Ellen counted Elizabeth Cabot as part of the team. "Mrs. Cabot's eyes seem to have exercised a blessed magic upon "Sovereignty of Ethics," she reported to Edith.[63] Waldo by this point offered few substantial contributions, even as he went through the motions. As they prepared "Sovereignty of Ethics" in April, Waldo read one set of proofs, while she and Cabot "worked on the other." Waldo eventually approved Ellen and Cabot's choices. "I don't know where you found all this, but it improves upon acquaintance," Ellen reported him saying. "So Mr. Cabot and I, besides the great delight of the work itself, have the delight of success with Father himself," Ellen explained to Elizabeth Hoar the day before she died.[64]

Ellen's delight in the work did not mean the frustrations of collaborating with and caring for her aging father had disappeared. "Each correction is his where he could understand what was wanted; in some instances I have showed him the trouble seven different days in vain," Ellen said of "Fortune of the Republic."[65] Sometimes it was just not Waldo's confusion but his obstinance that frustrated her. Ellen preferred it when she, Cabot, and Waldo were in one place to do this type of work. Physical proximity meant there was less room for misunderstanding, plus she valued the sense of community. She scolded her father, therefore, when he insisted on leaving Naushon the previous summer just as she arrived to work on the proofs of "Perpetual Forces." Ellen bid Lidian to tell him, "If he would have stayed three or four days longer the proofs could have been thoroughly and satisfactorily attended to. I am very anxious lest something went wrong in this formidable separation of the three authors."[66] Even in her frustration, her pride in identifying herself as one of the "three authors" shines through.

While Ellen and Cabot formed the core team, they consulted not just with Elizabeth Cabot but a wide number of people in the Emerson circle. This was helpful, but could lead to complicated conversations, as the discussion around "Fortune of the Republic" makes clear. Ellen had told Edith in January 1878 that she and Cabot were working "to make" it "a first-class lecture."[67] Waldo delivered it first on February 25, 1878 at Old South Church in Boston, then a revised version on March 30 at Cyrus Bartol's home.[68] When the *Atlantic* declined to publish it, Lily Keyes suggested, "Why not print it as a little vest-pocket edition book?"; Cabot and Ellen, in consultation with Will, decided to issue the lecture as a pamphlet.[69]

Ellen and Cabot sought Will and his father's suggestions because their "political enlightenment ... is greater than Mr. Cabot's and we want to be sure not to leave any marks of this paper's being anti-diluvian."[70] The scarlet fever crisis delayed the Forbes' contributions. By the time Edith responded, Ellen had provided them with two versions of the text; Edith sent detailed line edits and questions about word substitutions, stating she liked what she thought was Waldo's version better. She was confused; Ellen and Cabot were responsible for both versions. The essay was a "collection of every general remark on the country from many lectures of many dates, each full of the moment when it was written and so adapted to that occasion and no other that scarcely a page entire could be saved," Ellen explained. She continued, "Father never had these things combined, so he never had any order for them. I thought so and so did

Mr. C. that the final arrangement was truer and easier for the mind, but maybe it isn't so."[71] Even with that explanation, Edith lobbied for the earlier version, saying her sister-in-law Sarah Forbes agreed with her.

Will had specific concerns that reflected his political positions. He objected to the term "paternal," Edith explained, in the phrase, "Humanity asks that government shall not be ashamed to be tender and paternal." He felt "it has a temporary slangy sort of meaning to denote exactly what . . . he is fighting tooth and nail to prevent the government from being—a sort of meddling with everyone's private affairs," likely a reference to the Forbes fights against business regulation.[72] Ellen and Cabot took some of the Forbes' advice, reverting to the phrase "serious care of criminals," from "judicious treatment," which Edith condemned as "like the overseers of the poor." "Paternal," however, remained, perhaps an indication that Ellen thought the government should be more involved with the care of its people than did her capitalist brother-in-law.

Ellen's pledge of abstinence from public service came to a joyful end in September 1878 when she attended the National Unitarian Conference in Saratoga Springs, New York. This trip was combined with "domestic business," however, as Waldo came with her. Beforehand, they traveled to Niagara Falls, where Ellen convinced her reluctant father to spend a quarter to take the ferry to the Canadian side. They were glad he did. "I think I shall remember what I have seen today while I live in this world, and the next too," Waldo told her, a poignant statement from an aging man losing his memory.[73] The conference was everything for which Ellen hoped. "The joys of Saratoga socially and intellectually were all that had been promised," she told Edith. "To dwell in a fairy palace, in the best & gleefullest of company, to see every friend lay or clerical from every part of the world that you almost ever had . . . raises one's spirits continually."[74] The Sunday *Herald* mistakenly reported that Waldo was to be a delegate, and Ellen took great pleasure in disabusing person after person of that notion. Waldo, who had spilt off from Ellen to visit the poet George Tufts on the way from Niagara Falls and then taken a night train, slept through much of the conference.

Scarlet fever chased down the Forbes once more, on Naushon. Don came down with the dreaded disease in September, just after Will had left for a trip to Colorado. Edith immediately sent Violet, Ralph, and Edward to her in-laws, keeping Don and, so he could "comfort Don and me," Cameron. She decided she had to tell her mother-in-law Sarah Forbes a secret that only Ellen and Lidian knew; she was pregnant. It was earlier than she wanted to share the news. Edith asked Ellen to tell Annie and Edward, as her mother-in-law "may have already published" the information in letters.⁷⁵ Tending to the third wave of scarlet fever while fighting morning sickness, with an absent husband, wore down even the ever-optimistic Edith; she longed just to go to bed and read.⁷⁶ Her mood changed when Will returned. "Life wears quite another aspect down here, now my Will is at home," she declared.⁷⁷ Thirteen years into their marriage their love had not dimmed.

Waldo Emerson Forbes was born February 28 at 3:20 p.m. As the family adjusted to a new baby for the first time in five years, Ellen stayed in Milton for a month. Edith declared the new arrival "perfect—as lovely & good as could be," but she once again struggled after the birth. "I am comfortable but make no headway against my old trouble and have as little prospect of getting up fast as ever," a reference to her chronic rheumatism.⁷⁸ Edith did not sit up for two weeks and only came downstairs in mid-April.

Mid-April also brought the death of Edward's fifteen-month old son John, the second child Edward and Annie had lost. An abscess in his gums set off John's dramatic decline. Edith, still largely immobile in Milton, did not learn of John's fate for a week. Edward, knowing she could not come to the funeral, did not telegraph, and Ellen's letter got stuck at the post office.⁷⁹ "The terrible news yesterday came as a most sudden and undreamed of shock . . . I had not thought of being anxious about that dear strong little boy with his beautiful promise," she wrote to Ellen.⁸⁰

The rhythm of life in Milton was changing, and not just because of baby Waldo. Will, as of January 1879, was the president of the newly formed National Bell Telephone Company. He and other businessmen invested a combined $850,000 in the venture, and it required his time and energy.⁸¹ Meanwhile, Edith, at her father-in-law's request, was involved in efforts to reopen the private Milton Academy, which had been shuttered since 1866. Wanting a private academy at which to educate his grandchildren, John Forbes leaned on Edith and her sisters-in-law Mary and Sarah.⁸² Edith confided, "Mr. Forbes says he must leave the work and the plan to us." "Full of schemes," she wanted to "have methods discussed & the ideal school sketched out before the endowment is begged for." She enlisted "dear Miss Harriet Ware," a prominent Milton resident, with whom she "plotted" to woo donations from influential Miltonians.⁸³

There was a growing public awareness of Waldo's decline. "Among the inconveniences of age, Mr. Emerson now finds an infirmity of memory which somewhat interferes with his literary work, though it does not wholly impede it," an article titled "Emerson's Old Age" and signed "Scribner" declared. Originally appearing in the Boston *Advertiser* in the fall of 1878, it was republished in papers as far as Wisconsin and Missouri.[84] The article went on to praise "Fortune of the Republic" as evidence of Waldo's continuing abilities to write, but word of the Emerson factory was spreading. Waldo himself helped circulate this information. When Allen Thorndike Rice, editor of the *North American Review*, visited Bush in January 1878 and mentioned "Perpetual Forces," Waldo "let every cat in the house out of the bag, told him he never did anything about it that Mr. Cabot & I compiled these things &c &c.," Ellen told Edith. Ellen silently raged at his indiscretion, but ultimately decided, "it was all true & truth does no real harm."[85]

While the University of Virginia debacle put an end to longer trips, Waldo continued to lecture locally. People were grateful to see him speak, tacitly acknowledging his decline and that every event might be his last. There was "great clapping" when he stood to read the Declaration of Independence at Concord's 1879 Independence Day celebration. [86] The launch of the Concord School of Philosophy a few weeks later brought Waldo another opportunity. Organized by Bronson Alcott and Franklin Sanborn, the school offered formal lectures by speakers including Alcott, Ednah Dow Cheney, and Thomas Wentworth Higginson, along with scheduled discussion time and informal debate.[87] When Waldo delivered "Memory" on August 2, the crowd swelled so large the event had to be moved from Orchard House to the vestry of the Episcopalian church.[88] Audience members recognized Ellen's contributions to shepherding her father through these events. "His daughter Ellen was present with her usual careful anxiety that all her father's wants should be gratified," William Sloane Kennedy noted after Waldo delivered "The Preacher" at Harvard Divinity School on May 5, 1879.[89]

Ellen and Cabot, even as their contributions became known, tried to stay true to Waldo's ideas. This aim was particularly important as they worked on "The Preacher" for publication in *Unitarian Review*. Cabot wrote to Ellen in June 1879, "I quite agree with you as to the greater responsibility for care respecting writings of your father's on religious subjects, especially before printing them, and in a religious magazine. If there is any mistake it will mislead far more people than any other would."[90] They both wanted to make sure the essay expressed Waldo's religious beliefs, rather than their own. As Cabot noted, in a problematic analogy, "To you and me Christianity seems like white skin in Ethnology—we have no contempt for the black, the yellow, or the copper coloured, but cannot think them of equal rank, *He* sometimes seems to think that some other colour may be richer and more satisfying."[91] If Ellen responded to the racism in Cabot's analogy, it has not been found. Certainly, his vision of accepting other religions, but thinking them inferior, fit with Ellen's worldview.

Despite their caution, it was perhaps inevitable that Ellen's and Cabot's personal philosophies worked their way into the essays they collaboratively produced with Waldo. Christopher Hanlon has argued that Ellen and Cabot's contributions offer a "conduit toward reading Emerson anew" that illuminates existing threads that push against his more famous ideas of individualism and self-reliance.[92] He explains, "Ellen mined Emerson's notes and lectures for material, selecting and sometimes accentuating passages that spoke to a more communitarian, cooperative account of intellectual life than Emerson had previously emphasized in his published work."[93] She did not make up the ideas out of whole cloth, but as a person who loved committee work and treasured her partnerships with her sister and Cabot, she shone a brighter light on them when she encountered them in her father's work.

The sense that Waldo was entering his last years inspired the sculptor Daniel Chester French to ask Waldo to pose for a bust in 1879. French had earned acclaim for his Minute Man statue, but he was still early in his career, and it took him months to gather the courage to make the request of Waldo. The process took twenty sittings in Bush, with French taking "countless measurements," and aiming to capture the "'lighting up' that people noted in Emerson's face."[94] Lidian, meanwhile, sat for a pastel portrait for the British artist Jessie Noa. Noa, who was living in Boston, had done pastels of Mary Peabody Mann and Elizabeth Peabody.[95] Louisa Sanborn read to Lidian during the sessions, and, Ellen reported, "I conclude she likes it very much."[96] The family felt the works captured Waldo and Lidian as close as it was possible for art to do. Lidian said of French's bust, "the likeness is perfect."[97] Of Noa's portrait, Ellen declared, "it is remarkably true as to features, and has a delicate look, like Mother, and after all is better than portraits are apt to be."[98] While the bust became a famed image of their father, the Emersons made sure Lidian's old age was memorialized as well.

Ellen and Lidian found new outlets for intellectual engagement even as Waldo's abilities faded. While Ellen wanted essays published under her father's name to represent his philosophy, she continued to develop her own ideas. She put aside family responsibilities to attend the Unitarian Grove Meeting at New Hampshire's Lake Winnipesaukee in the summer of 1879. "I heard more clearly than I had before the advantages, the joys, the light of Unitarianism," she said of one speaker.[99] Back in Concord, she found a session of the School of Philosophy "so excellent" that she regretted "not arranging to go all the time." She was surprised it "was to cultivate new senses and give one an enlarged outlook."[100] Lidian, along with Waldo, also "took very kindly" to the school, and professors and attendees were frequent guests in Bush.[101] "The regular rising and regular walking to & fro, the new interest and the extremely social life she won great benefit from," Ellen remembered.[102]

Lidian's engagement with the School of Philosophy was part of a renaissance that she underwent in 1870s, as she became more energetic, engaged, and content than she had been in over twenty years. "The long lane had completely turned," Ellen remembered. While acknowledging it likely began earlier, she first noticed the change when Waldo's cousin Charlotte Haskins Cleveland visited in the mid-1870s. Charlotte was an Episcopalian, and she and Lidian got into heated, day-long debates over theology. That spirited interaction caused Lidian to become more social in Concord after Charlotte left. "With the social life, her spirits rose, her ill-health passed away, and she became a happy person," Ellen declared.[103] The winter before Alcott's school was founded, Lidian had attended the course in philosophy run by Elizabeth Peabody, now living in Concord. Now that she had "studied about Sophocles," Ellen reported, "she finds she thinks he was less hateful to Xanthippe than she supposed."[104] In this era she also became involved in the Massachusetts Society for the Prevention of Cruelty to Animals, serving as an officer and contributing to its journal.[105]

Lidian and Ellen were not the only women whose intellectual lives were enriched by the School of Philosophy. Women made up the majority of the attendees.[106] Edna Dow Cheney was a lecturer the first year; in future sessions, Elizabeth Peabody and Julia Ward Howe, among others, joined her.[107] The school, therefore, "carried on the rich Transcendentalist tradition of conversation as a means of cheap and accessible education for women."[108] Moreover, as Tiffany Wayne argues, the female speakers and audience at the school highlighted the thread of transcendentalist thought that "emphasized the importance of human relations and, in fact, the dangers of egoism or a focus on the 'solitary self,'" a concept that was important to feminist thinkers.[109] The *Woman's Journal* promoted the opportunity each year, publishing the schedule of speakers, suggestions for travel and lodging, and reports after the event, even as other periodicals ran satirical articles about the gathering. While Ellen continued to oppose suffrage, she embraced this opportunity; the emphasis on human relationships resonated with her ideas about community and she had always valued education for women.

Ellen still harbored hopes of putting out another volume of her father's work. In early 1880, she "attacked Mr. Cabot on the subject of publishing a new book" when he and Elizabeth visited. Ellen believed a publishing deadline would spur them to work faster. Cabot opposed the plan, arguing that Waldo had decided earlier not to publish the remaining material, and they should honor his choice; moreover, "the lustre of his works" diminished with each "second-rate" volume. Elizabeth Cabot felt the volume might be better published after Waldo's death. "Posthumous publications the author isn't considered responsible for and they are received with pleasure, as the last people can get who are in the mood to be thankful for anything," she argued. For the time being, Cabot agreed to keep working with Ellen on editing any remaining essays, to alleviate her fears that the job would fall into other hands if he and Ellen died. Ellen was pleased with the results of the conversation and her and the Cabots' ability to talk through their differences. "I feel now quite satisfied and happy and hope to work hard and steadily and keep Mr. Cabot coming twice a month," she wrote. Her response suggests her motivation to have Cabot commit to a volume was as much from the pleasure she got from working with both Cabots as her desire to publish her father's work.[110]

The Emersons again whiplashed between joy and sorrow in the spring of 1880. Edith was pregnant with her seventh child, due in October.[111] On April 28, Annie gave birth to her first girl, who became the third Ellen Tucker Emerson, often called Ellen Jr. by the family. Aunt Ellen was thrilled with the honor, singing the praises of her robust namesake, born at nine pounds and with a head of curly hair.[112] A month later, Edward and Annie's son Charles declined over two terrible weeks after catching the croup, dying on June 8.[113] The death of a third son in five years devastated all the Emersons. The morning after he died, Ellen asked Waldo to accompany her to Edward's house. "Edward wants someone better than me, someone full of life," he protested, although he did eventually go.[114] Edward castigated himself when he lost any patient, and his guilt over the loss of his children worried his sisters.

Five months later, Thanksgiving brought a packed house and happier times. Haven and Susy Emerson arrived with their six children, and Will brought six of the Forbes children. There was now a seventh. Ellen Randolph Forbes, known as Rosebud, was born October 26, 1880, her elder sister's thirteenth birthday. While Edith stayed in Milton with the baby, Ellen was delighted as all the visiting Emersons and Forbes squeezed into Bush.[115]

Ellen threw herself a "ball" at the Town Hall for her forty-second birthday, February 24, 1881. She rejoiced that "many a frolicking matron & grayhaired swain showed that the party was taking a right course." Ellen was thrilled that

Waldo came for most of the night and that so many men wore their dress coats, noting "I could write a volume on the pleasure I had in folks's [sic] clothes that night."[116] "The love for Miss Ellen" flowed through the room.[117] Dancing the Virginia Reel with her brother-in-law-was a highlight for Ellen, but Violet was the only Forbes to accompany Will. Illness had once again overwhelmed the Milton house.

The measles hit the Forbes on January 16, disrupting life as scarlet fever had three years earlier. Edward, Don, Cameron, Waldo, Ralph, and Violet fell like dominos. Edith sent the baby to quarantine in the "Green Room" with a servant, Miss Alger. Will was away during the first few days of the siege, but he threw himself into caregiving when he came home.[118] While Will's return and hiring a nurse helped, the children all wanted their mother, who bathed their faces with bay rum and moved from bed to bed during the night. The separation from her darling Rosebud wore on her. She had to disinfect herself for each visit—washing herself with carbolic water and putting on clean clothes—and some days was too busy and exhausted to visit. "My sweet dear baby—I miss her so much," Edith confessed.[119]

As the household began to right itself, and the baby came down from quarantine, a new threat arrived in the form of diphtheria. Edith believed that the disease snuck in via their refrigerator, which had a pipe connected to the sewer.[120] Ralph and Violet succumbed first, while once again Rosebud was isolated upstairs. On March 20, Edith was staying in Boston with Don and Waldo to visit a specialist for Waldo's on-going ear-infection when the news arrived that, despite all the precautions, Rosebud was sick. Edith rushed home, sending young Waldo to Concord. The baby turned out to have pneumonia, not diphtheria, and their doctor assured the anxious parents that Rosebud would be fine. Edith failed to believe him, as "demoralized by care and anxiety" it struck her that the child was in "very bad condition."[121] Tragically, her mother's intuition proved correct. Rosebud died on March 30. Ellen, informed by telegram, was in Milton before the end of the day.[122]

Rosebud's death was the worst moment thus far in Edith and Will's unusually blessed marriage. They held a funeral service on April 1, even though they did not yet have a cemetery plot.[123] Lidian sent a letter offering her advice for recovering from the loss of a child. She explained that once when she was "suffering so deeply that I believed I could never again take any interest in any earthly thing" she read the Bible and suddenly, "every cloud dispersed and I saw clearly *all* is well, now and forever, that in the plan of God the darkest dispensations are the highest prosperity." Lidian continued, "Your prosperity through life has been exceptionally great, and thankful as I am to God who has loaded you with earthly blessings, I firmly believe this bitter loss of the darling baby, is the greatest blessing you have yet received." Lidian closed by saying she realized her words might not offer consolation, as "minds are so differently constituted."[124] Edith knew her mother and likely took it in the spirit it was intended, but she was not one to take comfort in philosophy but willed optimism and action.

Even in this dark time, Edith and Will tried to maintain the commitment to happiness to which they had pledged themselves during their engagement. In the immediate aftermath of Rosebud's death, the children stayed with other family members; when they reunited a week later, Edith felt it was "delightful to us to have our flock together." She and Will selected a plot and commissioned a cabinet to hold "those things which have the most associations with her and keep it in the green room where she spent so much of her life, and where she died."[125] They also hoped a change in scenery would help them recover.

On April 23, Edith and Will's family set off on a cross-country train trip to California, accompanied by John Forbes, Will's cousin Annie Anthony, and the servants Mrs. Turple and Minnie. Edward, Annie, and Ellen Jr. joined them in Chicago. Edward had been hesitant to accept the invitation, aware of what he already owed Will, until he realized it was really "a request to come to your aid and comfort."[126] While Will's "preliminary homesickness" had depressed Edith to her "lowest pitch," she rebounded by the time they reached Syracuse.[127] "We are getting on famously—Waldo enchanted with his bed. The little boys radiant," she wrote.[128] In Chicago, they switched to a larger car; Edward's family had their own stateroom. The Forbes could not out-run their grief, however. Edith asked Ellen to send her Helen Hunt Jackson's poem "When the Baby Died" and the sight of Edward's young daughter undid Will. "I think he is better for having broken down thoroughly and had it out," Edith confessed.[129] Unfortunately, a stomach virus spread through the children, leading the trip from Chicago to Los Angeles to be "a series of hospital days of more or less anxiety."[130]

While the children's illnesses shadowed much of the trip, the two families still found themselves restored in body and mind after eighteen difficult months. "Edward looks a great deal brighter now.... At last my dear Will is looking well & bright & sings and rejoices in the air the scenery and everything else. He is a great deal better—the grey look is gone," Edith reported.[131] The landscape fed Edith's soul, inspiring her to fill letters with detailed descriptions of flowers, plants, and trees. The travelers went from Los Angeles to San Francisco, visiting their cousin Lizzie Barber at her home in San Rafael. Annie and Edward stayed there, as Ellen Jr. was still recovering, while the Forbes went on to Yosemite. Even Edith's "rubber cushions" could not make bumping along sixty-eight miles via stagecoach comfortable, but seeing Vernal Falls and Nevada Falls made the trip worth it. They were "splendid, brilliant, snowy white, perfectly graceful and beautiful, and having a worthy setting of deepest blue sky, wonderful rock, mountains around," Edith raved.[132] By May 30, the troop was en route to Massachusetts, with a brief detour to Lake Tahoe.

Thoughts of Rosebud were never far away, but life got back on track. The Forbes now had the *Hesper*, a forty-six-foot sloop, and Will passed his love of sailing to the boys; Edith felt it too "idle," but in general time on the water was a balm to the family. They would add the schooner the *Merlin* in 1889, and Edith, as her children grew older, came to look forward to sailing up the East Coast. She often read to her family and friends from her father's work on the deck.[133]

While Will took comfort on the water, Edith and Ellen scrambled for help with servants. Ellen concocted a scheme to help them and others face a shortage of cooks. Working with Caroline Brooks Hoar, she arranged for Juliet Corson to run a cooking school in the Concord school building from September 15 through October 2. Corson was the author of *Fifteen Cent Dinners for Workingmen's Families* and founder of the New York Cooking School.[134] In Concord, the school offered a free course and one that charged a sliding scale of one to three dollars. Corson "talks very slowly while she prepares her meat and vegetables, and we write down the words of wisdom," Ellen reported. She attended the classes, along with paying the tuition for Annie McLaughlin, a Scottish woman working at Bush.[135] Ellen also oversaw the administrative duties, finding it took "all day, morning and afternoon, to attend to its various requirements."[136]

The same year Ellen organized the cooking school she became a founding member of the Women's Parish Association. The association's aims included encouraging "the organized work of women for the various objects needing their help."[137] While some women protested the association was stepping into men's territory, Ellen was not one of them; her signature is the first on the membership list.[138] The monthly meetings included a talk or reading of a tract by a member. Ellen presented several times, including reading a temperance tract in 1886 and giving a talk on Religious Education of Children in 1887.[139] As with her roles on the school committee and the cooking school, Ellen justified this public work as falling within women's sphere of faith and home, with her desire to participate not shaking her stance against suffrage. She in fact was excited when the anti-suffragist Kate Gannett Wells spoke to the Women's Parish Association in 1886, telling Edith she would not invite her because she knew she disapproved.[140]

On October 28, the shared birthday of Violet and Rosebud, the Forbes "had a very lovely day together—though it was hard."[141] Edith strived to make the "dear birthday" a happy one for Violet, who turned fourteen.[142] Edith, Ellen, and Will had made a trip to New York to buy her special gifts, and friends and family showered her with presents. Still, Violet and Will were in tears at times and everyone thought of Rosebud throughout the day.[143] When Edith, Will, Waldo, Ralph, and Violet went to her grave, they found Don and Edward also there to visit their sister. Sarah Forbes, Edith's sister-in-law, also remembered Edith, sending her a camel hair bed jacket embroidered with the same rose garland design used on Rosebud's coat.[144]

As the Emersons became blunter about Waldo's failing mind, they grew increasingly concerned about preserving his legacy. When a request came in for Waldo to lend support to an unknown issue in August 1881, Edith warned Ellen, "Will says by no means let Father sign that letter—he should not put his name to any public matters now—especially as it is known his mind is failing."[145] The siblings again entered into cahoots with Elizabeth Cabot to pressure James Elliot Cabot to become Waldo's biographer. He had rejected the invitation in 1877, believing a biography should not be written for several decades to give critical distance.[146] Now, Elizabeth instructed them to temp him with the family archival treasures. "The moment that Mr. Cabot gets the mass of materials into his hands, and that ought to be this month, Mrs. Cabot says will be the time for an advance upon him on all sides," Ellen reported to Edith.[147] Once he was hooked on the family history, the plan called for his wife "to throw all her weight in our behalf," the Forbes to invite the Cabots to visit to underscore the friendship between the families, Ellen and Edward to make "stringent requisitions" and even for Nina Lowell "to urge and extort him."[148] Ellen took heart when Elizabeth Cabot told her "he found it hard to get to bed," because the "antiquities in the big brown paper bundle and the papier-mache tea chest" that he took home fascinated him.[149] Surrounded on all sides, he eventually agreed.

Edith did not have her usual verve for family schemes and visits that spring. At the age of forty-one, she was pregnant with her eighth child, due in late May.[150] Other events weighed on her, as well. Haven's daughter Elizabeth Hoar Emerson and Violet's best friend Madge Cunningham died of scarlet fever early in the year, and Will's nephew Howland Russell almost died of the disease in early April. "These days are very hard for Will to bear—it is like last year all over again," Edith confided.[151] Will did not want his family to go to Concord while scarlet fever was circulating.[152] Charley Emerson, meanwhile, was staying with Edith after his wife Therchi was committed to a mental asylum, another heart-wrenching situation.[153] Edith and her offspring finally got to Bush in mid-April, but she was uncomfortable seven months into her pregnancy and all six children had colds. "I am sorry you are gone, you singular and plural. And wish I knew how to make your visits pleasanter to you," Ellen wrote once Edith left.[154]

Edith soon had cause to be glad she made the pilgrimage, despite its hardships. Waldo came down with pneumonia on April 20. Two days later, Edward warned, "it is the beginning of the end."[155] Edward slept by his father's bed, and Ellen spent her days at his side. Waldo often thought he was not in Bush, but he seemed peaceful. "The Power of our life has been very kind," he said to Ellen; of his descendants, he declared there was "not one rascal among them."[156] Edith and Will arrived on Sunday, Will helping Edward with the physical care. With Edith's "confinement being very near," a worried Edward soon sent them back to Milton.[157] Ralph, Violet, Cameron, and Don then came, "and the sight of the children each time they came into the room made Father smile."[158] A string of Waldo's friends made their final goodbyes, including Franklin Sanborn, James Elliot Cabot, Judge Ebenezer Hoar, and Bronson Alcott. At times he was coherent, at others his family and friends struggled to make sense of the great author's words. By late afternoon on April 27, his pain led Edward, in consultation with Dr. Charles Pickering Putnam, to give him ether. He died at "ten minutes of nine," a month before his seventy-ninth birthday.[159] First Parish tolled its bell seventy-nine times at 9:30 p.m. that night to announce his death.[160]

The fire in Bush had marked the beginning of a challenging era for the Emersons and the Forbes. Watching a man renowned for his words and his mind lose the ability to write and speak was emotionally exhausting. The deaths of Edward and Edith's children were heartbreaking, especially in a family still shaped by the "miseries" that had followed young Waldo's death. Yet those years also offered opportunities. There was travel and the cerebral and social rewards of working with Cabot and on *Parnassus*, a way for Ellen and Edith to combine caregiving with intellectual labor. Now the work of caring for Waldo's body was done; the work of caring for his reputation was only beginning.

CHAPTER SEVEN

"In Reading a Biography I Always Like Best the Personal Parts"

(1882–1892)

Waldo's death was a private family matter, an occasion of mourning for Concord and the nation, and an international news story. The Emersons did not see it as a tragedy, feeling "the great comfort of his peaceful release from all the clouds and infirmity which he bore with such sweet patience and dignity."[1] Lidian, after a few fitful nights, "feels determined to live as long as she can, for she sees how it would leave me forlorn" if she were to die, Ellen reported.[2] Still, entering the post-Waldo era called for adjustments. Lidian and Ellen would build a new community in Bush, Edward would set off on a new career, and all three Emerson siblings would take up the work of shaping and preserving their father's legacy.

On April 30, the family held a private ceremony at Bush followed by a public one at the church. "It seemed to us most beautiful, most affecting, the great concourse, and most of the things that were said and done satisfied us," Ellen informed Clara Dabney. She added "the papers will tell you about the funeral."[3] The event was well-covered and well-attended. The Fitchburg railroad scheduled extra trains to accommodate the deluge of mourners, and the church reinforced the floor and galleries to withstand the weight of the crowd. The town draped public buildings in black, and a committee of Concord women festooned homes along the funeral procession with black and white rosettes.[4]

People from all stages of Waldo's life participated. Edith "could not stay away," despite the doctor's caution.[5] William Furness, a Unitarian minister who attended the Boston Latin school with Waldo, led the private service. In the church, pine boughs surrounded a spray of yellow jonquils contributed by

Louisa May Alcott. Judge Ebenezer Hoar and James Freeman Clark spoke, and Bronson Alcott read a sonnet. Pallbearers included Charley and Haven Emerson, James Elliot Cabot, Will and, at age fifteen, Ralph. At Sleepy Hollow Cemetery, the family was gratified to find Concord's "young people" had lined the grave with "hemlock twigs, and a bed of green at the bottom."[6] Reverend Samuel Haskins, Waldo's cousin, read the Lord's Prayer, the mourners raising their voices to say, "deliver us from evil." The grandchildren tossed flowers into the grave at the end of the ceremony.

"Edith has a son. All well," Will telegraphed his father on May 14.[7] Waldo's fame exponentially expanded the amount of work required after his death, but for now it was time to honor new life. Will and Edith, while disappointed in a boy, gave thanks for a healthy child, named Alexander, after the devastating loss of Rosebud. Ellen stayed in Milton until the end of the month. It was not an ideal time to leave Lidian, but Cousin Sarah Haskins Ansley's extended stay in Bush gave Ellen some flexibility.[8]

In this complex moment of mourning and celebration, the Emerson family wrestled with how to memorialize Waldo. The first hurdle involved Waldo's correspondence with Thomas Carlyle. Plans to publish the exchange had long been in the works. After, at Edith's insistence, Waldo collected and had transcribed Carlyle's letters to him, he gave the documents to Charles Norton in 1873, to do with as he saw fit; Norton obtained Carlyle's permission to publish them. Edith had arranged for Carlyle to bequeath to her Waldo's letters to him, receiving them after his death in 1881. Edith argued Cabot should incorporate the correspondence into his biography. Cabot, however, thought it would overwhelm the focus on Waldo; he wanted the book to "avoid all side-lights & exclude collateral figures" and "to give as near may be an autobiography instead of a Life and Times."[9] His plan won out, with Norton going ahead with the volume of correspondence.[10]

The letters soon caused more drama. On review of the material Carlyle willed to Edith, it became clear at least thirty of Waldo's letters were missing. The correspondence soon began to appear in British publications. Moncure Conway, living in England, discovered that Carlyle's assistant Frederick Martin had stolen the letters and was selling them under cover of the business "William Anderson, dealer in autographs and manuscripts." Conway managed to buy four of the stolen missives and copy over twenty more. Sir James Stevens, one of Carlyle's trustees, cautioned against taking legal action. In the introduction to the two-volume edition, published in February 1883, Norton obscurely thanked

Conway for his "energetic and successful effort to recover some of Emerson's early letters which had fallen into strange hands."[11] Letters continued to be recovered, and in 1886, Norton published an updated edition of the correspondence that included all of the known letters; on Edith's urging, he also published a stand-alone volume of the newly recovered letters for "the benefit of owners of the early edition."[12]

In Concord, Ellen and Lidian were finding their new rhythm. Widowhood largely suited Lidian, who was energized by the visitors who continued to fill the house.[13] Reverend Benjamin Bulkeley, Concord First Parish's new minister, stayed at Bush until his January wedding and was a "daily delight" to her. Still, Ellen noted, "If I attend to my work I omit her. If I attend to her I do nothing else."[14] That work included tasks generated by the Carlyle correspondence and answering condolence notes. In August, she reported had she made a "desultory attack on the huge pile of letters due."[15]

Waldo's will established a complex partnership between the Emerson children and Cabot. It appointed Cabot "literary executor" and gave him "authority, acting in cooperation with my children, or the survivors or survivor of them, to publish or withhold from publication, any of my unpublished papers."[16] It was unclear, in other words, who held the ultimate authority. Ellen had helped her father with the will, and she may have structured it this way to ensure her partnership with Cabot continued.[17] The partnership was now in flux, however, and not just because of Waldo's death. Edward gave up his medical practice and became a major player on the team. He had been a good doctor, valued by the community, but the work exhausted him physically and mentally. He turned to painting, editing his father's papers, and writing and lecturing on Concord's history and literary figures.[18] The team needed to learn how to function in this new configuration.

Despite Cabot's continuing objections, the Emerson siblings prioritized issuing a new edition of their father's complete works, including a collection of unpublished essays. Nancy Simmons suggests financial gain was a motivating factor, particularly for Edward. He no longer had the income from his medical practice and, with the birth of Florence in October 1882, now had a second daughter.[19] The decision to publish a "definitive" collected works, however, was also critical to the siblings' desire to preserve and shape their father's legacy. They well-remembered Waldo's panic at the prospect of an unauthorized volume of unpublished essays. William H. Channing's letter to Lidian less than two weeks after Waldo's death heightened their concern. "You can not *too promptly* decide upon the most trusted Publisher and editor to bring out a 'Complete Edition of Works'—arranged after some definite order," he wrote.[20] The Emersons overcame Cabot's resistance, and by September, Houghton Mifflin agreed to publish the volumes.[21] The team turned the project around quickly, issuing eleven volumes by December 1883. These volumes, along with a twelfth published a decade later, came to be known as the Riverside edition. The first eight required relatively few decisions, as they consisted largely of re-publications of existing works, including *Letters and Social Aims*, with new introductions. The final three, however, were another story.

Poems, the ninth volume, fell largely to Edward, launching his second career as editor and chronicler of the Concord of his youth and its eminent citizens. Setting aside Waldo's organization of the 1876 *Selected Poems*, he focused on a "comprehensive new edition including all but twelve of the previously published poems ... supplementing these with a 62-page Appendix of drafts and fragments drawn from the notebooks."[22] In the process, the poem "May-Day" reared its head again, with Edward trivializing Ellen's earlier work to justify his revision. "If Father allowed one of his children to make a different arrangement it might not be going too far if another of them, who perhaps knew more than the first of out-door events, should revise it," he wrote to Cabot.[23] Edward's dismissive attitude toward Ellen's contributions is out-of-character for a brother who regularly expressed his gratitude to his sister. The most generous interpretation is that Edward, among all the Emersons, was making the biggest adjustment after Waldo's death, as he left one career, started another one, and took on the mantel of patriarch. The road was not always smooth.

Edward acted more in character when addressing the issue how to distribute the income from Waldo's work. Waldo distributed much of his property equally between his children and ensured Lidian and Ellen could stay in Bush. He, however, left "the copyrights and plates and ownership of all my published writings" only to Edward. The will also assigned to Edward "for his own benefit all my contracts for the publication of said writings." Edward created a more equitable arrangement with his sisters for the unpublished work. He and Ellen would share the profits from any of Waldo's previously unpublished work, while Edith would receive the profits from *Parnassus*. All three would have an equal "voice in the disposal" of their father's work, something Edith wanted clear before agreeing to the plan.[24] She did not need the money, but she wanted her say in the family legacy.

While *Poems* was Edward's domain, the tenth and eleventh volumes fell to the larger "Emerson factory." These two books, eventually titled *Letters and*

Biographical Sketches and *Miscellanies*, respectively, involved more than reprinting existing essays with new introductions. The team needed to decide what material to publish and, as they had been doing with individual publications, organize essays out of lecture notes and journal entries, at times connecting and expanding Waldo's writing with their own prose. Despite Cabot's reluctance, his earlier collaborations with Ellen and his familiarity with Waldo's inventories of his work meant he went into the project with a good sense of what to include. There were still a number of issues to work out, however, editorially and personally.[25]

Tensions arose as the editors moved quickly with similar but not completely aligned agendas. In May 1883, for instance, Ellen and Cabot poured over her suggested changes to "Education" at Bush, with Cabot agreeing to all but one. When Edward arrived, however, he wanted Cabot to "yield" on that change as well. Ellen protested, "Mr. Cabot was chosen by Father because he knew what should be published and what not, and he ought to have the say in the end." Invoking the language of the will, Edward retorted, "Father added 'acting with my children' so that we might have our way too."[26] While Cabot conceded that point, over the summer Edward's strong opinions about how the preface to *Letters and Social Aims* should handle Waldo's mental decline and the arrangement of the final two volumes also frustrated him. Things only calmed down when the publisher Henry O. Houghton spoke to Edward, and Ellen and Edward traveled to Cabot's summer home in Beverly Farms, Massachusetts, to work things out.[27] Ellen, who treasured her and Cabot's ability to talk through their differences, was relieved Edward and Cabot had been able to do so as well.

As Cabot and Edward hammered out their relationship, Ellen again insisted on covering up her contributions. Regarding the preface for the Riverside *Letters and Social Aims*, she told Cabot, "It should not go in that I had anything to do with it because it was only a thing of proximity not of taste." She continued, "My lines lie in a different direction. I never knew Papa as a literary man, nor had the slightest knowledge of nor interest in his work."[28] Neither she nor Cabot address the irony that she claims to know nothing of her father's work as part of her argument that her efforts on editing that work be obscured.

Ellen's assertion is one in a long chain of claiming not to be literary-minded or familiar with her father's work while simultaneously providing evidence to the contrary. Her motivations had evolved since her earlier focus on shielding Waldo's reputation, however. She now wanted the aid Waldo received acknowledged, but she wanted it credited to Cabot and "his family."[29] She even pushed Cabot to take more credit, reminding him of his contributions to "Carlyle."[30] Ellen's desire to deflect attention from herself, even while asking her male partner to claim recognition, is part and parcel with her ideas about women's roles in society. While she justified efforts for the school committee and church conventions as still within the domain of appropriate service for women, she did not want public attribution for her editorial contributions. She cast them as another part of the caregiving through which she defined herself rather than an individual accomplishment. "When necessity threw it for those few years into my hands I did as anyone would in my place, but that was an accident, and a fleeting thing, already past. Let it pass," she firmly declared.[31]

The collective effort that Ellen tried to hide has made the final Riverside volumes and *Letters and Social Aims* problematic for Emerson scholars. Since the 1970s, as Harvard University Press began to issue the volumes of *The Collected Works of Ralph Waldo Emerson*, there has been a growing acknowledgment of the contributions of Cabot and the Emerson children to his later essays; there has been also a growing concern over how to understand these pieces as part of Waldo's body of work.[32] The issue came to a head in 2015. Ronald A. Bosco and Joel Myerson argued in *Uncollected Prose Writings*, the tenth volume of Harvard's *Collected Works*, that because "virtually nothing delivered by Emerson or published under his name during or after the 1870s came directly from his hand" they were "obliged to exclude . . . all items that appeared in print under Emerson's name for the first time between 1876 and his death in 1882 and include here only five items that appeared in print between 1870 and 1875."[33] The very reasons that "obliged" the Emerson editors to exclude these essays, however, make them valuable when focusing on the Emerson children. Their choices illuminate their vision of their father's legacy.

"Mary Moody Emerson," which appears in *Letters and Biographical Sketches*, highlights this conundrum and the complexities of the canon. While it draws from a lecture on his aunt Waldo delivered, Bosco and Myerson argue the published version "presents one of the most extreme examples of the involvement of Cabot, Ellen, Edward, and even the Emersons' distant relations in the preparation of a work posthumously attributed to Emerson" and "holds no authority as an original work" by Waldo.[34] The manuscript "betrays multiple hands (at least one unidentifiable) at work rearranging the order of Emerson's original pages, drafting different versions of transitional prose for use between disconnected prose passages Emerson drew from Mary's personal writings and fashioning more elaborate prose descriptions of Mary's character for inclusion in the essay than the hastily improvised descriptions that Emerson drafted for delivery."[35] The Emerson factory, Phyllis Cole argues, however, drew from the many passages Waldo had copied from Mary's almanacs into his journals and his dedicated "M.M.E." notebooks; his active role in making those selections before his decline complicates the rejection of the essay from the canon.[36] The "distant relations," moreover, were Waldo's first cousins—the Haskins—who had cared for Mary in Brooklyn and had helped ensure that Ellen receive important family papers; the siblings sought feedback from them on the depiction of family history. That consultation, the expansion of biographical information and "more elaborate prose descriptions of Mary's character," and their choice to publish this essay in the *Atlantic Monthly* to draw attention to the publication of the volume, indicate the Emersons' strong desire to place family at the center of Waldo's legacy.

The Riverside edition began to appear in September, two volumes at a time. Houghton Mifflin praised the team, as it was rare for such a complex project to come in without charges for extra corrections.[37] The publisher, however, balked at the 650-page length of *Lectures and Biographical Sketches*. Eventually all parties agreed to a plan to remove material for use in a twelfth volume later.[38] For the first eleven volumes, Houghton Mifflin issued two versions of the collected works—the regular set and a large "Edition de Luxe" edition, limited to five hundred copies, which sold out. Nancy Simmons explains that the volumes "marked an important step in shaping Emerson's lengthened shadow. Here was Emerson in formal dress, fitted out for public audiences, his legacy made available for future generations," the Emersons' ultimate goal.[39]

In the fall, a disagreement between the sisters illuminated how much their priorities beyond family caregiving had diverged. Edith was thrilled Milton Academy was finally opening its doors in the fall of 1883. Ellen worried the institution was too small and had qualms about wealthy people educating their children separately from the rest of the population.[40] Edith was irate, revealing not only her concern for her children's education but also her ugly prejudices. "I cannot appreciate your regret that I do not send my children to school with the Irish population," she wrote. Edith added, "the public schools are principally carried on by committees selected by the Irish vote," who would not, in her opinion, prioritize preparing students for college and providing the "classical education" she felt her children needed.[41] So abhorrent was the idea of educating her children in public schools that when first funding raising for the Academy years earlier, Edith had declared her "Milton home hangs on" the school's existence.[42]

Edith expressed anti-Irish sentiment throughout her life, particularly regarding Irish Catholic servants. She preferred to hire Scottish or Norwegian immigrants and did not feel "quite contented when we have any Catholics in the house."[43] Her prejudices were common in white, privileged Protestant women, who complained that Irish servants were poorly trained, unclean, and greedy, while also worrying they would try to convert their children.[44] Waldo helped instill anti-Irish prejudice in his family and in the country, arguing, for instance, for the superiority of "Saxons," as he defined English people and New Englanders of English descent, over "Celts" in works such as *English Traits*.[45] Ellen grew up in the same culture, and she did at times complain about Irish servants and worried that Irish boys would upset town social events.[46] But her ideas evolved as she served an observer for the Concord school examinations and then on the school committee. "It is so edifying to hear these Irish children especially, whose Fathers and Mothers can't read, recite in high English branches, and even in Latin. It is a great step forward in one generation," she explained.[47] While her sentiment is still condescending, Ellen allowed evidence from her experience to change her mind. Edith's ideas calcified. Cossetted by the Forbes' wealth, she actively worked to build more barriers between her family and Irish immigrants by helping reopen the private academy.

Even with this tension, the sisters still supported one another. Edith regularly flooded Bush with flowers from her garden, a way for someone who cherished every plant to send a physical embodiment of her love. When Edith and Will took Cameron and Violet on their first trip to Washington, D.C. in 1884, Alexander and Waldo, along with their nurses, stayed in Concord.[48] Ellen and Edith both rejoiced when Annie and Edward had a son, named William Forbes Emerson in May.[49] And Edith was delighted when Ellen and Lidian agreed to stay in Milton for month over the Christmas and New Years holidays.[50]

"I have been free and had all my time to myself, and Mother has been taken care of," Ellen gloated in March 1885.[51] Her freedom was a gift from Edith, who had hired a nurse to care for Lidian. Perhaps observing her mother and sister up close over the holidays had convinced Edith help was needed. The timing was excellent, because work on the biography was ramping up. Cabot had put it aside as he dealt with the declining health of his mother, Eliza, and his son Ted's diagnosis of diabetes.[52] Following Eliza Cabot's death on March 2, 1885, Cabot turned his full attention to the project. By the end of the month, Elizabeth Cabot had given Ellen eighty pages she had copied from the manuscript, which she found "very interesting, not dry but sparkling."[53] Edith, Ellen, and Edward began to collect material Cabot requested, including essays and family letters, and record stories from their cousins. Cabot had written at least two-hundred pages as September rolled around.

There was other work to do. Three years after Waldo's death, the siblings decided on his grave marker. It was Edward's vision. He had hoped to find "big beryls in their natural bed of quartz" but had "given up and brought a big piece of quartz."[54] Edward, Ellen, Edith, and Will had a "family council" and determined, as the stone was "too hard and brittle to be worked" to "set it up rough and have a bronze plate sunk in it."[55] Several years later, they added an epitaph consisting of lines, after debating other options, from Waldo's poem, "The Problem": "The passive master lent his hand, To the vast Soul which o'er him planned."[56] Waldo wrote the lines eleven months after delivering his final sermon, and they acknowledge the ministry's "attractions" to him and his ultimate inability to reconcile himself to it and need to find God elsewhere.[57] The choice of verse underlined their respect for their father's beliefs, even if Edith's and especially Ellen's were quite different. While some in their circle expressed confusion at the unusual tombstone, Ellen loved it and took guests to see it. "I think of it when I am away from it, and when I am there cannot contemplate it enough," she wrote to Edith.[58]

The fall brought Edith a moment of transition, as Ralph started Harvard. Edith decorated his rooms on Mt. Auburn Street with the same care as her homes, paying attention to details down to the curtain tassels. She also invested in furniture that she hoped would see all the boys through college. As her eldest child took steps towards independence, her youngest's "college days don't seem far off," she wrote wistfully to Ellen.[59] After twenty years of marriage and nineteen years of child-rearing, the departure of her first born marked a significant milestone.

The autumn of 1885 also saw the 250th anniversary of Concord's founding and Waldo and Lilian's fiftieth wedding anniversary. As in 1835, when Waldo had delivered "A Historical Discourse" on September 12 in Concord then traveled to Plymouth to marry Lidian on September 14, the family linked their civic and personal celebrations. The Emersons and Forbes gathered for the Concord commemoration, then moved en-masse to Plymouth to commemorate Waldo and Lidian's marriage. While traveling with Lidian presented challenges, the trip proved a great success. Lidian, a Plymouth girl at heart, rallied as she showed her descendants around her hometown. "She remembers her visit with delight, especially the united family part," Ellen reported to Edith.[60]

"Mr. Cabot's Life of Father is almost finished... we read it aloud together and criticize and enjoy at leisure," Ellen reported to Clara Dabney in April 1886.⁶¹ The process continued to be a collaboration. As Ellen explained, "Mr. Cabot means to revise it all by the light of the notes he takes on these occasions and then it will be ready to publish."⁶² The process was overall a friendly one, but signs of strain arose in the final stages. Edith tried to steer the book towards the vision she wanted to promote of her father, while Cabot demanded more material from Ellen than she had time, or perhaps will, to give.

"As far as I have read there is no portrayal of the happy home life and social ties in Concord," Edith worried about the book.⁶³ To remedy the situation, she planned a strategic campaign, betting the biographer needed material to flesh out the work as he rushed to finish and wrapping her pressure in the trappings of feminine deference and humility. "I think he is in the mood to to accept more than he was before he got so far ," she suggested to her brother. She urged Edward, whose son Raymond would be born in November, to forward extracts from Waldo's "letters to the family."⁶⁴ She employed the bonds of female friendship, reaching out to Elizabeth Cabot with letters filled with family memories. "I thought I would write to you and tell you some of the things I recall, and it may remind Mr. Cabot of some things he might like to look up & use," she wrote to "Cousin Lizzie," knowing well the influence Elizabeth had already used to promote the Emersons' desires to her husband.⁶⁵ Edith then wrote up a reminiscence to send directly to Cabot. In July 1886, she gave "every moment I could to my everlasting reminiscences" and to marking up Cabot's manuscript with her suggestions. She also created an index to allow Cabot to identify her suggestions quickly. Edith assumed a deferential air, explaining she only "boldly" sent them "because you have asked for them" and asked him to "please understand that I did not write them for publication, but to give you the most intimate possible acquaintance with Father." But she was clear with her wishes, saying she hoped he used the suggestions and memories "because in reading a biography I always like best the personal parts."⁶⁶

Edith's long account, combined with her letters to Elizabeth, illuminates her view of her father and her experiences as his child, the "personal parts" she wanted in the book. She complained, "perhaps a little too much is said about his difficulty in society," noting she never observed her father having trouble with conversation "except as a sign of aging."⁶⁷ She wanted Cabot to stress Waldo and Lidian's tight financial circumstances for the first decade or so of their marriage, in part because their "poverty" stemmed from their financial support of their relatives. Most importantly, she wanted her memories to serve as a corrective to the lack of family in the memoir. "I do not expect to have any of these hasty scrawls used, except to remind Mr. Cabot" that, with the exception of his brothers, there was no mention of "Father's domestic side," she explained to Elizabeth. Edith added pointedly, "He loved his children so."[68]

Soon after Edith sent her material, Cabot reported to Edward that he had "introduced the domestic & enlivening element to a considerable extent" as he "revisited" the manuscript.[69] Cabot in fact quoted a long excerpt of one of Edith's letters, crediting it to "one of" Waldo's "children," including the lines, "a baby could not be too young or too small for him to hold out his hands instantly to take it into his arms."[70] Elsewhere, Cabot rejected Edith's requests. Regarding *Parnassus*, she wanted it clear that "almost entirely the selections were made before there was any failure of his powers."[71] The published volume, however, notes "some pieces were admitted which at an earlier time he would probably have passed over" right before publication, a more accurate depiction of events.[72] While Cabot agreed with "Edith's objections to the resumés of lectures—nobody reads them," he did not see "any way to omitting them."[73] He was willing to work with the Emersons, but did not want to lead readers astray and wanted the publication to be useful to future scholars.

While Edith forged ahead, Ellen fell behind on fulfilling Cabot's requests. In July 1886, he thanked her for, "what you sent me about Miss Hoar, & for what you promise." But in the same letter he scolded her for what must have been push-back on supplying more memories of her father. "And with what face can you ask me to collect with labor & pains & to print & publish reminiscences at second hand & at arms length when you refuse to give what must be so much closer to the fact? I hope you will think better of it," he declared.[74] Scholars have interpreted Cabot's brusque language as a breach between him and the Emersons.[75] Certainly, tempers were wearing thin under the pressure to finish the project. But in their decade of working together, Ellen and Cabot had often teased one another as they pushed through the stress of editing and deadlines. Cabot moved from this scolding tone to tell Ellen about his sons' camping trip and his eczema. He returned to the biography at the end of the letter. "Pray remember always that our (biographical) metal is all in the crucible & that the casting must soon take place. If there are any gaps & flaws I shall always say that it is all your fault," the final line surely part of the partners' history of jesting.[76] Joke or not, his prodding worked. "Much obliged for the bountiful packet you sent me," he wrote to Ellen ten days later.[77]

"For my part I feel like a novice on a toboggan-slide, nervous about the pitch," Cabot wrote to Ellen soon after signing the contract for the biography with Houghton Mifflin in February 1887.[78] Cabot still wanted more information on Waldo's 1872 visit with Carlyle and was trying to select images, but he and the Emersons needed to make final decisions immediately. The anxious biographer asked for support from his long-term partner. "You must set me right before it is too late. It is really frightful," he confessed.[79]

The book was published in two stages. On May 25, 1887 a select circle of friends received prepublication copies of *A Memoir of Ralph Waldo Emerson*.[80] These early copies, released on Waldo's birthday, allowed the Emerson siblings to honor their father and the friends and colleagues he had valued. Of course, many in the selected circle possessed significant cultural influence, and getting the book to them first helped promote it. The memoir was then officially published in September. By the end of the year it had sold 3,654 copies.[81]

"Annie told me last night that Edward had read to her his Life of Father and that it had charmed her more than she expected," Ellen reported in March.[82] This was not Cabot's book—Edward had written his own sketch of his father, which he first presented in February and March over three meetings of the Social Circle, a conversational club made up of Concord's prominent men. The club had requested a memorial sketch soon after Waldo's death, assigning it to Edward and Ebenezer Hoar. Why Edward only delivered it four years later, just as Cabot was finishing his book, is unknown; in their vast correspondence, the Emersons make almost no reference to it, until Ellen records Annie's response. Ellen also noted that Annie said "it is wonderful to see the different effects produced by Mr. Cabot and Edward with the same material."[83] While the Emersons had pushed Cabot to include more about Waldo as a family man with some success, his book was still, ultimately, a portrait of Emerson the thinker and writer. Edward's sketch put family and Concord life at the center of its understanding of Waldo. Two years later, the "sketch" would appear as the final entry in *Memoirs of Members of the Social Circle in Concord, Second Series, from 1795 to 1840*, distributed only to club members and friends, and as *Emerson in Concord*, published by Houghton Mifflin and sold to the public.[84]

The biography was done, the tombstone erected, the Riverside collected works (largely) published. While they would always keep an eye on the past and on their father's legacy, Edith and Ellen could take a breath and look forward. For Ellen, this took the form of a relationship with one of her "dear pals" entering a new stage.[85] Anna McClure first appears in Ellen's correspondence in 1882, when Ellen declared, "She is a vision of delight. Happy are they who can behold her."[86] Anna's brother-in-law Samuel Emery served as director and moderator of the Concord School of Philosophy in its first year, which brought the family to Concord and into the Emerson orbit.[87] Anna eventually became a frequent visitor to Bush. She was good at calming Lidian, singing with her and playing the guitar, but was also one of the few people for whom Ellen was willing to sneak away. While it seemed "impossible, or at least improper," to take up Anna's invitation to "dine on the river" in October 1885, for instance, Ellen ultimately went and reveled in the "gorgeous trees and very soft little clouds, and meadows with sun on them."[88] Anna was living in Boston by early 1887, but that September moved into Bush for a month.[89] Her presence was officially to help Lidian during a break in coverage from the rotation of hired nurses. While Edith did offer to pay Anna, the family understood she was more than a hired hand and even more than merely a friend to Ellen.[90] "I am most happy that your Mother thinks me a blessing to you," Anna wrote Ellen in July. She added, "My Mother and her daughter Anna know you are to me."[91]

Even while Anna lived in Boston, the women maintained a strong connection. She hung a drawing of Ellen in her room, keeping her "in sweet memory (were it needed) a hundred times a day."[92] They found ways to show their commitment to and care for one another. While unpacking from a visit to Bush, Anna discovered Ellen had secretly mended her nightgown and "really cried over your goodness to me." In the same letter, Anna warned, "Do not let your hospitable feelings get the better of your judgement," as she feared Ellen would exhaust herself with social activities.[93] Edith, of course, looked out for Ellen, but she also depended on Ellen's help. Ellen was attracted to Ida Agassiz, but there is no evidence that Ida felt more than devoted but platonic affection. Anna wanted to take care of Ellen, with attending to Lidian part of that care, and she cherished Ellen's care of her. For all of Ellen's dear friendships, her letters with Anna are the only ones which suggest that she was in a romantic relationship with a woman who returned her feelings.

In 1887, Edith celebrated the completion of yet another house. The previous summer, the Forbes decided to tear down their Naushon home and rebuild in the same location. Edith's in-laws pushed for the project, deeming the earlier structure unsightly.[94] Edith's feelings were more complex. She cherished her memories of raising children—and giving birth to one of them—there and did not like the idea of too ostentatious a home. Leaking pipes made it easier to say goodbye; the fact that her beloved garden would be salvaged also softened the blow.⁹⁵ By the summer of 1887, the new house, designed by cousin William Ralph Emerson, was ready. Ellen's assurances that she liked it and did not think it too fancy comforted her sister. "I was willing to have the grandeur of space if it could be simple & easy to take care of & I think it is," Edith explained.⁹⁶

"We have already had enough fun to pay for the voyage in spite of the awful weather we have had," Edith wrote to Annie on March 14, 1888.⁹⁷ She was writing from the Grosvenoor Hotel in Chester, England. She, Will, Violet, Edward, Waldo, and Alexander, along with their servants Mary Fiske and Minnie, had sailed for Europe on the SS *Germanic* on March 1. As they began their three-month tour through England, France, Italy, and Scotland, Edith's health flagged almost immediately. In London, she wrote letters from bed while everyone else went to the National Gallery.⁹⁸ She spent almost two weeks laid up in Venice, where the Forbes extended their stay to help her recuperate. Edith praised her family's caregiving, particularly that of Will and Violet, as she managed her shopping from her rooms. Will arranged for "Salviati's men," from the famous Murano glass maker, to bring samples to her; Minnie "proved to have a taste and talent for bargaining," and purchased things Edith had spotted before her collapse.⁹⁹ Edith finally ventured outside to lounge in a gondola during their last days in Venice.¹⁰⁰

Edith's health again shaped the agenda when the group spent a month in Bath, where the city's thermal water attracted people looking for relief for aches and aliments.¹⁰¹ Edith entered the care of Dr. Kerr, a "pleasant youngish Scotchman" who "has plenty of cases like mine sent to him by doctors of women."¹⁰² He found her knee to be "grating very harshly" and pronounced her "all out of condition" and overweight. Dr. Kerr put her on a strict diet, consisting of dry toast, small portions of meat, a "green vegetable" at dinner, and "Solas water, (which is the spring water aerated) and half an orange." She took baths every other day at the spa, sitting for twelve minutes in ninety-nine-degree water. At the end, an attendant sprayed her back with a hose, which felt like "a powerful, warm, & velvet soft hand rubbing most deliciously," then wrapped her in a "scorching hot towel and sheet." Will, who had developed a tingling in his arms, also sought treatment.¹⁰³

Edith had despised her first water cure decades earlier. Bath's genteel Georgian buildings and gardens, however, appealed to her much more than the dingy bathhouse in New York. While she resented the diet, and her rapid weight loss caused dizzy spells, some combination of factors did help her. When the Forbes moved to Edinburgh in June, she was able to climb the steep incline of Arthur's Seat "without losing my breath in the painful way" that had plagued her for two years. Hair also sprouted in her bald spots, although to her displeasure some of it was gray.[104]

In Concord, Ellen and Lidian greeted each letter from Edith with joy during a season of challenges. The spring brought the petty irritations of a March snowstorm and the "Road-Commissioners" being commanded "to insult the town by nailing up at every corner boards inscribed in large letters with ugly & inappropriate names they have chosen to give the streets."[105] More seriously, March also saw, within days of one another, the deaths of Bronson and Louisa May Alcott. Still, Lidian was relatively calm and happy, telling Ellen she was a "comfort" and calling Edith "another good daughter." Ellen found these compliments "a great pleasure."[106] As the Forbes sailed for home in July, the sisters anticipated a summer of family reunions and the pleasure of sorting through the treasures Edith brought from Europe.

"It is hard to tell you that our dear Don died this evening at quarter before nine o'clock," read the letter Ellen received on August 27.[107] Edith could have phoned or telegraphed her sister with this devastating news, but, true to a sisterhood built on correspondence, she wrote out these heart-breaking words. Don had collapsed on Naushon four days earlier from "inflammation of the bowels of the worst kind," suffering from diarrhea, vomiting, high fever, and moments of delusion.[108] While he had been ill throughout the previous year, everyone thought he had recovered; the worst consequence seemed to be that studious Don failed the Harvard entrance exam in June, while less-academic Cameron passed. When he became sick again in August, Edith and Will nursed him non-stop for three days. Only after the doctor assured them their son was out of danger did the exhausted parents take a break. In the few hours Edith and Will were outside, Don fell into a "state of collapse." He died soon after they returned.[109] Ellen found the news "too sudden a breaking of the family circle for us even to contemplate, much less accept as fact."[110] She flew to Naushon, finding the flags at half-mast and "the family all in tears or just holding them back."[111]

Don's funeral took place on Wednesday August 29 in Milton. The day before his brothers had carried his coffin, wrapped in the Forbes tartan, to a boat, and the family sailed with him to the mainland.[112] Edward Emerson arranged for a photograph and "cast" of Don's face.[113] Lidian, so reluctant to travel, made her way to say goodbye to the boy cherished as "loving, patient, and sweet."[114] For his headstone, the family selected a boulder from Don's favorite camping spot.[115]

"We miss our Don so constantly and the family seems so small and broken without him," Edith confessed to her mother in September.[116] The day after the funeral, the Forbes had returned to the comfort of Naushon. Edward and Cousin Sarah Haskins Ansley cared for Lidian so Ellen could care for her mourning sister. Edith, in turn, cared for Will; she apologized for not going to Concord for Lidian's birthday because, "it would be too hard for Will to have me go away yet—he is so sad and so dependent on my presence."[117]

By October Edith and Will, though in deep mourning, were trying to honor their commitment to a happy home. "We sometimes wonder if our guests or servants can guess or know how much we feel, for life goes on as usual, and, as we wish to have it, the house is cheerful," Edith explained to Ellen.[118] Organizing always helped Edith feel in control, and finding the right spots for the treasures she had brought home from Europe offered a distraction. Cameron heading off for his first year at Harvard, looking "so handsome," was a bright spot. But Don was always on her mind. She and Will commissioned Daniel Chester French to sculpt a marble bust of him, and Edith cherished the stories people shared about her son, particularly the tales from his friends.[119] She and Will answered over ninety condolence notes.[120]

The Forbes chased comfort throughout 1889. In March, Edith, Will, Violet, Waldo, and Alexander, along with the nanny Martha, traveled to Florida. Some of the family, including Don, had visited in 1885, and the trip brought back fond memories. Edith experimented with her Kodak #1, released the year before.[121] The box camera came loaded with a roll of film with 100 exposures; once finished, the photographer mailed the camera and film to Kodak, which returned the reloaded camera, along with the developed photographs. Edith turned her lens most often to her children, another way to document her family. She also had started a new project organizing family letters, reading them and marking them for copying. But mostly Edith was happy "to see Will loafing and content to loaf."[122]

A disturbing incident brought home the downside of the continuing power of Waldo's reputation in October 1889. "Last Saturday night someone opened Father's grave and dug down to the box which was broken open but the coffin was not opened," Edward wrote to Edith on October 15.[123] He continued, "It seems almost the act of a lunatic." He and his brother-in-law Prescott Keyes arranged to have "great thick slabs with enormously heavy blocks of split granite around and above it, all joined by Portland cement."[124] They watched the entire process, which took from dawn until after dusk, and managed to keep the incident out of the press. Waldo was safe.

The tragedy of another family changed the make-up of Bush. On March 2, 1889, Tom Sanborn, the eldest child of Franklin and Louisa Sanborn, committed suicide in their home. The twenty-four-year-old Harvard graduate, a poet and journalist, had returned to his parents' as his physical and mental health declined.[125] The Emersons' relationship with Franklin suffered after his ugly reaction to Edith's rejection of his proposal, but Louisa was one of Ellen's closest friends and a regular guest in the Emerson parlor. The whole family mourned for her. In June, wanting to distance themselves from the scene of the death, the Sanborns rented out their home for three months; Louisa settled into Bush and Franklin traveled, moving his desk into the Emerson home and using it as a base.[126] The arrangement allowed Ellen and Lidian to comfort Louisa, even as she helped care for Lidian.

The Sanborns were not the only guests. Ever since Waldo's death, Bush had hosted a rotating series of visitors, along with the nurses Edith hired. Waldo's first cousins Sarah Haskins Ansley and Charlotte Haskins Cleveland visited frequently; Mary Miller, a young cousin of Lidian's who had been studying at Vassar, arrived in August 1890 and became a family intimate.[127] Helen Legate, a teacher, began boarding at Bush in the late 1880s.[128] These women were critical to the Bush ecosystem. Now in her late eighties, Lidian's health was more delicate than ever. She also had cognitive issues, thinking her grandsons were her childhood playmates. The women who visited and lived in Bush helped Ellen with the physical reality of caring for her aging and sometimes difficult mother, while also supporting her with their companionship. "I am enjoying the daily spectacle of Mother surrounded by her attendant ladies," Ellen explained to Edith in September 1890. "There are now so many of them that it makes a fine show. Cousins Sarah & Charlotte, Caroline Cheney, Miss Leavitt, Helen & I. Every one of the six considers it her own special business to look out for Mother, and Mother seldom leaves her chair or asks for water, a blanket or a handkerchief, that at least four don't jump."[129]

Anna McClure's name is notably absent from the "attendant ladies" Ellen listed in September 1890. She had been at the center of the care network for years, and central to Ellen's emotional life, but now she was in Quincy, Illinois, where her sister Mary had settled. She had not planned on a long stay, but an illness causing severe swelling, perhaps pelvic peritonitis, prevented her return to Boston. While she had hoped to be home by mid-November, instead she had surgery on November 17 to relieve the pressure.[130] From that point on, Anna was unable to write herself, and her brother Edward and niece Constance Ellis Emery took over her correspondence.

"Dear Miss Ellen she is very ill. The doctor has told us so and we are trying to face the result with courage, whether the end will be soon we cannot tell,"

Constance informed Ellen on November 18.[131] Ellen sent Edith a letter confessing her distress via Will's office, but he forgot to pass it on until December.[132] Edith's unexplained silence must have made the following weeks even more painful for Ellen. As Anna's condition grew worse, the McClures acknowledged Ellen's role in her life. Constance wrote, "In all our pain and sadness Mama and I think constantly of you and what you are bearing and wish that we might be together and that you might be with Auntie."[133] When Anna died on December 6, her brother telegraphed Ellen immediately.

Both women's families recognized the enormity of Ellen's loss. "Do be assured however it may have served in the stress of her going that the love of her for you and you for her in which she felt so substantially united with your dear self was a pillar and delight for her soul," Edward McClure informed Ellen. Edith wrote to Ellen, "I grieved that you have to bear the parting from your friend," adding that Anna was a "great blessing" to both Ellen and Lidian and that Edith "should have been glad to have her live with you always."[134] "I know how you valued her love … I have an idea what a joy has gone out of your life," Cousin Sarah Ansley commiserated.[135] While Ellen debated going to Illinois, she decided to hold her own "funeral" at Bush instead. Joined by Lidian, Louisa Sanborn, and the nurse Miss Leavitt, they read the Episcopal Service, in honor of Anna's faith, and shared reminiscences of her. "Now all is over, except the memories and, I hope, her influence for good," Ellen wrote Edith later that day.[136] In Quincy, Anna's family slipped Ellen's last, unopened letter "under the lace on her breast" before burying her, "thinking that the fittest place for it."[137]

Edith's on-going mourning for Don may have deepened her sympathy for Ellen. While committed to a "cheerful house," she missed her son terribly. When Will traveled to Honduras for three months, Edith, Violet, and the younger boys rented a home on Boston's Mount Vernon Street. Will had proposed the move, worried Edith would feel too lonely in their home. He was right. When the family returned to Milton for a weekend, Edith found "without Will the house is sadly empty and I miss Don most on the Sundays."[138] Don's death had drawn Will and Edith even closer together. "I wish my dearest Will were here today—I know he wishes it. We find parting harder every time now & the comfort of being together very satisfying," she wrote to Ellen on the twenty-fifth anniversary of her engagement.[139]

Both sisters struggled to keep up their correspondence. While they did have demands on their time, there were other factors. The telephone would eventually disrupt written communication across the world, but this technology came to the

Forbes family early, given Will's involvement with the Bell Telephone company. The sisters never abandoned their tradition of the journal letter, but they picked up the phone to make travel arrangements or convey time-sensitive bits of news. Edith, meanwhile, had always been critical of her own correspondence skills compared to Ellen's, but grew even harder on herself. She warned Ellen that she was writing "the stupidest letters" that were full of "facts with no ornamentation or colouring." She added, "as you luckily have imagination enough for three you will read between the lines and dress up these facts as you know they should be adorned to be true to life."[140] The woman who had once said she was documenting her children's lives in letters to so she could later remember them later now told Ellen she hoped she was not sharing her letters or keeping them for posterity. "It is killing to all one's ideas to think of all the people who are to see what one is writing," she complained.[141]

In April 1891, Edith's doctor sent her to bed when she could not shake an illness. It had been a difficult spring, marred by the death of Sarah Coffin Jones Forbes, the wife of Will's brother Malcom. Edith declared Sarah had been the "heart and soul of the whole family" and worried about Sarah's fifteen-year-old daughter Margaret.[142] Edith's sickness, however, proved to be more than grief or another bout of rheumatism. She felt nauseous and drained, had a metallic taste in her mouth, and lost feeling in her feet and hands. Her doctors eventually diagnosed her with arsenic poising, contracted through "a new wrapper, made of the peppermint candy-looking flannel."[143] Confining her to her room, where she likely swaddled herself in the wrapper for warmth, had been the worse choice of treatment. Only after the cause was identified and Edith was moved from to another room did she start to recover. It took six months for her to approach her pre-sickness level of energy.

Will spared no expense or effort in Edith's care. She had three doctors and two nurses, and her wardrobe was tested for arsenic. Will reserved a "parlour car with state room" on the train to New Bedford and arranged for a doctor to accompany them when they moved to Naushon.[144] Edith reported that when she suffered a setback in July, a terrified Will "dropped all other cares to stay with me & consult with the doctors, and guard me from every possible difficulty."[145] Violet and Mary Fiske took over housekeeping in Milton and Naushon. Violet did not love the work, and Edith's own history of caring for an ill mother must have made her particularly appreciative of her daughter's efforts.[146]

Ellen, while making a few brief visits, is surprisingly absent from Edith's recuperation. "I am very sorry you are sick and I cannot come," Ellen wrote in late May.[147] When Will alerted her to Edith's relapse in a letter received on Monday July 6, Ellen only promised to visit for a half hour, acknowledging to Edith it "seems monstrous not to come to you."[148] Afraid to leave eighty-nine-year-old Lidian for long, however, Ellen prioritized her mother over her sister. The devotion of Violet and Will, along with the medical team the Forbes could afford to hire, likely made this decision easier. Edith understood, but she missed the devotions of her older sister.

In a sign of how much they both valued her, Edward and Edith negotiated over how Ellen should spend her vacation from Bush in August. Edward argued that, rather than Naushon, Ellen would enjoy "the more unusual fun" of Coffin Beach, the stretch of the Massachusetts coast where his family vacationed. Edith deferred to him. She made sure Ellen knew, via a letter to Lidian, however, that "I wanted her and Will exclaimed with horror at our not getting the good of her vacation, and wished me to tell her how reluctantly we resigned the chance of having her."[149]

Ellen did in fact love the trip, thinking of it as a "community experiment." She invited a large party of women, including her cousins Sarah Ansley and Alice Jackson and Alice's daughter Lidian, valuing the chance to give the group of women a vacation. She "enjoyed the most heavenly weather and ideal bathing every single day in a place singularly suited to my taste" and "saw an orange clear dawn on a dark blue still ocean" and "clear as crystal a grand aurora borealis." As each of the woman was "a housekeeper in active service as well as by nature" they even enjoyed cleaning the small house together. On the final night, they danced on the beach under the moonlight.[150]

The fall was a happy one. Cambridge was packed with the next generation. Edward Forbes and his cousin William Emerson, Haven's son, entered Harvard; Cameron started his last year of college, while Ralph began his final year of Harvard Law School. Lidian and Ellen were thrilled when Edith and Violet came for an extended stay in November; Alexander had already been attending school in Concord all fall, staying with Edward's family, as Edith traveled to Washington, D.C. and New York with Will and tried to get up to full strength. Thanksgiving was joyous, as the Harvard students poured in and Haven traveled up from New York. Edith apologized for not being of more help, but her restored health was all Ellen wanted.

Care of Lidian fell squarely on Ellen's shoulders the following winter. Edward set off on a lecture tour, while Edith, Will, Violet, Waldo, Alexander, and, for part of the trip, Cameron sailed to the Caribbean. Ellen was thrilled that her brother had found a happier direction and delighted in the letters that Edith sent describing Nassau, Jamaica, and Trinidad.[151] She worried about Lidian, however. "I feel thankful for every day of Edward's absence that passes and leaves her still well, for now she is so old, and especially now that someone dies in Concord every week," she confessed.[152] The specter of death drew closer when John Clahane, the Emerson's long-time handy-man and gardener, died unexpectedly of pneumonia on March 21. "I see at every turn his shovel which he expected to use Wednesday night, his basket in which he meant to bring Mother her wood before tea, his potatoes he had just sorted, the woodpile he had just framed," Ellen wrote, indicating how central he had been to the running of Bush.[153]

The approach of the tenth anniversary of Waldo's death spurred an odd conflict between the sisters. Edith complained that Ellen did not read Waldo's books, suggesting it was a sign she did not care for their father.[154] It was the case that Edith did regularly read her father's work aloud to her children and to guests, while Ellen almost never mentioned doing the same. The question is still odd, given that Edith knew as well as anyone how much Ellen had done for their father. Ellen's response is equally odd. "The reason I don't read those books is not because they are his, it is because they are books," she wrote. She then provided an overview of her version of her reading history:

> Have I ever looked at one of the great authors of this age or any other, except for special purposes? . . . With you & Una & Uncle George I have read Tasso & Manzoni, with Aunt Lizzy Dante & Homer; for the High School Class I have read some hundred pages of Carlyle, and once to mother a part of Sartor at her request. My Milton & Shakespeare I got at school & from Father, and so on. In my early days on R.R. journeys I read the French memoirs that my school lessons started me on, Coventry Patmore at Father's desire; and I am acquainted with a dozen devotional books. There is a history of my life's reading . . . [s]tories & poems I have heard read or read to mother.[155]

Ellen's letters over the years document a much more extensive reading history, but even if this did comprise all she had read, it is an impressive list. Still, she concludes, "I have yet to open my first book of real reading."[156]

Ellen seems to define "real reading" as serious study done with no distractions, for no other reason than the life of the mind, and with no social element such as discussion with others. Waldo's "privileging of self-reliant, inviolate consciousness as the acme of intellectual integrity," through his most famous works surely shaped this definition of what "real reading" entailed.[157] Ellen's responsibilities made that relationship to the written word impossible. That, however, did not make her reading less meaningful, and her discussions of what she read in fact deepened her connection to and enjoyment of it. For nineteenth-century women, largely cut off from institutions of intellectual authority like universities and the pulpit, "the initiating and continuing scene of action was a woman reading, responding, and taking part in conversation, whether directly or through exchange of letters and journals."[158] Even if she dismissed her own efforts, Ellen had carved out a life of the mind amid her caregiving work.

The exchange cleared the air, and there were soon things to celebrate. Cameron earned his bachelor's degree from Harvard; Ralph graduated from the law school and passed the Massachusetts bar. Both sisters beamed with pride as their brother delivered the lecture "Lessons of the Soldier," about Charles Lowell, to the Concord schools on Decoration Day. Malcolm Forbes married Rose Dabney, Clara Dabney's niece. Edith and Ellen, both friends with Rose, were thrilled to have their family bound closer to the Dabneys.[159]

The most joyous moment of the fall was September 20, when Lidian turned ninety. While she was increasingly confused and was often ill enough that Ellen called Edward to the house, "from the beginning to the end we had a happy day."[160] All morning family and friends took turns visiting Lidian's room, filling it with flowers. Ellen was thrilled when she rallied to come downstairs for cake dressed in a "new gown and prettiest things."[161] Soon after that celebratory day, however, Lidian "failed steadily"; by November, Ralph and Violet were the only grandchildren she recognized and she rarely left her bed and barely spoke.[162]

The three Emerson siblings had shared the care of their mother for decades, but Ellen and Lidian were alone when the end came. On November 12, Lidian developed a "rattle" in her throat. Edward did not sense any immediate danger on the afternoon of November 13 and went home. Ellen, attempting to comfort her, read aloud a letter from Waldo to Thomas Carlyle and tempted her with hot milk and brandy punch. Just after 7 p.m., "the rattling in her throat stopped, she opened her eyes" and Ellen "saw she was dying, for they were dead." At 7:35 p.m., "she breathed her last."[163]

In these last moments, Ellen's thoughts turned not to her father or siblings, but to Anna McClure. Anna had hoped that after she passed "she might be able when the rest of us died to come to help us through." The idea had provided

Lidian "great relief," and she had believed, "Anna will come to me!" As Lidian took her last breaths, Ellen thought Anna "was perhaps here and helping Mother with the same gentle skill and strength that used to be such a comfort to her."[164] Anna had once again provided Ellen solace.

"I liked to think of dear Mamma happy & not suffering or tired any more," Edith wrote to Ellen after the family gathered for Thanksgiving.[165] They had held a "strictly private" funeral on November 16, followed by a quiet holiday.[166] As with their father, Edith, Ellen, and Edward saw their mother's death as a blessing, a release from suffering. Still, her passing marked a new era even more starkly than the one marked by Waldo's death. Now fifty-three and fifty-one, Ellen and Edith had cared for their parents for almost four decades, with increasing help from Edward in recent years. To determine what shape their parentless lives would take, all three siblings turned to Europe, sailing literally and metaphorically into their next acts.

FIGURE 1. Ellen and Edith by Caroline Hildrith, c. 1847. The original hangs in their parent's bedroom in Bush. Courtesy Concord Free Public Library.

FIGURE 2. Ellen and Edith, circa 1858. Emerson Family Photographs and Miniatures, MS Am 2911, item 11. Houghton Library, Harvard University.

FIGURE 3. Edith Emerson Forbes and William Hathaway Forbes in March 1865, shortly after their engagement. Courtesy Concord Free Public Library.

FIGURE 4. Edith with the first five of her eight children, c. 1876. Clockwise from Edith are Edward, Ralph, Edith (Violet), John (Don), and Cameron. The Forbes often wore tartan in honor of their Scottish heritage. Courtesy Concord Free Public Library.

FIGURE 5. Ellen leads Edith on Gloriosa, Ellen's donkey. Gloriosa arrived from the Azores in 1876. Courtesy Concord Free Public Library.

FIGURE 6. The Emersons and Forbes in front of Bush, 1879. Courtesy Concord Free Public Library.

FIGURE 7. Ellen with Edward Emerson's family in Antibes, France, 1893 or 1894. From left, William, Ellen, Jr., Edward, Raymond, Ellen, Florence, and Annie. Courtesy Concord Free Public Library.

FIGURE 8. Edith, c. 1910. Her eulogy declared, "Wherever she went, she planted a garden." Courtesy Concord Free Public Library.

FIGURE 9. Ellen, who often struggled with knee pain, with her crutch around 1900. Courtesy Concord Free Public Library.

FIGURE 10. "Nachmittagstee," or afternoon tea, on board the SS *Kleist*, en route to the Philippines in 1910. Edith is the second woman on the right. Courtesy Concord Free Public Library.

CHAPTER EIGHT

"Be Content to Remain a Dove and Let Me Remain a Cat"

(1892–1897)

"I am delighted that the old home is to be kept up and by you and it will be the greatest pleasure to all of us that it should be kept up just as it has been," Will wrote to Ellen in late November 1892. He added, "But I hope that we see to have an era of long visits from you—and before any more of the children grow up out of sight."[1] Knowing Ellen would fret about money, the Forbes took pains to make sure she felt secure. Edith insisted Ellen have her share of the "income" from Lidian's investments the siblings inherited as "I haven't a want & it is the only way I could enjoy using it."[2] She and Will had done the calculations, and between Ellen's own income and Edith's, Ellen would have three thousand dollars a year, enough to live comfortably in Bush. Ellen would not be alone. Helen Legate would continue to live with her, and she was hopeful for at least one other border.[3] She did not find Bush lonely. "The house does not seem to me so different as people think it must. Life looks as full and as interesting as it did before," she assured Clara Dabney.[4] Still, she took up Edith's invitation for Christmas and New Year's and Edward's to live with his family in January.[5]

The sisters soon went farther afield. Just weeks after Lidian's death, Will sailed to Europe with Cameron and Ralph to scout for horses and art on a long-planned trip.[6] The separation was difficult as Edith mourned her mother, and she arranged to join them, along with Violet and Alexander, in April; Waldo and Edward would come after school let out. "I have taken passage on the *Teutonic* 5 April—and if you will join us your stateroom is ready," Edith informed Ellen.[7] She was thrilled, if surprised, when Ellen agreed to go. "Oh won't you & I have fun if we get together to enjoy people & sights & shops & learning," Edith rejoiced. She continued, "You can read one book & I another and tell each other so as to prepare our minds or we can read aloud—We shall want to study up what we are to see."[8] Ellen, who decided to rent out Bush, wrote to Haven, "I am more occupied with the somewhat melancholy task of pulling up my roots, but very likely I shall enjoy the whole business, and at any rate to be with my family is sweet."[9] Not since their trips to Newport as teenagers had the sisters traveled together without responsibility for their parents or small children. Now, with Waldo and Lidian gone and Edith's youngest child aged ten, the trip allowed them time to enjoy one another's company and honor this new stage in their life.

From April to August, the Forbes and Ellen crisscrossed Western Europe, with stops including London, Cambridge, Oxford, Venice, and Paris, and travels through Wales and Scotland. Ellen laughed at the family being in London on April 19, the day Concord celebrated its critical role in the American Revolution.[10] In Paris, Edith took charge of ordering new dresses for herself, Ellen, and Violet, along with suits for the boys. Will insisted he pay for Ellen's "black street jacket" from the Paris dressmaker and, later, "a fawn-coloured ladies-cloth garment, to cover me from chin to foot" in London.[11] The sisters negotiated their differences through these purchases, with Ellen giving her sibling credit for allowing her "to assert my own taste to a degree which I know must cost my dear Edith some effort."[12] They would be well-dressed for this new era of their lives, both on their own terms.

Ellen cherished the opportunity to spend time with her niece and nephews. In the past few years—as they grew older and busier and Lidian occupied her time—she felt like they had become strangers to her. "I enjoy my dear children every day and love to watch the beauty in their faces, and their resemblances" to their ancestors, she reported; she was thrilled that Waldo, Edward, and Alexander loved philosophy and history.[13] Her trek to the Trossachs on Loch Lomond with Cameron, Ralph, and Violet was a highlight.[14] It was the worst moment of the trip for Edith. She and Will were still in London with Alexander, who came down with scarlet fever. It was a mild case, but it terrified the Forbes, who could not help but think of Rosebud and Don.[15]

When the Forbes boarded the RMS *Majestic* on August 30, Ellen was not with them. She had decided to stay in Europe and meet up with Edward and his family, who would come in October. "Oh my dear sweet Ellen, it breaks my heart to leave you & not to have you near me for so long," Edith wrote on the day she left, one of the most emotional statements in their life-long correspondence.

She added, "I knew I did not like the idea, but I find it quite horrible."[16] Edith did admit she felt the adventure would be good for both Ellen and Edward, who was thrilled his sister was joining him.

It was a significant choice for Ellen to remain in Europe. She was choosing to rent Bush for another year, choosing not to be near Edith, choosing to be away from her beloved church and Sunday school and the Concord social scene. For someone whose life had been defined by caring for others, it was a bold step. She would be on her own in England for over a month, spending the time in Manchester and Salisbury. Of course, Ellen was not truly alone. Her inherent curiosity about people, along with her status as Waldo's daughter, guaranteed her interesting conversations and new friendships. In Manchester, she connected with the editor Alexander Ireland, who had invited Waldo to England in 1847, and his family; she also befriended the Halls, a Unitarian family, and Mr. Hall showed her his large scrapbook of clippings about Waldo.[17] Both Hall and Ireland explained the vote on Home Rule in Ireland to Ellen. She came to agree with their pro-Home Rule position, one more step in the evolution of her thinking on the Irish.[18] In Salisbury, while boarding with a local family, she studied the history of the town at the public library and was "at home and happy ... so curious that I look sharply into every open door & window, and many pretty things do I see!"[19] The funny, inquisitive tone that had always lurked in Ellen's letters, under the layers of duties and tasks, bubbled to the surface as she experienced a life without daily chores.

A controversy caused by Franklin Sanborn turned Ellen's attention back to Concord. Sanborn had published Lidian's scathing "Transcendental Bible" in his *A. Bronson Alcott: His Life and Philosophy*. Before she left, Ellen specifically told Louisa Sanborn that Franklin could not use it; Louisa had told her, "Mr. Sanborn wouldn't give it up, that nothing would avail that I might say on the subject" and so Ellen had forbidden him to credit it to Lidian.[20] In the volume, Franklin refers to Lidian as "a lady closely allied" with transcendentalism's "great apostles."[21] Her text is used to highlight the extremes of transcendentalism, which might have pleased Lidian. Edward, however, was furious, his reaction made more intense because Ellen had forgotten to tell him about her conversation with Louisa. Ellen's response was more equanimous, but still damning to Sanborn. "I am very sorry about it, but most because it lowers him in our esteem; the mere publication of it without name in a book which may have few readers does less harm."[22] All three children were proud of their mother's intellect and spirit, but they did not want this angry side of her to be public. Sanborn's dismissal of their wishes made the situation worse, stirring memories of his bad behavior after Edith rejected his proposal.

Ellen was waiting at the Alexandra Dock in Hull when Edward and his family sailed into port on October 6. "Well, it was indeed a great sight, one's own family," she wrote to Edith.[23] They quickly moved on to France, speeding through Paris to the warm weather in Antibes. Annie took charge of the housekeeping, while Ellen tried to help in any way Annie would let her. The Emersons celebrated an American-style Thanksgiving and hung family pictures on the walls; Ellen privately marked the one-year anniversary of her mother's death and hoped others remembered it.[24]

Edith eagerly followed her sibling's travels while keeping an eye on Concord. She shared Ellen's letters with guests; when each missive came to a close, "no readers of a sensational serial were more dismayed."[25] Edith was also dismayed with what she found in Bush, where the tenants had rearranged the furniture and had housekeeping standards far below hers. They "have done no irreparable harm but were dirty & shiftless," and the mother of the family "was not at all conscientious in her use of things." Edith spent a day "withdrawing things & locking them up & taking charge of things to be mended."[26]

Edith had a project to celebrate. In October, Roberts Brothers published *The Children's Year-book: Selections for Every Day in the Year*, a collaboration between Edith and Louisa Sanborn. The volume was "compiled for the use of children from seven to fifteen years old" with "the hope that it may help them to form the habit of reading each day at least a few sentences from the Bible, or some religious book."[27] Edith and Louisa had begun work in January, with assistance from Edith's cousin Lidian Jackson. By the time Edith sailed, she had "attended personally to the arrangement of the first six months" of the volume, along with "holidays and anniversaries," meaning days of special significance to the family.[28] For the dates on which Don, Rosebud, Lidian, and Waldo died, she included passages read at their funeral services. She did not feel these selections were ideal for children, however, and planned to change them in later editions. Edith largely handed over the project to Louisa when she went abroad but notes occasional efforts while traveling in her datebook.[29] Louisa made choices from texts Edith had chosen but not assigned to a specific day, occasionally consulting with Edward. Edith credited Louisa with the large number of Emerson quotes. She explained, "Mrs. Sanborn has filled gaps with sentences from Father more than I should, so that I appear very partial to my Papa—and who has a better right?"[30]

Despite the collaboration, the title page credits only "Edith Emerson Forbes" as compiler. The choice was strategic, insisted on by the publishers and, according to Edith, Louisa, as her two famous last names would attract attention and spur sales.[31] It worked. The *Boston Evening Transcript*, for instance, opened its review with, "It is pleasant to find the name of the daughter of Ralph Waldo Emerson attached to one of the new books of the year, and it is pleasant to be able to congratulate her on her literary workmanship."[32] She had feared the Forbes family would disapprove of her using their name, but Will had been thrilled when she asked him about it.[33]

The project was perfect for Edith, combining her love for organizing and anthologizing with her concern for children, as well as giving her a way to memorialize loved ones. She was annoyed the publisher had "taken the liberty to disobey my order about the shape" of the volume she had requested, but she found the experience "very satisfactory on the whole."[34] That the publisher realized the print-run had been too small and ordered a second, allowing Edith to make some of her desired changes immediately, made it all the more satisfying.[35]

In the same letter in which Edith described the division of labor on the yearbook, she mentioned "Houghton & Mifflin sent me *The Natural History of the Intellect*. I'm glad to have it."[36] At long last the twelfth volume of the Riverside edition was out. Including material cut from the eleventh volume, the title essay came from Waldo's 1870s lecture series. Ellen and Edith do not seem to have been actively involved in the final stages of this volume and were in fact abroad in the months leading up to its publication. As Nancy Simmons explains, "the book's origins and timing have never been explained."[37] While the volume earned only passing mention in the press and in the Emerson correspondence, it was a significant milestone. The effort Edith and particularly Ellen had put into the lectures years earlier was now out in the world, and the Riverside series was finally complete.[38]

As when their father died ten years earlier, moments of tension burst out as Edith and Ellen adjusted to their motherless reality. Ellen's decision to stay in Europe made her independence from home—and thus also from Edith—starker and may have intensified the conflict. Religion was again at the center of one of their worst quarrels. In October, Ellen decided to attend the annual Salisbury Conference, a religious gathering during which one speaker encouraged the audience to serve as missionaries, rather than visit Stonehenge. A furious Edith wrote she was "frightened that you seem to be so easily influenced & to feel that this person spoke with the authority of Christ to you." She argued, "you have a sphere of your own to fill where you are most useful & have your own poor and young to help," adding, "you are unsuited to the doubtful good of foreign missionaries, and your health not good enough for Edward and me to feel at all easy in letting you go beyond our care."[39] Edith's sentiments echoed those of twenty-seven years earlier, when Ellen's insistence on teaching Sunday School instead of staying home with her and infant Ralph infuriated her. Again, she combined genuine concern for Ellen's health with blindness to the significance of Ellen's faith and curiosity about the faith of others to her sister's sense of self and well-being.

Ellen was too upset to respond to this letter, but she did reply to one Edith sent a month later, which criticized Ellen for focusing too much on housekeeping. "I cannot wholly answer your first scolding letter; I am sorry, but I cannot; I do not quite know how. But this last one I can," she wrote.[40] "Imagine yourself for a moment obliged by me to adopt my approach to housekeeping," Ellen suggested, and "you will thereby be enabled to understand how hard it would be for me to adopt yours. You must be content to remain a dove and let me remain a cat."[41] She explained she wanted to focus on housekeeping under Annie as a way to understand the experience of servants. "I wish to know the monotony, the inevitableness, the inconveniences, the wear upon one's self will in doing your mistresses way instead of your own," she explained. She realized it was not something Edith would ever do, but added, "I am also sensible that you care for me and for that reason hate to have me do foolishly. On the other hand it hurts when you supposed me for foolish."[42] The subject of religion and faith was too close to Ellen's heart for her to answer Edith. She transferred her argument to the discussion of housekeeping, framing her housework in the context of sacrifice and learning, to help Edith understand her choices in both realms. Ellen was hoping they could come to a place, as they did with her clothing order in Paris, where they could respect one another's differences rather than letting their differences drive them apart now that they were no longer bonded by the project of caring for their parents.

When Ellen had left the Agassiz school for the last time in 1860, she had "felt as if nothing could be so good as to go straight back and continue such a charming life till age made it ridiculous."[43] Now, thirty-four years later, she finally had the opportunity to return to school, at least briefly through the Oxford Summer Meeting. The meeting was part of Oxford University's Extension School, which had offered lectures across the country, in collaboration with local organizations, since 1878.[44] While originally aimed at working class men, women soon flocked to the opportunity for higher education. The Summer Meeting, started in 1888, brought together extensions students from across the country, along with people like Ellen who enrolled for just one summer session. Ellen decided to take the course "The History, Literature, Philosophy, and Art of the 17th Century," which would run from July 27 through August 24. She began to read the suggested books in advance, including Theophile Lavallee's *Histoire des Francais* and John Richard Green's *Short History of the English People*.[45] "I am having a good time reading my history for the summer-school," she wrote to Cameron. Edith added, "I am much interested to take a position where I can get a bird's eye view of a century and see what happened in it from the beginning to end."[46]

"You don't know what a charming room I have. A beautiful window, plenty of sky, a sofa on which I often sleep when I can't read for nodding, pretty pictures and many handsome possessions of the student, best of all his writing-table!," Ellen raved to Violet soon after arriving in Oxford.[47] Thirty four years before Virginia Woolf delivered the lecture that would become *A Room of One's Own* in Cambridge, Ellen reveled in a space where she could read and think, with little else to occupy her. She was boarding with Mrs. Chamberlain at 9&10 High Street (now St. Clements), taking over the accommodations of a student gone for the summer. It was a short walk over the river and past Magdalen College to 90 High Street, which housed the University Extension Offices. Ellen was delighted to find two women from Concord—Blanche Wheeler and Fanny Rolfe—among her fellow students.[48] She quickly made friends with other students as well. Ellen had "inclined to be an old lady from the country, unconnected with Father," but soon word was out that she was the daughter of Ralph Waldo Emerson, and she was "invited to meet several people on the strength of my name."[49] She attended the daily lectures, made the rounds of different church services, and when she felt up to it, went to the events organized for the Extension students at night; a heated debate about temperance thrilled her.[50] She also eagerly joined in the excursions organized by the school, including tours of Oxford's famous colleges.[51]

Ellen loved studying history. "It is a great privilege to be here and hear these men," she wrote to Edith. She continued, "The extent and accuracy of their historical knowledge, their feeling of personal acquaintance with the personages of the XVII century is glorious, and the broad view of the work of the Century for the world beyond my hopes, while they speak perfectly naturally and with delight in what they tell."[52] At the end of the term, after listing the historic "personages" she had studied, Ellen wrote, "In all this high company as you will perceive from their names I have been very happy, and I have gained some sense of how they lived and how they felt." She applied the same curiosity about human nature and people's experiences that drove her to interview everyone from missionaries on ships to John Brown's daughters as she studied the past. Reflecting on the experience, she concluded, "It has been quite worth my while to come, especially if my memory proves to have vigor enough to retain what I have gained."[53]

Edith and Edward recognized what a wonderful opportunity the Oxford session was for Ellen. They encouraged her interest from the beginning, with Edward telling her she might never have such a chance again.[54] Just before the session started, he visited Oxford with his family, and they all took delight in touring what Florence called Ellen's "college," the building where the Extension school met.[55] Edith cherished the letters Ellen sent, sharing them far and wide. "I received on Saturday your excellent letter telling me about the good you have received from your stay most interesting & I should think it was well worth while and it does ignorant me good to know you are really in your element absorbing knowledge," Edith wrote.[56] Her sister's sense that Ellen "was in her element" at Oxford makes it clear that Edith recognized Ellen as, at heart, an intellectual, or at least someone who could have been an intellectual in other circumstances. She could not help herself from cautioning Ellen from overexerting herself. "Do heed my beseeching that you will only go to interesting lectures that will be worthwhile & not to evening meetings for righteousness sake—You will only break down & make yourself an invalid," she scolded.[57] Ellen laughed as she read this warning. She must have forwarded the letter to someone else, for she wrote a note dismissing Edith's claims on the bottom: "E has written me a letter of advice not to spend my evenings at Temperance Meetings! One might have supposed that in fifty years of experience of me my sister would have discovered that it is my habit to avoid evening meetings & go to bed."[58] Of course, Ellen had in fact gone to those Temperance meetings. The sisters could support one another without fully understanding one another.

Back in the United States, Edith had a full house, even though several of her children were now adults. Ralph, at twenty-eight, had rooms in Boston, but often stayed in Milton. Cameron, aged twenty-four, broke his collarbone and, during a long and difficult recovery, moved home. Violet, twenty-seven, was her mother's right hand, helping with daily chores, social events, and the move to Naushon. Edward was still at Harvard, but he, and his cousins and fellow Harvard students William and Haven Jr., Haven Emerson's sons, regularly visited. All of the older Forbes children had active social lives, but even as their friends began to marry, Edith's letters hold no hints of her children's romantic interests. Meanwhile, concerned about Waldo's health, she had pulled him from Milton Academy. Louisa Sanborn gave him private lessons to keep him, at age fifteen, up to speed with his classmates. Alexander, twelve, was lively and quick, and continued at the Academy; he had adopted a crow, which Edith detailed exhaustively in letters to Ellen.[59]

Edith also kept her eye on Bush and Concord relatives, including those in Sleepy Hollow. She hated that the flood of pilgrims to Waldo's grave left the area without "a spear of grass" and that the angle of the bronze plaque on his gravestone attracted a great deal of guano, cleaning it off herself.[60] She threw herself into the preparations for her cousin Lidian Jackson's wedding, likely underwriting some of the expense.[61] She continued to be bothered by the idea of tenants in Bush and was particularly dismayed at them having access to Waldo's study. This concern was sentimental but also practical, as she worried that people would steal the valuable first editions housed there.[62] Ellen, on the other hand, had "made up my mind to see some devastation," and urged Edith not to worry.[63] Her attitude was a sign of how much Ellen was able to corner off her normal concerns and focus on making the most of her time abroad.

Will, Edith, Violet, and Ralph greeted Ellen and her seventeen pieces of luggage when the SS *Buffalo* sailed into Boston Harbor on October 20. They accompanied her to Concord, where the house was lit up and Edith and Violet had arranged "delightful surprises of the housekeeperly sort," including fresh paint, cleaned carpets, and flowers filling the rooms.[64] Edith invested in the work to ensure Ellen not lose the benefits of her time away by drowning in housework immediately. Ellen quickly took in Helen Legate and Grace Heard, another Concord teacher, as boarders.[65] Even by Emerson standards, Thanksgiving was a huge gathering, with the Forbes, Haven's family, and the Haskins cousins from Brooklyn all pouring in. Only Edward and his family, still in Europe, were missing.[66] Waldo and Lidian were gone, but Bush remained the family homestead.

Ellen plunged back into Concord life. She gave a talk to the Women's Parish Association about her trip in January 1894, with one hundred percent attendance, and helped organize a series of University Extension lectures in the summers of 1895 and 1896.[67] She took back up the mantle of family historian, diving into family letters and collecting stories from older relatives. When visiting her cousin Phoebe Haskins Chamberlin in Brooklyn, for instance, she "was allowed about ten minutes to talk with her" and "made the most of it to hear about our Grandmother Ripley."[68]

Ellen soon expanded her historical project. "My hand must be saved for Mother's story so I write with pencil as easier," Ellen reported to Edith and Edward in August.[69] She had turned from her general interest in family history to a more formal project of writing a biography of Lidian. The idea started to brew in June when Lizzie Weir, a Concord friend, recounted a conversation she had with Franklin Sanborn, in which they agreed that some of Waldo's ideas "he learned from Mrs. Emerson." This sentiment reminded Ellen of a conversation in which Caroline Downe Brooks announced, "Mr. Emerson wouldn't be the man he is if it weren't for Mrs. Emerson. People have no idea how much he owes to his wife."[70] After the years spent shaping her father's legacy through her collaboration with Cabot, she now focused on memorializing her mother.

Ellen had Edith's full support. "Please do save some time for your writing and stop this universal hospitality for a time," she urged her sister.[71] Rather that setting off another squabble, this time Ellen agreed with Edith. She arranged to go to Nina Lowell's home in Magnolia, Massachusetts, for two weeks on what was essentially a writing retreat. She committed to writing twelve pages a day and kept socializing to a minimum. "Nina pushes me on with zeal," Ellen reported, and was "as good as her word and secured me long days to write."[72] Part of her process was clearly reading over her vast correspondence with her sister, as some passages come almost word-for-word from letters to Edith. Ellen was able to draft the biography up to her parent's wedding day by the time she left Magnolia, but realized she needed to do more research about her mother's life in Plymouth and to "consult" with "Mr. Watson and Cousin Mary [Watson]" there.[73] Over the next year, she made pilgrimages to Plymouth and carved out time to write in Bush, then returned to Nina's the following summer to continue her work.[74]

Will had urged Edith to select a "gorgeous ornament" as a gift for their thirtieth anniversary in October 1895, but she did not decide on what she wanted until January 1897. She finally commissioned a pearl necklace of three strands "with various stones set in every inch and a half." She desired "American jewels" and was "able to have seven American out of twelve."[75] Will loved to see her wear it, a sign of both their love and their wealth, and she was excited to show it off at a ball thrown by Malcolm and Rose Forbes in honor of twenty-year-old Margaret. The gift "was received with the greatest approval" of Edith's friends, but Will was not there to share in the admiration.[76] He had cracked his ribs during a fall while ice skating and was plagued with a cough, so he stayed home.

Will's cough continued to bother him, but he was not the only person suffering that spring. Edith took to her room with a lingering cold, using the time to organize family letters. Ellen's stiff knee made it difficult for her to get around. In April, the sisters travelled to Hot Springs, Virginia, to partake in yet another water cure; Lizzy Bartlett joined them.[77] As always when traveling, Edith decorated the cottage they stayed in to make it feel like home, bringing her own photographs, plants, and even a Morris chair.

By early May, Ellen had returned home, delighted she could run up the stairs once again.[78] Edith and Lizzy stayed in Virginia so Will, still with his bothersome cough, could join them. They moved into the main hotel, the Morris chair hoisted in through their window. Rather than improving, after a series of chilly days in Virginia, Will "stopped making progress" and "had a stiff red throat."[79] Edith and Will postponed their departure at least once in the hopes that he would improve. His lungs did seem better, but his throat remained "angry."[80]

Will's stalled recovery upended the Forbes' summer plans. As wet air worsened his symptoms, they decided to rent a place in Dublin, New Hampshire, rather than subject him to the sea air on Naushon. They consulted a host of doctors, all of whom agreed with this change, but Will was irritated and depressed. "How he hates any interference with his liberty," Edith lamented.[81] They waited to move until after the May 31 dedication of the memorial to Robert Gould Shaw, sculpted by Augustus Saint-Gaudens, in Boston. John Forbes had chaired the committee for the memorial, and Cameron and Ralph served as mounted aids during the ceremony; while John, now eighty-four, did not attend, Will rallied to sit on stage during the event.[82]

The Forbes pulled strings and spent money to make the trip as easy as possible. Cameron arranged for them to ride in the company director's car on the Boston and Maine Railroad, which had a "good wide bed" where Will could lie down. A doctor rode with them. They rented a "dark green home" on a "hilltop" and immediately had a telephone installed.[83] Will and Edith slept outside in a tent on some nights, advised that the fresh air would help him recover. Alexander, Waldo, Edward, and Violet were in residence, and Ralph and Cameron visited when their jobs and activities allowed. "We are blest with the presence of all our dear children, who gladden our eyes & hearts as they play golf, football, baseball, fly kites & adorn the lawn," Edith reported when the entire family assembled in August.[84] They read *Rob Roy* and *Ivanhoe* aloud, had family concerts, and took tromps through the woods; the children scrambled up Mount Monadnock. Annie and Edward were staying nearby, another source of comfort for Edith.

For all the mountain breezes and familial love, Will failed to make more than temporary progress. Every chilly, damp day set him back. When the Forbes learned that Sir William Osler, physician-in-chief at and a founder of the Johns Hopkins Hospital and Johns Hopkins Medical School, was in Canton, Massachusetts, Ralph tracked him down and convinced him to travel to Dublin.[85] Osler, like other doctors, found Will's lungs had largely recovered and his heart was strong, but Will's painful throat and weakness continued.[86] At times, he could barely eat. Edith lost her legendary optimism and fell into a "stupor of anxiety."[87]

Ellen spent little time in New Hampshire, save for a flying one-day visit. She had caregiving of her own, tending to Mary Miller, the young Vassar student who had helped nurse Lidian, and Susan Jackson, the widow of her uncle Charles, both of whom were very ill. Edith had hoped Ellen would spare herself the Aunt Susan duties, writing, "you have had enough strain taking care of the old . . . I do not want you to take a burden that does not belong to you."[88] She did, however, pay for Mary's doctor bills and her board at Ellen's. From afar, Ellen helped by taking on errands and tasks for Edith that could be accomplished in Boston or by mail. Her sister thanked her for relieving "my tired mind of my Harassment by shifting it on to you."[89] Ellen did come at the end of the summer to help Edith pack up.

In September, with their doctors' permission, Edith and Will moved to Naushon. They planned to travel to California later in the autumn, but everyone agreed the crisp fall air would not hurt Will and returning to his own home would raise his spirits. He did take great joy in reading on the piazza and even venturing onto the *Merlin* for a sail. Dr. Vincent Bowditch served as his primary physician, and Dr. Frank Perkins, a friend of the Forbes and Bowditch, stayed on Naushon to keep Will under observation.[90] Dr. Arthur Klebs, an expert in treating tuberculosis, came to examine him as well. Edith first mentioned the word tuberculosis in the letter to Edward that detailed the invitation to Klebs. That is what Will proved to have—tuberculosis of the throat, a rarer form of the disease than that of the lungs. Klebs pronounced he was "much pleased with several features of Will's case" and felt like he was making progress.[91]

Despite the doctors' optimism, Will's increasing weakness drained Edith of hope. Her intuition, as with Rosebud, proved correct. Will died on October 11, 1897, three weeks before his fifty-seventh birthday and just a week after his thirty-second wedding anniversary. Obituaries praised his war service, his business acumen, his wide circle of friends, and his generosity, almost always noting he had married the daughter of Ralph Waldo Emerson.[92] None of them captured the great love he and Edith had shared, in a marriage that had, even in the worst of times, lived up to their promise to one another to build a happy home.

CHAPTER NINE

"Thank You Over and Over for Helping Me Out"

(1898–1903)

When Ruth Emerson's husband died, it was a financial disaster for the family. Edith mourned her beloved Will, but, unlike her grandmother and many other women, she did not need to worry about money. Will had left her and her children wealthy. Edith also was not alone as she decided what shape her life would take. She had her children, her many Forbes in-laws, her brother Edward and cousin Haven and their children, and, of course, Ellen, the person with whom she first formed a partnership. Ellen and Edith, both in their fifties, were far from slowing down. In the coming years, they would go on new adventures, reshape their households, and find new ways to support one another as they entered a new century. They took different paths, as Ellen focused on reconfiguring her life in Concord and Edith increasingly left Milton behind. Each, however, offer examples of the under-told story of women reimagining their lives at the stage of life when caregiving for children and aging parents is largely over.[1]

While Edith's story was far from over, even the eternal optimist needed a period of secluded reflection after the sad season that ended in Will's death. "It was a real rest not to see people, and unsocial as it seemed, it did me good," Edith wrote to Ellen after a quiet Thanksgiving at Bush. She acknowledged it was the first break she had "taken for a long time," thanking her sister for doing the work and shielding her from social obligations.[2] Will was always on her mind. Edith was relieved when Rose Forbes' new baby was a girl, "for I am not yet ready to have a nephew named for Will and Mrs. Forbes was most anxious to have a boy to be named for him."[3] When a cold kept her to her room for much of the winter, she welcomed it as a "vacation"; she used the time to organize letters and page through "a delicious pile of florist's catalogues from all parts of the country."[4] A March trip to Hygeia, a sanitarium in Citronelle, Alabama, known for its healing waters, helped her ease back into a social life.[5] Her companions included her niece Margaret Forbes, whose ongoing respiratory problems spurred the trip, and her cousin Mary Watson. Arnold Klebs, one of the doctors who had treated Will, was a founder and physician-in-residence at the sanitarium.[6] Edith praised the attentive staff, but Klebs's attention was inspired by more than medical concern; he soon proposed to Margaret.[7]

Edith and Will had always been generous with her family, but now Edith became even more so, perhaps because she had more control of the money. A "beautiful, glorious" new sewing machine, with a mahogany case and a ruffler function, arrived in Concord in January, thrilling Ellen.[8] Ellen was less thrilled with the contribution of a new wagon to Bush, finding it ostentatious. Edith, however, insisted it was necessary for the "old wagon is nearly impossible to the heavy and stiff, I am both, you are one, and most of our contemporaries are one or the other."[9] Ellen did soon acknowledge people in their circle, like Louisa Sanborn, appreciated the more comfortable ride.[10] Ellen was also grateful for the bequest Will left her. "I shall try to use it according to his & your wishes, and see that with increasing decrepitude it may be very necessary," she wrote to Edith.[11]

International affairs occupied the thoughts of the Emerson siblings in the spring and summer. The Spanish-American war horrified them all. While the United States was theoretically coming to the aid of the Cubans in their fight for independence from Spain, anti-imperialists saw the conflict as a thinly disguised attempt to expand American power overseas and a betrayal of the principle of self-government celebrated by the Declaration of Independence. Edith declared, "How grievous and humiliating is the conduct of our government—I am not at all reconciled to this unrighteous war."[12] The vote to annex Hawaii in mid-June only stoked anti-imperialist fears. The Emersons' response was common within their circle. Moorfield Storey, an attorney who was a close friend of Edward's from Harvard, delivered a speech at the country's first large gathering of anti-imperialists, held on June 15 at Boston's Faneuil Hall; he served as president of the American Anti-Imperialist League beginning in 1902, a position William James held from 1904 through 1910.[13] Storey, who later helped found the NAACP, credited Waldo with shaping his thinking on civil rights and anti-imperialism.[14] In August 1900, Edward joined Storey in Indianapolis to participate in the Liberty Congress of Anti-Imperialists, one of the few times he was actively involved with politics.[15] The Congress endorsed William Cullen Bryan for President as "the most effective means of crushing imperialism."[16]

Six years after their mother's death, the Emerson siblings were still debating the design and epitaph for Lidian's tombstone. For their father, they had let the large, rough boulder and the tablet reading "Ralph Waldo Emerson" in large letters announce his importance. For Lidian, someone on whom many fewer words had been spilled in obituaries and other testimonies, the siblings planned a long, permanent tribute carved in stone. They had been discussing the wording since 1893, when they had also erected stones for their brother Waldo, their grandmother Ruth Emerson, their uncle Robert Bulkeley Emerson, and their great aunt Mary Moody Emerson in the family's plot.[17] In 1898, the siblings were finally closing in on the design and epitaph with the artist and stonecutter Newton Mackintosh. They were all happy with Mackintosh's general design, which included tulips on the top half of a rounded off stone. Ellen, however, felt that "dividing" the epitaph across the stone's two sides caused a "more disagreeable effect than I expected." She hated that there was no mention of Lidian's name on one side, meaning anyone who approached from that direction would not know to whom the "she" in the memorial referred.[18] They also debated the wording. Should it start, "To her children she seemed in native ascendancy & unquestioning courage a queen, in elegance & delicacy a flower," for instance, or simply begin, "in her native ascendancy."[19] In the final design, one side of the stone reads "Lidian Emerson," and the other reads, "LIDIAN, Wife of Ralph Waldo Emerson." "To her children" remains, the siblings again insisting that family was at the heart of the Emerson enterprise; the inscription also notes "the love and care for her husband and children was her first earthly interest." But the stone goes far beyond remembering her as a mother and wife. The inscription ends, "with overflowing compassion her heart went out to the slave, the sick, and the dumb creation. She remembered them that were in bonds as bound with them."[20] The Emerson children ensured that their mother's activism and compassion were the final words in this last tribute. "I am delighted with Mother's stone—it is beautiful," Edith announced when it was finalized in April 1899.[21]

Ellen was also finishing up her other memorial to her mother, the biography. In early March, she went for another writing retreat, this time at the Cabots in Brookline. Elizabeth Cabot set up "a big writing table with ink and trays, pens, pencils, paperweights, blotting paper, writing paper ... and two empty drawers for my portfolio and the Life." While Elizabeth was not as strict a taskmaster as Nina Lowell, Ellen still wrote thirty-five pages in three days. She reported, "It is already finished except fussing over ordering it and adding scraps" and went home feeling the project was done. [22]

Ellen's biography offers a thoughtful, detailed portrait of her mother that celebrates Lidian's strengths while acknowledging her complexity. The woman that emerges is principled and intelligent but suffers from what today would likely be called depression and obsessive behaviors. Ellen spends significant time on her mother's early life, giving a sense of how Lidian thrived as a single woman and entered her marriage as an opinionated, mature adult. Ellen does not skirt from the tension between her parents, but her depiction of their marriage is more loving than many found in Emerson biographies. Ellen is clear-eyed about Lidian's challenges running Bush and raising small children. Her mother expended an "amazing amount of indignation and shame" on "little difficulties and failures of a housekeeper," she explains. [23] Ellen also traces the lifting of Lidian's depression in the 1870s, when "she suffered much less both in mind and body."[24]

The manuscript documents the material culture of Bush and the Emersons' lives as well. Ellen includes renovations of the house; the provenance of pieces of furniture; and descriptions of dresses she, Edith, and Lidian wore. Small scraps of fabric from some of those clothes are pasted into the manuscript. Ellen instinctively knew what later historians of women have argued: material culture is a critical source for understanding women's lives. "Studying the things that women made, bought, used, and desired," as Meha Priyadarshini explains, is a path to "accessing women's experiences." Analysis of these sources can illuminate that "in a patriarchal society" women "found ways to create and maintain identities for themselves through their material belongings."[25]

Ellen's choice to include Lidian's "Transcendental Bible" reveals how she rethought her mother's life through writing about it. The siblings condemned Sanborn for publishing the piece in 1893. Now, Ellen incorporated the full text, along with Lidian's complaints about hosting the pilgrims to Bush and the evidence from Lidian's letters and Elizabeth Hoar to support her vision of her experience. She frames it by using her father's description of it as "a good squib" to take away some of its sting, but his quip does not dilute the power of Lidian's writing or, ultimately, Ellen's choice to include her mother's manifesto.[26] By including the "Bible," she presents Lidian as a thinker and writer.

During her mother's life, Ellen's letters make it clear she is more concerned about the physical and emotional realities of caring for Lidian than engagement with her philosophy. Now, reading through her mother's letters and recording reminiscences of people who knew her, Ellen had the time and mental space to appreciate her as Lydia, the Plymouth intellectual, rather than Lidian, the mother and wife. She underscores that Lidian was happier when intellectually engaged, recounting her enjoyment of the School of Philosophy and how debating religion with Charlotte Haskins Cleveland invigorated her.

Ellen also pays heed to her mother's reform work. She describes her as a "zealous member" of the Concord Female Anti-Slavery Society and documents her efforts for the Massachusetts Society for the Prevention of Cruelty to Animals, including the fact Lidian "once told me that she herself wrote articles to be published" in the society's journal, *Our Dumb Animals*. Notably, Ellen adds, "I have long regretted that I did not follow this up, learn what which they were and secure those numbers in which they appeared, for they did appear."[27] The society was founded in 1868 and Lidian was active with it throughout the 1870s, when Ellen was in the house; it seems shocking that not only that she, as the family archivist, did not save Lidian's publications, but that she was not even aware of them. The journey from that omission to the writing of "The Life of Lidian Jackson Emerson" illuminates the distance Ellen traveled in her posthumous appreciation of her mother. It is a journey twenty- and twenty-first century scholars have also taken, as there is increasing recognition of Lidian's influence on her husband's thinking. As Randall Fuller has written, "To consider Emerson's life and work without a full appreciation of his wife is like reading only the canonical portions of *Essays*—certainly possible, even heuristically satisfying, but also certainly incomplete."[28] Ellen's biography of her mother has served as a critical source as scholars have traced that influence.

While Edith supported Ellen's project, she had strong opinions about some of the content. In response to Ellen's claim that "it seemed to me that for the next thirty years sadness was the ground-colour of her life, but it was not unrelieved," Edith wrote what she titled "A Protest."[29] It is tipped in after page eighty-four of the original manuscript. "I think the picture of Mother's sorrow is too dark and decided," she declared. While acknowledging their mother had "dark hours," Edith insisted that "she was of too hopeful and healthy a mind naturally to always be sad." Edith argued that she had been with her mother a great deal when Ellen was at school in Lenox and Cambridge and was not "so unobservant a person that I should have failed to feel the sad atmosphere if she had always been so deeply unhappy."[30] She detailed the ways in which Lidian served the community and took care of people who were struggling, and, in a fifteen-page letter also attached to the manuscript, focuses largely on Lidian's social connections, another way to contest the depiction of her mother as sad and isolated.[31] This last echoed her complaint to James Elliot Cabot that Waldo was more social than he depicted. Her own commitment to optimism may have led Edith to stress this theme as she reflected on her parent's lives.

Ellen did not pursue publishing the book, but she did stage readings of it for family and friends beginning in 1896, including one in Bush to commemorate Lidian's ninety-sixth birthday. Edith showed her enthusiasm for the memorial to her mother, whatever her disagreements, by arranging readings at her Milton home for family favorites including the Cabots and Ida Agassiz Higginson.[32] To some extent, these events were an extension of the sharing of family letters that often was central to Emerson and Forbes family gatherings, as well as an expansion of the long epitaph on Lidian's tombstone. Ellen had taken the mantel of family historian from Mary Moody Emerson over three decades earlier. Now with a summer of study of history at Oxford under her belt, she took that role more seriously than ever.

The biography was just one example that the intellectual engagement Ellen had kindled in Oxford had not dimmed. She enthusiastically took part in what she called a "history class," a study group made up of Concord women who reported on different subjects each week. "I tasted the advantage of having travelled, for, when the story of the Popes at Avignon was told by Miss Jenny Leavitt I was doubly interested, because I had explored their palace, and had also been at Siena and seen the house of St. Catherine," she noted after one class.[33] In the fall she began a similar course on Dante. "Doesn't that sound like a new departure and very cultivated—or cultivating?" she asked Violet.[34]

Edith and her children made it through the first year without Will, always finding ways to remember him. There was good news, including Waldo graduating as valedictorian from Milton Academy and his acceptance into Harvard; the furniture Edith had invested in when Ralph started college, as she had hoped, filled Waldo's rooms in Cambridge. When Alexander did well on his exams, the older brothers "were all very sweet in their congratulations" as "they all felt Papa would have hugged and petted him on the joyful occasion."[35] Ralph made sure to spend the weekend that marked the tenth anniversary of Don's death with Edith, taking her on a carriage ride and a sail.[36] Edith mourned when her sweet son Edward set off to study in Europe for at least a year, but she knew it was the fulfillment of the plans he and Will had made together for his future.[37] She put on her editor's hat again to compile a book of Will's contributions to the Game Club, a social group the Forbes had attended for years, in which attendees wrote poems quickly based on prompts.³⁸ But the anniversary of his death on October 11 was made all-the-harder by the death of her father-in-law John Forbes, who had long been in ill-health, the next day.

Lidian and Waldo's descendants gathered in Milton for New Years. Edward Forbes was in Rome, and Cameron and Waldo were touring the western United States, but the rest of the family made the most of the gathering. Edward Emerson read from lectures he had delivered in Chicago, and Ellen read from "1848 to 1853 in Mother's Life." Hearing the section on their childhoods, Edward gave "many stories of his infancy recalled by it." As is often the case with siblings, "we kept finding we three remembered things differently."³⁹

Ellen turned sixty on February 24, 1899. She planned to celebrate with a quiet tea at Edward and Annie's house, but her "circle of friends" planned a surprise party.⁴⁰ The road to the house was "black" with those making the pilgrimage to celebrate one of Concord's favorite daughters, as visitors poured into Bush bearing gifts and treats. Edith's rheumatic knee kept her in Milton, but she sent glass tumblers, flowers, and a "magnificent cake covered with soft frosting"; the enclosed note offered "congratulations to (myself and) your family that sixty years of so dear a sister have been granted us."⁴¹ The usually self-effacing Ellen did not try to hide her delight.

The excitement and disruption of a trip west is what had aggravated Edith's knee. In January, she visited the newlyweds Margaret Forbes and Arnold Klebs, who had relocated to Chicago and were expecting a baby. She was swept along to Burlington, Iowa, when Charles Perkins invited her to join the Klebs at his mansion, named Apple Trees. Perkins was Will's cousin and president of the Chicago, Burlington, and Quincy Railroad for whom Edward had briefly worked.⁴² Edith reported, "Among the most cherished traditions of this house is the story of Father's visit." His refusal of a free railroad pass was the stuff of legend. Edith, however, was perfectly happy to accept Perkins' offer of a pass, "because I think as a Forbes my family have done enough for the railroad to deserve the free rides."⁴³ The statement encapsulates how far she had traveled from the philosophy of her childhood home.

Edith soon headed home in part to encourage Violet to take up Edward's invitation to join him in Italy and travel to Greece. Well-meaning friends had cautioned Violet against leaving her mother for an extended time, but Edith waved away such concerns. Alexander was still with her, after all. Moreover, while in her Milton home, "I am never unmindful of Will's care and protecting love which seems to me as strong and real as ever."⁴⁴ Ellen's life of caring for Lidian may have been on her mind when she insisted her only daughter travel. She did not want Violet to fall into what Edith felt was the drudgery of caregiving, even if that was far from how Ellen understood her life.

While she encouraged her children's adventures, Edith also loved when they were together. The Forbes soon had a new place to gather. Cameron, who had joined the Forbes firm, and Edith had purchased a ranch in Sheridan, Wyoming. Waldo was to stay in the area for health reasons in the summer and fall of 1899, and the ranch would allow him to learn the cattle business as he recuperated.[45] Construction of a house on the property had begun, giving Edith the type of project she loved. She spent much of the spring ordering the "household affairs" and planning the summer.[46] The focus was a welcome distraction when news came that Margaret Forbes Klebs, to whom Edith had grown close, died on May 29, just weeks after giving birth to a daughter. In July, Edith, Alexander, Violet, and Edward started off from Wyoming on the train, again receiving personal service from railroad officials en route.[47]

The family with such deep New England roots, who usually rushed to their island home and took to the ocean, thrived in land-locked Wyoming. Edith cherished having so many of her children together in the "cosiest daintiest little house that can be."[48] Once Cameron arrived in August, only Ralph, working in Boston, was missing. Words such as "joy" and "delight" infuse her long descriptions of the two months on the ranch. One night, "the boys and Violet sang on the piazza and frolicked and laughed and made extempore verses to their songs—and delighted my very heart as I wrote just inside," Edith reported to Ellen.[49] Her inner naturalist was thrilled by the landscape, such as the fields "gay with enchanting sunflowers which kept me in a state of joy all the way" to Sheridan on a provisions run.[50] She also marveled at "the velvety foothills" and the "perfect purple or azure mountains" and found them a "constant delight."[51] While Edith would always love her homes in Milton and Naushon, this dramatic change in landscape, with no associations with Will, helped her move on.

Edith detailed the Forbes' Wyoming adventures in long, lively missives that thrilled Ellen and everyone with whom she shared them. "All your letters are as good as a novel," Ellen raved.[52] Those back in Massachusetts were enthralled with Edith's tales of a rattlesnake in the blacksmith shop, the elaborate engineering project that piped mountain water into the "bathing room," picnics in the mountains, Edward and Alexander's work laying out a polo field, and "the boys'" adventures driving cattle and fishing for dinner.[53] Edith made sure to note, when they went for target shooting, "my capable daughter is apt to do best at it."[54] Edith and Violet toured Yellowstone Park just before leaving for home. They bonded with a group of fellow travelers, including a Scottish colonel named Alexander Pirie and the artist Charles Frederick Ulrich and his wife Margarethe. When eventually Edith revealed she was Waldo's daughter, Colonel Pirie declared, "Oh Mrs. Forbes.... Why didn't you tell us before that I might fall down before you and call you my father and my mother?"[55]

Edith's letters reveal her ugliest attitudes as well. She claimed John Evans, a Black man who served as the cook, did not wash the utensils, ruining the food's taste. Edith was often harshly critical of her servants, but now she spewed overtly racist language, describing Evans as "our grotesque monkey-like cook."[56] Edith did not always describe Black people in such vile terms. When Thomas Wentworth Higginson introduced her to Maria Baldwin, the first Black head of a Cambridge public school, Ellen described her as "the much respected head of the Cambridge Grammar School, whose subordinates and scholars are white" adding, "she rules all with perfect success and dignity."[57] She had happily hired Edmonia Lewis to sculpt a bust of Violet, and she would donate to a variety of organizations founded to aid Black Americans, including the Tuskegee Institute and the NAACP.[58] But these facts do not erase the ease with which she reached to racist ideas when in conflict with a Black person, which is of a piece of her prejudice towards Irish Catholics. Also like her anti-Irish attitudes, her sentiments were not out of line with her contemporaries, even those in the abolitionist circles in which she was raised. As Kerri Greenidge notes, "white reformers' dedication to Black people as a moral obligation to be fulfilled did not always translate into a belief that Black people were intellectually and politically capable."[59] Like many white, privileged females, Edith envisioned making room for white women of her class—and a few others like Lewis and Baldwin who could demonstrate their ability to succeed in a racist, sexist world—without disturbing the existing power structures from which she directly benefited.[60]

Ellen, now sixty, still had friendships from her school days that sustained her. She visited her Sedgwick classmate Addy Manning and her partner, the sculptor Anne Whitney, in Boston and accepted the couple's invitation to spend ten days with them in Shelburne, New Hampshire in August. Addy and Anne had lived together for over thirty years, first in Europe and then in Boston.[61] Ellen does not comment on their relationship in her letters, and always refers to Anne as "Miss Whitney," but she clearly felt comfortable in their company. The couple ensured that she saw "the finest views" of the White Mountains, and Ellen and the sculptor had a friendly debate about the merits of Robert Browning's poetry.[62] Did Ellen see in them what might have been for her and Anna McClure if Anna had not died? She does not say, but she was happy to have this friend from her girlhood in her social circle.

Her friendship with Sally Hopper Gibbons Emerson, the Sedgwick friend who had been so briefly married to her cousin William before his death, also grew deeper. Sally, who never remarried, served alongside her mother Abby as a nurse in military hospitals in Virginia, Maryland, and New Jersey during the Civil War. Abby died in 1893, and in 1897 Sally published the two-volume biography *The Life of Abby Hopper Gibbons: Told Chiefly through Her Correspondence*.[63] Ellen was thrilled when Sally came to Thanksgiving at Bush in 1899. While the schoolmates had always stayed in contact, Sally usually turned down invitations to Concord, perhaps finding it too painful a memory of her short marriage. Now, with her mother gone and over three decades past since William's death, she found comfort in the Emersons. "You delighted me by coming and liking it; make up your mind to keep coming for the future," Ellen wrote her soon after the holiday.[64] Ellen, of course, had many friends. But the shared threads of her and Sally's paths—from the Sedgwick School to their lives as companions to their mothers to the desire to memorialize those mothers in biographies—made their friendship especially resonant as they entered their sixties.

Ellen's advice to other single women like Sally illuminates her strategic approach to shaping her life as she aged. After Sally's mother died, Ellen suggested how to set up a household that would provide companionship and privacy. "Find a teacher or other business woman to board with you that you may have company at meal-times and at night, and yet your house to yourself some hours of the day. It works well in every imaginable way I find," she advised.[65] She also urged Sally and Mary Miller, now a teacher in New York City, to invest their money. She wrote to Mary, for instance, "As soon as you have any money to invest send it to me and the Forbes will invest it far better than you could for they understand business methods and look closely into the management of all the property.... In Sav Bank you would never get more than 4% on it and they find stocks for me that give 5 and even 6."[66] For several years, Ellen was in regular correspondence with both women about their investments, managed for all three women by her nephews Ralph and Cameron and other Forbes employees. A lifetime of watching the family books, and a sense of the precarious position of single women who did not have her support network, made Ellen yearn to share the good fortune of her connection to the Forbes.

"I do not know what I should have done without you—and thank you over and over for helping me out ... the fact that I was going for six months, all moth time, increased my cares very much," Edith wrote to Ellen from a train "probably in Indiana" on April 3, 1900.[67] Ellen had helped Edith pack and prepare for two adventures that together would keep her away from home for half a year. The first stage was a train voyage to California with Violet, Edward, and Alexander, along with her sixteen-year-old nephew William. She then planned to head to Europe, again accompanied by Violet, Edward, and Alexander, with Waldo following in October.[68] The long sabbatical from Massachusetts illustrates how flexible Edith's life had become. Alexander, now eighteen, had finished at Milton Academy and was postponing college. While still active in her Milton and Boston circles, without Will she prioritized quiet time alone in her room as much as social activities. She felt some remorse thinking of how her mother-in-law would miss her and Violet, but she did not have the loyalty to Sarah Forbes that she had to her own mother or even John Forbes. She was free to go.

The Forbes traveled through San Francisco, Santa Barbara, Yosemite, and Seattle, where they met with Cameron who was in town for business. They then headed up to British Columbia, and back east across Canada. William Emerson's presence allowed the Forbes to see the adventure with new eyes. "His going makes all the difference. We travel so much no journey can be an event of life, but it will be to him, and through him to us," Violet told Ellen.[69] Even having their plans briefly upended when William came down with the German measles did not diminish their delight in having their polite and less-worldly relative along for the ride.[70] Edith did acknowledge her "enthusiasm for the vegetation is rather a bore to him," as he preferred, like her children, to sail, ride horses, or scramble up a mountain than admire the landscape from a wagon. But she herself found, "old age only increases my powers of admiration and enjoyment," adding "I care so much more than any of the young, I believe they find my childish enthusiasm a bit wearisome." She promised, "Next time I come I shall try to have one companion as old and childish as myself!"[71]

While they loved their adventure, the California party was sorry to miss the celebration of the 125th anniversary of the Battle of Concord. The town, as it had been for the centennial, was in a state of excitement as the day approached. The renovation of First Parish, including the installation of electric lights, was a major part of the preparations, with the work concluded on April 11. That night a fire broke out. Ellen ignored the fire bell at first, but when it was still ringing at 4:30 a.m. she went to the window in Lidian's room. "I thought I ought to see the church, but didn't. . . . It was inconceivable. It was too true," she reported to Edith.[72] The church was second only to Bush in Ellen's heart, and for the second time she had lost a beloved building to fire. Despite the devastation, the town rallied for the battle commemoration just seven days later. The ceremony was shifted to the "Orthodox" (Episcopalian) church, where Ellen was proud when Edward's poem brought tears to the eyes of many in the crowd. Within days, the parish voted to have the church "rebuilt substantially on the old plan to look much the same."[73]

After a brief swing through Milton, Edith set sail from New York on the *First Bismarck* with Violet and Alexander on May 31, 1900.[74] Edward, who had joined Ralph earlier in England, came aboard at Plymouth, then the Forbes de-embarked in Cherbourg. For the next five months, they crisscrossed Western Europe, visiting France, Switzerland, Holland, Belgium, Scotland, and England, with Waldo joining them for a time. In Paris, Edith hired Madame Ancell-Lecoy as a "courier-maid," to care for her clothes, help with packing and setting up each hotel room, and run errands; she ended up doing much more, including writing business letters and handling travel details such as securing good train seats and scouting for good inns, jobs Will would have handled. "She has been a real comfort to me . . . taking every care she can think of . . . and is always ready to do anything in the world I can suggest," Edith raved.[75]

The European trip again fed Edith's "enthusiasm for vegetation," as she relished seeing flowers, plants, and trees from train windows and out of funiculars and filling her hotel rooms with blooms at each stop. As they walked through a Swiss meadow, "It was a delight to see and touch the flowers I had always before seen from car windows."[76] In the Swiss Alps, the altitude bothered Edith, but she gamely rode a cogwheel train part way up the Matterhorn; though it embarrassed her to do so, she then hired two men to carry her in a chair to the lookout when she saw "my suffering would so delay and distress the children."[77] She found Brussels to be "a handsome, spacious, airy looking city" and declared, "The Dutch are so much nicer than the French! Faces, manners, habits, houses, and *voices*, or I should qualify that say calmness in the use of them."[78] Edith did enjoy the Paris Exposition, even if she used a wheelchair to get around.[79] Still, she made sure to note it was "delicious . . . to arrive in dear England," when they left the Continent behind in mid-September.[80]

Distressing news made its way across the ocean. On July 1, Ralph and Cameron were sailing the *Hesper* near Cape Cod when a strong wind washed a sailor, Charles H. Cheney, overboard; the mate Charles R. Peterson took out a lifeboat to find him, but both men drowned. Ralph, the sensitive, responsible eldest son, was devastated. "The grief went deep with him—I hate to stay away so long," Edith mused.[81] Cheney was British, and Edith visited his mother in London, where "she held my hand tight and cried."[82] The Forbes faced a further blow when their matriarch Sarah Swain Forbes died on October 4. "I am so grieved and disappointed that we shall not see Mrs. Forbes again, and that she did not have the pleasure of welcoming us home," Edith wrote, feeling particularly bad that her mother-in-law had not had Violet nearby in her final days.[83]

Neither incident led Edith to consider cutting her trip short, a sign of her priorities in this new stage in life. Instead, she returned to Bath for much of her final month, joined by Lucia Bartlett, a Plymouth woman who had taught at Milton Academy. Working again with Dr. Kerr, "the treatment was almost entirely directed at my heart to strengthen it—and reduce the work it has to do in supporting pounds of superfluous fat," she told Ellen, a change from her usual focus on her aching knee and back. She loved the effervescent baths and massages; she and Lucia both hated the newfangled Dowsing Electric Baths, which consisted of laying for forty minutes on an "asbestos bed covered with Turkish toweling" while "electric heat is turned on to heat the bed to 350 degrees" and their heads hung out in the "cool air."[84] This was her first mention of heart trouble, although her light-headedness and frequent exhaustion could have been signs of it. Edith did feel better than she had in ages by the end of the month. She spent two of her final weekends abroad in Oxford, visiting Edward, who had begun a course in English Literature at New College. Edith, knowing how much she would miss him, took comfort that she had seen his room, met his tutor, and could envision his daily life.[85]

Back home, Ellen was thrilled at Edward's choice, revealing how much she still cherished her time studying in England. She wrote of her nephew, "He will henceforth feel a certain property in Oxford & enthusiasm for it just as I do."[86] Her home life had undergone a significant change while Edith was traveling. Waldo's cousin Samuel Moody Haskins, the minister at St. Mark's Church in Williamsburg, Brooklyn, for over sixty years, died in March 1900.[87] His sisters Sarah Ansley, Charlotte Cleveland, and Hannah Parsons, who had been frequent visitors in Bush, were all widows in their seventies and eighties who lived with him at the time of his death. "Some six or seven years ago I told Cousins Hannah, Sarah, and Charlotte that I desired them to make their home with me for the rest of their lives after Cousin Samuel should die," Ellen reported to Haven when he expressed concern about the women. Samuel had left them in "comfortable circumstances," so they would be able to pay board.[88] By the fall they had settled in, although Sarah wanted to consider her real home her daughter's but still spend several months at Bush each year. Some of Ellen's "ladies," such as Helen Legate, stayed as well, making for a bustling household. The desire to welcome her elderly cousins fit with the model of caregiving through which she had long defined herself. Neither Edward nor Edith raised much objection to the arrangement, although in recent years they had tried to persuade her to cut back on such duties. Whether they believed taking on the care of these aging cousins was the right thing for a family to do or had accepted that it was what Ellen wanted for herself is unclear. For Ellen, it was another stage of building a community of women in her home.

"First of all, let us rejoice together over Ralph and Elise," Ellen wrote to her nephew Edward in November.[89] Ralph, thirty-four years old, had just announced his engagement to Elise Cabot, the daughter of James Elliot Cabot's brother Walter. The news was especially welcome after Ralph's despair at the deaths on the *Hesper*. That the marriage bound the Forbes and Emersons closer to the Cabots was one more reason to celebrate. The same month, Haven's daughter Ruth and his son Haven Jr. announced their own engagements. The last marriage in the Emerson family had been Charles to Therchi in 1871, which had taken place quietly in Europe.[90] The next generation had been slow to start building their families; now there was a flood of new members.

"Simple and unconventional was the wedding" of Ralph Forbes and Elise Cabot on January 16, 1901, at First Parish in Brookline, Massachusetts, the Boston *Evening Transcript* reported.[91] The bride wore a "beautiful gown," and a "piece of rare old lace thrown carelessly over her head and falling below the waist." The new couple had decided to settle in Milton. While she at times had resented staying so close to her own in-laws, Edith was thrilled her eldest child would be nearby. Edith arranged the house for the couple's first night, setting the table and packing the dining room windows with plants. Soon after the newlyweds arrived, Edith, Violet, and Alexander carried embers from Edith's fireplace to Ralph's. "We've brought you fire from the ancestral home," Edith cried from the parlor. "How delightful," Elise responded.[92] Elise fit easily into the family, serving as a companion to Edith and Violet as well as Ralph. Edith, for the first time since Don had died, began to refer to "my seven" children.[93]

Ralph's wedding was just the first of several celebrations in 1901. Ellen Jr. graduated from Smith the same June weekend that Haven Jr. married Grace Parish, the great, great granddaughter of the abolitionist Lucretia Mott.[94] Ruth

Emerson married Henry Fletcher, an English architect; while the family liked Henry, Ruth's move to London caused dismay. The dedication of the rebuilt Concord First Parish took place on October 3, with Edward reading a poem he wrote for the occasion.[95] Florence had a coming-out party in Boston in December. Edith was actively involved in the preparations for both Ruth and Florence, buying linens and clothes for Ruth's trousseau and dresses for Florence.[96] Ruth and Florence both adored Edith, and she loved to help, but at times their mothers may have thought Edith overstepped. Regarding the purchases she made for Ruth, Edith wrote, she and her mother were "both content though I know they would not have chosen as interesting designs themselves." And when a dressmaker thought she was Florence's mother, Edith, "plumed myself and wouldn't deny that this was my daughter" even though Annie was right there.[97]

"Mother I think you'll like to come over now—Elise is under ether." Ralph said these words over the telephone at quarter past four on the morning of February 21, 1902. Edith "did not stop for questions but flew into my clothes" and hurried over to Ralph and Elise's home to be there when her first grandchild arrived. When Elise saw her, she cried, "Dear Mother!" in the "sweetest tone ever heard."[98] For the next hour, Edith hovered between her daughter-in-law's bedroom and dressing room, leaving to call Elise's parents at 5:30. She heard the cries of the newborn while on the phone with her in-laws. As the doctors attended to the new mother, Edith wrapped the baby boy in the blanket she used for all eight of her children as newborns, followed by another blanket of Alexander's, and finally a new blanket Ellen had made, then cradled him in front of the fire for an hour. Ralph and Elise took weeks to decide on a name, but announced in March he would be William Hathaway Forbes. "Ralph waited to make sure that I should like it, and Edith and Cameron—and that no one had objections to make," Edith explained to Ellen. "We are very glad," she added.[99]

At the age of sixty, thirty-five years after her first child was born, Edith was overjoyed to become a grandmother. In the weeks leading up to Will's arrival, she had been in a state of anticipation, embroidering a new cover for the baby basket Sarah Forbes had bought in New York City for Ralph and bleaching all of Ralph's baby clothes to give to Elise.[100] Following the birth, she often read to Elise and Ralph stories from the letters she had written when her children were young, prompting Ralph to ask her to write similar missives about his son; he was "gratified" to learn that she had already been sending such letters to Ellen.[101]

Edith's worries as a parent continued even as she took on her new role. Alexander had an appendectomy the previous fall, interfering with his first semester at Harvard. Edward ended up in a hospital in England in the spring, perhaps due to a head injury playing football. And over the summer, Ralph had typhoid fever, keeping him from baby Will for several weeks.[102] She was also concerned about Waldo's career plans. He, encouraged by Cameron, announced he would go into "business" in part to help look after his mother's financial interests. Edith had felt business was the correct path for Cam, but recognized Waldo's scholarly nature and thought it would be a "horrible waste of his fine mind." She and Violet "had much rather be poorer" than "sacrifice Waldo to Mammon," Edith told Ellen, adding they could easily hire someone to watch their affairs.[103] He did eventually follow his mother's advice, becoming his uncle Edward's co-editor in the massive job of editing his grandfather's journals for publication.

Edith was devoted to her grandson, but she agreed to leave him for a month to travel to the Wyoming ranch. All her children except Ralph were there for part of August, along with Edward Emersons' daughter Ellen and son William. Cameron had bought out Edith's share of the ranch and had big plans for it. These included building a new house for the family which could serve as "a health resort to be ready at all seasons at a moment's notice," a sign of how Will's death still haunted the family.[104] He took great interest in his mother's happiness, ordering her a side saddle, lowering a barn roof six-and-a-half feet so it did not interfere with her view, and making a "present to the family of very perfect waterworks, so that we have plenty of hot and cold clear water in my dressing room and kitchen and the bath tub."[105] Edith delighted in seeing prairie dogs and porcupines for the first time, as well as hearing her children sing in the evenings. There were more polo games and the excitement of visiting the livestock and identifying the western flora. Edith sewed curtains and made the day-long excursion to Sheridan for provisions. She was relieved when the new wagon arrived, for the old "spring" wagon was intolerable even after she took a shot of bourbon and brought her rubber cushion along for the ride.[106]

As the Forbes moved the family forward, Ellen continued her campaign to document its past. In April, while visiting Dr. Richard Cabot, she began the manuscript, "What I Can Remember About Father." A shorter companion to her biography of her mother, this account places Waldo in the context of his ancestors and his immediate family. She pointedly includes details seen in neither Cabot's nor Edward's biographies. Ellen notes, for instance, that "Uncle William actually stood to him in the place of a Father, he tells him everything," adding, "Yet I don't see it mentioned at all in either Life of Father, so I will set it down here."[107] Despite the title, in the first thirty pages, out of fifty, she focuses more on Waldo's brothers and his sister, who died at the age of three. Much of the second half is focused on the experience of being his child, particularly how safe he made his children feel and how he encouraged their studies.

In April 1903, Violet announced her engagement to Kenneth Webster, an English professor at Harvard. Edith had known since February, when she noted cryptically in her diary, "V. told me."[108] Originally from Halifax, Nova Scotia, Kenneth earned a BA from Harvard in 1893, followed by a PhD in 1902.[109] Violet was thirty-six years old, but there is no explanation in the Forbes and Emerson correspondence for her relatively late marriage; she and Kenneth may have waited for him to finish his dissertation before the engagement. Some expressed concern for Edith, as Violet had been one of her closest companions, especially after Will's death. But Edith, whose own marriage had brought her such happiness, stressed that she and "the boys" supported the union.[110] The announcement of Florence Emerson's engagement to Gerrit Forbes later the same month increased the family's jubilant spirit.[111] Gerrit was the son of William's brother Malcolm, and Edith and her children were thrilled the Emersons and the Forbes would be bound even closer together.

The planning for Violet's wedding, set for August, began immediately, and Edith also was preparing for another trip to the Wyoming ranch in June. The Emersons first faced a major milestone, however. May 25, 1903 marked the centennial of Waldo's birth. While the Emerson family regularly honored the birthdays and anniversaries of their ancestors, this birthday was a national event. "Citizens throughout the nation ratified the canonization of Emerson as a genuine American saint whose testament would provide the way, the truth, and the light that would help guide the nation's destiny in the 20th century," Len Gougeon explains of the celebrations.[112] The Congress of Religion called for "ministers of all denominations ... to observe Sunday May 24 or any near date that may be convenient as the Emerson centenary, either by preaching sermons reflecting the thought, appropriate to the occasion, of our common indebtedness to Emerson, or in such other manner as may appeal to their judgement and taste."[113] The Society of Authors held a dinner for 200 at the Waldorf Astoria in New York; a letter by President Theodore Roosevelt, who had rowed Waldo in Egypt as a child, was read at the event, praising "a man to whom American literature, American philosophy, and American citizenship owe so much."[114] Harvard laid the cornerstone for Emerson Hall, a new building to house the philosophy department, and Harvard's president Charles W. Eliot delivered an address organized by the American Unitarian Association at Boston's Symphony

Hall on May 24. Concord claimed the actual anniversary, with the Social Circle organizing day-long "Memorial Exercises"; speakers included Samuel Hoar, Charles Norton, Thomas Wentworth Higginson, William James, and, of course, Edward, who delivered the keynote at the dinner for 150. The town, and Bush itself, was a site of pilgrimage. "Emerson's grave at Concord, his home and his haunts will all be visited by thousands during the centennial observances," the *Boston Evening Transcript* reported.[115]

The attention made it clear that, in the two decades since his death, Ralph Waldo Emerson's reputation had only grown. But while the country embraced Waldo as a saint whose "testament would provide the way, the truth, and the light," Americans had very different opinions about what that way was. Harvard's president employed Waldo's concept of self-reliance to justify racial hierarchies and American imperialism and to demonize labor unions; others, including Franklin Sanborn, used their platforms to stress, and perhaps exaggerate, his career as a reformer. Moorfield Storey and William James invoked Waldo in the cause of anti-imperialism.[116] What is clear is that the siblings' attempt to put family at the center of Emerson's legacy had largely failed. There was little room in the narrative of a secular saint for his home life.

Edith and Ellen were surprisingly uninvolved in the commemoration, particularly given the attention they usually paid to their family legacy. Edith was caught up in her grandchild and trip west. Ellen, meanwhile, seemed unaware at the end of April of the schedule of events in Concord and Boston. Edith warned her that the Social Circle was unlikely to allow her to invite the Haskins cousins to the dinner and that, given the events in Boston, "there will not be a week of festivities in Concord as you seem to expect."[117] The published program for the Social Circle event indicates that Ellen and Edith were honored guests but not integrated into its planning.[118] Ellen admitted of the speeches, "sleep overcame me soon after Mr. Higginson's began, and caught me again in the same way during my dear William James.'" She laughed that so many of the speakers she did hear quoted the same passages. "I suppose that shows which of Father's verses have really been chosen as best by the world at large," she concluded.[119]

It was a different story for Edward. Not only was he an active club member given a prime speaking slot during the dinner, but he had taken on the task of preparing a Centenary Edition of his father's works. The first two volumes appeared in May, in time for the anniversary: *Nature; Addresses and Lectures*, which includes a short biography of Waldo, and *Essays, First Series*. In the introduction to *Nature*, he praises James Elliot Cabot's work on the Riverside

Edition, saying that that earlier project made Edward's "work lighter." He notes that Houghton Mifflin first approached Cabot in the summer of 1902 about the new edition; he "felt unable to undertake the task" and "advised" Edward to take it on. Cabot had died in January, sadly correct about his inability to do the work. There is no mention of Ellen and Edith's earlier contributions, but Edward does praise Elizabeth Cabot, noting the "help of" Cabot's "wife" is "gratefully remembered."[120] Edward worked tirelessly on the project, which included annotating the material with, for the first time, references to Waldo's journals. He promised in the introduction of Nature to publish eventually portions of the journals as well.[121] Ellen was not the editorial partner she had been to Cabot, although she answered his questions and aided him in locating manuscripts.[122] The timing suggests Ellen may have started "What I Can Remember About Father" to help him with the biographical profile that appeared in Nature.

Edith scrambled after the Centenary to make final preparations for the move to Wyoming, and, with significant packing help from Ellen, was on the train by May 29. Violet and Cameron were with her, along with Florence Emerson. Other guests that summer included Gerrit Forbes and Gertrude and Moorfield Storey. Moorfield's speech at the Centenary had placed him firmly in the camp of depicting Waldo as a crusader for social justice. He had also included his remembrance of Waldo's "grave and gracious" behavior at a dinner at Bush, when Moorfield was still a college student, and the genuine curiosity with which he drew out his young visitor's opinion.[123] This personal note likely charmed all the Emerson children, depicting the same warm, family-oriented Waldo they wanted to promote. Edith and her children were certainly happy to have the Storeys with them. "We were so happy in this perfect scenery—and enjoyed every moment," she raved after one excursion with her guests.[124]

During her third summer in Wyoming Edith was more aware of life beyond the ranch. She visited a "Government School" for Native Americans with Florence, Gerrit, and a Mr. Gillette. "They take the children whether parents wish it or not," she reported to Ellen, condemning "the matron" as "cold and uninterested" in the children and the "squalor" of the public areas of the school.[125] Perhaps the presence of Storey, who had just argued that Waldo's legacy should be a push for social justice and was involved in the Indian Rights Association, caused her to reflect on the experiences of Native Americans in the schools and the parents who lost their children, even if her condemnation is ultimately light. Edith also thought about the lives of white women in Wyoming, noting how it must be terrifying for mothers to live so far from the closest doctor.[126]

Back East, the Emerson commemorations continued, most notably with the Emerson Memorial School. Organized by the Free Religious Association, it consisted of thirty lectures held at Concord Town Hall in the mornings and the Massachusetts Institute of Technology in the evenings over the last two weeks of July. Speakers included Franklin Sanborn, William L. Garrison Jr., Julia Ward Howe, William James, Moorfield Storey after his return from Wyoming, and, of course, Edward. Ellen attended "all the beautiful lectures about Father" with her cousins, at least those in Concord.[127] She also welcomed groups of Emerson pilgrims to the house. Showing Bush to the Essex County Emerson Club and telling them about Waldo gave her "a coveted chance to say that most newspaper stories about him were false." She was particularly happy to disabuse them of the notion that her father "wrote his lectures on old envelopes & odd scraps of paper."[128] As the summer ended, Ellen reflected, "The whole long celebration of his hundredth year has been to me not only delightful but most impressive. I have learned much of what he is to the world."[129]

The Emersons and Forbes turned their attention from earlier generations to those of the future, celebrating Violet and Kenneth's marriage on Naushon on August 15. Violet wore the same muslin dress in which Edith had married Will. Everyone pitched in to decorate the first floor with the plants, flowers, and tree branches the Forbes brothers had gathered from the around island, and Kenneth picked flowers for his bride's bouquet.[130] Edith also wore white muslin and must have missed Will as she watched her daughter say her vows.

Edith and Ellen took different roads as they entered their sixth decades. The five years since Will's death had untethered Edith from Milton. With her youngest children now adults, her parents and in-laws gone, and her responsibilities as Will's wife behind her, she traveled the world, by rail and by sea. It was a trend that would only increase, even as she embraced her role as a grandmother. Ellen, on the other hand, was more rooted in Concord than ever. She had loved her time in Oxford and her adventures in Europe, and the intellectual renaissance it had inspired within her continued, but she returned to Bush ready to focus on her home and hometown. She put her energies into documenting her family and creating a community of women who could support one another in a world not designed for women to live alone.

CHAPTER TEN

"I Am So Glad We Had So Much Time Together"

(1904–1909)

A bad knee drove Ellen to Milton for much of the first half of 1904. Helen Legate covered the day-to-day care of the house and her "ladies" in Bush while she recuperated. The timing meant Ellen could support Edith as she adjusted to life without Violet, who was setting up house in Cambridge. Edith and Ellen were not alone. Edward had allowed Raymond to attend Milton Academy, sponsored by and living with Edith, and Julia Emerson, Haven's daughter, came to help with Edith's gardens and copying family manuscripts. There was also a new baby—Ralph's daughter Ruth had been born the previous October. "I look back on my winter with great interest, and delight in every touch of family life I have felt," Ellen wrote after she returned home.[1] Edith responded, "I am so glad we had so much time together."[2] For sixty years, Ellen and Edith had rejoiced in one another's company while helping each other negotiate life's twists and turns. They would continue to do so as they entered one final act.

They also helped their brother. During the extended visit, Ellen and Edith collaborated in providing Edward information as he edited the Centenary edition of *Poems*. Edward was again annotating what was close to the Riverside text, incorporating passages from Waldo's journals and other contextual information. The sisters provided their memories of things their father had said about the origins of the poems and their meanings, some of which Edward integrated directly into his text. Ellen wrote him, for instance, of the poem "Brahma," "you know as well as I that when people said it was puzzling Father said, 'If you tell them to say Jehovah instead of Brahma, they will not feel any perplexity.'"[3] The annotation to the poem quotes the statement exactly, noting Waldo said it to his "daughter."[4] In response to a question about the crafting of "Forerunners," Ellen pointed her brother to "What I Can Remember About Father," a reminder of the effort she had already put into documenting her father's life and work.[5] But the sisters in general were happy to help Edward, worried the project "seemed to wear hard on his strength."[6]

In February President Theodore Roosevelt asked Cameron to serve as Commissioner of Commerce and Police of the Philippines. The family took it as an honor, although they debated the offer's pros and cons. Ellen summed up the arguments in a letter to Haven:

> We have all, of course, had a very good time with him over it, and while first, we all of us wish he were an anti-imperialist, and, second, we cannot shut our eyes to the objections, the distance, the climate, the ten best years of his life, we are happy in the unusual chance given him to exercise his powers in the service of Civilization and we earnestly hope Justice, Mercy, and all good; we, being mother & cousins & aunts, feeling as if these powers were adequate to the Call.[7]

As Ellen indicated, Cameron did not harbor the fierce anti-imperialistic feelings of his elders, even though he had welcomed Moorfield Story to his ranch the year before. As one of the five members of the commission appointed to oversee the archipelago on behalf of the United States, in fact, his task was to expand the American imperialist project, helping the country to govern and develop the islands while "civilizing" its residents. Edith's concerns were less about his politics than the separation from her son, but she had long felt that Cameron was her child who inherited the ambition and vision of his Forbes grandfather. She would soon go beyond maternal support to turn her back on anti-imperialism and endorse his actions and beliefs.

A family crisis almost derailed Cameron's appointment. Malcolm Forbes died following complications from surgery on February 19.[8] He was Will's brother and Edith's children's uncle, the father of Florence's fiancé, and, as the head of J. M. Forbes & Company, Cameron's boss; his death upended the family. Cameron was an executor of Malcolm's will, which appointed him trustee of his property and guardian of his children, and he considered turning the Philippines appointment down.[9] When given an extra four months to arrange the Forbes affairs before leaving, however, he determined to go.[10] In June, just before he departed, Edith hosted a dinner at her Milton home for a delegation of forty-three men from the Philippines.[11] Florence and Gerrit, with the encouragement of their mothers, also went ahead with their wedding on June 18.[12]

A regime of "massaging & baking & electrifying" allowed Ellen to avoid surgery and return home in May, even if she had to be on crutches for the summer.[13] While Ellen grew stronger, Edith's duties as aunt-of-the bride and mother-of-the-commissioner, along with a bad case of the "grippe" in February, had exhausted her.[14] She returned to Bath for another round of the water cure after Alexander's graduation from Harvard. By the end of July, she had "improved very much thanks to Nurse Drummond's wonderful massage and my much-loved Nauheim baths."[15] Following their treatment, the women traveled throughout Britain, including Edinburgh and London; Edith spent a week in Sussex with Haven's daughter Ruth, who now had two daughters of her own. Edith wrote Ellen less than in earlier expeditions, as "everyone preaches no writing" to combat her exhaustion and sending letters to Cameron was her priority.[16] She summed up a tour of Edinburgh as, "visited colleges and quadrangles and the river and beautiful bridges and lawns—as you doubtless remember. Then I will say no more."[17]

The Emersons and Forbes were spread across the world in 1905. Cameron was in the Philippines, and Edward Emerson, with the Centenary edition completed, traveled to Europe with Annie and Ellen Jr. Waldo Forbes met up with the Emersons in Greece; upon his return, he and Alexander set off to the Wyoming ranch, where Florence and Gerrit and their new baby also made a long visit. Haven and his daughter Helena were in England, where Ruth had been diagnosed with tuberculosis and sent to a sanatorium.[18]

As always, the family depended on letters to knit them together over distance, a habit the next generation had embraced. Edith employed new methods to keep up her correspondence with the far-flung clan. She began to use a "triplicate block," which made carbon copies of her letters, to send out to various children and other family members. Edith hated how they looked, referring to a "miserable looking penciled document with two blue impressions," but it did help keep everyone informed.[19] She also kept journal letters for Cameron, sometimes sending them first to Ellen to catch her up, along with bribing Ellen to come to Milton with the promise of reading the journal letters Cameron himself sent.[20]

Ellen needed bribing as she was largely bound to Concord, again caring for aging relatives in cognitive decline. Bush had "pretty much become a quiet retreat for feeble age," she wrote to Sally Emerson. She continued, "We have very little going on and my rule is to stay at the house all the time."[21] Hannah was going blind and had difficulty remembering things; Sarah was regularly confused, having frequent "interviews" with her grandfather.[22] Ellen made light of it in her letters, noting that Sarah thought a loaf of bread was a baby, and did gain satisfaction from caring from her elderly cousins. The situation, however, limited the physical and intellectual freedom she had found after Lidian's death and reminded her of the challenges of caring for her father. At age sixty-six, moreover, the work of caregiving taxed her more physically than it had in the earlier decades. Edith paid for a nurse, an enormous help. Still, Ellen turned down most overnight invitations and feared her cousins would soon not recognize her.[23]

Ellen ruled the roost at Bush, but Edith, now sixty-four, was clearly the matriarch of the Forbes and Emerson families. Her role was even more prominent as, given the early deaths of a generation of Forbes men and Edward Emerson's delicate health, there was not a strong patriarchal figure in either branch. She was generous with her time and wealth, not just to her siblings and nieces and nephews, but also to Haven Emerson's four children. The next generation regularly wrote to thank her for gifts, trips, invitations to Naushon, and her time and attention. Edward's children called her a fairy godmother, and Ruth Emerson Fletcher and Florence Emerson Forbes turned to her for advice as they began their families. "I can't say how it touched me that you should have been willing to write so intimately to me of your own experiences & feelings & what you call mistakes, indeed I do mean to profit by what you tell me," Ruth wrote.[24]

Not everyone appreciated Edith's advice. Her perfectionism, so like her mother's, could cause tension. Annie Emerson expressed relief that Rose Forbes, Gerrit's stepmother, had taken charge of acquiring table linens for Florence's dowry; Edith "cares so much about having it exactly so and in such quantities that it is a great labour to see to it," she confessed to Rose.[25] While her daughter-in-law Elise had welcomed Edith's presence in the early days of her marriage, she wanted distance by the time her third child, Margaret, was born in May 1905. "The Baby is intentionally kept in seclusion by her mother, as well as nurse," Edith complained in the summer of 1906; in her opinion, that isolation led Margaret to be less "developed" than Florence's daughter Helen, who was the same age.[26] Edith continued to report long tales about William, and some of Ruthy, but baby Margaret is largely absent from her letters.

Elise soon got the distance she wanted. "Here is a secret. I am going to Manila next month," Edith confided to Ellen in September 1906. She had already sped through Europe from February through May; in addition to a month in her beloved Bath to ease her chronic knee problems, she had traveled to Italy and Scotland and visited Ruth Emerson Fletcher in London. Margaret Laighton, Edith's twenty-one-year-old secretary, accompanied her. Margaret was the daughter of an innkeeper on Appledore Island in the Isle of Shoals, and the niece of the author Celia Laighton Thaxter. Edith, often tough on the women who worked for her, raved soon after hiring Margaret, "I foresee she will be a treasure, intelligent, businesslike, and ready."[27] Will's sister Alice Forbes Cary also came along, but a case of the grippe had confined Alice to an English nursing home while Edith and Margaret continued on to Scotland and eventually home without her.[28] By this point, Edith had been to Europe so often that the trip, even with a disruption like Alice's illness, barely phased her.

This next voyage was a different undertaking. She would not just go to Manila, but Hong Kong, Japan, and India; she decided to come back via Greece and England, thus going around the world. She would be gone for over six months and traveling to places unfamiliar to her. Ralph did not want her to go, but Alexander and particularly Edward encouraged the trip.[29] It was a "secret" because Edith hoped to avoid long goodbyes by only telling her inner circle until the last minute. It was a new stage of the life of a traveler she had embraced since Will's death.

Cameron, of course, was her prime motivation. She missed him and was worried he would break down under the climate and the pressure of his job. As when Edward was at Oxford, she wanted to see the place her son lived. She recruited a group of younger women as her companions: her nieces Ellen Emerson, who was twenty-six, and Ellen Forbes, twenty, along with Susan Hallowell, the twenty-two-year-old daughter of family friends, and Mary McKay, her thirty-three-year-old maid, originally from Scotland.[30] Margaret Laighton rounded out the party. Margaret, however, would not be traveling as Edith's secretary, at least not on the second half of the adventure. She and Edward, now thirty-six, became engaged in October, after the trip was largely planned; Edward would join them in Manilla, where the couple would marry. The Emersons and Forbes celebrated their new family member, those who knew her sharing Edith's high estimation and everyone thrilled that gentle, scholarly Edward had found happiness.[31]

The party shot off at a whirlwind pace in late October, starting with a transcontinental train trip that brought them to their ship in San Francisco. In their few hours there, they ran around buying underwear, stockings, and toiletries after they realized several pieces of luggage had not been loaded on the train and would have to be sent on a separate steamer.³² It was then off to Honolulu on the SS *Coptic*, on which the two Ellens won prizes in a shooting competition. John and Agnes Galt met them at the boat and served as their guides during their few days on Oahu; John was a financier and Agnes was the granddaughter of one of first missionaries in Hawaii and the sister of George Carter, the second territorial governor of Hawaii. A friend of Cameron's arranged the connection, and it was the first of the many ways Cameron's circle and influence eased the path of his mother as she made her way to him. "Almost every tree except palms was new to me," Edith wrote with awe of a drive to Nu'uanu Pali Lookout. "I can't begin to give you any idea of the wonderful beauty of that view," she continued.³³

The *Coptic* next took them to Yokohama, Japan, where Cameron's personal secretary Conrad Hatheway greeted them. Cameron had sent Conrad and his wife Mable to escort the party. Mabel ushered Edith and her "girls" through excursions, shopping trips, and appointments with tailors, with Edith noting that the Hatheways "do everything for us." She continued, "Mrs. Hatheway helps us by going with us, and Conrad takes all cares."³⁴ Their tour included Tokyo, Kyoto, and Kobe, but, aside from the gardens, Japan did not capture Edith's imagination. At a "Shogun's Palace," she proclaimed, "I had seen enough and was not interested." She and the Hatheways "went out to toast ourselves in the blessed sunshine like true Philistines, such as I am."³⁵ In Japan the group picked up Langdon Warner, a friend of Waldo's from Harvard, whom the Museum of Fine Arts Boston had sent to Japan to study Asian art. Despite her open dislike of museums, Edith bonded with Langdon, who came with the Forbes party to Manila, finding him "charming, and most entertaining, and witty . . . a very cozy companion."³⁶ In Hong Kong, Edith was thrilled as they "mounted" into the air and "saw the harbour all dotted with steamers and little boats on the blue; and velvet mountains with light yellow tops on the ridges, shading into brown" from the funicular.³⁷ All of the sights and adventures of Hawaii, Japan, and Hong Kong, however, were merely a prelude to the main event waiting for her in the Philippines.

"I could make out Cameron (all white) sitting on the forward rail . . . the happy moment when my eyes could distinguish Cameron's eyes and smile soon came. And he called to me," Edith wrote of her sailing into the Manila harbor.³⁸ She loved his home in Manila, raving that "the whole decoration of the house is affecting me"; she particularly appreciated the photographs of the Emersons and Forbes found throughout the house. Cameron shared his mother's and Lidian's attention to detail; he had stocked a writing desk with paper and pens and a chair cut to the height he knew his mother preferred.[39] As the daughter of Ralph Waldo Emerson and the wife of William Forbes, Edith had grown used to receiving attention because of her association with the men in her life. The tradition continued in the Philippines. Throughout her stay, she was feted as the mother of Cameron Forbes at dinners, receptions, and calling hours of American expatriates.

Edith, once an anti-imperialist, saw only things to praise in Cameron's work. While noting that Filipinos had good reason not to like many Americans, she felt Cameron "is very courteous and courtly with them, and I think he has a great many friends among them."[40] Racist statements in his diaries suggest a different story. Manuel Quezon, a politician involved in the fight for independence, declared that Cameron loved Filipinos "in the same way the former slave owners loved their Negro slaves."[41] Cameron advocated for the "prosperity policy," arguing that developing the economy and infrastructure was more important than Philippine independence and that, moreover, Filipinos were not ready to control their own country.[42]

Edith's support of Cameron was due to more than motherly love. Her rant about the Irish in public schools and racist comments about her Black cook in Wyoming evidence a belief in white superiority that also undergirded American policies in the Philippines. Her prejudices about Irish and Black Americans were ugly, but they were not uncommon. Her imperialist position was different in that it was an active choice to reject the anti-imperialist stance she had once embraced and that was supported by people in her circle including her brother and friends William James and Moorfield Storey. She also could not claim ignorance of the violence that undergirded America's control. Six months before she left on her trip, debate over the morality of the American military's massacre of hundreds of people at Bud Dajo had played out in American newspapers; Storey published an outraged letter in the Boston *Daily Advertiser*.[43] Edith carefully tracked news of the Philippines, and how Cameron was covered, and she would have certainly known of this atrocity. Her embrace of imperialism was a far cry the declaration Lidian made in a letter to her children that, until the Emancipation Proclamation, she had always felt, "the Stars and Stripes were on the Flag of a nation at war against the dearest and most sacred rights of Humanity; to which I was sad to belong."[44]

Cameron's broad mandate included attracting investors, building roads and railroads, and helping develop the "winter capitol" of Baguio. This final item was a passion project for Cameron; he promoted and oversaw its development in the mountainous area 150 miles north of Manilla. He and other American leaders felt the town would be healthier during the heat of the summer and promote tourism. To bring the vision to fruition, the government seized fourteen thousand acres of land from the Igorots, the region's Indigenous people.[45] Cameron selected Daniel Burnham, the architect behind the "White City" at the World's Columbian Exposition, to plan this city, which included "large governmental buildings, commanding views" and "a grand axis cutting through the Baguio meadow."[46] Cameron founded the Baguio Country Club, which included a golf course and a polo field; only 6 of the original 161 members were Filipino. The historian Daniel Immerwhar describes it as "the architecture of power, plus golf."[47] Cameron also built his own home, Topside, in the area. While his family fretted that he was overworked, he noted in his diary in 1908 that in Baguio he and his colleagues only convened every few days for an hour or so. Baguio was certainly and most importantly part of the American imperialist project, but on the individual level it is also evidence of Cameron's connection to the world building of his mother and of Lidian. All three felt the need to shape and perfect their environment. But Cameron, a wealthy white man in an age in which America strove to make shows of strength beyond the borders of the continental United States, had an exponentially larger—and more devastating—canvas on which to work.

News of a family tragedy arrived from Concord. Florence Emerson Forbes died on December 30, at twenty-four years old. She had given birth to her second daughter, Edith Emerson Forbes, in September. The young mother had been "at the height of happiness, living in her Dedham house with Gerrit and her two delightful babies, enjoying them, enjoying life, enjoying keeping house, enjoying seeing and using her pretty things," according to Ellen.[48] But a case of the flu turned into pneumonia, and, despite the care of her father and several other doctors, seventeen days into her illness she passed away. Edward and Annie, enduring the loss of a fourth child, stoically gave thanks for the happiness Florence had during her short life. Having Ellen Jr., along with Edith, so far away made the difficult time even harder, however. Edith worried Ellen Jr. would always regret that she had decided to go on the journey, but Ellen did not feel her namesake should feel guilt. Her letters, Ellen told her sister, "did more for her family than her presence during Florence's sufferings would have," a true testament to the power with which the Emersons imbued correspondence.[49]

After consulting with her brother William via telegram, Ellen Jr. decided to cut her trip short but wait until after Edward and Margaret's wedding on January 29 to leave.[50] The ceremony at Cameron's Manila home was a joyous moment in the midst of mourning. Edith had asked Ellen to send her the marriage service from the King's Chapel prayer book, so that Bishop Charles Brent, an Episcopalian and friend of Cameron's who performed the ceremony, could read from it. Brent did insist on mentioning the Trinity, but Edward and Margaret were still happy to hear the words with which they were familiar.[51] Edith stood on the bride's side, having promised Margaret she would act as her mother and give her away. Cameron filled his home with flowers and plants—he had even brought in bamboo trees for the occasion—and everyone wore white. "Under the graceful bamboos our dear children in their snowy whiteness and lovely earnestness, making their vows which they are so sure to keep—every prospect of happiness before them," Edith reported to the family.[52] Edith's own marriage had been a source of ongoing pleasure, and she was thrilled when her children made their own partnerships. After the ceremony, Cameron presented the couple with a book containing the raft of congratulatory telegrams sent from the United States pasted into it; it included one from, in Edith's words, "the other six," meaning Ralph, Violet, Waldo and Alexander, along with Elise and Kenneth. Margaret was now a Forbes, and Edith counted herself as having nine children.[53]

While Edith welcomed a new family member, Ellen said goodbye to another. Cousin Hannah died "on the last hour" of Ellen's sixty-eighth birthday, marking a new stage in Ellen's life as she entered a new year.[54] Hannah, who was ninety-two, had broken her hip five weeks earlier and never gotten out of bed again. Ellen took Hannah's body to New York for burial. During the calling hours at St. Mark's Church in Brooklyn, Ellen insisted on opening the coffin so everyone could see "how beautiful" Hannah looked. She stayed with Haven, cherishing the chance to catch up with all of his family.[55] Ellen Jr. reported to Edith, "Apparently 'escorting Cousin Hannah to New York' was a most delightful journey to her & she saw all the cousins to the 10th & 12th degree & had a fine time."[56] With Hannah gone and Cousin Sarah no longer recognizing Ellen, she felt freer to leave Bush. Edith wanted to make sure this remained the case. "Don't take up any new duties—wait and let us have you," Edith wrote on hearing the news of Hannah's death.[57]

By the time Edith learned about Cousin Hannah, she was in Athens. On the way there, her travels had taken her, Ellen Forbes, Sue, Mary, Edward, and Margaret through Singapore, India, and Egypt. On the way to Calcutta, the Duke of Connaught, Queen Victoria's seventh child, was their fellow passenger; he was charmed as "the girls" looked for books in the ship's library and brought over a pile of "Illustrated News, Punch, and Daily and Weekly Graphics, which he said they had picked up in Singapore, and put them in Margaret's lap, asking if we would like to see them—in the pleasantest way."[58] If Japan had bored her, India delighted and surprised Edith. "And off we went through the finest and most exhilarating scenery—trees, pines, forests, wonderful engineering in zigzags and loops and double loops, climbing all the time, and looking through deep blue valleys, and fine mountain glooms occasionally—out to wide spread blue misty plain, melting into blue sky. It was all most beautiful near and far, trees of fine shades and heights trimmed with great creepers—once or twice a beautiful white trumpet flower," she raved about the Darjeeling Himalayan Railway.[59] It was cloudy when they visited the Taj Mahal, but "the Taj is the Taj, and beautiful in all lights," Edith concluded. She was also fascinated with the women's quarters at the Agra Fort and the "many provisions for entertaining the noble ladies who must not be seen by man."[60] In Egypt, she did "enjoy seeing the pyramids," but was disappointed that the light was behind the Sphinx and found the masses of tourists and beggars distracting. Once in Greece, the pace slowed a little. Edith found a day at the Acropolis "was more beautiful than anything yet, to me—though we have seen such various and wonderful landscapes and buildings." She continued, "We strolled about looking at the pictures framed by the golden columns, and I wished we might stay and spend every day there." She even enjoyed the Acropolis Museum, "especially grave stones with their family scenes."[61] A sore throat kept her from visiting the Delphi, but Edith welcomed the time to rest, especially as a heap of letters had arrived from home. On the train to Olympia, the party "had a 'competition' of writing out a list of all the flowers we remembered seeing in Greece," certainly Edith's idea of fun.[62]

Then it was off to Italy. Edith was thrilled to learn about pistachio trees, but complained of *The Last Supper*, "I liked it less than last year, and cannot understand why it is so highly rated."[63] Margaret and Edward headed to Rome, finally having time to themselves three months after they married. Meanwhile, Edith, Ellen Forbes, Sue, and Mary went to France and England. "Oh, how sweet and homelike England looked," Edith declared. She, of course, visited Ruth, whose health continued to flag. She did not make another pilgrimage to Bath, even as she complained the trip had caused her hair to fall out and her face to wrinkle.[64]

"I am glad to know your long circumnavigation has been happily accomplished," Haven wrote to Edith soon after her return via the S.S. *Arabic* in early May.[65] Edith had been away from home for ten of the last fifteen months.

She now focused on her family, sailing on the *Merlin* to Maine and enjoying Naushon with her descendants and siblings. Even as her children aged, she continued to worry. Ralph was hospitalized in the fall, and Alexander, now in Harvard Medical School, had developed hearing loss that she feared would interfere with his career as a doctor.[66]

A seemingly innocuous request from the New England Women's Club in November set off a debate about appropriate ways to memorialize Lidian. The club wanted to publish images of Waldo and Lidian in their next yearbook. Ellen only wanted to send an image of her father, believing Lidian's memory should be kept as "a private person."[67] While this association of women with the private sphere fit with her anti-suffrage stance, it seems at odds with Ellen's efforts to document her mother in her biography and even her tombstone. It does suggest why, unlike Sally Emerson, she never attempted to publish her book. Ellen read the manuscript to people in their circle, which in her estimation kept her mother's life private in a way publishing the biography would not. Edith had a different view, writing an ardent justification for publishing the picture which reads like an argument for women's history. "A man's choice of a wife is a large part of his history—and we do not half know it without seeing her. We have every reason to be proud of Mother and it is greatly to Father's credit that he had such a wife, and it seems only fair to both that his beautiful wife should be seen," she wrote to Ellen. She added, "in another edition of the memoirs or Edward's book, it would be only justice to her to stop hiding her, and let the world see she was worthy of him & she would think so herself I believe."[68] Her son Edward agreed with her, she made sure to include; when it turned out Edward Emerson also concurred, the siblings agreed to the publication of Lidian's image. Ellen had strong opinions and was not afraid to express them, but she valued harmony with her siblings above all.

"I do hope you will give me as much time as possible, and not keep running away," Edith wrote to Ellen while lobbying for her to spend Christmas and New Years in Milton. "Concord must be broke of 'expecting you,'" she added bluntly.[69] When Cousin Sarah Ansley died on Christmas Eve, it seemed as if Edith would have her wish. Edith began to plot to take Ellen to Wyoming for the summer. Edward Emerson and Waldo Forbes, meanwhile, wanted editorial help. Edward was in the process of making good on the pledge to publish his father's journals, assisted by Waldo, who would receive credit as co-editor. They called for an "Olympian Symposium" on Naushon during which family members would "spend ten days or two weeks in considering the journals and having an uninterrupted and peaceful time together."⁷⁰ The symposium did come to pass in March, with Edward, Waldo, Annie, Ellen and Edith spending days reading the material and voting on the inclusion of each passage Waldo and Edward had selected.⁷¹ The volumes were a family affair, even if only the names Waldo Forbes and Edward Emerson appeared on the title page.

Despite Edith's vision for the summer, it soon became clear that Ellen would not be up to any grand plans and could not even keep up with her regular duties. Her knee again hobbled her, and she was exhausted. In April, Edith escorted Ellen to the Homestead Hotel in Hot Springs, Virginia, where the sisters had gone in 1897. "Edith decreed that it was better for me not to keep house this summer and Edward agreed with her, so I submitted and she has taken me in hand and brought me here first to stay a month," Ellen explained to Mary Miller.⁷² Ellen stayed until September, while Edith went to Naushon. Freed from housekeeping, Ellen turned to historical analysis, critiquing Mary MacDermot Crawford's *Madame de Lafayette and Family*. "He doesn't understand the art of historical writing, and keeps thwarting me by leaving things at loose ends," she complained, assuming that Crawford, appearing as M. MacDermot Crawford on the title page, was a man. "I am diligently trying to correct and improve his book. It is perplexing work to unravel his snarls," she continued.⁷³ Ellen may not have wanted to publish her biography of her mother, but she had strong opinions as an author and editor, and as an Oxford student of history, about how to shape historical narratives.

The sisters had much to celebrate in the summer and fall. Ellen, as Edith had hoped, did spend the summer on Naushon. Cameron made a trip home, meaning Edith had all her children together. In June, Ellen was well enough to accept Anne Whitney's invitation to visit her in Shelburne, New Hampshire, even as she warned Whitney that she could not walk more than a half mile.⁷⁴ There were two babies: Margaret gave birth to Rosamond on October 14, and David, Ralph and Elise's fourth child, arrived fifteen days later. Ellen was thrilled to help with Edith's plan to sneak a baby basket into the nursery to surprise Margaret the week before Rosamond's birth and was honored when she was given the chance to meet the little girl on October 20 and hold her on her lap.⁷⁵

Perhaps the biggest news was that Cameron was promoted to Vice Governor of the Philippines. Again, the news generated chatter and debate among his relatives. Ralph was openly critical. He had "hoped to persuade him to never go back" from the summer visit and was "sure first that he will lose his health irrevocably" and that "all his labor and interest there will count for nothing and vanish like a cloud in a year or two after he gets through," Ellen reported to her brother and Annie. Edward Forbes and even Edith agreed "in some measure," although they were "delighted for Cameron's sake." In writing her brother, Ellen pronounced, "I supposed you agree entirely with Ralph," suggesting Edward's anti-imperialist views had not softened to support his nephew.[76] Despite the family qualms, Cameron accepted the position and headed back. While he was still in Boston, he gave a speech at the Twentieth Century Club, "headquarters of anti-Imperialists," according to Edith, where she cheered his ability, in her estimation, to cut down their arguments with humor and charm.[77]

"In the past fortnight, there has been a sudden [increase] of symptoms hard to explain and causing much discomfort."[78] Edward gave Anne Whitney this grim update on Ellen on November 6, 1908. Ellen had collapsed during a visit to Violet and Kenneth, with a doctor ordering her to bed in their Ash Street home. Edith soon arranged to move Ellen to Milton, settling her in the "green room" and hiring day and night nurses. While the arrangement made Ellen more comfortable, by the middle of the December her doctors only allowed her one visitor a day and she did not have the energy to write or even dictate letters.[79] She was eventually diagnosed with ovarian cancer.[80] As it became clear he would not see her again, Haven, who had suffered a stroke in February, wrote a touching note to Edith reflecting on his last visit with Ellen. "It was a great pleasure to us," he wrote, "as it has been all my life to talk with her, although I have not always had so large a share in it."[81]

"We all stood round Aunt Ellen's bed on New Year's Day, and each in turn received her New Year's greeting—and Good-bye," Violet reported to Cameron. Understanding she would not recover, Ellen asked that her family gather together in her sick room on January 1st. Ellen "rejoiced" to see her nieces, nephews, grandnieces, and grandnephews together, with only Cameron missing. Ellen cuddled the babies and hugged and kissed each family member, wishing them a Happy New Year individually and sometimes whispering "goodbye." Violet had worried it would be impossibly sad, but Ellen "did not make it a leave taking, and regarded it as the festival [so] that it was not hard to bear as I had feared it would be."[82]

The end came two weeks after Ellen's "festival." Edith and Edward were her constant companions in her final days, when she rarely spoke. The siblings' editor instincts helped them through this limbo, as they planned her funeral service while Ellen floated on morphine. Edith "took the service book and collected detached single sentences and arranged them to describe Ellen's life in the first person."[83] "It is a stroke of genius," Edward marveled when he read it. Edward "welded" together the selections from their father's journals that he, Edith, and Waldo had chosen for the service.[84] On the evening of January 14, five weeks before Ellen's seventieth birthday, "a beautiful look of perfect peace came over the dear face" as she passed.[85] In Concord, the church tolled its bell sixty-nine times to announce her death, reviving an old tradition for a favorite daughter. "The town may truly mourn—she was an influence and a presence such as will never be there again," Edith reflected.[86]

The funeral service was held on Sunday, January 17. Despite hail and snow, mourners filled a "special car" from Boston and Concord folks marched through the storm to fill the church. Violet draped Ellen's body in a shroud so "beautifully" that she looked like a "statue of a holy saint." Ellen's nephews served as pall bearers, carrying the coffin covered with flowers sent by friends. "How much her bearers would have pleased her," Edith mused. Ellen's pew was filled with white roses. Ned Bartlett, one of Edward's oldest friends, managed the ceremony and Loren MacDonald, the Concord minister since 1895, led the service. Edith and Edward made it a "keynote of the day" that Ellen's death should not be mourned. Though it was a "sad breakup and loss" for them, Edith reminded people that "it would have been sadder yet to have her suffer old age or invalid life."[87] In the evening, Edith read aloud some of Ellen's 1866 letters to friends and family, an appropriate way to pay homage to the sister whose correspondence had been a touchstone of her life.[88]

The woman who devoted much of her time to memorializing others was much memorialized herself. Obituaries and death notices appeared not only in Boston papers, but across the country. The headlines and main thrust of these pieces focused on her relationship with and care for her father, but many noted the other ways she served her community. The Boston *Globe* referred to her Sunday School teaching and participation in the Union Bible Society; Ellen's genealogist's heart would have been broken by the fact that the obituary identified Edith as the widow of J. Malcom Forbes, not William.[89] The *New Orleans Times-Democrat* took the opportunity to lobby for Bush to be preserved, noting, "The Home of Emerson should be kept as a sacred historic place, to which his lovers might always make their reverent pilgrimage."[90] The Fitchburg *Weekly Sentinel*, meanwhile, felt compelled to include, "She was not one who followed woman's dress fashions closely, but she was respected none the less."[91]

Longer tributes appeared in the following months. Elizabeth Powell Bond, the first dean of Swarthmore College, and A. W. Jackson, a Unitarian minister, wrote extensive remembrances for, respectively, the Quaker *Friends' Intelligencer* and the Unitarian *Christian Register*. Loren MacDonald delivered a memorial service at the Concord church on January 24. James Herbert Morse, a poet and the brother-in-law of Sally Gibbons Emerson, wrote a tribute to Ellen found in her papers, although it is unclear where he delivered it.[92] Not surprisingly, these tributes focus on her faith, her care for her parents, and her devotion to and love of her family and Concord. They also depict her as the embodiment of her father's ideas about individualism. Jackson notes, "in her the Emersonian philosophy of life became flesh and dwelt among us," and MacDonald states she was "eminently true to her own nature, frankly loyal to her own thought, even when it led her to differ from the views of him she loved and honored."

Oddly, these authors all stress that Ellen was not a writer. "She has not written books nor made pictures nor statues but she has lived the best that is in books and in the artist's achievements," Bond concludes, while Morse claims, "she never wrote a line for publication." Jackson contrasts the idea that she was the fleshly embodiment of her father's philosophy with the statement, "She wrote no Consuelo, no 'Middlemarch,'" and MacDonald says her genius was not in the form of "literary expression." This stress on what she did not do would be strange in any case, given that obituaries usually focus on what their subjects *did* accomplish. But it is even stranger in Ellen's case, given her work on her father's essays and her biography of her mother. The authors all knew Ellen even if they were not in her inner circle, and they must have been aware of these efforts. Jackson in fact quotes Oliver Holmes' biography of Waldo, which referred to Ellen "bringing order to the chaos of his manuscript" as Waldo's memory failed. The tombstone that Edward and Edith erected continued this theme, even though they certainly knew the extent of her efforts. As wordy as Lidian's, it states that while "of a fine mind" Ellen "cared more for persons than books."[93] These tributes do capture essential parts of Ellen's life. But they also obscure a critical element of her contributions.

One remembrance differs significantly. Edith and Edward printed a booklet that gathered the texts from Ellen's funeral service and MacDonald's memorial sermon, along with a sketch of Ellen's life.[94] They asked Elizabeth Hoar Storer, Elizabeth Hoar's niece, to write the biographical sketch. Storer wrote more than they expected, and took longer than they hoped, but she ran everything by Edward, who made only slight "additions and alterations."[95] Storer, who had also gone to the Agassiz School, stresses Ellen's education and her travel, not just her faith and caregiving. Listing her schools, Storer explains Ellen "made her mark as a girl of high ability and principle." Including extensive biographical information on Lidian, she notes pointedly that while Ellen's connection to and inheritance from her father is "well known ... perhaps the large part taken by her mother in the forming of her character may not be fully recognized." Ellen's work with her father's later essays is also acknowledged. "For ten years Ellen was to her father eyes, hands, and memory. Her straightforward simplicity made it seem pleasant and natural for her to watch over him, and to help him with suggestions and in the arrangement of his papers in his later lectures," Storer writes. The committees on which Ellen served, her role as family historian, her deep connection to her siblings and nieces and nephews, her insight as a reader, and her love of dancing all rate specific mention. "We do not know why the forces of rare inheritance, influence, and opportunity made our Ellen Emerson, but we are glad she was made exactly the person she was, and we rejoice that we have known her to love and delight in her," she concludes.[96]

Given her negative response to the New England Women's Club's request to publish Lidian's portrait, and her belief that women's lives should remain "private," Ellen may have been dismayed by these public tributes. But she did also memorialize herself, through her will. She left funds to the Massachusetts Society for the Prevention of Cruelty to Animals, an organization dear to Lidian's heart; to the Concord Manual Training School; to the Concord First Parish's Committee on Domestic Charities; and to the campaign for playground and parks in Concord, a cause for which Edward had been raising money.[97] She thus honored her family, her town, and her church, the three pillars of her life. Her contribution to the First Parish was very specific. She left $3,500 to fund an annual gift to "a daughter (or daughters) who living at home are supporting parents in straightened circumstances." She asked that the donation go to the same woman each year until her parents died, then be given to another family; the money, she hoped, would "save them much corroding anxiety."[98]

This final bequest allowed Ellen to honor her life as a single woman and caregiver. Her sister's wealth and her father's fame had eased her path, even when faced with the challenges of caring for elderly people with memory loss. She had been able to stay in Bush after her parents' deaths and even make a home for other single women and widows. But, as her advice to Sally Gibbons Emerson and Mary Miller about investing and setting up a household makes clear, the financial security and happiness of single women concerned her. She wanted her legacy to include helping those in her community feel valued for the work they did in caring for their families, while easing their financial worries. This was the memorial Ellen created for herself.

CHAPTER ELEVEN

"Wherever She Went, She Planted a Garden"

(1909–1929)

Edith was sixty-seven when Ellen died. While she and her brother were grateful Ellen had been spared a long decline, soon the depth of the loss hit them. As Edward wrote to Edith in May, "I begin to feel Ellen's absence now—at first the relief was too great."[1] Edith's loss, however, did not mean she was done being a force in the world, nor did it mean she was alone in the world. Her roles as mother, grandmother, sister, aunt, traveler, lively and cherished correspondent, and editor continued to develop throughout the twenty years she survived Ellen.

Edith dealt with her grief over Ellen with the same tactics she had handled other losses—putting things in order and staying on the move. Within a week of her sister's death, she and Annie began gathering Ellen's clothes for distribution among friends and charities.[2] They also set aside small tokens, such as books, that Ellen had wished given to her friends and family. Edith outfitted Lidian's room with a new bed, washstand curtains, and furniture covers.[3] She invested in the property because Ellen's "ladies" Helen Legate and Grace Heard were remaining in Bush. After days spent working through Ellen's things, Edith, Annie, and Edward often sat down to reminisce with Helen and Grace and read Ellen's letters.

Edith had bigger plans for the letters. She had decided to assemble a typescript of Ellen's correspondence for the family, a more formal version of the gathering and copying of family letters she had done for years. Edith often notes in her diary that she is reading and marking the letters, at times working with Violet. When Edith and Waldo made their way to Florida, she used her travel time for this task.[4] She had the letters that Ellen had sent her, but she also collected them from friends and family members.⁵ "Miss Bessie," a Scottish woman serving as Edith's secretary whose name was Margaret Neill, typed them.⁶ As Ellen had with her biography of her mother, Edith took the project of memorializing her sister through her letters seriously.

The original letters held in the Houghton Library at Harvard and the Massachusetts Historical Society bear the marks of Edith's work. She added dates, marked letters with "omit" and "start" to indicate what to include, and sometimes penciled in brief contextual information. The final typescript runs seventeen volumes, dated from 1850 through 1908, plus a few letters about Ellen written after her death; the Houghton and the Concord Free Public Library both hold copies. The volumes include at least partial transcriptions of the majority of the letters found in the *Ellen Tucker Emerson Correspondence*; some letters found in the Forbes correspondence; and correspondence, primarily to friends, where the location of the originals is not known. While most of the letters are by Ellen, Edith occasionally inserted letters from others—often Edward—that provide information about her sister and context for the events in Ellen's correspondence. Throughout the typescript, someone has traced the illustrations Ellen added to her originals onto the typing paper, capturing her whimsy and artistic skill.

Edith made editorial decisions with an eye towards a family audience. Many of the letters are only short excerpts, often with a focus on details about the Forbes children or other family concerns. In the lead up to her father's death, for instance, Edith edits the letters to tell primarily the trajectory of his illness, cutting out social news and details about work with Cabot to keep the narrative on Waldo's final days.⁷ In other cases, however, she includes multi-page letters, such as those to Clara Dabney in which Ellen spells out her ideas about religion and morality in more detail than in letters to her family.⁸ Some of Edith's choices seem not motivated by narrative clarity, but to protect a family member or erase a negative memory. In a letter Ellen wrote during the 1878 scarlet fever siege at the Forbes House, she noted, "Mother says Scarlet Fever never created any panic in her house. She thinks it won't in yours."⁹ The remark is inexplicable, particularly given young Waldo's death. Edith edited it out.¹⁰

While Edith dealt with her grief by keeping busy, her brother and oldest son worried about her hectic schedule. They consulted with her doctor, "plotting" to encourage her to slow down. When she agreed, Edward thanked her for her "willingness to try to go at a pace more safe for your years." He added, "you are very dear to me, to us, and we want you *long*."¹¹ Edward soon had more reason to fear tragedy lurked around the corner. His son William Forbes Emerson died on June 24 after a short, steep decline from pneumonia while working in Chicago. It was shocking that the vibrant twenty-five-year-old, "remembered as the most energetic and active man" in his Harvard class, should go so quickly.[12] And it was heartbreaking that Edward and Annie should endure the loss of a fifth child. As with Ellen, Edith helped Edward and Waldo identify passages from her father's journals for the service, then found another way to memorialize her nephew.[13] William had wanted to install electric lights in his parent's home, and Edith honored his memory by underwriting the project. Edward thanked her for her "most characteristically ingenious and large beneficence in wishing to carry out William's plan for his Mother's comfort of lighting the house."[14]

"I was alone & breakfasting in my room & reading Cameron's words at his inauguration—when Alexander telephoned" with the news that Violet "had a daughter," Edith wrote in her journal on November 24, 1909.[15] Cameron had been promoted to governor-general of the Philippines earlier in the month, and the formal inauguration took place that day. On most days, in most families, that would be the main news. But Violet giving birth to her first child, named Edith Emerson Forester, rivaled or even surpassed it. At forty-two, Violet was just a year younger than Edith when she gave birth to her eighth child, and the baby arrived at least a month early.[16] But the little girl was healthy at seven pounds. Edith appeared in Cambridge "with a carriage load of baby baskets" within hours.[17] She already had five grandchildren, including two granddaughters, but this daughter of her daughter was a special joy. "Thanksgiving Day Indeed!" Edith started her journal the day after the baby's birth, as some of the family gathered for the annual feast.[18] In addition to Cameron's inauguration and Violet's baby, the month had brought the news of Waldo's engagement to his cousin Ellen Forbes, Malcolm and Sarah's daughter.[19] In a year that started with loss and weathered more, the family gave true thanks that they now had so much to celebrate.

Despite her promise to slow down, Edith's life moved at a good clip in 1910. Waldo married Ellen Forbes on January 20.[20] In June, Alexander graduated from Harvard Medical School and married Charlotte Grinnell after a six-month engagement.[21] Now all of Edith's children except Cameron were settled down and living near her. There were more grandchildren; Margaret gave birth to John Murray Forbes on July 14 and Waldo and Ellen were expecting a baby in December.[22] As much as Edith adored her descendants, however, she was not going to limit her life to that of doting grandmother. By March, she was planning another around-the-world tour, hoping to convince Ellen Jr. to go with her.[23]

Edith set sail on the SS *Arabic* at the end of August. For her second circumnavigation of the globe, she sailed east across the Atlantic. Only her maid Mary McKay accompanied her on the ship, but Edith had arranged for a series of companions on different legs of the trip.[24] Her first stop was England, where she had a heart wrenching duty. Ruth Emerson Fletcher had succumbed to tuberculosis in April, and Edith visited her widower and his two daughters in the English countryside. It was then on to her beloved Bath, where she found the water cure "as delicious" as ever.[25] Eleanor Whiteside, a friend who was the sister of Boston doctor George Shattuck and the widow of businessman Alexander Whiteside, joined her.[26]

"I saw a loaded omnibus coming and leaned out and read E.W.F. on top of the load!" Edith reported to her family in early October.[27] Edith spotted the luggage from her window in London's Garlant's Hotel, where she moved from Bath while Eleanor headed home. The omnibus also brought the luggage's owner—Edward Waldo Forbes—and "the girls": Ellen Jr., now thirty, and Charlotte Hemenway, the twenty-year-old daughter of Boston philanthropists and family friends Harriet and Augustus Hemenway.[28] Ellen Jr. had been hesitant to leave her parents after their difficult losses, but Edward was grateful his dutiful daughter had this opportunity. "I am most thankful that the doors of youth, which seemed shutting to some extent, owing to Ellen's work and Concord's limited supply of young people, have been, on this trip, driven open wide again," he wrote Edith.[29] Eleanor Greene, age twenty-two, would join them in Genoa; she was going to visit her brother Warwick, Director of the Bureau of Public Works in Manila.[30] Edith cherished the opportunity to give younger people an opportunity to travel. Just as when her nephew William accompanied her to California years earlier, seeing places through new eyes kept her from being jaded. She also loved youthful chatter and gaiety, sounds she had grown used to as she raised her large family.

After a few days of shopping, including buying Ellen and Charlotte each a "party cloak" at Liberty's of London, the group took off across Europe at Edith's usual breakneck pace for a fortnight. A train strike in France caused them to change their route, so they streaked through Amsterdam, Cologne, Basel, and Milan. "It was good by to dear Edward" in Milan; he headed to his job as director of Harvard's recently founded Fogg Art Museum. They boarded the *SS Kleist* in Genoa on October 20, joined by Eleanor, Mary Williams, the daughter of a Boston banker, and Mary Boreham, one of the Dabneys.[31]

Over the next month, the *Kleist* wended its way from Genoa to Hong Kong, with ports of call including Port Said, Ceylon (now the Democratic Socialist Republic of Sri Lanka), Penang, and Singapore. Edith loved Ceylon, where they took "a ride that was most exciting and thrilling to us all—so beautiful and different from any we had ever seen."[32] The Penang botanical gardens disappointed her, however, because "they had taken a fine piece of wild land with beautiful native plants and left many of them but did not consider them worth labeling."[33] Onboard activities included an "exercise room" where Edith was "'vibrated' by the steward with a metal electric fist" while Mary Boreham sat in a machine that "vibrates thoroughly both arms and legs"; the younger members of the party rode an electric camel and electric horse.[34] Edith needed the treatment because she had fallen and hurt her knee while chasing down the purser to complain about Mary McKay's accommodations.[35] Mary Boreham began to teach everyone but Edith Spanish. Charlotte and Eleanor charmed a group of German midshipmen "being sent out to the Asiatic Squadron," playing cards with them while the older women chaperoned.[36] Mary Williams and Mary Boreham disembarked at Colombo to set off on a tour of India.

Even as Edith traveled around the world, her sister was on her mind. Edward had urged her not to carry "trunks of work" with her, but she spent much of her time editing Ellen's letters.[37] One batch was ready by the time she parted with Eleanor Whiteside, who took them to Milton for Miss Bessie to type.[38] On the *Kleist*, Edith spent time "inking over some of Aunt Ellen's pencil letters," which she "found so charming" that she devoted a whole day to reading Ellen's correspondence from 1877 and 1878.[39] Once in Manilla, she read Ellen's letters aloud to others for entertainment.[40] Memory of Ellen must have inspired Edith to read *Angel in the House*, along with Waldo's essay "Fate," to Charlotte and Eleanor while still onboard. Ellen was the one who had loved the poem and lobbied to include it in *Parnassus*, and Patmore's depiction of demure, female domesticity was closer to Ellen's ethos than Edith's; Edith loved her home, her children, and her marriage, but she did not tend towards self-sacrifice. Choosing to read it to the "girls" was another tribute to her sister.[41]

The final few days on the *Kleist* exhausted everyone. "I should say the Flood had arrived, it is called a Monsoon here," Edith reported.[42] As the ship slowed to eight knots an hour Edith's room was as "dark as a pocket," and she found sleep elusive as the wind "roared so and whistled through the night."[43] They did not need to worry about missing their connection at Hong Kong, though. Cameron had arranged for the SS *Zafario* to delay its departure for Manila until his mother arrived, to the dismay of its other passengers.[44] Once they finally sailed into port, reliable Conrad Hatheway, again sent by Cameron, was there to assist with the transfer of their large pile of luggage between ships.[45]

The "rattle of the anchor chains" woke Edith at five in the morning on November 21. After three more rough days at sea, the *Zafario* had made it to Manila Bay. She soon spotted Cameron headed towards them on a "chair in the middle of the forward deck" of a launch; he ran up the gangway and Edith "had him at last."[46] Cameron's elevated status was immediately evident. He now lived in the sprawling Malacañan Palace, the official residence and workplace of the governor-general. The robin's-egg blue walls of his bedroom, which he gave over to Edith, were again covered with photographs of Forbes and Emersons, along with sketches and watercolors of Concord, Manadnock, Milton, and Naushon; a picture of Daniel Chester French's *The Minute Man* hung over a wardrobe, apparently without irony. "As before the pictures that make his home are very affecting to me," Edith reported to her other children.[47] Now, however, his private quarters rested among a sprawling complex of government buildings. Before Edith hosted her first reception, she searched for a spot "where we could make a home corner in these great halls" and contemplated "how to take away the public building aspect."[48] She eventually decorated the music room with flowers, books, and textiles purchased on her trip and rearranged the furniture to make a welcoming space.

Edith was feted as "Señora Madre" throughout her time in Philippines. The honors given to her increased over her last trip, commensurate with Cameron's higher status. Cameron was not married—and would never marry—and Edith served as his hostess and representative; when she was too tired, Ellen Jr. stepped in. She visited not just Manila and Baguio but locations throughout the archipelago, as they sailed to different provinces on the SS *Rizal*. Edith was showered with gifts at receptions, dinners and lunches, reviews of military troops, and tours of schools, hospitals, and orphanages. While many were small tokens—such as flowers, silk handkerchiefs, and pieces of embroidery—some were valuable, including an enormous diamond ring sent to her by one of the provincial governors.[49] Edith accepted them all unquestioningly as her and Cameron's due, a way to honor her for raising such a fine son and honor the work he had done. That these gifts were a way to earn his favor did not enter her mind.

Edith remained stalwart in her support of Cameron's mission and American actions in the Philippines. "I am so proud of his tact and skill like Grandpa Forbes and Papa who would have been so proud of him!" she announced in a letter home.⁵⁰ In 1898, Edith had said of the Spanish-American War, "how grievous and humiliating is the conduct of our government."⁵¹ Now she was all praise when touring Bilibid Prison, concluding, "I suppose the prisoners never had such good food, good care of their health and opportunity to do good work and have fresh air and exercise combined, and teaching as they do now."⁵² She dismissed any criticism of Cameron and spoke derisively of anti-imperialists, despite the fact that they filled her inner circle.

Filipino nationalists did court Edith, making their criticism impossible for her to ignore completely. Simeon Mandac, the former provincial governor of Ilocos Norte who had been sentenced to prison for twenty years after leading an uprising in the province of Nueva Vizcaya that autumn, sent her a "flowery welcome" asking her to use her "influence with the Governor" to "restore" him to "the arms" of his wife and children. Edith instead reported to her own children that a "murderer" had contacted her.⁵³ Edith liked Gregorio Aglipay, a revolutionary and former Catholic clergyman who had founded the Philippine Independent Church, calling him the "cheerful comfortable priest." On his invitation, she agreed to meet with him and Cameron. Aglipay presented an "Inserecto," or a "call on the people to rise and overthrow the government." Cameron responded, in Spanish, "It would turn out like the other rising made by his friend Mandaue!" a reference to a city in which American troops killed the municipal president in 1901.⁵⁴ These direct appeals, and her son's offhand reference to American military violence, did no more to change her mind than her close association with anti-imperialists did. She paid more attention to the polo community Cameron helped build up, both in Manila and Baguio. She cheered him on at matches on the polo fields he had helped establish in both cities. She reported, with no skepticism, "Everyone from Gen. Duvall down tells me nobody ever did so much for Manila as Cameron in giving this polo field, and it makes such a difference in the life."⁵⁵

Edith's shocking statements appear in her long journal letters to her family. Side-by-side with her pro-imperialist views are her detailed descriptions of what she encountered. There were technical wonders, such as watching an "aeroplane" take off and circle the crowd at the Carnival in Manila.⁵⁶ She loved the glass-bottom boats which allowed her to see aquatic life, marveling at the "beautiful colours below, the beds of heliotrope or lilac corals or sea anemones, or weeds, brown ferns, white and green and brown or blue coral or sponges, and fishes ... striped with yellow black red green and blue like Roman sashes or one way of a Scotch plaid."⁵⁷ She took care to record small delights such as a "speedy crab rushing across the beach to the water, or going as smoothly and fast as an automobile."⁵⁸ Of course, it was still the flora to which she responded the most. When she packed to leave at the beginning of March, her luggage included a trunk stuffed with plants.⁵⁹

On March 4, "a crowd of friends and officials" came to see off Edith, Ellen Jr., and Eleanor Greene, with Conrad Hatheway along to help them in Hong Kong.⁶⁰ There, they switched to the SS *Korea* for the month-long trip to California. The president of the shipping company had arranged for Edith to book a suite on the same terms of a regular stateroom, because "the Company was indebted to the Governor-General for so much help."⁶¹ She enjoyed the stop in Shanghai. A lover of gardens and gravesites, she was fascinated to report, "The country is most singular wherever there are not houses—are vegetable gardens and graves, every bit of space between the groups of graves is utilized for raising things for market. The graves therefore are not in consecrated ground but everywhere."⁶² In Kyoto, there was a joyful reunion with Mary Boreham and Mary Williams, along with Langdon Warner. She was happy to have Langdon's "careful vigilance" at a temple, where she found herself "an especial object of curiosity and wonder with my grey hair and black clothes and bonnet" and one of the "pilgrims" "pulled my veil hard behind!"⁶³ The final stop was Honolulu, where the sea creatures at the Aquarium, with "all its wonders of beauty, grace, horror, freaks, and funniest flights of fancy," fascinated her. She also collected more plants at the Government Agricultural Station for her greenhouse. John Galt made sure "a basket of strange fruits," including pineapples, papayas, and water lemons, was in her stateroom as the ship pulled out for the last stage of the voyage.⁶⁴

Edith had enjoyed her trip but was anxious to get home, and she jumped on a train the day after the *Korea* sailed into San Francisco on April 6. On April 13, "my two Edwards came on board the train" in Worcester, Massachusetts, to accompany her for the final leg. Edward Forbes, joined by Alexander at the Milton station, drove Edith to the house in which she still felt Will's presence protecting her. "Ralph & his elder four, Violet and Baby Edith, Margaret, Rosamond & John, Waldo & Ellen & Baby Stephen & Charlotte were on the doorstep," as they pulled up. "The sight of three mothers with babies in arms and five children standing before them & my four sons & four daughters was too beautiful."⁶⁵ The scene included two new grandchildren. Waldo and Ellen's Stephen had arrived in December, and Elise had given birth to Pauline while Edith was on the train home.⁶⁶ Alexander's wife Charlotte had a son, Lawrence, four days after Edith's return, but he died the same day.⁶⁷ Helen Forbes, Edward's six-year-old granddaughter whom he and Annie had been raising since Florence's death, died in May, of blood poisoning stemming from pneumonia.⁶⁸ In this whiplash between joyous reunions and celebrations of new life and the mourning of two young souls, Edith was again immersed in the throes of domestic life.

Edith had taken care to preserve and organize Ellen's letters, gathering them from friends, editing them, and creating a typescript for her family. She gave her own correspondence for her "trips around the globe" the same treatment, curating edited typescripts. For the first trip she interspersed, delightfully, her "Kodaks" as well. In the Edith Emerson Forbes and William Hathaway Forbes Collection at the Massachusetts Historical Society, the typescripts are nestled in folders next to the original letters, along with invitations, programs, ships manifests, and other ephemera collected on the trips. Edith saw the value in her experiences and ensured her record of them was preserved, for her children and for future generations.

The correspondence from the second trip is the last major collection of Edith's letters. If someone collected her correspondence from her final years, it did not make it to the archives. There are dozens of folders in the Forbes collection dated after 1911, but they are primarily letters to Edith—from her children, from cousins and friends, sometimes from mere acquaintances. Only a few scattered missives written by Edith herself are interspersed among them. The collection includes her daily diaries, but she was an inconsistent and concise diarist. She did not use journals primarily to reflect on her feelings or inner thoughts, but to record events. In the small books, allotting at most a page for each day, she sometimes filled out each entry for weeks in a row, but she often skipped months or almost whole years; there are no journals after 1924. Her experiences can be pieced together through the diaries and the correspondence of her circle, along with sources like newspaper articles and financial records. But without her letters, the thoughtful, loving, funny, and at times caustic and offensive, voice that documents her experiences in novelistic and exhaustive detail disappears for the last eighteen years of her life. Yet her life in those years contained significant events worthy of examination, even if at a distance.

Edith swerved between her domestic life in Milton and her life as a traveler in the years following her second trip to the Philippines. When home, she focused on her family, loving the time she spent with her growing number of descendants. On September 3, 1911, for instance, she labeled her diary entry "Perfect Day." Edith took a drive around Naushon with Violet and Edward, collected moss for her garden, worked on her Japanese garden with Violet, and hosted Ralph and his children for dinner. She capped off the day by reading to her grandchildren, a favorite activity since her own children were small.[69]

Such days were satisfying—perfect—but they did not quell Edith's travel bug. Her father's life had faded as he lost his memory and ability to speak, her mother, for all her intelligence, at times retreated to her bed chamber, her dynamic husband's life had been cut short. Edith was determined to remain active and seek out new experiences. She would not be her mother, and she would honor her husband in doing what he did not have the chance to do.

In 1912, Edith explored Portugal and Spain for the first time, again with Eleanor Whiteside, along with Bessie Neill and Mary McKay. In Seville, they met with Alice Gould, a forty-four-year-old graduate of Bryn Mawr who had also studied mathematics at Massachusetts Institute of Technology and written a biography of Louis Agassiz. Alice was researching Columbus, and she took the party to the Archives of the Indies to see the "Papal Bull dividing the world between Portugal & Spain & autographs of many kings and explorers" and the Columbian Library to see Columbus' "own writing and books."[70] Gould accompanied the group to Paris. Edith, Eleanor, and Bessie then traveled to Bath, yet again, while Mary visited her family in Orkney. Edith reunited with Alexander and Charlotte in England, where Alexander was finishing up a year of working with British scientists on human reflex pathways in Liverpool and Cambridge; he was returning to Harvard to teach in the Department of Physiology. Cameron joined them in London, sailing to Boston with his mother, brother, and sister-in-law on the SS *Lusitania* on April 27. The sinking of the *Titanic* less than two weeks before they left shook them, but not enough to keep them from heading home.[71] Ralph, Edward, and Waldo met their ship in Boston and Edith was overjoyed to see "my five sons together." The following day she met her newest grandson, Frederick Augustus Webster, born to Violet on April 3.[72]

The next year proved difficult for the Forbes. In January, Waldo had surgery to remove a tumor the same week Alexander needed surgery to repair a broken arm.[73] Edith was felled by the flu and jaundice on a trip to California with her brother Edward and Annie in March; her children waited anxiously for updates from across the country.[74] Haven Emerson, so close to Ellen, Edith, and Edward their entire lives, died on May 4.[75] The election of Woodrow Wilson in November 1912 ended Cameron's position in the Philippines; the new president, a Democrat, asked for the resignation of Cameron, a Republican appointee, by September 1, 1913.[76] Most devastatingly, Alexander and Charlotte's baby, Robert

Irving, died soon after his birth on February 11, the second son they lost as a newborn. "I am filled with sympathy for the poor young parents & for you, dear friend. Our children's sorrows are harder to bear than our own," Eleanor Whiteside wrote to Edith in condolence.[77]

In the midst of six brutal months, there was some happy news. Raymond Emerson wed Amelia Forbes, the daughter of Sarah and Malcolm, on April 12. Before her marriage, Amelia served as a nurse in missionary hospitals in Newfoundland. "Leaves Labrador to Wed: Amelia Forbes, Society Girl Nurse, to Marry Raymond Emerson," the *New York Times* announced.[78] Edith helped facilitate the union. As Will had done for Edward Emerson in 1871, she gave Raymond a gift of money that allowed him to feel financially secure enough to set a date. "We hope to be married sometime this year and your help to me at this time has made a great deal of difference," Raymond wrote his aunt in January. He invested the money and committed to spending only the interest, hoping to pay forward his good fortune. He explained, "I shall make a point of using it at some time in the future to lend a hand to some other fellow and if it can bring half the happiness I know that it will bring me I think that it will be mighty well invested."[79] While Edith could be overbearing, her generosity also could make a genuine difference in people's lives.

In 1914, Edith busied herself with tributes and memorials, for her own family and those of others. On May 23, she and Edward attended the celebration for the unveiling of Daniel Chester French's full-size sculpture of a seated Waldo in the Concord Free Public Library.[80] A committee had spent over the decade to raise the money to pay French, the Concord native who had found fame through *The Minute Man* and his bust of Waldo. Edith lent French her father's long dark blue robe, a marble replica of which hangs over the chair in the piece.[81] Edith donated the clay model of French's bust of Waldo to Harvard in 1916 and paid for a bonze version to be cast; it was displayed in Emerson Hall.[82]

Edith also put her energies towards memorializing another Concord family. Sophia and Una Hawthorne each died in England in 1871 and 1877, respectively, and were buried in London's Kensal Green in London. Edith wanted to clean up the Hawthorne lot in Sleepy Hollow, add a marker explaining where Sophia and Una were interred, and landscape the London Hawthorne site and add a stone for Una. Edith first corresponded about the issues with Rose Hawthorne Lathrop, Una's younger sister, in 1902. Rose, a widow, had converted to Catholicism and founded the Servants of Relief for Incurable Cancer, a religious order serving impoverished patients, and was now called Mother Mary Alphonsa. She valued Edith's efforts, but was focused on her nursing work and worried about the money. Although the first effort faded away, Edith took it up the again in 1914. She eventually got Kenneth Havers, the secretary of the General Cemetery Company which oversaw Kensal Green, to agree to make repairs using funds available through the Dilapidated Monuments Act of Parliament and to give her permission to install Una's stone. Edith also finally arranged for the Sleepy Hollow markers, likely underwriting everything.[83] "Not only the living rise up and call you beloved, but the dead also," Rose wrote Edith in thanks in 1918, as the Sleepy Hollow work came to a close.[84]

On June 9, 1914, Edith again sailed for Britain, looking forward to a restful, restorative summer in Scotland and Bath. She was traveling with Lucia Bartlett, the Plymouth woman who had taught at the Milton Academy. "I am anticipating some happy weeks," Lucia told Anne Whitney. She explained they would first spend time "motoring to lovely places" in Scotland and "go to Southern England."[85] The world had other plans. Edith and Lucia had barely arrived when the Serbian nationalist Gavrilo Princip assassinated Archduke Franz Ferdinand on June 28 in Sarajevo. A series of alliances throughout Europe began to topple the continent into a devastating war, but for most of the summer Edith and her family show no evidence of concern. The Forbes in New England sent breezy reports about the grandchildren and time on Naushon. Edward Forbes' missives came from Berlin, where he was doing research and seeking treatment for the digestive issues suffered by his four-year-old son John; Margaret and their daughters Rosamond, now five, and Mary, age one, were also with him. As late as July 12, Edward was encouraging Edith to visit them in the villa they had rented in Weggis, Switzerland; on July 29, the day after Austria-Hungary declared war on Serbia, he was still considering returning to Berlin and traveling to Vienna. "The war may have something to say about that," he did acknowledge. "It is almost impossible for me to believe that England, France & Italy will really be dragged into this miserable squabble in the Balkans. But apparently those who know are much more afraid that it will happen," Edward conceded.[86]

Edith was still in Bath when Britain declared war on Germany on August 4. By that time, she and her family were worried that Edward might get trapped in Switzerland. Throughout Europe, a crush of Americans tried to find boats home, as passenger ships were pressed into military service. Even if one could get a spot, in an age of submarines, torpedoes, and airplanes, there were risks to taking to the seas; at the same time, rumors swirled of coming food shortages in England if the war continued through the winter. Edward, urged to leave Switzerland by Cameron, was finally able to get on trains organized to evacuate American citizens first to Paris, then to Dieppe, where there were boats, again for Americans, to England. The trip, with three small children, was chaotic, but it led to an ecstatic reunion with Edith in England.[87] "What a joy it was to see you when we arrived. It made all the difference," Margaret wrote her mother-in-law.[88] Edith finally boarded the RMS *Olympic* on September 16, with Edward's family sailing two weeks later. Edith's fellow passengers included Cornelius Vanderbilt and Massachusetts Senator Henry Cabot Lodge.[89]

Edith, who turned seventy-three in November, had vivid memories of the Civil War. Now she contributed to this war effort, even before the United States entered the fray. Her biggest efforts came through collaborating with Mary Miller, the cousin who had helped care for Lidian. Miller, a teacher, had married Rene Engel, a French chemical engineer, in 1912. He was required to return to France to serve in the military. Mary, encouraged and funded by Edith, soon went to France herself, and she quickly set up the Le Soldat et Sa Famille, as part of the Oeuvre de Guerre relief effort "organized under the auspices of the French government." It was part of the "marraines de guerre" initiative, in which women wrote to soldiers, but she also collected and distributed goods such as rubber boots, clothing, and food. "Mrs. Forbes sent me important sums of money," Mary recounts in her memoir.[90] As the war wore on, Edith also funded Mary's home for children in Chateau Maleffre, near Alencon, as a refuge from the bombing in Paris and underwrote accommodations for soldiers on leave. When Mary returned to the United States for six months, Edith arranged for Bessie Neill, her former secretary who was back in her native Scotland, to take over Mary's work. "Any need I saw and communicated to her she always told me to undertake to alleviate. She wrote that she was glad to have an agent through whom she could distribute her gifts to the needy," Mary explains.[91]

There were other contributions closer to home. Edith helped fund the ambulance that Amelia and Raymond sponsored through the American Field Service in honor of William Forbes Emerson. "Everyone has been so generous and you above all," Amelia wrote in thanks.[92] Boston papers record her donations to the New England Belgium Relief Fund, the Cardinal Mercier Fund, which also aided Belgians, and the Ever Ready Bible Class of the Ruggles Street Baptist Church, which knit clothing for soldiers in France; she also organized fundraisers for The Little House, a settlement house in South Boston, to aid its war relief work.⁹³ The stream of money suggests the war was at the forefront of her mind long before the United States entered the conflict.

In November 1916, Edith launched a project not related to the war, publishing *Favorites of a Nursery of Seventy Years Ago: And Some Others of a Later Date* with Houghton Mifflin. The volume combined many of her interests: editing and curating, honoring her ancestors and promoting their memory, and the importance of reading to children. Edith wanted to make the nursery rhymes of her childhood, many long out of print, available to a new generation. She pointedly dedicated *Favorites* to the "descendants of Lidian Emerson." As she told Mary Miller Engel, "I have felt that it is especially associated with my Mother who I think selected the earliest editions to read to my cousins Sophia & Frank Browne and knew them all by heart."⁹⁴ Her preface also honors the women who had written and published the verses in earlier eras, carefully naming them and their publications.

While the book explicitly honors Lidian, Edith also quietly tips her hat to her father. She includes an uncredited poem titled, "A Nonsense Verse of Eighty Years Ago." It begins, "Little Red Robin / Spinning white bobbin / Whistled his time away / How could Robin rejoice / Amid such a noise / For he lived on London quay."⁹⁵ A quarter of a century earlier, she included the same poem in the reminiscence she wrote while James Elliot Cabot collected stories for his biography, explaining her father had "made" it "for Cousin Abby Adams." "I believe this has never been written before and I do not remember having heard it more than once nearly forty years ago but I think it is just as he said it . . . though I forget it for entire years at a time I find it still."⁹⁶ The poem in *Favorites* is largely the same, with a few small changes. Edith had sent the poem to Cabot as part of her campaign to push her father's humanity and commitment to family to the center of the biography. Now, given an opportunity to publish it herself, she kept his name out of print, although she understood as well as anyone the attention it could bring the volume. Given that she did not have a manuscript and remembered it slightly differently each time, she may have hesitated to bring attention to it as a work of her father's. But she still wanted it recorded.

Edith's publishing ventures were not done. The following year she and Edward collaborated on an edition of *Slovenly Peter*, a translation of German nursery rhymes by Heinrich Hoffmann. The publication includes facsimiles of the rhymes written in Ellen's hand, drafted for her nephews, and illustrations by Edward, a true family affair.⁹⁷ Edith reunited her siblings between the covers of the book and honored their commitment to the roles of an aunt and uncle.

Edith carefully recorded "book money" in the back of her diary most years, including the funds Edward sent as her share of her father's estate, the revenue from the yearbook, and now the proceeds from *Favorites* and *Slovenly Peter*. In 1922, for instance, she noted selling sixty-seven copies of *Favorites* and forty-six copies of *Slovenly Peter*, earning $118.55.[98] These funds are minuscule compared to the Forbes fortune that underwrote her comfortable life and her generosity to others. Her careful accounting of this money suggests the pride she took in her efforts and in the money she earned herself. Edith also made sure to donate a copy of *Favorites* to the Concord Free Public Library, saving the certificate of acknowledgment she received.[99]

America declared war on Germany on April 6, 1917, an outcome for which many in Ellen's circle had hoped. But the Forbes soon had a private tragedy to contend with. Waldo Forbes died June 17, 1917, at the age of thirty-eight. Edith had always worried about Waldo's health, and the previous year he had gone to Cuba to recover from an illness.[100] He left his wife Ellen and three children: Stephen, age seven, Waldo Jr., five, and Amelia, three. He had published *Cycles of Personal Belief*, a work of philosophy, just weeks before his death.[101] His mother's wish that he become a scholar had come to pass, but that career was cut short. Edith surely mourned him as she had Don and Rosebud, but her archive is silent on the loss.

On November 11, 1919, Edith was a "patroness" of the "Victory Ball" held at Boston's Copley-Plaza Hotel to celebrate the one-year anniversary of the end of the war.[102] She had lost Waldo, but the rest of her descendants had survived the conflict and the flu pandemic that had raged in 1918. There was another a heartbreaking loss on the horizon, however. Ellen Tucker Emerson Jr., who was a social worker, had married the Boston attorney Charles Davenport in November 1920 at the age of forty. Less than a year later, on August 5, 1921, she died abruptly from a cerebral embolism while at her parents' summer house in Fitzwilliam, New Hampshire; she was pregnant.[103] Edith doted on all her nieces and nephews, and on Haven's children, but she had been particularly close to Ellen Jr. Both she and her sister had always admired Ellen's combination of quick intelligence, quirky humor, and devotion to family and service, and Ellen Jr. and Edith built a strong bond on their two trips to the Philippines. "What a terrible blow has come to us all in the loss of our dear and wonderful Ellen. I know how heavily it must have borne upon you," Cameron wrote to his mother.[104] It was devastating, of course, for Edward and Annie. Raymond was the last of their seven children still living. The death of his daughter largely marked the end of Edward's working life, the grief too much to bear.[105]

In July 1922, Edith finally took to the seas again, heading to England with Annie Anthony and Mary McKay. She made a beeline to Bath, declaring "this place more beautiful than ever" in her diary.[106] She was eighty years old and no longer zipped from country to country, often choosing to read and rest in her rooms. The appearance of Edward Forbes and his family, who arrived at the end of August to stay for several months, did liven up the London portion of the trip. So did the telegraph on September 12 from Alexander announcing, "Son born all well."[107] The baby, also named Alexander, proved to be the last of Edith's grandchildren. She took one last transatlantic trip to England and France in 1924, traveling with Mary Miller and Rene Engel; she underwrote the Engels' trip and read her father's essays to them in her cabin.[108]

On November 15, 1922, the week before her eightieth-first birthday, Edith stood in front of the Women's Alliance at Milton's First Parish and made her declaration that "It was a very happy home."[109] The Alliance had asked Edith "to speak of Concord and my Father, and if I liked, read some of his poems," allowing her to deliver her last, and most public, effort to shape Waldo's legacy.[110] Decades earlier, she had scribbled furious notes about him for James Elliot Cabot, hoping to focus his biography on the "personal parts" and "domestic side" of her father's life. Now she made the case herself. It was a success. "Hardly a day goes by that I do not hear an echo of your Alliance talk from someone who speaks to me in appreciation," Edith Stebbins, the First Parish minister's wife, reported to Ellen.[111] Following the Milton presentation, Edith read the paper in the vestry of Concord's First Parish to the Women's Alliance and at the Armory Hall in Plymouth.[112]

In her talk, Edith, like Ellen before her, put Waldo in his larger family context, with particular attention to the women in his life. She praises Waldo's mother Ruth for keeping "the wolf from the door" after her husband died, perhaps thinking of how her experience of widowhood differed from her grandmother's.[113] Lidian, and Waldo's love of Lidian, take center stage at several points. "Our Mother was a queenly woman, tall and graceful, and as my Father desired me to notice, walked beautifully," Edith writes. "I must insert a few stories of my Mother as a child in Plymouth," she continues, detouring the narrative away from Waldo.[114]

"I have always thought of my Father as very wise in dealing with children," Edith writes when she turns to her childhood toward the end of the talk. She explains that when she was "silly or giggling" at the table, Waldo asked her to "run out to the front gate and look at the clouds," to help her calm down, a story she had told the Cabots. She discusses the family's "long walks in the woods" on Sundays, when her father would "croon his verses lately written."[115] Edith also recounts hours spent learning poetry with him in his famous study; like Ellen, she depicts this as a space for family, not just one for the Sage of Concord to think and write in solitude. To underscore the importance of home and family to her father, she concludes with a long passage from his essay "Domestic Life" in which he turns to his childhood with his brothers.

Edith joined forces with Edward to honor their father in another way the same year she gave the speech. Along with the Heywood and Hoar families, they donated over 80 acres surrounding Walden Pond to create a "reservation" originally overseen by Middlesex County; it became a state park in 1975.[116] They aimed to preserve the area as a site of quiet contemplation. The deed declares, "No part of the premises shall be used for games, athletic contests, racing, baseball, football, motion pictures, dancing, camping, hunting, trapping, shooting, making fires in the open, shows and other amusements, such as are often maintained at or near Revere Beach and other similar resorts, it being the sole and exclusive purpose of this conveyance to aid the Commonwealth in preserving the Walden of Emerson and Thoreau, its shores and nearby woodlands for the public who wish to enjoy the Pond, the woods nature, including bathing, boating, fishing, and picnicking."[117] While it was a joint effort, a plaque embedded in a large rock near the pond credits the gift to "Edith E. Forbes et al and C. Fey Heywood" and again stresses that it was "to preserve the Walden of Emerson and Thoreau." Edith was written into the landscape she had helped preserve.

Edith, who had written the passionate defense of her mother's significance to Ellen, also wrote her mother into the landscape by sponsoring the development of Brewster Gardens in Plymouth. The land had been apportioned to Elder William Brewster in 1620. Four hundred years later, Edith collaborated with a group of Plymouth women, including the physician Helen Pierce, to develop a garden on the site.[118] "Isn't it fine that this spot in the centre of this historic part of the town, made beautiful by you, is ever to be cared for," Pierce wrote to Edith.[119] Edith arranged for the installation of a plaque honoring Lidian and her brother, Dr. Charles Jackson, in the park. In 1924, the National Society of New England Women erected a bronze statue titled *Pilgrim Maiden* in the gardens, dedicated to "those intrepid English women whose courage fortitude and devotion brought a new nation into being."[120] A memorial made of flowers and honoring Plymouth foremothers was the perfect tribute to Lidian, who passed her love of gardening to her daughter and never ceased to identify as a child of Plymouth.

Edith, as her comments to Mary Miller Engel during World War I and her contributions to the Brewster Gardens and Walden Pond indicate, felt compelled to direct her wealth to where it could do good. She had always been generous, through donations to official charities and gifts to friends and relatives, and by channeling money and work to people, particularly women, she knew were hard on their luck. In her last years, these impulses if anything increased. In 1922, she gave over $6,700 spread across 140 charities, ranging from the American Indian League to the Society for the Protection of Native Plants to the Milton Women's Alliance. Some of her choices honored her friends and family circle. She donated, for instance, to the Elizabeth Peabody House, which worked for the "Americanization" of immigrants in North Boston; after Pauline Agassiz Shaw died in 1916, Edith made annual contributions to the North Bennet School, founded by Shaw.[121] She funneled money into the Fogg Museum, for which Edward thanked her for relieving him from the burden of fundraising. Edith also continued to shower her friends and family with flowers and bushels of apples from her gardens and greenhouses. Often the floral gifts served as a way to remember those who had passed. She sent Helen Legate, still living in Bush, and Ida Agassiz Higginson, for instance, boxes of flowers every year on Ellen's birthday.

"Our Violet had a very happy life—and no one ever used her opportunities to enjoy and help others more than she did," Edith wrote to Mary Miller Engel in June 1926.[122] Violet had died at the age of fifty-eight on April 28, 1926, after an illness—likely cancer—of several months.[123] Describing her as a "cushion" to all her family and friends, Edith acknowledged, "there is no one who can begin to fill the place she enjoyed, using all her opportunities to just 'lend a hand' to us all."[124] Her daughter's death intertwined with her sister's in Edith's mind, a sign of the bond she shared with both of them and perhaps of growing confusion. "It is strange that I had the feeling that I had lost both my sister Ellen and my dear daughter at once. It was so strong a fancy that I believe I have spoken of it as if it were true," Edith explained.[125] Edith, at eighty-five, had outlived four of her children, her sister, and her husband, along with many in her circle, and her memory was beginning to fail.[126] Yet, her optimism and love of life never fully left her. In the wake of Violet's death, her sons circled around her, as Edith "deserted" her home and was "gadding about to the young households" of her boys and their children, enjoying game nights and the joyful sound of youthful voices echoing through the halls.[127]

The letter honoring Violet's life is the last piece of correspondence in Edith's hand found in the Forbes or Emerson papers, although she lived for three more years. She had begun to complain of memory problems in 1918, which, while not slowing her down immediately, may have limited her in her final years. The loss of Violet, moreover, could have been a blow from which she did not recover. The archives hold almost no record of this time—no letters or diary entries by her and only brief references to her in her children's and brother's letters. The great correspondent is erased from the page. The stock market crashed on October 29, 1929, but Edith was likely beyond caring. She died three weeks later, on November 20, two days before her eighty-eighth birthday. Edward Emerson passed on January 27, 1930; Annie had died in 1928. The Emersons of Bush were gone.

"Wherever she went, she planted a garden." These words opened Edith's eulogy, read by Vivian T. Pomeroy, the minister at Milton's First Parish. The service was held at Edith's home on November 22, her birthday. The short tribute put her talent as a gardener within the context of her devotion to her children and her work collecting nursery rhymes and gathering "memories for her friends, the dignity and grace of the past."[128] She tended to plants, people, and her family's legacy. The service, like Ellen's, included passages from her father's work, including "Threnody," the poem about grief he had written for young Waldo. Edith lived for eighty-seven years after that much-mourned boy's death, her commitment to happiness a counter to the "miseries" that engulfed her childhood home in the wake of his passing. Her wide circle of friends and family would miss her, but they would also, as she and Edward had done for Ellen, give thanks for a life well-lived.

Ellen and Edith's lives stretched over nine dramatic decades in American history. The railroad did not go to Concord when Ellen was born in 1839; Edith lived to see a war in which battles were fought in the sky. Their father's fame, along with Edith's marriage into the powerful Forbes family, made their lives in many ways extraordinary, and those are the reasons many people might be drawn to their story. But at heart, their lives offer a chronicle about the roles women play in keeping a family together and preserving its memories as members pass away. Their letters bound them together over distance and now allow their lives and contributions to be told.

NOTES

Preface

1. Phyllis Cole, with Jana Argersinger, "Introduction," in *Toward a Female Genealogy of Transcendentalism*, ed. Jana Argersinger and Phyllis Cole (Athens: University of Georgia Press, 2014), 11.
2. EWE to ETE, Jan. 26, 1892, LLJE, xxi; ETE to EEF, July 18, 1877, ETE Correspondence.
3. Ralph Waldo Emerson, "Self-Reliance," in *The American Transcendentalists: Essential Writings*, ed. Laurence Buell (New York: The Modern Library, 2006), 214.
4. Laurence Buell, *The American Transcendentalists* (New York: The Modern Library, 2006), 208.
5. ETE to Clara Dabney, Feb. 28, 1877, ETE Correspondence.
6. James Perrin Warren, *Culture of Eloquence: Oratory and Reform in Antebellum America* (University Park: Pennsylvania State University Press, 1999), 102.
7. ETE, "What I Can Remember of Stories of Our Ancestors Told Me by Aunt Mary Moody Emerson," EF Papers (357); ETE, "What I Can Remember About Father," unpublished manuscript, Houghton.
8. James Slater, "The First Edition," in *The Correspondence of Emerson and Carlyle*, ed. James Slater (New York: Columbia University Press, 1964), 64–67.
9. Edith Gregg, "Introduction," LETE, xiii.
10. EEF to ETE, Nov. 10, 1907, FP, Carton 5.
11. Kyla Schuller, *The Trouble with White Women: A Counterhistory of Feminism* (New York: Bold Type Books, 2021), 4. See also: Kerri Greenidge, *The Grimkes: The Legacy of Slavery in an American Family* (New York: Liveright Publishing, 2023); Susan Goodier, *No Votes for Women: The New York State Anti-Suffrage Movement* (Urbana: University of Illinois Press, 2015); Susan Marshall, *Splintered Sisterhood: Gender and Class in the Campaign Against Woman Suffrage* (Madison: University of Wisconsin Press, 1997); Shirley Yee, *Black Women Abolitionists: A Study in Activism* (Knoxville: University of Tennessee Press, 1992.)
12. Carlos Baker, *Emerson Among the Eccentrics: A Group Portrait* (New York: Viking, 1996), esp. 350–60.
13. Ronald Bosco, "Historical Introduction," in *Letters and Social Aims* (Cambridge: Harvard University Press, 2010), xix-ccxii; Ronald Bosco and Joel Myersson, "Historical Introduction," in *Uncollected Prose Writings* (Cambridge, MA: Harvard University Press, 2013), xxv–xcv; Christopher Hanlon, *Emerson's Memory Loss:*

Originality, Communality, and the Late Style (New York: Oxford University Press, 2018); Nancy Simmons, "Arranging the Sibylline Leaves: James Elliot Cabot's Work as Emerson's Literary Executor," *Studies in the American Renaissance* (1983): 335–89; Nancy Simmons, "Philosophical Biographer: James Elliot Cabot and 'A Memoir of Ralph Waldo Emerson,'" *Studies in the American Renaissance* (1987): 365–92; Joseph Thomas, "Late Emerson: Selected Poems and the 'Emerson Factory,'" *ELH* 65, no. 4 (1998): 971–94.

14 Bosco, "Historical Introduction," *Letters and Social Aims*, xxxiv.
15 Bosco and Myerson, "Historical Introduction," *Uncollected*, xxx–xxxi.
16 Hanlon, 13.
17 Robert Habich, *Building Their Own Waldos: Emerson's First Biographers and the Politics of Life-Writing in the Gilded Age* (Iowa City: University of Iowa Press, 2011), 99–120.
18 Argersinger and Cole, ed., *Towards a Female*; Noelle Baker and Sandra Petrulionis, "The Almanacks of Mary Moody Emerson: A Scholarly Digital Edition," Women Writers Project, Northeastern University, https://wwp.northeastern.edu/wwo/; Kathleen Lawrence, "The 'Dry-Lighted Soul' Ignites: Emerson and His Soul-Mate Caroline Sturgis as Seen in Her Houghton Manuscripts," *Harvard Library Bulletin*, 16, no. 3 (2005): 37–67; John Matteson, *Eden's Outcasts: The Story of Louisa May Alcott and Her Father* (New York: W.W. Norton, 2007); John Matteson, *The Lives of Margaret Fuller* (New York: W.W. Norton, 2012); Megan Marshall, *Margaret Fuller: A New American Life* (New York: Houghton Mifflin, 2013); Megan Marshall, *The Peabody Sisters: Three Women Who Ignited American Romanticism* (New York: Houghton Mifflin, 2005); Sandra Petrulionis, *To Set the World Right: The Antislavery Movement in Thoreau's Concord* (Ithaca, NY: Cornell University Press, 2006), Patricia Valenti, *Sophia Peabody Hawthorne: A Life*. 2 vols. (Columbia: University of Missouri Press, 2004, 2015); Tiffany Wayne, *Woman Thinking: Feminism and Transcendentalism in Nineteenth-Century America* (Lanham, MD: Lexington Books, 2004); and Sarah Wider, "'How it All Lies Before Me Today': Transcendentalist Women's Journeys into Attention," *Towards a Female*, 157–76.
19 SLLJE.
20 LETE; *North American Women's Letters and Diaries* (Alexandria, VA: Alexander Street, 2001).
21 ETE Letters.

Chapter One

1 RWE to Elizabeth Hoar, Feb. 24, 1839, *LRWE*, 2:185.
2 *LLJE*, 77.
3 Robert Richardson, *Emerson: The Mind on Fire* (Berkeley: University of California Press, 1995), 3–5.
4 RWE, *Journals and Miscellaneous Notebooks*, ed. A.W. Plumstead and Harrison Hayward (Cambridge, MA: Harvard University Press, 1969), 7:170.
5 *LLJE*, 77.
6 Tiffany Wayne, "Ralph Waldo Emerson," in *Critical Companion to Ralph Waldo Emerson*, ed. Tiffany Wayne (New York: Facts on File, 2010), 4.

7 JEC, *A Memoir of Ralph Waldo Emerson* (Boston: Houghton, Mifflin & Co., 1895), 1:249.
8 The dedication was supposed to take place on April 19, 1836, but was delayed a year. Alberta J. von Frank, *Ralph Waldo Emerson: The Major Poetry* (Cambridge, MA: Harvard University Press, 2015), 129–31; Tiffany Wayne, "'Hymn: Sung at the Completion of the Concord Monument, April 19, 1836' (1837)," in *A Critical Companion to Ralph Waldo Emerson*, 135.
9 For an in-depth biographical treatment of Ralph Waldo Emerson, see Robert Richardson, *Emerson*.
10 There is not extensive data available on the marriage age in the United States between 1800 and 1850; age of first marriage in 1850 was around 21.5 years. Catherine Fitch and Stephen Ruggles, "Historical Trends in Marriage Formation: the United States, 1850–1990," in *Ties that Bind: Perspectives on Marriage and Cohabitation*, ed. Linda Waite (Hawthorne, NY: Aldine de Gruyter, 2000), 59–88.
11 Delores Bird Carpenter, "Introduction," *SLLJE*, xii. Bird's introductions to her editions of *SLLJE* and Ellen's biography of her mother, along with the biography of herself, provide the most extensive biographical profiles of Lidian. See also, Randall Fuller, "Lydia Jackson Emerson," in *The Oxford Handbook of Ralph Waldo Emerson*, ed. Christopher Hanlon (New York: Oxford University Press, 2024), 489–504.
12 *LLJE*, 23, 24.
13 *LLJE*, 41.
14 *LLJE*, 37.
15 LJE to Charles T. Jackson, Feb. 28, 1832, *SLLJE*, 18.
16 *LLJE*, 43.
17 *LLJE*, 47.
18 *LLJE*, 47.
19 RWE to LJE, Jan. 24, 1835, *LRWE*, 7:232.
20 Richardson, *Emerson*, 207.
21 Gross, *The Transcendentalists and Their World* (New York: Farrar, Straus and Giroux, 2021), 309.
22 Barbara Downs Wojtusik, "Concord," *Critical Companion to Ralph Waldo Emerson*, 318–19.
23 Tiffany Wayne, "Emerson, William (1769–1811)," *Critical Companion to Ralph Waldo Emerson*, 334.
24 RWE to LJE, Feb. 1, 1835, *LRWE*, 1:435.
25 While the story that Waldo wanted to change her name because he did not like the pronunciation of it as "Lydiar" has been often repeated, there is not contemporary evidence to support that theory. Richardson, *Emerson*, 192.
26 Gross, *Transcendentalists*, 261. Gross provides a detailed history of the town of Concord from 1820s through the 1850s in *Transcendentalists*.
27 Gross, *Transcendentalists*, 129–45.
28 *LLJE*, 95.
29 *LLJE*, 106.
30 RWE to LJE, May 12, 1836, *LRWE*, 2: 18–19
31 For biographical information on Elizabeth Hoar, see, Elizabeth Mayfield-Miller, "Elizabeth of Concord: Selected Letters of Elizabeth Sherman Hoar to the Emersons,

Family and the Emerson Circle (Part 1)," *Studies in the American Renaissance* (1984): 229–98.
32 Richardson, *Emerson*, 175; *LLJE*, 32, 51.
33 *LLJE*, 76.
34 LJE to Elizabeth Peabody, Jan. 8, 1837, *SLLJE*, 53.
35 RWE to Waldo Emerson, March 19, 1840, *LRWE*, 2:263.
36 RWE to Lucy Jackson Brown, Nov. 22, 1841, *LRWE*, 2:465.
37 LJE to Lucy Jackson Brown, January 1841, *SLLJE*, 100; RWE to William Emerson, Dec. 4, 1841, *LRWE*, 2:469.
38 Ronald A. Bosco, "Historical Introduction," in *Society and Solitude* (Cambridge, MA: Harvard University Press, 2007), xxviii.
39 Tiffany Wayne, "Essays: First Series (1841)," ed. Wayne, *Critical Companion to Ralph Waldo Emerson*, 97.
40 *LLJE*, 79.
41 Sarah Freeman Clarke to James Freeman Clarke, Feb. 28, 1835, quoted in *LLJE*, 49.
42 *LLJE*, 80.
43 *LLJE*, 80.
44 *LLJE*, 80.
45 Ellen includes the text of the "Transcendental Bible" in *The Life of Lidian Jackson Emerson*, which Delores Bird Carpenter published in 1992. She also published the text along with an analysis of it in the context of Lidian's religious views in *Studies in the American Renaissance* in 1980. Ellen Tucker Emerson, *Life of*, 81–82; Delores Bird Carpenter, "Transcendental Bible," *Studies in the American Renaissance* (1980): 91–95.
46 LJE, "Transcendental Bible," quoted in *LLJE*, 83.
47 *LLJE*, 83.
48 *LLJE*, 79
49 *LLJE*, 83.
50 Richardson, *Emerson*, 329.
51 Megan Marshall, *Margaret Fuller: A New American Life* (New York: Houghton Mifflin Harcourt, 2013), 177–82.
52 Kathy Lawrence, "The 'Dry-Lighted Soul' Ignites: Emerson and His Soul-Mate Caroline Sturgis as Seen in Her Houghton Manuscripts," *Harvard Library Bulletin* 16, no. 3 (2005): 42.
53 LJE to RWE, Feb. 3, 1843, *SLLJE*, 125.
54 RWE to Mary Moody Emerson Jan. 28, 1842, *LRWE*, 3:7.
55 LJE to Lucy Jackson Brown, Feb. 4, 1842, *SLLJE*, 104.
56 *LLJE*, 88.
57 Richardson, *Emerson*, 356–57.
58 RWE to LJE, Feb. 10, 1842, *LRWE*, 3:11–12.
59 LJE to Lucy Jackson Brown, March 15, 1842, *SLLJE*, 111.
60 LJE to RWE, March 10, 1842, *SLLJE*, 109.
61 LJE to RWE, after Feb. 26, 1842, *SLLJE*, 105, and RWE to LJE, Feb. 10, 1841, *LRWE*, 3:12.
62 RWE to William Emerson, June 26, 1842, *LRWE*, 3:68.
63 *LLJE*, 90.

64 LJE to RWE, Jan. 15, 1843, *SLLJE*, 116.
65 ETE to EEF, March 22, 1894, ETE Correspondence.
66 LJE to RWE, Dec. 21 [1845?], *SLLJE*, 135.
67 RWE, "Experience," *Ralph Waldo Emerson: The Major Prose*, ed. Ronald Bosco and Joel Myerson (Cambridge, MA: Harvard University Press, 2015), 228.
68 RWE, "Threnody," in *Ralph Waldo Emerson: The Major Poetry*, ed. Albert J. von Frank (Cambridge, MA: Harvard University Press, 2015), 121.
69 Margaret Fuller, Journal, Sept. 1, 1842, quoted in Joel Myerson, "Margaret Fuller's 1842 Journal: At Concord with the Emersons," *Harvard Library Bulletin*, XXI, no. 3 (1973): 330–31.
70 Myerson, "Margaret Fuller's 1842 Journal," 331–32.
71 Richardson, *Emerson*, 267.
72 *LLJE*, 127.
73 RWE to Margaret Fuller, July 11, 1843, *LRWE* 3:184
74 RWE to E.C. Goodwin, April 16, 1846, *LRWE* 3:331.
75 LJE to RWE, Jan. 10, 1843, *SLLJE*, 113.
76 ETE to RWE, Jan. 15, 1843, LJE to RWE, Feb. 1, 1843, ETE to RWE, Feb. 3, 1843, *SLLJE*, 117, 122.
77 LJE to RWE, Feb. 17, 1843, *SLLJE*, 130–131.
78 LJE to RWE, Feb. 17, 1843, *SLLJE*, 129–130.
79 ETE to RWE, Feb. 3, 1843, *SLLJE*, 122.
80 LJE to RWE, Dec. 21 [1845?], *SLLJE*, 135.
81 EEF to ETE, Spring 1886, FP, Carton 3.
82 Tiffany Wayne, "Essays: Second Series (1844)," in ed. Wayne, *Critical Companion*, 99.
83 Richardson, *Emerson*, 335–36, 391.
84 Gross, *Transcendentalists*, 548–49.
85 Sandra Harbert Petrulionis, *To Set the World Right: The Antislavery Movement in Thoreau's Concord* (Ithaca, NY: Cornell University Press, 2006), 42–47.
86 Richardson, *Emerson*, 399, 405.
87 LJE to RWE, May 15, 1848, *SLLJE*, 150.
88 EWE to EEF, July 10, 1919, EWE Papers, Box 3.
89 LJE to RWE, May 15, 1848, *SLLJE*, 150.
90 EWE, *Emerson in Concord: A Memoir* (Boston: Houghton Mifflin Co., 1889), 169, 171.
91 RWE, *Journals and Miscellaneous*, 8:306; EWE, *Emerson in Concord*, 169.
92 *LLJE*, 103.
93 *LLJE*, 103–4.
94 EWE, *Emerson in Concord*, 169.
95 EWE, *Emerson in Concord*, 171.
96 ETE, "What I Can Remember About Father," unpublished manuscript, Houghton Library, Harvard University, MS Am 1280.227.
97 ETE, "What I Can Remember About Father."
98 RWE to William Emerson, Oct. 16, 1843, *LRWE*, 3:213.
99 ETE, "What I Can Remember About Father."
100 Louisa May Alcott, "In Memoriam: Sophia Foord," *The Woman's Journal*, April 11, 1885: 117.

101 Eve LaPlante, *Marmee and Louisa: The Untold Story of Louisa May Alcott and Her Mother* (New York: Simon and Schuster, 2012): 142; John Matteson, *Eden's Outcasts: The Story of Louisa May Alcott and Her Father* (New York: W.W. Norton, 2007), 183.
102 ETE to EEF, Nov. 8, 1858; *LRWE*, 8:255n91.
103 *LRWE* 8:258.
104 RWE to George Ripley, Dec. 15, 1840, draft, *LRWE*, 2:370.
105 RWE to George Ripley, Dec. 15, 1840, draft, *LRWE*, 2:370; Laura Dassow Walls, *Henry David Thoreau: A Life* (Chicago: University of Chicago Press, 2017), 119–20.
106 Noelle Baker, "Family," *Emerson in Context*, ed. Wesley Mott (New York: Cambridge, MA, 2013), 157–58; Matteson, *Eden's Outcasts*, 85, 173, 232.
107 Patricia Valenti, *Sophia Peabody Hawthorne: A Life, Volume 2, 1848–1871* (Columbia: University of Missouri Press, 2015), 1–2, 79, 94, 198, 272.
108 RWE to William Emerson, Aug. 30, 1847, *LRWE* 3:415; Richardson, *Emerson*, 441–458; Walls, *Henry David Thoreau*, 231.
109 EEF, "Childhood with Thoreau, as Remembered in 1882," in *Thoreau in His Own Time*, ed. Sandra Petrulionis (Iowa City: University of Iowa Press, 2012), 43.
110 Henry David Thoreau to RWE, Dec. 29, 1847, in *The Correspondence of Henry David Thoreau*, ed. Robert Hudspeth (Princeton, NJ: Princeton University Press, 2013), 1:332–33.
111 Henry David Thoreau to RWE, Nov. 14, 1847, in *The Correspondence of Henry David Thoreau*, 1:314.
112 Walls, *Henry David Thoreau*, 232–34.
113 Henry David Thoreau to RWE, Nov. 14, 1847, in *Correspondence of Henry David Thoreau*, 1:313.
114 ETE, EEF, EWE, and LJE to RWE, Nov. [29?], 1847, *SLLJE*, 138–39.
115 LJE to RWE, May 15, 1848, *SLLJE*, 149.
116 David Henkin, *The Postal Age: The Emergence of Modern Communications in Nineteenth Century America* (Chicago: University of Chicago Press, 2006), 3.
117 Theresa Strouth Gaul and Sharon Harris, introduction to *Letters and Cultural Transformations in the United States* (Routledge, 2009), 7; Nan Johnson, "Dear Millie: Letter Writing and Gender in Postbellum America," *Nineteenth-Century Prose* 27, no. 2 (Fall 2000): 22–46.
118 Celeste-Marie Bernier, Judie Newman, and Matthew Pethers, introduction to *The Edinburgh Companion to Nineteenth-Century American Letters and Letter-Writing*, ed. Celeste-Marie Bernier, Judie Newman, and Matthew Pethers (Edinburgh: Edinburgh University Press, 2016), 13.
119 Kassia Waggoner and Adam Nemmers, eds., *Yours in Filial Regard: The Civil War Letters of a Texas Family* (Fort Worth, TX: TCU Press, 2015), 14–15.
120 Robert N. Hudspeth, "Letter Writing," *Oxford Handbook of Transcendentalism*, ed. Joel Myerson, Sandra Petrulionis, and Laura Dassow Walls (New York: Oxford University Press, 2010): 309. See also, David Greenham, "Corresponding Natures; Ralph Waldo Emerson's Letters," in *Edinburgh Companion*, 319–31 and Magdelena Nerio, "'The Epistolary Medium': Friendship and Civil Society in Margert Fuller's Private Letters," in *The Edinburgh Companion*, 332–46.
121 RWE to LJE, May 4, 1848, *LRWE*, 4:68
122 RWE to LJE, June 8, 1848, *LRWE*, 4:83, and RWE to LJE, April 20, 1848, *LRWE* 4:54.

123 RWE to Henry David Thoreau, Dec 2, 1847, *LRWE*: 8:136; RWE to LJE, June 8, 1848, *LRWE* 4:83.
124 Henry David Thoreau to RWE, Feb. 23, 1848, in *Correspondence of Henry D. Thoreau*, 1:345.
125 Henry David Thoreau to RWE, Feb. 23, 1848, in *Correspondence of Henry D. Thoreau*, 1:345.
126 Walls, *Henry David Thoreau*, 239.
127 Henry David Thoreau to RWE, Nov. 14, 1847, *Correspondence of Henry D. Thoreau*, 1:313.
128 Quoted in Wells, *Henry David Thoreau*, 239.
129 Carol Faulkner, *Unfaithful: Love, Adultery, and Marriage Reform in Nineteenth-Century America* (Philadelphia: University of Pennsylvania Press, 2019), 2.
130 RWE, [Dec.?] 1840, journal, in Joel Porte, ed. *Emerson in His Journals* (Cambridge, MA: Harvard University Press, 1982), 249.
131 Richardson, *Emerson*, 366, 368.
132 Faulkner, *Unfaithful*, 7.
133 Richardson, *Emerson*, 369.
134 James Marcus provides a nuanced analysis of the ebbs and flows of the Emerson marriage. James Marcus, *Glad to the Brink of Fear: A Portrait of Ralph Waldo Emerson* (Princeton, NJ: Princeton University Press, 2024), 94–107.
135 Henry David Thoreau to RWE, before March 24, 1848, in *Correspondence of Henry D. Thoreau*, 1:353.
136 RWE to LJE, March 8, 1848, *LRWE*, 4:32.
137 *LLJE*, 104.
138 LJE to ETE, June 25, 1849, *SLLJE*, 161.
139 LJE to ETE, Sept. 3, 1849, *SLLJE*, 167.
140 EEF to ETE, June 17, 1849, EF Correspondence, 3504.
141 EEF to ETE, June 25, 1849, *SLLJE*, 161.
142 Edith E.W. Gregg, "Emerson and His Children: Their Childhood Memories," *Harvard Library Bulletin* XXVII, no. 4 (1980): 417
143 EWE to EEF, Nov. 22, 1906, EWE Papers, Box. 3.
144 ETE to EEF, March 22, 1894, ETE Correspondence.
145 EWE to EEF, Nov. 22, 1906, EWE Papers. Box 3.
146 EEF, "A Protest," in Ellen Tucker Emerson, "Life of Lidian Jackson Emerson," manuscript, EF Papers (358).

Chapter Two

1 RWE to Caroline Sturgis Tappan, Aug. 26, 1852, *LRWE*, 8:327.
2 Mary Kelley, *Learning to Stand and Speak: Women, Education, and Public Life in America's Republic* (Chapel Hill: University of North Carolina, 2006); Jamie Osterman Alves, *Fictions of Female Education in the Nineteenth Century* (New York: Routledge, 2009); and Barbara Miller Solomon, *In the Company of Educated Women: A History of Women and Higher Education in America* (New Haven, CT: Yale University Press, 1985).

3 EEF to Elizabeth Cabot, 1886, EF Correspondence (3500).
4 ETE to RWE, December 29, 1852, ETE Correspondence.
5 RWE to Caroline Sturgis Tappan, Oct. 13, 1852, *LRWE*, 8:337.
6 Elizabeth Sedgwick, "Teaching," *Friend's Intelligencer*, June 25, 1868, 333.
7 Lucinda Damon-Bach, "Inspiration or Competition: Catharine Sedgwick's Influence on Nathaniel Hawthorne," *Nathaniel Hawthorne Review* 41, no. 1 (2015): 1–32; Les Olson, "Elizabeth Buckminster (Dwight) Sedgwick, 1801–1864" *The Catharine Maria Sedgwick Society Newsletter* (Summer 2017): 2–4.
8 ETE to EEF, June 1, 1853, ETE Correspondence.
9 Lenox History, "15 Cliffwood Street, Francis Farley House, c. 1850," *Lenox History*, Sept. 2014, http://lenoxhistory.org/lenoxhistorypeopleandplaces/lenoxhistoryplaces/15-cliffwood-st-francis-farley-house-c-1850/; Richard Francis, *Transcendental Utopias: Individual and Community at Brook Farm, Fruitlands, and Walden* (Ithaca, NY: Cornell University Press, 1997), 43.
10 ETE to LJE, June 5, 1853, ETE to RWE, June 14, 1853, ETE Correspondence.
11 ETE to Charlotte [Haskins Cleveland], June 4, 1853, ETE Correspondence
12 Margaret Hope Bacon, *Abby Hopper Gibbons: Prison Reformer and Social Activist* (Albany: SUNY University Press, 2000), 71; Edith Gregg, "List of School Friends," *LETE*, 1: xxii. Ellen Emerson addresses Abby Adeline Manning as "Addy" throughout her life.
13 ETE to RWE, June 14, 1853, ETE Correspondence.
14 RWE to ETE, June 21, 1853, *LRWE*, 4:369–370.
15 RWE to ETE, July 8, 1853, *LRWE*, 4:372.
16 LJE to ETE, June, 28, 1853, *SLLJE*, 180.
17 LJE to ETE, July 6, 1853, *SLLJE*, 181.
18 ETE to LJE, March 27, 1854, ETE to LJE, August 10, 1853, ETE Correspondence; LJE to ETE, March 21, 1854, *SLLJE*, 199.
19 ETE to LJE, April 9, 1854, ETE Correspondence.
20 ETE to LJE, Feb. 12, 1854, ETE Correspondence.
21 ETE to LJE, June 12, 1853, ETE Correspondence.
22 ETE to LJE, Aug. 21, 1853, ETE Correspondence.
23 LJE to ETE, Aug. 26, 1853, *SLLJE*, 185.
24 ETE to EEF, May 26, 1853, and ETE to EEF, Dec. 25, ETE Correspondence.
25 ETE to EEF, June 29, 1853, and ETE to RWE, July 23, 1853, ETE Correspondence.
26 EEF to ETE, June 26, 1853, EF Correspondence, (3507).
27 EEF to ETE, July 10, 1853, EF Correspondence, (3510).
28 ETE to LJE, Dec. 31, 1853, ETE Correspondence.
29 RWE to LJE, Jan. 9, 1854, *LRWE*, 4:414.
30 Ronald Bosco and Joel Myerson, *The Emerson Brothers: A Fraternal Biography in Letters* (New York: Oxford University Press, 2005), 225.
31 LJE to ETE, Jan. 3, 1854, *SLLJE*, 192.
32 LJE to RWE, Jan. 11, 1854, *SLLJE*, 195.
33 ETE to LJE, Feb. 26, 1854, ETE Correspondence.
34 ETE to LJE, March 5, 1854, ETE Correspondence.
35 LJE to ETE, Feb. 28, 1854, *SLLJE*, 198.
36 Kathleen Lawrence, "The 'Dry Lighted Soul' Ignites: Emerson and His Soul-Mate Caroline Sturgis as Seen in Her Houghton Manuscripts," *Harvard Library Bulletin*

16, no. 3 (2005): 39. Beginning in the Gilded Age, "biographies of Emerson insisted on imaging his life as loftily detached from all social and historical reference." Randall Fuller, *Emerson's Ghosts: Literature, Politics, and the Making of Americanists* (New York: Oxford University Press, 2007), 28. See also, ETE to LJE, March 5, 1854, ETE Correspondence.
37 Elizabeth Sedgwick to RWE, March 5, 1854, Ralph Waldo Emerson Letters from Various Correspondents, MS AM 1280, (2882), Houghton.
38 RWE to ETE, March 20, 1854, *LRWE*. 4:434; ETE to LJE, Jan. 18, 1854, ETE Correspondence.
39 ETE to LJE, July 2, 1854, ETE Correspondence.
40 RWE to ETE, Aug. 2, 1854, *LRWE* 4:454.
41 RWE to Abel Adams, Aug. 7, 1854, *LRWE*, 4:455.
42 *LLJE*, 32.
43 EWE to EEF, Nov. 22, 1906, EWE Papers, Carton 3.
44 Susan Haven Emerson to LJE, Feb. 6, 1848, EF Papers, (2802).
45 LJE to RWE, March 6, 1848, *SLLJE*, 140.
46 ETE to Charlotte Haskins Cleveland, July 26, 1855, Emerson Family Additional Correspondence, Compositions, and Photographs, MS 2982 (4), Houghton.
47 Ann Douglas Wood, "'The Fashionable Diseases': Women's Complaints and Their Treatments in Nineteenth Century America," *The Journal of Interdisciplinary History* 4, no. 1 (1973): 26.
48 Catharine Beecher, *Physiology and Calisthenics for Schools and Families* (New York: Harper and Brothers: 1856), 164.
49 Jennifer Lunden, *American Breakdown* (New York: Harper Wave, 2023), 5.
50 Lunden, *American Breakdown*, 5.
51 Douglas, "The Fashionable Diseases," 31–32.
52 Charles Brown to LJE, July 11, 1854, EF Papers, (3171); LJE to EEF, Jan. 11, 1864, *SLLJE*, 224.
53 *LLJE*, 32, 108, 127.
54 ETE to Charlotte Haskins Cleveland, Feb. 18, March 12, 1855, Emerson Family Additional Correspondence, Compositions, and Photographs, MS2982 (3), Houghton; *LLJE*, 125–126.
55 Faye Dudden, *Serving Women: Household Service in Nineteenth Century America* (Middletown, CT: Wesleyan University Press, 1983), 79.
56 *LLJE*, 87.
57 Laura Dassow Walls, *Henry David Thoreau: A Life* (Chicago: University of Chicago Press, 2017), 118.
58 ETE to LJE, July 24, 1853, ETE Correspondence; LJE to ETE, Aug. 5, 1854, *LLJE*, 184. Sarah Wider, "The Children of Transcendentalism: Caroline Sturgis's Drawings and Stories," (paper) presented at Transcendental Intersections: Literature, Philosophy, Religion, Heidelberg, Germany, July 28, 2018.
59 RWE to William Emerson, Aug. 21, 1854, *LRWE* 4:456.
60 ETE to LJE, Sept. 3, 1854, ETE Correspondence. For more on Beecher, see: Karen Kish Skylar, *Catharine Beecher: A Study in American Domesticity* (New Haven, CT: Yale University Press, 1973).
61 ETE to LJE, Aug. 6, 1854, ETE Correspondence.
62 ETE to Cousin Charlotte [Haskins Cleveland], Sept. 24, 1854, ETE Correspondence.

63 ETE to Emma Stimson, Oct. 8, 1854, ETE Correspondence.
64 ETE to Charlotte Haskins Cleveland, Feb. 18, March 12, 1855, EF Papers, 3.
65 ETE to Emma Stimson, November 6, 1854, and ETE to Emma Stimson, Dec. 21, 1854, ETE Correspondence.
66 ETE to Charlotte Haskins Cleveland, Feb. 18, 1855, EF Papers, 3.
67 ETE to Emma Stimson, Dec. 21, 1854, ETE Correspondence; Louisa May Alcott, *Flower Fables* (Carlisle, MA: Applewood Books, 2005).
68 ETE to Emma Stimson, Dec. 21, 1854, ETE Correspondence.
69 Franklin Sanborn, *Recollections of Seventy Years* (Boston: Gorham Press, 1909), 2:441.
70 John Matteson, *Eden's Outcasts: The Story of Louisa May Alcott and her Father* (New York: W.W. Norton, 2007), 26–27.
71 Kenneth Walter Cameron, "Sanborn's Preparatory School in Concord (1855–1863)," *American Renaissance Literary Report* (1989), 39; Sanborn, *Recollections*, 2:441–442.
72 ETE to Haven Emerson, April 7, 1855, in *LETE*, 1:88–89. The original is not found in the ETE Correspondence.
73 ETE to Emma Stimson, June 7, 1855, ETE Correspondence.
74 *LRWE*, 8:448–449n97.
75 For information on the Agassiz School, see: Christoph Irmscher, *Louis Agassiz: Creator of American Science* (Boston: Houghton Mifflin, 2013), 283–286, and Lucy Allen Paton, *Elizabeth Cabot Agassiz: A Biography* (Boston: Houghton Mifflin, 1919), 45–46.
76 Louis Agassiz to RWE, April 2, 1855, *LRWE*, 8:428.
77 RWE to Caroline Sturgis Tappan, Oct. 13, 1857, *LRWE*, 8:536. For information on Emerson and Agassiz's friendship and the Saturday Club, see: James Schlett, *A Not Too Greatly Changed Eden: The Story of the Philosophers' Camp in the Adirondacks* (Ithaca, NY: Cornell University Press, 2015), 56–58.
78 RWE, "Address at the Woman's Rights Convention, 20 September 1855," *The Later Lectures of Ralph Waldo Emerson, 1843–1871*, ed. Ronald A. Bosco and Joel Myerson (Athens: University of Georgia Press, 2001), 2:15–29.
79 Quoted in Bosco and Myerson, *Later Lectures*, 15.
80 Gilbert, Gougen, and Zwarg position the lecture as strong support for women's rights. Cole argues that Waldo's support for women's rights was limited, acknowledging the potential for his ideas to inspire women's rights advocates, which Eckel also stresses. Phyllis Cole, "The New Movement's Tide: Emerson and Women's Rights," *Emerson: Bicentennial Essays*, ed. Ronald Bosco and Joel Myerson (Boston: Massachusetts Historical Society, 2006), 117–52; Leslie Elizabeth Eckel, "Gender," *Ralph Waldo Emerson in Context*, ed. Wesley T. Mott (New York: Cambridge University Press, 2014), 188–95; Armida Gilbert, "'Pierced by the Thorns of Reform': Emerson on Womanhood," *The Emerson Dilemma: Essays on Emerson and Social Reform*, ed. T. Gregory Garvey (Athens: University of Georgia Press, 2001), 93–114; Len Gougeon, "Emerson and the Women Question: The Evolution of His Thought," *New England Quarterly* 71, no. 4 (Dec. 1998): 570–92; Christina Zwarg, *Feminist Conversations: Fuller, Emerson, and the Play of Reading* (Ithaca, NY: Cornell University Press, 1995). Cole bases her argument on the text appearing *Later Lectures of Ralph Waldo Emerson* (2001), published after Gourgeon, Zwarg, and Gilbert's analyses. She notes its publication "may require revising some of the critical judgement based on Edward

Emerson's text from the Century Edition," which may have been closer to his 1860 and 1869 speeches. Cole, "The New Movement's Tide," 139.
81 RWE, "Address at the Woman's Rights Convention," 20.
82 ETE, "What I Can Remember About Father," 1902, manuscript, Houghton Library, Harvard University, MS Am 1280.227.
83 RWE, "Address at the Woman's Rights Convention," 22.
84 ETE to Emma Stimson, Sept. 29, 1855.
85 For information on women's nineteenth-century relationships, see: Rachel Hope Cleves, *Charity and Sylvia: A Same-Sex Marriage in Early America* (New York: Oxford University Press, 2014); Sharon Marcus, *Between Women: Friendship, Desire, and Marriage in Victorian England* (Princeton, NJ: Princeton University Press, 2007); Lisa Merrill, *When Romeo Was a Woman: Charlotte Cushman and Her Circle of Female Spectators* (Ann Arbor: University of Michigan Press, 1999); Carol Smith-Rosenberg, "The Female World of Love and Ritual: Relations Between Women in Nineteenth-Century America," *Signs* 1, no. 1 (1975): 1–29; and Martha Vicinus, *Intimate Friends: Women Who Loved Women, 1778–1928* (Chicago: University of Chicago Press, 200).
86 ETE to Addy Manning, Jan. 22, 1856, ETE to EEF, [Dec. 1855], ETE Correspondence.
87 Erica Hirshler, *A Studio of Her Own: Women Artists in Boston, 1870–1940* (Boston: Museum of Fine Arts Boston, 2001), 33.
88 ETE to Emma Stimson, Dec. 14, 1855, ETE Correspondence.
89 ETE to Emma Stimson, Feb. 15, 1858, ETE Correspondence.
90 LRWE, 5:13n51; Charles Bahne, *Chronicles of Old Boston: Exploring New England's Historic Capital* (New York: Museyon, 2012), 234.
91 ETE to Haven Emerson, Dec. 15, 1855, ETE Correspondence.
92 ETE to Haven Emerson, Dec. 15, 1855, ETE Correspondence.
93 ETE to EEF, Nov. 9, 1855, ETE Correspondence.
94 EEF to ETE, Nov. 12, 1855, FP, Carton 1.
95 EEF to ETE, Thursday, Dec. 1855, FP, Carton 1.
96 ETE to Haven Emerson, Dec. 15, 1855, ETE Correspondence.
97 ETE to LJE, Jan. 1856, ETE Correspondence.
98 ETE to Addy Manning, Jan. 22, 1856, ETE Correspondence.
99 ETE to EEF, Feb. 15, 1856, ETE Correspondence.
100 RWE to Caroline Sturgis Tappan, Sept. 6, 1840, quoted in Eleanor M. Tilton, "The True Romance of Anna Hazard Barker and Samuel Gray Ward," *Studies in the American Renaissance* (1987): 69.
101 Tilton, "The True Romance," 69.
102 ETE to Anna Barker Ward, Samuel Grey Ward and Anna Hazard Barker Ward Papers, 1823–1934, Houghton Library, Ms AM 1456 (297).
103 ETE to Emma Stimson, May 8, 1856, ETE Correspondence.
104 ETE to Sally Gibbons Emerson, Oct. 15, 1856, *LETE*, 121.
105 LLJE, 125.
106 ETE to Addy Manning, Sept. 8, 1856, ETE Correspondence.
107 ETE to Addy Manning, Sept. 8, 1856, ETE Correspondence.
108 Sandra Petrulionis, *To Set this World Right: The Antislavery Movement in Thoreau's Concord* (Ithaca, NY: Cornell University Press, 2006), 41.
109 Lilian Clarke to EEF, Oct. 30, 1856, Lilian Clarke to EEF, Nov. 21, 1856, FP, Carton 1.

110 ETE to Haven Emerson, Aug. 21–Sept. 7, 1857, ETE Correspondence.
111 ETE to William Emerson, Jr. Nov. 17, 1857, ETE Correspondence.
112 ETE to Haven Emerson, May 7, 1858, ETE Correspondence.
113 Albert J. von Frank, *An Emerson Chronology*, (Albuquerque, NM: Studio Non Troppo, 2016), 2:761–62.
114 ETE to RWE, Aug. 3–9, 1858, ETE Correspondence.
115 RWE to William Emerson, June 8, 1859, *LRWE*, 5:152.
116 Joel Myerson details the Emersons' financial picture, arguing they were well off, despite the anxiety. Joel Myerson, "Money," *Ralph Waldo Emerson in Context*, ed. Wesley Mott (New York: Cambridge University Press, 2014), 213–20.
117 RWE to William Emerson, Oct. 18, 1858, *LRWE*, 5:121.
118 ETE to EEF, Dec. 6, 1858, ETE Correspondence.
119 EEF to ETE, Nov. 29, 1858, FP, Carton 1.
120 ETE to Emma Stimson, Jan. 22, 1859, ETE Correspondence.
121 EEF to ETE, Nov. 1, 1858, FP, Carton 1.
122 EEF to ETE, Nov. 16, 1858; EEF to ETE, Nov. 29, 1858; and EEF to ETE, Feb. 1, 1859, FP, Carton 1.
123 EEF to EWE, Dec. 15, 1858, FP, Carton 1.
124 EEF to ETE, Dec. 6, 1858, and EEF to EWE Dec. 15, 1858, FP, Carton 1.
125 EEF to ETE, Feb. 3, 1859, FP, Carton 1.
126 RWE to William Emerson, Oct. 18, 1858, *LRWE*, 5:121.
127 ETE to EEF, Feb. 15, 1859, ETE Correspondence.
128 EEF quoted in Edith Gregg, "Emerson as Remembered by His Children," *Emerson in His Own Time*, ed. Ronald A. Bosco and Joel Myerson (Iowa City: University of Iowa Press, 2003), 166.
129 ETE to EEF, Feb. 24, 1859, ETE Correspondence.
130 ETE to EEF, March 3–March 5, 1859, ETE Correspondence.
131 ETE to EEF, April 19, 1859, ETE Correspondence.
132 ETE to EEF, Feb. 5, 1859, ETE Correspondence.
133 ETE to EEF, Feb. 5, 1859, ETE Correspondence.
134 Merrill, 148. Merrill is discussing the actress Charlotte Cushman.
135 William Ellery Channing to Franklin Sanborn, March 19, 1959, quoted in Sanborn, *Recollections*, 2:331–32.
136 Megan Marshall, *Margaret Fuller: A New American Life* (New York: Houghton Mifflin, 2013), 214–15, 262.
137 ETE to Emma Stimson, Sept. 15, 1859, ETE Correspondence.
138 ETE to LJE, Aug. 24, 1859, ETE Correspondence.
139 ETE to Emma Stimpson, Sept. 15, 1859, ETE Correspondence.
140 EEF to ETE, Aug. 6, 1858, FP, Carton 1.
141 John Haddad, *America's First Adventure in China: Trade, Treaties, Opium, and Salvation* (Philadelphia: Temple University Press, 2013), 172–76.
142 EEF to Suzy Loring, May 31, 1859, FP, Carton 1.
143 ETE to LJE and EEF, Aug. 9, 1859, ETE Correspondence.
144 EEF to Suzy Loring, July 18, 1860, FP, Carton 1.
145 ETE to Emma Stimson, Sept. 15, 1859, ETE Correspondence.
146 RWE, "Courage," *New York Tribune*, Nov. 8, 1859. See also David Reynolds, *John Brown: Abolitionist* (New York: Knopf, 2005), 363–69.

147 Jeffery Rossbach, *Ambivalent Conspirators: John Brown, the Secret Six, and a Theory of Slave Violence* (Philadelphia: University of Pennsylvania Press, 1982).
148 RWE to Sarah Forbes, Oct. 26, 1859, *LRWE*, 5:179, RWE to Franklin Sanborn, Oct. 23, 1859, quoted in Franklin Sanborn, *Recollections*, 1:196. See also, Petrulionis, *To Set This World Right*, 127–34.
149 ETE to Addy Manning, Oct. 8, 1860, ETE Correspondence.
150 ETE to RWE, Feb. 11, 1860, ETE Correspondence.
151 ETE to RWE, Feb. 11, 1860, ETE Correspondence.
152 RWE to ETE, Feb. 18, 1860, *LRWE*, 5:200–1.
153 ETE to Haven Emerson, Feb. 22, 1860, ETE Correspondence.
154 ETE to Haven Emerson, Feb. 22, 1860, ETE Correspondence.
155 EEF to Suzy Loring, July 18, 1860, Forbes Correspondence, Carton 1.
156 ETE to Agnes, April 4, 1860, ETE Correspondence; John Shepard Keyes, "The Autobiography of John Shepard Keyes, Transcribed," Concord Free Public Library, Nov. 10, 2010. https://concordlibrary.org/special-collections/keyes-autobiography.
157 EETE to Agnes April 4, 1860, ETE Correspondence.
158 ETE to EEF, May 29, 1860, ETE Correspondence; Franklin Sanborn to Benjamin Smith Lyman, April 22, 1860, quoted in Kenneth Walter Cameron, ed., *Young Reporter of Concord* (Hartford, CT: Transcendental Books, 1978), 24.
159 ETE to Addy Manning, Oct. 8, 1860, ETE Correspondence.

Chapter Three

1 ETE to LJE, April 15, 1861, ETE Correspondence.
2 ETE to EWE, April 16–April 19, 1861, ETE Correspondence.
3 LJE to EEF, April 20, 1861, *SLLJE*, 209.
4 JEC, *A Memoir of Ralph Waldo Emerson* (Boston: Houghton Mifflin, 1893), 2:601.
5 LJE to "My Dear Children," July 15, 1862, *SLLJE*, 216
6 Louisa Leavitt Sanborn to EEF, July 20, 1861, FP, Carton 1.
7 EEF to EWE, July 19, 1861, FP, Carton 1.
8 ETE to William Emerson [Jr.?], Oct. 28, 1861, ETE Correspondence.
9 RWE to William Emerson, Nov. 6, 1861, *LRWE*, 5:256.
10 RWE to William Emerson, Dec. 6, 1861, *LRWE*, 5:259.
11 EEF to EWE, Nov. 7, 1861, FP, Carton 1.
12 ETE to William Forbes, [Jr.?], October 28, 1861, ETE Correspondence.
13 ETE to EEF, Jan. 10, 1861, ETE Correspondence.
14 Phyllis Cole, *Mary Moody Emerson and the Origins of Transcendentalism* (New York: Oxford University Press, 1998), 298
15 ETE, "What I Remember of Stories of Our Ancestors told me by Aunt Mary Ellen Moody," EF Papers (357).
16 RWE to William Emerson, Nov. 6, 1861, *LRWE*, 5:257.
17 Carol Faulkner, *Lucretia Mott's Heresy: Abolition and Women's Rights in Nineteenth-Century America* (Philadelphia: University of Pennsylvania Press, 2011) 178–79.
18 ETE to RWE, Feb. 3, 1862, ETE Correspondence. See also, Willie Lee Rose, *Rehearsal for Reconstruction: The Port Royal Experiment* (New York: Oxford University Press, 1976).

19 EEF, "Childhood with Thoreau, as Remembered in 1882," in *Thoreau in His Own Time*, ed. Sandra Petrulionis (Iowa City: Iowa University Press, 2012), 44.
20 EEF, "Childhood with Thoreau," 44.
21 Harmon Smith, *My Friend, My Friend: The Story of Thoreau's Relationship with Emerson* (Amherst: University of Massachusetts Press, 1999), 181–83.
22 RWE, "Thoreau," *The Atlantic*, August 1862, 240.
23 EEF, "Childhood with Thoreau," 44.
24 Carol Bundy, *The Nature of Sacrifice: A Biography of Charles Russell Lowell, 1835–1964* (New York: Farrar, Straus and Giroux, 2005), 214; George Haven Putnam, *Memories of My Youth, 1844–1865* (New York: G.P. Putnam's Sons), 89–92.
25 ETE to Mary Waterman, May 7, 1862, ETE Correspondence.
26 EEF to EWE, June 3, 1862, FP, Carton 1.
27 LJE to EWE, June 3, 1862, *SLLJE*, 214.
28 EEF Diary, March 2, 1861, FP, Carton 24.
29 Franklin Sanborn to LJE, March 9, 1862, Ralph Waldo Emerson Correspondence with Franklin Benjamin Sanborn and Other Letters. bMs Am 2932, Houghton. Joel Myerson published the exchange. Joel Myerson, "'retracting nothing & reaffirming all': F.B. Sanborn, the Emersons, and a Courtship Gone Wrong," *Harvard Library Bulletin* 10, no. 4 (1999): 3–18.
30 RWE to Franklin Sanborn, July 18, 1862, Ralph Waldo Emerson Correspondence with Franklin Benjamin Sanborn and Other Letters. Ms Am 2932, Houghton.
31 LJE to Franklin Sanborn, Aug. 7, 1862, Ralph Waldo Emerson Correspondence with Franklin Benjamin Sanborn.
32 In 1927, Bill Perry thanked the bookseller George Goodspead for showing him the Emerson and Sanborn correspondence around the incident, promising to keep it confidential. He noted the correspondence answers questions he had about "certain allusions which Edward Emerson often made to Frank Sanborn and which I was quite at a lost to account for until I read this correspondence." Bill Perry to George Goodspead, May 23, 1927, curatorial file for Ralph Waldo Emerson Correspondence with Franklin Benjamin Sanborn.
33 Jane Knopp and Scott Bowden, *Sarah Freeman Clarke, 1808–1896* (Marietta, GA: Cobb Landmarks and Historical Society, 1993).
34 RWE to ETE, July 13, 1862, *LRWE*, 5:281.
35 ETE to LJE, July 9, 1862, ETE Correspondence.
36 LJM to "My Dear Children," July 15, 1862, *SLLJE*, 217.
37 RWE to ETE, July 13, 1862, *LRWE*, 5:281.
38 ETE to LJE, July 9, 1862, ETE Correspondence.
39 ETE to Haven Emerson, July 12–23, 1862, ETE Correspondence.
40 ETE to Mary Waterman, Aug. 26, 1862, ETE Correspondence.
41 EEF to EWE, July 10, 1862, FP, Carton 1.
42 ETE to Haven Emerson, July 12–23, 1862, ETE Correspondence.
43 ETE to Haven Emerson, July 12–23, 1862, ETE Correspondence.
44 ETE to Haven Emerson, September 25, 1872, ETE Correspondence.
45 RWE to William Emerson, Oct. 14, 1862, *LRWE*, 5:290–291.
46 EEF to Susy Loring, Feb. 1862, and EEF to EWE, Oct. 24, 1862, FP, Carton 1.
47 ETE to Mary Waterman, Nov. 1862, typescript, EF Papers, 703.

48 ETE to Haven Emerson, Nov. 18, 1862, ETE Correspondence.
49 ETE to Haven Emerson, Nov. 3, 1862, ETE Correspondence.
50 ETE to LJE, Nov. 1862, ETE Correspondence.
51 ETE to Edith Davidson, Sept. 8, 1874, ETE Correspondence.
52 *Concord, MA, 1892.* Concord, MA, USA: E. H. Smith & Co., 1892, digital image, Ancestry.com; Massachusetts, U.S., Death Records, 1841–1915, digital image, s.v. "Isabella Davidson" (c. 1820–1896), Ancestry.com.
53 ETE to Susan Haven Emerson, Jan. 6, 1863, *ETE Letters.*
54 ETE to RWE, Jan. 17, 1863, *ETE Letters.*
55 ETE to Susan Emerson, Jan. 6, 1863, *ETE Letters.*
56 EWE to ETE, Dec. 19, 1862, EWE Letters, Box 1.
57 EEF to EWE, [January 1863?], FP, Carton 1.
58 ETE to Haven Emerson, Feb. 20, 1863, ETE Correspondence.
59 ETE to EEF, March 24, 1863, *ETE Letters.*
60 RWE, *Journals and Miscellaneous Notebooks of Ralph Waldo Emerson,* (Cambridge, MA: Harvard University Press, 1982), ed. Linda Allardt and David W. Hill, 15:343.
61 ETE to Charlotte Haskins Cleveland, April 27, 1863, Emerson Family Additional Correspondence, Compositions, and Photographs, Houghton Library, MS Am 2982, 9.
62 ETE to Haven Emerson, May 5, 1863, ETE Correspondence.
63 ETE to Haven Emerson, May 5, 1863, ETE Correspondence.
64 ETE to William Emerson, May 19, 1863, *ETE Letters.*
65 ETE to LJE, July 15, 1863, *ETE Letters*; Richard Birdsall, "Emerson and the Church of Rome," *American Literature* 31, no. 3 (1959): 273.
66 ETE to Haven Emerson, July 14, 1863, *ETE Letters.*
67 ETE to RWE, July 17, 1863, *ETE Letters.*
68 RWE to ETE, July [12?] 1863, *LRWE,* 9:111.
69 Margaret Hope Bacon, *Abby Hopper Gibbons: Prison Reformer and Social Activist* (Albany, NY: SUNY Press, 2002), 113–17.
70 ETE to Haven Emerson, July 14, 1863, ETE to RWE, July 17, 1863, and ETE to Sally Hopper Gibbons Emerson, August 5, 1863, *ETE Letters.*
71 ETE to Mary Waterman, Nov. and Dec. 1864, ETE Correspondence
72 Alfred Habegger, *The Father: A Life of Henry James Sr.* (Amherst: University of Massachusetts Press, 2001), 441–42.
73 Sage Stossel, "Voluntaries," *The Atlantic Monthly,* Feb, 2012, *Gale Literature Resource Center.* Accessed Sept. 9, 2018. https://shorturl.at/uuCgg
74 RWE to Francis Shaw, Sept. 10, 1863, *LRWE,* 9:113–14.
75 Mark Howe, *A Great Private Citizen: Henry Lee Higginson* (Boston: Atlantic Monthly Press, 1920), 24.
76 EEF to ETE, Sept. 17, 1863, FP, Carton 1.
77 ETE to Mary Higginson, Sept. 22, 1863, ETE Correspondence.
78 ETE to Mary Waterman, Jan. 8, 1864, ETE Correspondence.
79 ETE to Mary Elizabeth Waterman, Nov. and Dec. 1864, ETE Correspondence.
80 James Baker, *Thanksgiving: The Biography of an American Holiday* (Hanover, NH: University Press of New England, 2008).
81 RWE to George Bradford, Nov. 11, 1863, *LRWE* 9:120.

82 Haven Emerson to EEF, Nov. 22, 1863, FP, Carton 1.
83 RWE to William Emerson, Feb. 15, 1864, *LRWE*, 5:352.
84 EEF to [ETE?], Dec. 1863, fragment, FP, Carton 1.
85 EEF to ETE, Dec. 21, 1863, FP, Carton 1.
86 EEF to [ETE?], [Dec. 24?], 1863, fragment, FP, Carton 1.
87 James Whorton, *Nature Cures: The History of Alternative Medicine in America* (New York: Oxford University Press, 2002), 84–97.
88 EEF to ETE, Dec. 1863, FP, Carton 1.
89 Harry Weiss and Howard R. Kemble, *The Great American Water-Cure Craze: A History of Hydropathy in the United States* (Trenton, NJ: Past Times Press, 1967), 95–97.
90 EEF to [ETE?], Dec. 1863, fragment, FP, Carton 1.
91 . EEF to LJE, Jan. 5, 1864, FP, Carton 1.
92 EEF to ETE, Jan. 26, 1864, FP, Carton 1.
93 LJE to EEF, Jan. 11, 1864, *SLLJE*, 224–25.
94 RWE to William Emerson, Feb. 15, 1864, *LRWE*, 5:352.
95 ETE to EEF, Jan. 2, 1864, *ETE Letters*.
96 ETE to EEF, Jan. 19, 1864, *ETE Letters*.
97 ETE to EEF, Feb. 25, 1864, *ETE Letters*.
98 ETE to EEF, Jan. 8, 1864, *ETE Letters*.
99 EEF to ETE, Jan. 14, 1864, FP, Carton 1.
100 EEF to ETE, Jan. 26, 1864, FP, Carton 1.
101 ETE to EEF, Dec. 18, 1863, *ETE Letters*.
102 ETE to Mary Waterman, Nov. and Dec. 1864, ETE Correspondence.
103 EEF to ETE, Feb. 7, 1864, FP, Carton 1.
104 EEF to ETE, Feb. 29, 1864, FP, Carton 1.
105 ETE to Mary Waterman, Jan. 8, 1864, ETE Correspondence.
106 EEF to ETE, March 2, 1864, FP, Carton 1.
107 EEF to LJE, March 22, 1864, FP, Carton 1.
108 ETE to Haven Emerson, April 12, 1864, *ETE Letters*.
109 Haven Emerson to EEF, May 23, 1864, FP, Carton 1.
110 RWE to [Thomas Hill?], May [8?], 1864, *LRWE*, 5:376.
111 EEF to EWE, July 13, 1864, and EEF to EWE, May 12, 1864, FP, Carton 1.
112 EWE to RWE, 1864, EWE Papers, Box 1.
113 *LLJE*, 142.
114 Bliss Perry, "Edward Waldo Emerson," *Essays, Addresses, and Poems of Edward Waldo Emerson* (Privately Printed, 1930), xi.
115 Julian Hawthorne, "Memories of the Alcott Family," *Alcott in Her Own Time*, ed. Daniel Shealy (Iowa City: University of Iowa Press, 2005), 192.
116 Una Hawthorne to EEF, Sept. 21, 1864, FP, Carton 1.
117 Una Hawthorne to EEF, Sept. 21, 1864, FP, Carton 1.
118 Albert J. von Frank, "Monadnoc," *Poems: A Variorum Edition* (Cambridge, MA: Harvard University Press, 2011), 118. The name is commonly spelled Monadnock, but the Emersons did not use the "k."
119 ETE to EEF, June 29, 1866, ETE Correspondence.
120 ETE to Haven Emerson, Aug. 18, 1865, ETE Correspondence.

121 Tiya Miles, *Wild Girls: How the Outdoors Shaped the Women Who Challenged a Nation* (New York: W.W. Norton, 2023), 45.
122 ETE to Mary Waterman, May 1865, ETE Correspondence.
123 ETE to Mary Waterman, Jan. 14, 1865, ETE Correspondence.
124 EEF to LJE, Jan. 18, 1865, FP, Carton 1.
125 EEF to WHF, April 4, 1865, and EEF to WHF, April 7, 1865, Box 7, FP.
126 RWE to B.B. Wiley, March 10, 1865, *LRWE*, 5:408–409.
127 ETE to Mary Waterman, April 19, 1865, ETE Correspondence.
128 "Unfortunate Affair at College," *Boston Evening Transcript*, Jan. 13, 1860.
129 Sarah Forbes to EEF, 1860, FP, Carton 1.
130 The declaration is reported in: Arthur Pier, *Forbes: Telephone Pioneer* (New York: Hobbs, Mead, 1953), 15.
131 WHF to Charles Perkins, Oct. 19, 1860, FP, Carton 27.
132 Sarah Forbes to WHF, March 4, 1865, FP, Carton 7.
133 Una Hawthorne to EEF, March 10, 1865, FP, Carton 7.
134 ETE to Mary Waterman, April 10, 1865, ETE Correspondence.
135 ETE to Haven Emerson, March 7, 1865, ETE Correspondence.
136 ETE to Mary Waterman, April 19, 1865, ETE Correspondence.
137 RWE to Caroline Sturgis Tappan, March 7, 1865, *LRWE*, 9:174.
138 RWE to John Forbes, March 13, 1865, LRWE, 5:410.
139 EEF to WHF, April 2, 1865, FP, Carton 7.
140 Sarah Forbes to EEF, March 4, 1865, FP, Carton 7.
141 EEF to ETE, March 28, 1865, FP, Carton 1.
142 LJE to Lucy Jackson Brown, March 25, 1865, EFC, Ms AM 1280.226, 488.
143 EEF to WHF, April 2, 1865, FP, Carton 7.
144 EEF to WHF, April 20, 1865, FP, Carton 7.
145 EEF to WHF, April 4, 1865, FP, Carton 7.
146 ETE to EWE, April 10, 1865, ETE Correspondence.
147 ETE to Sarah Forbes, April 10, 1865, FP, Carton 7.
148 ETE to WHF, April [18?], 1865, FP, Carton 7.
149 ETE to WHF, April 15, 1865, FP, Carton 7.
150 Sarah Forbes to Mary Russell, April 15, 1865, and WHF to EEF, April 16, 1865, FP, Carton 7.
151 ETE to Mary Waterman, April 19, 1865, ETE Correspondence.
152 EEF to WHF, April 20, 1865, FP, Carton 7.
153 RWE "A Plain Man of the People," quoted in *Building the Myth: Selected Speeches Memorializing Abraham Lincoln*, ed. Waldo Braden (Chicago: University of Illinois Press, 1990), 33.
154 EEF to WHF, April 20, 1865, FP, Carton 7.

Chapter Four

1 ETE to [Mary] Waterman, Jan. 5, 1866, ETE Correspondence.
2 ETE to [Mary] Waterman, Jan. 5, 1866, ETE Correspondence.
3 ETE to [Mary] Waterman, Jan. 5, 1866. ETE Correspondence.

4 EEF to LJE, Oct. 4, 1865, FP, Carton 1.
5 EEF to LJE, Oct. 4, 1865, FP, Carton 1.
6 ETE to [Mary] Waterman, Jan. 3, 1866, ETE Correspondence.
7 ETE to EEF, Oct. 10, 1865, ETE Correspondence.
8 Arthur Pier, *Forbes: Telephone Pioneer* (New York: Dodd, Mead, 1953), 62.
9 Una Hawthorne to ETE, Nov. 21, 1865, FP, Carton 1.
10 EEF to LJE, Dec. 13, 1865, FP, Carton 1.
11 John Keyes, "Autobiography of Hon. John S. Keyes," typescript, 131. Concord Free Public Library.
12 ETE to [Mary Elizabeth] Waterman, Jan. 3, 1866, and ETE to EEF, Nov. 3, 1865, ETE Correspondence.
13 EEF to EWE, Aug. 8, 1866, FP, Carton 2.
14 ETE to Alice Jackson, July 11, 1866, ETE Correspondence..
15 ETE to LJE, July 18, 1866, ETE Correspondence. Mrs. Rounsville may be Cornelia Rounsville. Year: *1865*. Census Place: Rochester, Plymouth, Massachusetts. Reel 26, Vol. 28. *Massachusetts, U.S., State Census, 1865* [database on-line]. Provo, UT, USA: Ancestry.com Operations, Inc., 2014.
16 LJE to EEF, July 12, 1866, *SLLJE*, 240.
17 ETE to LJE, July 11, 1866, and ETE to Edith Davidson, July 18, 1866, ETE Correspondence.
18 RWE to EEF July 11, 1866, *LRWE*, 5:471–472.
19 *LRWE*, 9:232n70; David Hologram, "Perkins, Charles," *The Biographical Dictionary of Iowa* (Iowa City: University of Iowa Press, 2008), 403–5.
20 ETE to EWE, July 12, 1866, ETE Correspondence.
21 LJE to RWE, March 15, 1848, *SLLJE*, 142.
22 EEF to LJE, Sept. 10, 1866, FP, Carton 1.
23 EEF to ETE, Sept. 9, 1866, FP, Carton 1.
24 ETE to EWE, Nov. 26, 1866, ETE Correspondence.
25 EEF to EWE, Nov. 18, 1866, FP, Carton 1.
26 ETE to LJE, Jan. 5, 1867, ETE Correspondence.
27 ETE to Haven Emerson, Jan. 18, 1867, ETE Correspondence.
28 Ashley Reed explains, "critics of women's writing have often taken for granted that religion can serve only as an oppressive force in women's lives rather than a matter of personal choice, as aspect of communal belonging, a vehicle for intellection and self-expression, and a sincere apprehension of the nature of the universe and human existence." Ashley Reed, *Heaven's Interpreters: Women Writers and Religious Agency in Nineteenth-Century America* (Ithaca, NY: Cornell University Press, 2020), 2
29 ETE to Haven Emerson, Jan. 18, 1867, ETE Correspondence.
30 ETE to EEF, June 14, 1872, ETE Correspondence.
31 ETE to Haven Emerson, Jan. 18, 1867, ETE Correspondence.
32 ETE to Haven Emerson, Jan. 18, 1867, ETE Correspondence.
33 ETE to Haven Emerson, Jan. 18, 1867, ETE Correspondence.
34 ETE to Haven Emerson, Jan. 18, 1867, ETE Correspondence.
35 ETE to RWE, Jan. 28, 1867, and ETE to RWE, Dec. 6, 1867, ETE Correspondence.
36 WHF to EWE, Nov. 22, 1866, and Dec. 7, 1866, WHE Letterbook, FP, Carton 28; Piers, 70.
37 ETE to EEF, June 4, 1867, ETE Correspondence.

38 EEF to ETE, May 20, 1867, FP, Carton 2.
39 EEF to ETE, Oct. 24, 1867, FP, Carton 2.
40 EEF to LJE, Oct. 1867, FP, Carton 2.
41 EEF to ETE, Nov. 8, 1867, FP, Carton 2.
42 ETE to EEF, Nov. 2, 1867, ETE Correspondence.
43 ETE to EEF, Nov. 2, 1867, ETE Correspondence.
44 EEF to LJE, "Thanksgiving Day" 1867, FP, Carton 2.
45 EEF to ETE, Aug. 23, 1868, FP, Carton 2.
46 RWE to LJE, Aug. 9, 1868, *LRWE*, 6:28.
47 ETE to Haven Emerson, Jan. 9, 1868, ETE Correspondence.
48 EEF to "Family," May 1, 1868, FP, Carton 2.
49 EEF to ETE, Aug. 23, 1868, FP, Carton 2.
50 EEF to ETE, Aug. 23, 1868, FP, Carton 2.
51 ETE to EEF, Sept. 3–4, 1868, ETE Correspondence.
52 EEF to ETE, Sept. [5?] 1868, FP, Carton 2. See also, ETE to EEF, Sept. 8, 1868, ETE Correspondence.
53 ETE to EEF, April 20, 1868, ETE Correspondence.
54 Ronald Bosco, "Historical Introduction," in *Letters and Social Aims* (Cambridge, MA: Harvard University Press, 2010), xxxix–xli.
55 Ellen later told James Elliot Cabot that by the mid-1860s Waldo "made mistakes" in his lectures and expressed frustration that he would not let her help him, but she does not begin to document that for a few years in her correspondence. Bosco, "Historical Introduction," clv.
56 RWE to Sarah Ann Clark, July 8, 1868, *LRWE*, 9:318–19.
57 EWE to ETE, Sept. 17, 1868, EWE Papers, Box 1.
58 ETE to EEF, [Sept.?] 1868, ETE Correspondence.
59 ETE to Haven Emerson, Oct. 24, 1868, ETE Correspondence.
60 ETE to Haven Emerson, Oct. 24, 1868, ETE Correspondence.
61 ETE to [Mary] Waterman, Dec. 10, 1868, ETE Correspondence. Ellen later told James Elliot Cabot that she was relieved to go the trip, to escape the pain of her father's failing memory and his rejection of her offers to help, but that timing is not reflected in her correspondence at the time, which had only begun to mention the lapses. Bosco, "Historical Introduction," clv.
62 EWE to EEF, Oct. 24, 1868, EWE Papers, Box 1.
63 EEF to ETE, Oct. 30, 1868, FP, Carton 2.
64 Mark Twain, *The Innocents Abroad* (Hartford, CT: The American Publishing Co, 1901), 50.
65 Daniel Dillard, "'The Delicious Sense of Foreignness:' American Transcendentalism in the Atlantic," *American Nineteenth Century History* 14, no. 2 (2013): 221. See also: Tammy Rose, "A Far Azore: Fayal and the Transcendentalists," July 9, 2022, YouTube video, 18:19, https://youtu.be/f4KTHbP9q4o?si=tXUS-827fqWITRCN.
66 EEF to ETE, Oct. 26, 1868, FP, Carton 2.
67 EEF to LJE, Nov. 4, 1868, FP, Carton 2.
68 *LRWE*, 6:63n46.
69 ETE to Edie Davidson, Nov. 26, 1868, ETE Correspondence.
70 ETE to Emma Stimson, Feb. 16, 1869, and ETE to Edie Davidson, Nov. 26, 1868, ETE Correspondence.

71 ETE to Haven Emerson, Feb. 11, 1869, ETE Correspondence.
72 RWE to EEF, Nov. 19, 1868, *LRWE*, 6:41–42.
73 RWE to EEF, Jan. 10, 1869, *LRWE*, 6:54.
74 RWE to James Thayer, Nov. 22, 1868, *LRWE*, 6:43.
75 RWE to William Forbes, Dec. 23, 1868, *LRWE*, 6:48.
76 Bosco, "Historical Introduction," cxliii.
77 EEF to EWE, Feb. 11, 1869, FP, Carton 2. See also Bosco, "Historical Introduction," cxliii–cxliv.
78 ETE to EEF, Feb. 16, 1869, ETE Correspondence.
79 ETE to Emma Stimson, June 16, 1869, ETE Correspondence.
80 ETE to Charles Emerson, Jan. 14, 1869, ETE Correspondence.
81 ETE to Clara Dabney, Dec. 13, 1869, ETE to Louisa Sanborn, June 12, 1869, ETE Correspondence.
82 ETE to Emma Stimson, Feb. 16, 1869, ETE Correspondence.
83 ETE to Ellen Stimson, Feb. 16, 1869, ETE Correspondence.
84 RWE to Anna Botta, March 16, 1869, *LRWE*, 6:62. Many of Ellen's Fayal letters were likely lost in the fire in Bush in 1872.
85 ETE to Haven Emerson, April 15, 1869, ETE Correspondence.
86 *LRWE*, 6:70n76.
87 ETE to EEF, Saturday [July?] 1869, ETE Correspondence.
88 ETE to EEF, June 29, 1869, and ETE to EEF, Aug. 5, 1869, ETE Correspondence.
89 ETE to EEF, Sept. 7, 1869, ETE Correspondence.
90 ETE to EEF, June 29, 1869, ETE Correspondence.
91 *LETE*, 1:524–25.
92 ETE to EEF, Aug. 5, 1869, ETE Correspondence.
93 ETE to EEF, "Wednesday morning," 1869, ETE Correspondence.
94 ETE to LJE, Aug. 31, 1869, ETE Correspondence.
95 ETE to LJE, Oct. 13, 1869; ETE to LJE and RWE, Feb. 11, 1870; and ETE to Haven Emerson, Feb. 17, 1870, ETE Correspondence.
96 ETE to RWE, Oct. 19, 1869, ETE Correspondence. Henry Henderson and Albert Henderson, *The Indomitable Spirit of Edmonoia Lewis: A Narrative Biography* (Milford, CT: Esquiline Hill Press, 2012).
97 ETE to [Clara] Dabney, Dec. 13, 1869, ETE Correspondence.
98 ETE to EEF and EWE, Dec. 6, 1869, ETE Correspondence.
99 ETE to "Monseigneur" [EWE] Jan. 21, 1870, ETE Correspondence.
100 LJE to ETE, Feb. 24, 1870, *SLLJE*, 265–66.
101 ETE to Haven Emerson, Feb. 17, 1870, ETE Correspondence.
102 ETE to LJE, Feb. 23, 1870, ETE Correspondence.
103 ETE to Haven Emerson, Feb. 17, 1870; ETE to LJE, March 28, 1870; ETE to Edith Davidson, May 24, 1870, ETE Correspondence.
104 ETE to RWE, March 24, 1870, and ETE to LJE, March 16, 1870, ETE Correspondence.
105 ETE to LJE, March 19, 1870, ETE Correspondence.
106 ETE to EEF, April 18, 1870, ETE Correspondence. See also Beth Van Duzer, "Voices, and Votes, for Women: Concord's Early Pioneers," *Discover Concord* (Spring 2020): 24.

107 Lori Ginzburg, *Women and the Work of Benevolence: Morality, Politics, and Class in the 19th-Century United States* (New Haven, CT: Yale University Press), 3.
108 ETE to EEF, May 18, 1870, and ETE to June 25, 1870, ETE Correspondence.
109 For more on *Parnassus*, see: Bosco, "Historical Introduction," esp. lxi–lxv, and Nikhil Bilwakesh, "Emerson's Decomposition: *Parnassus*," *Nineteenth-Century Literature* 67, no. 4 (2013): 520–45.
110 EEF to ETE, March 12, 1870, FP, Carton 2.
111 EEF to ETE, May [13?], 1870, FP, Carton 2.
112 EEF to ETE, May [13?], 1870, FP, Carton 2.
113 Bosco, "Historical Introduction," lxi, xxxv.
114 ETE to EEF, May 23, 1870, and ETE to Edith Davidson, May 24, 1870, ETE Correspondence.
115 ETE to Edith Davidson, May 24, 1870, ETE Correspondence.
116 ETE to EEF, May 23, 1870, ETE Correspondence.
117 ETE to EEF, May 27, 1870, ETE Correspondence.
118 ETE to Edith Davidson, June 11, 1870, ETE Correspondence.
119 ETE to EEF, June 25, 1870, ETE Correspondence.
120 RWE to EEF, June 14, 1870, *LRWE*, 6:120–21.
121 RWE to EEF, Aug. 10, 1870, *LRWE* 6:127. See also ETE to Sally Gibbons, Aug. 18, 1870, ETE Correspondence.
122 Bosco, "Historical Introduction," xxviii.
123 Bosco, "Historical Introduction," xc–xci; *LRWE*, 6:128n136.
124 ETE to EEF, Aug. 19, 1870, ETE Correspondence.
125 Bosco, "Historical Introduction," xciii.
126 ETE to Sarah Forbes, Sept. 6, 1870, ETE Correspondence.
127 EEF to ETE, Sept. 22, 1870, FP, Carton 2.
128 ETE to EEF, Oct. 25, 1870, ETE Correspondence.
129 ETE to EEF, Feb. 17, 1871, ETE Correspondence.
130 ETE to [Clara] Dabney, Feb. 15, 1870, ETE Correspondence.
131 ETE to EEF, Feb. 17, 1871, ETE Correspondence.
132 ETE to Edith Davidson, Dec. 28, 1870, and ETE to EWE, Jan. 5, 1872, ETE Correspondence.
133 Pier, *Forbes: Telephone Pioneer*, 65.
134 Pier, *Forbes: Telephone Pioneer*, 96–97.
135 Bosco, "Historical Introduction," xxix.
136 RWE to Samuel Eliot, April 6, 1871, *LRWE*, 6:147.
137 James Bradley Thayer, *A Western Journey with Mr. Emerson* (Boston: Little, Brown, 1884). See also Brian Wilson, *The California Days of Ralph Waldo Emerson* (Boston: University of Massachusetts Press, 2022) and Bosco, "Historical Introduction," ci.
138 Shannon Withycombe, "Unusual Frontal Developments: Negotiating the Pregnant Body in Nineteenth-Century America," *Journal of Women's History*, 27, no. 4 (Winter 2015): 165.
139 Thayer, 11; Wilson, 24–54.
140 Thayer, 15.
141 RWE to Ralph Forbes, May [21?], 1871, *LRWE*, 6:159–60.

142 RWE, April 11–April 21, Pocket Diary 22, in *The Journals and Miscellaneous Notebooks of Ralph Waldo Emerson*, ed. Ronald Bosco and Glen Johnson (Cambridge, MA: Harvard University Press, 1982): 16:408–9.
143 ETE to Edith Davidson, April 12, 1871, ETE Correspondence.
144 ETE to EEF, April 13, 1871, ETE Correspondence.
145 ETE to EEF, May 11, 1871, ETE Correspondence.
146 ETE to EEF, April 17, 1871, ETE to RWE, April 24, 1871, and ETE to EEF, May 13, 1871, ETE Correspondence.
147 ETE to RWE, April 24, 1871, ETE Correspondence.
148 ETE to EEF, April 26, 1871, ETE Correspondence.
149 EEF to WHF, May 3, 1871, FP, Carton 2.
150 ETE to EEF, May 20, 1871, ETE Correspondence.
151 "Local Brevities," *San Francisco Examiner*, May 18, 1871: 3.
152 EEF to ETE, May 20, 1871, FP, Carton 2.
153 EEF to ETE, May 20, 1871, FP, Carton 2.
154 EEF to ETE, May 20, 1871, FP, Carton 2.
155 EWE to WHF, Aug. 9, 1871, EWE Papers, Box 1.
156 EWE to EEF and WHF, Aug. 22, 1871, EWE Papers, Box 1
157 ETE to Haven Emerson, Sept. 21, 1871, ETE Correspondence.
158 EEF to EWE, Oct. 24, 1871, FP, Carton 2.
159 ETE to Haven Emerson, Sept. 21, 1871, ETE Correspondence.
160 EEF to ETE, Oct. 7, 1871, FP, Carton 2.
161 ETE to RWE, Jan. 11, 1872, and ETE to EWE, Feb. 6, 1872, ETE Correspondence.
162 Susan Goodier, *No Votes for Women: The New York State Anti-Suffrage Movement* (Urbana: University of Illinois Press, 2015), 5.
163 "Talk about the Tea-Table, IV" *Old & New*, July 1871:79.
164 Susan Marshall, *Splintered Sisterhood: Gender and Class in the Campaign Against Woman Suffrage* (Madison: University of Wisconsin Press, 1997), 29.
165 ETE to EWE, Oct. 30, 1871, ETE Correspondence.
166 ETE to EWE, Nov. 17, 1871, ETE Correspondence.
167 Marshall, *Splintered Sisterhood*, 19.
168 "Talk about the Tea Table, IV" 81. Phyllis Cole, "The New Movement's Tide: Emerson and Women's Rights," in *Emerson Bicentennial Essays*, ed. Ronald Bosco and Joel Myerson (Boston: Massachusetts Historical Society, 2006), 137–38.
169 Todd Richardson, "Another Protest That Shall Be 'Heard Round the World': The Woman's Journal and Women's Pilgrimages to Concord Massachusetts," *The Concord Saunterer* 24 (2015): 29.
170 Todd Richardson, "Pushing the Cause of Suffrage: The *Woman's Journal* Appropriation of Ralph Waldo Emerson in Postbellum American," *The New England Quarterly* 79, no. 4 (2006): 581–82; Sarah K. Bolton, "A Visit to the Sages," *The Woman's Journal*, Sept. 20, 1879: 299.
171 "Notes and News," *The Woman's Journal*, Nov. 8, 1902: 360.
172 *LETE*, 1:657.
173 EEF to ETE, Dec. 5, 1871, FP, Carton 2.
174 ETE to Clara Dabney, March 4, 1872, ETE Correspondence.
175 ETE to Clara Dabney, March 4, 1872, ETE Correspondence.
176 EWE to ETE, July 14, 1872, EWE Papers, Box 1.

177 EEF to EWE, March 2, 1872, FP, Carton 2.
178 ETE to EWE, April 7, 1872, ETE Correspondence; Pier, 84.
179 EEF to EWE, March 2, 1872, FP, Carton 2.
180 EEF to LJE, March 22, 1872, and ETE to EEF, March 19, 1872, FP, Carton 2.
181 EEF to ETE, April 19, 1872, FP, Carton 2.
182 ETE to EWE, May 14, 1872, ETE Correspondence.
183 Pier, *Forbes: Telephone Pioneer*, 86.
184 Pier, *Forbes: Telephone Pioneer*, 90.
185 EWE to ETE, July 14, 1872, EWE Papers, Box 1.
186 EWE to RWE, July 28, 1872, EWE Papers, Box 1.
187 ETE to Clara Dabney, March 4, 1872, ETE Correspondence.
188 ETE to EWE, Feb. 6, 1872, ETE Correspondence.
189 ETE to Clara Dabney, March 4, 1872, ETE Correspondence.
190 ETE to EWE, April 15, 1872, ETE Correspondence.
191 ETE to ETE, June 5, 1872, ETE Correspondence.
192 Bosco, "Historical Introduction," clv.
193 ETE to EWE, July 30, 1872, ETE Correspondence.
194 ETE to EWE, July 30, 1872, ETE Correspondence.
195 Anna Alcott Pratt, quoted in Bosco, "Historical Introduction," clxii.
196 Louisa May Alcott to Louisa Wells, July 27, 1872, quoted in Bosco, "Historical Introduction," clxii.
197 JEC, notebook, EF Papers, Box 79.
198 Anna Alcott Pratt, quoted in Bosco, "Historical Introduction," clxii.
199 ETE to EWE, July 30, 1872, ETE Correspondence.
200 ETE to EWE, July 30, 1872, ETE Correspondence.
201 ETE to Haven Emerson, Aug. 16, 1872, ETE Correspondence.
202 ETE to Sarah Forbes, July 30, 1872, ETE Correspondence.
203 ETE to EWE, July 30, 1872, and ETE to EWE, Aug. 6, 1872, ETE Correspondence.
204 Bosco, "Historical Introduction," clxiv–clxv. For a list of contributors, see Ronald Bosco and Joel Myerson, *Ralph Waldo Emerson: A Bicentennial Exhibition at Houghton Library of the Harvard College Library, 26 March to 3 June 2003* (Cambridge, MA: Houghton Library of the Harvard College Library, 2003), 46.
205 ETE to EWE, Aug. 6, 1872, ETE Correspondence.
206 ETE to Haven Emerson, Aug. 16, 1872, ETE Correspondence.

Chapter Five

1 EEF to EWE, Sept. 1, 1872, FP, Carton 2.
2 EEF to EWE, Aug. 20, 1872, FP, Carton 2.
3 Edward annotated a letter from Ellen to him, recounting Waldo's relief at learning the pressure from the publishers was off. ETE to EWE, Sept. 9, 1872, ETE Correspondence.
4 EEF to EWE, Oct. 8, 1872, FP, Carton 2.
5 EEF to EWE, Oct. 8, 1872, FP, Carton 2.
6 EEF to LJE, Oct. 24, 1872, FP, Carton 2.
7 LJE to RWE, October 23, 1872, quoted in Bird, *SLLJE*, 279.

8 EEF to LJE, Oct. 24, 1872, FP, Carton 2.
9 ETE to LJE, Oct. 1872, ETE Correspondence.
10 ETE to LJE, Oct. 1872, ETE Correspondence.
11 EEF to ETE, Nov. 18, 1872, FP, Carton 2.
12 LJE to RWE, Nov. 25, 1872, quoted in Bird, *SLLJE*, 285.
13 ETE to LJE and EEF, Oct. 1872, ETE Correspondence.
14 ETE to LJE, Nov. 4, 1872, ETE Correspondence.
15 EEF to LJE, Nov. 4, 1872, ETE Correspondence.
16 ETE to LJE, Nov. 6, 1872, ETE Correspondence.
17 EEF to LJE, November 4, 1872, FP, Carton 2.
18 EEF to ETE, Nov. 3, 1872, FP, Carton 2.
19 EWE to EEF, Oct. 20, 1872, EWE Papers, Box 1.
20 EWE to LJE, Nov. 10, 1872, EWE Papers, Box 1.
21 EWE to LJE, Nov. 10, 1872, EWE Papers, Box 1.
22 ETE to LJE, Nov. 16, 1872, ETE Correspondence.
23 ETE to EEF, Nov. 16, 1872, ETE Correspondence.
24 ETE to WHF, Nov. 14, 1872, ETE Correspondence.
25 EEF to ETE, Dec. 2, 1872, FP, Carton 2.
26 EEF to ETE, Dec. 15, 1872, FP, Carton 2.
27 ETE to LJE, Nov. 6, 1872, ETE Correspondence.
28 ETE to LJE, Nov. 16, 1872, ETE Correspondence.
29 ETE to EEF, Nov. 26, 1872, ETE Correspondence.
30 ETE to EEF, Nov. 26, 1872, ETE Correspondence.
31 ETE to EEF, Nov. 26, ETE Correspondence.
32 ETE to LJE, Dec. 4, 1872, ETE Correspondence.
33 ETE to EEF, Nov. 26, 1872, ETE Correspondence.
34 ETE to LJE, Dec. 4, 1872, ETE Correspondence.
35 ETE to EWE, Dec. 14, 1872, ETE Correspondence.
36 ETE to EEF, Nov. 14, 1872, ETE Correspondence.
37 ETE to EEF, Nov. 26, 1872, ETE Correspondence.
38 ETE to LJE, March 21, 1873, ETE Correspondence.
39 ETE to LJE, Dec. 4, 1872, ETE Correspondence.
40 ETE to LJE, March 11, 1873, ETE Correspondence.
41 ETE to EEF, Dec. 3, 1872, ETE Correspondence.
42 EEF to ETE, April 4, 1873, FP, Carton 2.
43 EEF to ETE, Dec. 10, 1872, FP, Carton 2.
44 EWE to ETE, Nov. 20, 1872, EWE Papers, Box 1.
45 EEF to ETE, Nov. 25, 1872, FP, Carton 2.
46 EWE to ETE, Dec. 18, 1872 EWE Papers, Box 1.
47 EEF to ETE, Dec. 26, 1872, FP, Carton 2.
48 EEF to ETE, Dec. 26, 1872, FP, Carton 2.
49 ETE to EWE, Dec. 14, 1872, ETE Correspondence.
50 RWE, *The Journals and Miscellaneous Notebooks of Ralph Waldo Emerson*, ed. Ronald Bosco and Glen Johnson (Cambridge, MA: Harvard University Press, 1982) 16:286; "Obituary: William Scoloway Whitwell," *Journal of the Associate of Engineering Studies* 24 (March 1900): 232–33.

51 ETE to LJE, Dec. 25, 1872, ETE Correspondence.
52 ETE to EWE, Jan. 1, 1873, *LETE*, 2:31. Ellen's letters from January and February 1873 are not in the 1873 folder in the ETE Correspondence.
53 ETE to EEF, Jan. 1, 1873, *LETE*, 2:34
54 RWE, *Journals*, 16:286.
55 ETE to EEF, Jan. 12, 1873, *LETE*, 40.
56 ETE to LJE, Jan. 29, 1873, *LETE*, 48.
57 RWE to Samuel Ward, Nov. 29, 1872, *LRWE*, 10:97. Robert Richardson and James Marcus stress the importance of the myth of Osisis to Waldo and his ideas about mourning, arguing that interest drove his desire to travel to Egypt. Robert Richardson, *Emerson: The Mind on Fire* (Berkeley: University of California Press, 1995), 568–69; James Marcus, *Glad to the Brink of Fear: A Portrait of Ralph Waldo Emerson* (Princeton, NJ: Princeton University Press, 2023), 239–41. See also Jennifer Sears, "Emerson's Egypt," *North American Review*, 306, no. 3 (2021), 66–74.
58 ETE to LJE, Feb. 19, 1873, in *LETE*, 56.
59 ETE to EEF, Jan. 21, 1872, in *LETE*, 41–42.
60 ETE to EWE, Jan. 31, 1873, in *LETE*, 51.
61 ETE to EWE, Jan. 31, 1873, in *LETE*, 52.
62 ETE to LJE, Feb. 19, 1873, in *LETE*, 55–57.
63 EEF to EWE, Jan. 31, 1873, in *LETE*, 53–55.
64 ETE to LJE, Feb. 19, 1873, in *LETE*, 57.
65 ETE to LJE, Feb. 19, 1873, in *LETE*, 59.
66 ETE to EEF, March 1, 1873, ETE Correspondence.
67 ETE to EEF, March 1, 1873, and ETE to LJE, March 11, 1873, ETE Correspondence.
68 ETE to LJE, March 11, 1872, ETE Correspondence.
69 ETE to EEF, March 18, 1873, ETE Correspondence.
70 ETE to LJE, March 11, 1873, ETE Correspondence.
71 ETE to EEF, March 18, 1873, ETE Correspondence.
72 ETE to EEF, April 14, 1873, ETE Correspondence.
73 ETE to LJE, April 1873, ETE Correspondence.
74 ETE to Edie Davidson, May 3, 1873, ETE Correspondence.
75 ETE to Clara Dabney, May 27, 1873, ETE Correspondence.
76 ETE to Clara Dabney, May 27, 1873, ETE Correspondence.
77 EEF to EWE, Aug. 5, 1873, FP, Carton 2.
78 ETE to Haven Emerson, July 22, 1873, typescript, EF Papers (703).
79 RWE to EEF, July 21, 1873, *LRWE*, 6:244.
80 EEF to ETE, Sept. 7, 1873, FP, Carton 2.
81 Elmus Wicker, *Banking Panics of the Gilded Age* (New York: Cambridge University Press, 2000), 16–33.
82 The Chicago, Wilmington and Vermillion Coal Company, owned in part by the Forbes, tried to save money by encouraging immigration of coal miners from Austria-Hungary to work as scabs in the mines in Braidwood, Illinois; the plan fell apart when the immigrants refused to work when they realized their role. Scott Reynolds Nelson, *A Nation of Deadbeats: An Uncommon History of America's Financial Disasters* (New York: Knopf, 2012), 170–73.
83 Arthur S. Pier, *Forbes: Telephone Pioneer* (New York: Dodd, Mead and Co., 1953), 101.

84 EEF to ETE, Sept. 18, 1873, FP, Carton 2.
85 ETE to EEF, Oct. 2, 1873, ETE Correspondence; Ronald A. Bosco, "Historical Introduction," in *Letters and Social Aims*, vol. 8 of *The Collected Works of Ralph Waldo Emerson* (Cambridge, MA: Harvard University Press, 2010), cxcii.
86 Ralph Waldo Emerson, "Address [At the Dedication of the New Building for the Concord Free Public Library, 1 October 1873]", in *Letters and Social Aims*, 513.
87 EEF to ETE, March 15, 1874, FP, Carton 2.
88 EEF to ETE, March 15, 1874, FP, Carton 2.
89 ETE to Sally Emerson, Feb. 3, 1874, *LETE*, 2:122.
90 ETE to Sally Emerson, Jan. 16, 1874, *LETE* 2:120.
91 EEF to ETE, April 26, 1874, EEF to ETE, April 30, 1874, and EEF to LJE, May 5, 1874, FP, Carton 2.
92 ETE to EEF, June 12, 1874, ETE Correspondence.
93 ETE to EEF, Aug. 1874, ETE Correspondence.
94 EEF to ETE, Aug. 1, 1874, FP, Carton 2.
95 EWE to EEF, Aug. 6, 1874, EWE Papers, Box 1; EEF to ETE, Aug. 1, 1874, FP, Carton 2; WHF to ETE, Aug. 1, 1874, FP, Carton 2. This note appears on the back of EEF's Aug. 1, 1874 letter to ETE.
96 ETE to EEF, Aug. 4, 1874, ETE Correspondence.
97 WHF to RWE, Jan. 19, 1875, and WHF to RWE, Jan. 28, 1875, WHF Letterpress Books, FP, Carton 28; Pier, *Forbes*, 74–76.
98 Pier, *Forbes*, 77–78; *LLJE*, 166.
99 *LLJE*, 166.
100 ETE to EWE, Aug. 17, 1874, ETE Correspondence.
101 ETE to Lily Ward von Hoffman, Nov. 8–Dec. 12, 1874, ETE Correspondence. Ronald Bosco has argued that these final changes disrupted the plan Waldo had earlier conceived for the volume, which largely corresponded with his ideas in "Poetry and Imagination." Ronald Bosco, "'Poetry for the World of Readers' and 'Poetry for Bards Proper': Poetic Theory and Textual Integrity in Emerson's 'Parnassus.'" *Studies in the American Renaissance* (1989): 288–89.
102 ETE to Lily [Ward von Hoffman], Dec. 12, 1874, ETE Correspondence.
103 EEF to ETE, Dec. 18, 1874, FP, Carton 2; Glen M. Johnson, Note to "Preface [Parnassus]," in *Uncollected Prose Writings* (Cambridge, MA: Harvard University Press, 2013), 893.
104 ETE to EEF, Sept. 15, 1874, ETE Correspondence.
105 ETE to EEF, Nov. 3, 1874, ETE Correspondence.
106 EEF to ETE, Nov. 17, 1874, FP, Carton 2; Joel Myerson, *Ralph Waldo Emerson: A Descriptive Bibliography* (Pittsburgh, PA: University of Pittsburgh Press, 1982), 699–700.
107 ETE to Clara Dabney, Dec. 22, 1874, ETE Correspondence; EEF to ETE, Nov. 17, 1874, FP, Carton 2.
108 EEF to ETE, Dec 18, 1874, FP, Carton 2.
109 ETE to Clara Dabney, Dec. 22, 1874, ETE Correspondence.
110 Myerson, *Ralph Waldo Emerson*, 699.
111 ETE to Lily Wald Von Hoffman, Nov. 8–Dec. 12, 1874, ETE Correspondence.
112 ETE to EEF, Oct. 19, 1874, ETE Correspondence.
113 EEF to ETE, October 18, 1874, FP, Carton 2.

114 Edward Waldo Forbes, "Edward Waldo Emerson (1844–1930)," *Proceedings of the American Academy of Arts and Sciences* 17, no. 10 (1936): 532.
115 ETE to Haven Emerson, April 24, 1875, ETE Correspondence.
116 Harold Holzer, *Monument Man: The Life & Art of Daniel Chester French* (Princeton, NJ: Princeton Architectural Press, 2019), 41–53.
117 David Little, "'Twas the Nineteenth of April in (18)75—and the Centennial Was Coming Unstuck," *American Heritage* 23, no. 3 (April 1972): 18–25.
118 ETE to JEC, July 17, 1883, ETE Correspondence. See also Johnson, *Uncollected Prose*, 899.
119 ETE to Haven Emerson, April 24, 1875, ETE Correspondence.
120 Louisa May Alcott, "Women's Part in the Concord Celebration," *Woman's Journal* 6 (May 1, 1875), 140. See also, Madeline Stern, "Louisa May Alcott's Feminist Letters," *Studies in the American Renaissance* (1978): 432, 438–41.
121 For examples, see: "Notes on the Concord Celebration," *Boston Daily Globe*, April 20, 1875; "Centennial Number," *Boston Evening Transcript*, April 20, 1875.
122 ETE to Sally Emerson, July 13, 1875, ETE Correspondence.
123 EEF to Annie Emerson, July 20, 1875, July 22, 1875, and July 25, 1875, FP, Carton 2.
124 EWE to EEF, 1875, EWE Papers, Box 1.
125 Nancy Simmons, "Arranging the Sibylline Leaves: James Elliot Cabot's Work at as Emerson's Literary Executor," *Studies in the American Renaissance* (1983), 342–43.
126 ETE to EEF, Aug. 1875, ETE Correspondence.
127 Simmons, "Arranging," 343.
128 ETE to EEF, Aug. 16, 1875, ETE Correspondence.
129 ETE to EEF, Aug. 16, 1875, ETE Correspondence.
130 ETE to Haven Emerson, Sept. 2, 1874, typescript, EF Papers, 703.
131 ETE to EEF, Aug., 1875, ETE Correspondence.
132 ETE to EEF, Sept. 8, 1875, ETE Correspondence.
133 ETE to EEF, Sept. 8, 1875, ETE Correspondence.
134 ETE to EEF, Sept. 25, 1875, ETE Correspondence.
135 ETE to EEF, Nov. 15, 1875, ETE Correspondence.
136 Myerson, *Ralph Waldo Emerson*, 331–32.

Chapter Six

1 Nancy Craig Simmons, "Arranging the Sibylline Leaves: James Elliot Cabot's Work as Emerson's Literary Executor," *Studies in the American Renaissance* (1983): 351; Joseph Thomas, "Late Emerson: Selected Poems and the 'Emerson Factory,'" *ELH* 64, no. 4 (1998): 971–94.
2 ETE to EEF, Nov. 15, 1875, ETE Correspondence.
3 The poetry volume was part of a *Little Classic Works* edition of Waldo's work. Only *Selected Poems* was not a reissue. Simmons, "Arranging," 348.
4 Albert von Frank suggests "certain forms of aphasia leave oddly intact... an aptitude for poetry and song." Albert J. von Frank, "Historical Introduction," *Poems: A Variorum Edition* (Cambridge, MA: Harvard University Press, 2011), xcvii. See also, Thomas, "Late Emerson," 971–94.

5 ETE to EEF, Sept. 29, 1876, ETE Correspondence.
6 Thomas, "Late Emerson," 977–79.
7 ETE to EEF, March 3, 1876, ETE Correspondence.
8 Thomas, "Late Emerson," 982–88; Von Frank, "Historical Introduction," *Poems*, xcix–c, "May-Day [1867 Version], 311–313, and, "Later Versions of May-Day," *Poems*, 683.
9 EWE to JEC, October 19, 1883, EF Correspondence (295).
10 ETE to Haven Emerson, April 1876, ETE Correspondence.
11 Ronald A. Bosco, "Historical Introduction," in *Letters and Social Aims* (Cambridge, MA: Harvard University Press, 2010), clxxxvii–viii.
12 Bosco, "Historical Introduction," xxxiv.
13 ETE to LJE, June 23, 1876, ETE Correspondence.
14 ETE to JEC, Sept. 26, 1882, in *LETE*, 2:666–67.
15 ETE to LJE, June 29, 1876, ETE Correspondence.
16 ETE to JEC, Sept. 26, 1882, in *LETE*, 2:668.
17 ETE to JEC, Sept. 26, 1882, in *LETE*, 2, 668.
18 Bosco, "Historical Introduction," clxxxviii.
19 Hubert H. Hoeltje, "Emerson in Virginia," *New England Quarterly*, 5, no. 4 (1932): 753–68.
20 ETE to EEF, Sept. 29, 1876, EEF Correspondence.
21 ETE to Clara Dabney, Oct. 23, 1876, ETE Correspondence.
22 ETE to EEF, Oct. 29, 1876, ETE Correspondence.
23 ETE to EEF, July 12, 1876, ETE Correspondence.
24 ETE to EEF, July 24, 1876, ETE Correspondence.
25 ETE to EEF, Feb. 17, 1875, ETE Correspondence.
26 ETE to EEF, Sept. 6, 1876, ETE Correspondence.
27 ETE to EEF, Sept. 6, 1876, ETE Correspondence.
28 Esther Schor, *Emma Lazarus* (New York: Penguin Random House, 2006), 54.
29 ETE to LJE, March 22, 1878, ETE Correspondence.
30 ETE to Clara Dabney, January 8, 1877, ETE Correspondence.
31 ETE to Clara Dabney, Feb. 28, 1877, ETE Correspondence.
32 ETE to Haven Emerson, [April 1876], ETE Correspondence.
33 ETE to EEF, April 10, 1876, ETE Correspondence.
34 ETE to EEF, April 18, 1877, ETE Correspondence.
35 EEF to ETE, April 1877, FP, Carton 2.
36 ETE to EEF, [April 1877], ETE Correspondence.
37 Ellen reported these comments to Edith. ETE to EEF, July 18, 1877, ETE Correspondence.
38 EEF to ETE, April 1, 1877, and EEF to ETE, Sept. 16, 1877, FP, Carton 2.
39 EEF to ETE, Aug. 22, 1875, and EEF to ETE, Sept. 26, 1876, FP, Carton 2.
40 EEF to ETE, Sept. 26, 1876, and EEF to ETE, May 5, 1877, FP, Carton 2.
41 ETE to EEF, May 5, 1877, FP, Carton 2.
42 ETE to EEF, Jan. 20, 1877, FP, Carton 2.
43 EEF to ETE, June 8, 1875, and EEF to ETE, Dec. 28, 1875, FP, Carton 2.
44 ETE to LJE, [Oct. 1877], ETE Correspondence.
45 EEF to LJE [Oct. 1877], FP, Carton 2.

NOTES TO PAGES 112–116   253

46 EEF to ETE Oct. 18, 1877, FP, Carton 2; Regina Morantz-Sanchez, *Sympathy and Science: Women Physicians in American Medicine* (Chapel Hill: University of North Carolina Press, 2000), 110.
47 ETE to EEF, Dec. 1877, ETE Correspondence.
48 EWE to EEF, Jan. 1878, EWE Papers, Box 2.
49 EEF to ETE, Feb. 1, 1878, EEF to ETE, Feb. 17, 1878, and EEF to ETE, 19, 1878, FP, Carton 2.
50 EEF to ETE, Feb. 17, 1878, FP, Carton 2.
51 EEF to ETE, Feb. 28, 1878, FP, Carton 2.
52 EEF to ETE, March 8, 1878, FP, Carton 2.
53 EEF to ETE April 14, 1878, FP, Carton 2.
54 EEF to ETE April 14, 1878, FP, Carton 2.
55 ETE to Haven Emerson, April 8, 1878, ETE Correspondence.
56 ETE to LJE and RWE, July 7, 1868, ETE Correspondence; ETE to Susan Emerson, Jan. 8, 1863, *ETE Letters*.
57 ETE to EEF, April 2, 1878, ETE Correspondence.
58 E. R. Hoar to WHF, July 25, 1878, FP, Carton 2.
59 EEF to ETE, July 31, 1878, and EEF to ETE, Dec. 5, 1878, FP, Carton 2.
60 ETE to Elizabeth Hoar, April 6, ETE Correspondence. For the "Emerson factory" work on "Perpetual Forces," see Christopher Hanlon, *Emerson's Memory Loss: Originality, Communality, and the Late Style* (New York: Oxford University Press, 2018), 99–116.
61 ETE to EEF, April 20, 1878, FP, Carton 2.
62 ETE to EEF, Feb. 1, 1878, ETE Correspondence.
63 ETE to EEF, Feb. 1, 1878, ETE Correspondence.
64 EEF to Elizabeth Hoar, April 6, 1878, ETE Correspondence.
65 ETE to EEF, May [18?], 1878, ETE Correspondence.
66 ETE to LJE, Aug. 16, 1877, ETE Correspondence.
67 ETE to EEF, Jan. 31, 1878, ETE Correspondence.
68 This lecture is distinct from the lecture of the same name delivered in 1863 and 1864. For a history of both lectures by this name, see "Ronald A. Bosco and Joel Myerson, eds., *The Later Lecturers of Ralph Waldo Emerson, 1843–1871* (Athens: University of Georgia Press), 2:319.
69 ETE to WHF, March 13, 1878, ETE Correspondence.
70 ETE to EEF, May 16, 1878, ETE Correspondence.
71 ETE to EEF, May [18?], 1878, ETE Correspondence.
72 EEF to ETE, May 26, 1878, FP, Carton 2.
73 ETE to LJE, Sept. 16, 1878, typescript, EF Papers (703).
74 ETE to EEF, Sept. 23, 1878, typescript, EF Papers (703).
75 EEF to ETE, Sept. 6, 1878, FP, Carton 2.
76 EEF to ETE, Sept. 10, 1878, FP, Carton 2.
77 EEF to ETE, Sept. 16, 1878, FP, Carton 2.
78 EEF to LJE, March 1879, and Susan Emerson to EEF, March 18, 1879, FP, Carton 2.
79 ETE to EEF, April 15, 1879, ETE Correspondence.
80 EEF to ETE, April 16, 1879, FP, Carton 2.

81 Arthur Pier, *Forbes: Telephone Pioneer* (New York: Dodd, Mead, & Company, 1953), 116–20.
82 Richard Walden Hale, *Milton Academy, 1798–1948* (Milton, MA: 1948), 37–40; "Milton Academy: History," *Milton Academy 1929–30 Catalogue*. (Milton, MA: 1929), 5.
83 EEF to ETE, Oct. 13, 1879, and EEF to ETE, Nov. 16, 1879, FP, Carton 2.
84 ETE to EEF, Nov. 4, 1878, ETE Correspondence; Scribner, "Emerson's Old Age," *Jefferson City Tribune*, Sept. 29, 1878: 2; Scribner, "Emerson's Old Age," *Green Bay Weekly Gazette*, Sept. 28, 1878: 1.
85 ETE to EEF, Jan. 30, 1878, ETE Correspondence.
86 ETE to EEF, July 5, 1879, ETE Correspondence.
87 Bruce Ronda, "The Concord School of Philosophy and the Legacy of Transcendentalism," *New England Quarterly* 82, no. 4 (2009): 575–607; "Concord School of Philosophy," in *Louisa May Alcott Encyclopedia*, ed. Gregory Eiselein and Anne Phillips (Westport, CT: ABC-CLIO, 2001), 62–63.
88 Ronda, "The Concord School of Philosophy," 587; S.H. Emerson and F.B. Sanborn, "The Concord Summer School of Philosophy," *Journal of Speculative Philosophy* 14, no. 2 (1880): 251–53.
89 William Sloane Kennedy, diary, quoted in Hendrick, George Hendrick, "William Sloane Kennedy Looks to Emerson and Thoreau," *ESQ*, no. 26 (1st Quarter 1962): 29
90 JEC to ETE, June 16, 1879, FP, Carton 2.
91 JEC to ETE, June 16, 1879, FP, Carton 2. In the end, they incorporated material from "The Rule of Life," a lecture that Waldo had given three times between 1867 and 1871. Ronald Bosco and Joel Myerson, "Textual Introduction," in *Uncollected Prose Writings and Addresses, Essays, and Reviews* (Cambridge, MA: Harvard University Press, 2013), cxv.
92 Hanlon, *Emerson's Memory Loss*, 8.
93 Hanlon, *Emerson's Memory Loss*, 13.
94 Daniel Chester French, "A Sculptor's Reminiscences of Emerson," *Art World* (October 1916): 44. Daniel Holzer provides a detailed history of the bust. Daniel Holzer, *Monument Man: The Life and Art of Daniel Chester French* (New York: Princeton Architectural Press, 2019), 87–94.
95 *Catalogue of Oil-Paintings, Water-Colors, and Engravings in the Art Exposition of the Twelfth Exhibition of the Massachusetts Charitable Mechanics Association* (Boston: Rand, Avery, and Co., 1874), 9; "The Late Mrs. Jesse Noa," *Boston Evening Transcript*, April 25, 1907: 12.
96 ETE to EEF, Oct. 4, 1879, typescript, EF Papers (703).
97 ETE to Daniel Chester French, July 26, 1879, quoted in Holzer, 92.
98 ETE to Sarah [Haskins Ansley], Dec. 23, 1879, ETE Correspondence.
99 ETE to EEF, July 24, 1879, ETE Correspondence.
100 ETE to EEF, July 24, 1879, ETE Correspondence.
101 ETE to EEF, July 18, 1879, and ETE to EEF, July 30, 1880, ETE Correspondence.
102 *LLJE*, 129, 182.
103 *LLJE*, 173.
104 ETE to Haven and Susan Emerson, Feb. 28, 1879, typescript, EF Papers (703).

105 *LLJE*, 167–68.
106 Todd Richardson, "Another protest that shall be 'heard round the world': The 'Woman's Journal' and Women's Pilgrimages to Concord, Massachusetts," *The Concord Saunterer* 23 (2015): 33.
107 Tiffany Wayne, *Woman Thinking: Feminism and Transcendentalism in Nineteenth-Century America* (Lanham, MD: Lexington Books, 2004), 114.
108 Ronda, "The Concord School of Philosophy," 590.
109 Wayne, *Woman Thinking*, 122.
110 ETE to EEF, Jan. 17, 1880, ETE Correspondence.
111 ETE to EEF, May 17, 1880, ETE Correspondence.
112 ETE to Sally Emerson, May 21, 1880, *LETE*, 2:378.
113 ETE to Mrs. Lewis, June 15, 1880, *LETE*, 2:384.
114 ETE to EEF, June 9, 1880, ETE Correspondence.
115 ETE to EEF, Dec. 1, 1880, ETE Correspondence.
116 ETE to EEF, Feb. 26, 1881, ETE Correspondence.
117 EEF to ETE, Feb. 28, 1881, FP, Carton 2.
118 EEF to ETE, Jan. 19, 1881, FP, Carton 2.
119 EEF to ETE, Jan. 27, 1881, FP, Carton 2.
120 EEF to ETE, March 26, 1881, FP, Carton 2.
121 Copy in Edith's hand of EEF to ETE, March 23, 1881, FP, Carton 2.
122 ETE to Haven and Susan Emerson, March 30-April 1, 1881, *LETE*, 2:419
123 ETE to Haven Emerson, May 7, 1881, ETE Correspondence, *LETE*, 2:423.
124 LJE to EEF, March 31, 1881, FP, Box 5
125 EEF to LJE, April 10, 1881, FP, Carton 2.
126 EWE to WHF, April 15, 1881, EWE Papers, Box 2.
127 EEF to ETE, April 24, 1881, FP, Carton 2.
128 EEF to ETE, April 24, 1881, FP, Carton 2.
129 EEF to ETE, April 24, 1881, FP, Carton 2.
130 EEF to ETE, May 7, 1881, FP, Carton 2.
131 EEF to ETE, May 13, 1881, FP, Carton 2.
132 EEF to ETE, May 23, 1881, FP, Carton 2.
133 EEF to ETE, Aug. 5, 1881, EEF to ETE, June 30, 1890, FP, Carton 2; Pier, *Forbes*, 182.
134 Andrew F. Smith, "Juliet Corson," in *Savoring Gotham: A Food Lover's Companion to New York City*, ed. Andrew F. Smith (New York: Oxford University Press, 2015), 145–46.
135 ETE to EEF, Sept. 14, 1881, ETE Correspondence; 1880 United States Census, Concord, Middlesex County, Massachusetts, digital image s.v. "Annie McLaughlin," *Ancestry.com*. See also ETE to EEF, Aug. 26, 1881, ETE Correspondence.
136 ETE to EEF, Sept. 14, 1881, ETE Correspondence.
137 "Constitution," manuscript, First Parish in Concord Records, Box V.1 (8), Concord.
138 Rebecca Morton Blodgett, "Women in the Parish," in *The Meeting House on the Green: A History of the First Parish in Concord and its Church*, ed. John Whittemore Teele (Concord, MA: First Parish, 1985), 157.
139 Women's Parish Association Annual Reports, 1886, 1887, draft, First Parish in Concord Records, Box. V.1 (4).
140 ETE to EEF, Concord, March 13, 1886, ETE Papers.

141 EEF to ETE, Nov. 1, 1881, FP, Carton 2.
142 EEF to ETE, Oct. 4, 1881, FP, Carton 2.
143 ETE to Sarah [Haskins Ansley], Sept. 15–Nov. 2, 1881, ETE Correspondence.
144 EEF to ETE, Nov. 1, 1881, FP, Carton 2.
145 EEF to ETE, Aug. 26, 1881, FP, Carton 2.
146 Nancy Simmons, "Philosophical Biographer: James Elliot Cabot and 'A Memoir of Ralph Waldo Emerson,'" *Studies in the American Renaissance* (1987)," 365.
147 ETE to EEF, Feb. 8, 1882, ETE Correspondence.
148 ETE to EEF, Feb. 8, 1882, ETE Correspondence.
149 ETE to Sarah [Haskins Ansley], Feb. 8, 1882, and ETE to EEF, Feb. 8, 1882, ETE Correspondence.
150 ETE to EEF, Jan. 21, 1882, ETE Correspondence.
151 EEF to ETE, April 19, 1882, FP, Carton 2.
152 EEF to ETE, March 7, 1882, FP, Carton 2.
153 ETE to Sarah [Haskins Ansley], Feb. 8, 1882. ETE Correspondence.
154 ETE to EEF, April 11, 1882, ETE Correspondence.
155 ETE to Sarah [Haskins Ansley], April 22, 1882, ETE Correspondence.
156 ETE to EEF, April 22, 1882, ETE Correspondence.
157 ETE to Clara Dabney, May 13- 19, 1882, ETE Correspondence.
158 ETE to Clara Dabney, May 13–19, 1882, ETE Correspondence.
159 ETE to Clara Dabney, May 13–19, 1882, ETE Correspondence.
160 "The Death of Mr. Emerson: Dying Peacefully after a Brief Illness," *New York Times*, April 28, 1882.

Chapter Seven

1 EEF to Sarah Forbes, May 10, 1882, FP, Box 8.
2 ETE to Clara Dabney, May 13–May 19, 1882, ETE Correspondence.
3 ETE to Clara Dabney, May 13–May 19, 1882, ETE Correspondence.
4 For a detailed description of the funeral, see: John Mcaleer, *Ralph Waldo Emerson: Days of Encounter* (Boston: Little, Brown, 1984), 662–65.
5 EEF to Sarah Forbes, May 10, 1882, FP, Box 8.
6 ETE to Clara Dabney, May 13–May 19, 1882, ETE Correspondence.
7 WHF to John Forbes, May 14, 1882, telegraph, FP, Box 8.
8 EEF to Sarah Forbes, May 10, 1882, FP, Carton 8.
9 JEC to Charles Norton, June 13, 1882, EF Correspondence (3250).
10 Norton chose James Osgood as the publisher, as he "offers the best terms, the stereotype plates to be made at his, O's, expense yet be Mother's property, and a royalty of 20 per dent on retail price paid her on all sales." ETE to WHF, Aug. 8, 1892, ETE Correspondence.
11 For discussion of the debate about publishing the letters and the recovering the stolen correspondence, see: Nancy Craig Simmons, "Philosophical Biographer: James Elliot Cabot and a 'Memoir of Ralph Waldo Emerson,'" *Studies in the American Renaissance* (1987): 365–92; and James Slater, "The First Edition," in *The Correspondence of Emerson and Carlyle*, ed. James Slater (New York: Columbia University Press, 1964), 64–67.

12 Charles Norton, ed., *The Correspondence of Thomas Carlyle and Ralph Waldo Emerson, 1834–1872, Supplementary Letters* (Boston: Ticknor and Company, 1886), i; EEF to ETE, Feb. 23, 1885, FP, Carton 3.
13 ETE to "Brethren and Descendants" Sept. 1, 1882, ETE Correspondence.
14 ETE to EEF, July 29, 1882, ETE Correspondence.
15 ETE to EEF, Aug. 21, 1882, ETE Correspondence.
16 "Last Will and Testament of Ralph Waldo Emerson," April 14, 1876, EF Papers, Box 83; Robert D. Habich, *Building Their Own Waldos: Emerson's First Biographers and the Politics of Life Writing* (Iowa City: University of Iowa Press, 2011), 163n41.
17 EWE to ETE, Aug. 29, 1903, EWE Papers, Box 3.
18 Edward Forbes, "Edward Waldo Emerson (1844–1930)," *Proceedings of the American Academy of Arts and Sciences* 70, no. 10 (1936), 533–34
19 Nancy Simmons, "Arranging the Sibylline Leaves: James Elliot Cabot's Work as Emerson's Literary Executor," *Studies in American Renaissance* (1983): 361–64.
20 William H. Channing to LJE, May 6, 1882, EF Papers (3266).
21 Simmons, "Arranging," 364. The agreement was laid out in a letter from Houghton, Mifflin to William Forbes. Edward signed the formal contract on March 15, 1883. Habich, *Building Their Own Waldos*, 105.
22 Albert J. von Frank, "Historical Introduction," in *Poems: A Variorum* (Cambridge, MA: Harvard University Press, 2011), xcviii–xcix.
23 EWE to JEC, Oct. 19, 1883, EF Correspondence, (295).
24 EWE to EEF, March 1, 1883, EWE Papers, Box 2.
25 Bosco and Myerson argue, "Relying on Emerson's multiple inventories and his and Ellen's recent essays printed under Emerson's name, Cabot almost certainly had the contents of *Letters and Biographical Sketches* and *Miscellanies* fairly well set in his mind before Emerson's death." Ronald Bosco and Joel Myerson, "Historical Introduction," *Uncollected Prose Writings* (Cambridge, MA: Harvard University Press, 2013), lxxii.
26 ETE to EEF, May 22, 1883, ETE Correspondence.
27 ETE to EEF, Aug. 14, 1884, typescript, EF Papers (703).
28 ETE to JEC, Aug. 1883, ETE Correspondence.
29 ETE to JEC, Aug. 1883, ETE Correspondence.
30 ETE to JEC, Aug. [11?] 1883, ETE Correspondence.
31 ETE to JEC, Aug. 1883, ETE Correspondence.
32 Simmons, "Arranging," 335.
33 Bosco and Myerson, "Historical Introduction," *Uncollected*, xxx–xxxi. For reflections on the complications of this decision, see Phyllis Cole, "The New Emerson Canon," *Resources for American Literary Study* 37 (2014): 261–73; Christopher Hanlon, *Emerson's Memory Loss: Originality, Communality, and the Late Style* (New York: Oxford University Press, 2018).
34 Bosco and Myerson, "Historical Introduction," *Uncollected*, lxxiv–lxxv, lxxvi.
35 Bosco and Myerson, "Historical Introduction," *Uncollected*, lxxvii.
36 Cole argues strongly against the removal of "Mary Moody Emerson." Cole, "The Emerson Canon," 268–70.
37 Simmons, "Arranging," 368.
38 Simmons, "Arranging," 368–70.
39 Simmons, "Arranging," 373.

40 ETE to Annie Emerson, Aug. 29, 1883, ETE Correspondence.
41 EEF to ETE, Oct. 2, 1883, FP, Carton 3.
42 EEF to ETE, Oct. 13, 1879, FP, Carton 2.
43 EEF to ETE, Jan. 27, 1881, FP, Carton 2.
44 Faye Dudden, *Serving Women: Household Service in Nineteenth-Century America* (Middletown, CT: Wesleyan University Press, 1983), 65–71.
45 Nell Irvin Painter, "Ralph Waldo Emerson's Saxons," *Journal of American History* 95, no. 4 (2009): 977–85.
46 ETE to RWE, Feb. 13, 1867, ETE Correspondence.
47 ETE to Susan Emerson, Feb. 15, 1865, ETE Correspondence.
48 EEF to ETE, March 26, 1884, FP, Carton 3.
49 EEF to ETE, May 28, 1884, FP, Carton 3.
50 EEF to ETE, Dec. 6, 1884, FP, Carton 3.
51 ETE to EEF, March 4, 1885, ETE Correspondence.
52 Habich, *Building Their Own Waldos*, 102; Nancy Craig Simmons, "Man Without a Shadow: The Life and Work of James Elliot Cabot, Emerson's Biographer and Literary Executor," PhD diss., (Princeton University, 1980), 429–30.
53 ETE to EEF, March 26, 1885, ETE Correspondence.
54 ETE to Clara Dabney, April [2?] 1885, ETE Correspondence.
55 ETE to Clara Dabney, April [2?], 1885, ETE Correspondence.
56 ETE to EEF, Oct. 27, 1892, ETE Correspondence.
57 Von Frank, *Poems*, 18–20.
58 ETE to EEF, Sept. 3, 1885, ETE Correspondence.
59 EEF to ETE, Aug. 22, 1885, FP, Carton 3.
60 ETE to EEF, Sept. 21, 1885, ETE Correspondence.
61 ETE to Clara Dabney, April [2?], 1886, ETE Correspondence.
62 ETE to Clara Dabney, April [2?], 1886, ETE Correspondence.
63 EEF to Elizabeth Cabot, 1886, EF Correspondence (3500).
64 EEF to EWE, July 14, 1886, and EEF to EWE, July 31, 1886, FP, Carton 3.
65 EEF to Elizabeth Cabot, 1886, EF Correspondence (3500).
66 EEF to JEC, July 24, 1886, EF Correspondence (3502).
67 EEF to Elizabeth Cabot, June 1886. EF Correspondence (3502).
68 EEF to Elizabeth Cabot, 1886, EF Correspondence (3500).
69 JEC to EWE, Aug. 4, 1886, EF Correspondence (3247).
70 ETE to Elizabeth Cabot, 1886, EF Correspondence (3502); JEC, *A Memoir of Ralph Waldo Emerson* (Boston: Houghton Mifflin, 1887), 2:486.
71 EEF to Cabot, July 24, 1886, EF Correspondence (3501).
72 Cabot, *A Memoir*, 2:652.
73 JEC to EWE, Aug. 4, 1886, EF Correspondence (3247).
74 JEC to ETE, July 17, 1886, EF Correspondence (3236).
75 Simmons, "Philosophical Biographer," 372; Habich, 106.
76 JEC to ETE, July 17, 1886, EF Correspondence (3236).
77 JEC to ETE, July 27, 1886, EF Correspondence (3237).
78 JEC to ETE, Feb. 16, 1887, FP, Carton 3.
79 JEC to ETE, Feb. 16, 1887, FP, Carton 3.
80 Habich, *Building Their Own Waldos*, 102.
81 Habich, *Building Their Own Waldos*, 118.

82 ETE to EEF, March 12, 1887, ETE Correspondence.
83 ETE to EEF, March 12, 1887, ETE Correspondence.
84 Habich speculates there was significant tension between Edward and Cabot, which explains the timing of the Edward coming forward with his memoir just before Cabot officially published his. Eventually, Houghton, Mifflin included both Cabot and Edward's biographies in Riverside edition sets. Habich, *Building Their Own Waldos*, 99–120.
85 ETE to EEF, June 27, 1882, ETE Correspondence.
86 ETE to EEF, Feb. 27, 1882, ETE Correspondence.
87 By 1880, Anna, born in 1848, was living in town with Samuel, her sister Mary, and her brother Edward. 1880 United States Census, Concord, Middlesex County, Massachusetts, digital image, s.v. "Anna McClure," *Ancestry.com*.
88 ETE to EEF, Oct. 3, 1883.
89 She appears to have worked in an orphanage or school for low-income girls, perhaps associated with the Boston Children's Friends Society. Anna McClure to ETE, July 1887, EF Correspondence (3778), Anna McClure to ETE, April 21, 1889, EF Correspondence (3782); Amy Morris Homens to ETE, Feb. 20, 1891, EF Correspondence (3658).
90 EEF to ETE, Aug. 16, 1887, FP, Carton 3.
91 Anna McClure to ETE, July 1887, EF Correspondence (3778).
92 Anna McClure to ETE, July 1887, EF Correspondence (3778).
93 Anna McClure to ETE, July 19, 1889, EF Correspondence (3788).
94 EEF to ETE, Sept. 24, 1886, FP, Carton 3.
95 EEF to ETE, April 1886, FP, Carton 3.
96 EEF to ETE, Sept. 11, 1887, FP, Carton 3.
97 EEF to Annie Emerson, [March 13–17, 1888], FP, Carton 3.
98 EEF to Annie Emerson, [March 13–17, 1888], FP, Carton 3.
99 EEF to ETE, April 18, 1888, FP, Carton 3.
100 EEF to ETE, April 18, 1888, FP, Carton 3.
101 Ian Bradley, *Health, Hedonism, and Hypochondria: The Hidden History of Spas* (London: Tauris Park, 2021), 131–66.
102 EEF to ETE, May 7, 1888, FP, Carton 3.
103 EEF to ETE, May 20, 1888, FP, Carton 2.
104 EFE to ETE, June 20, 1888, and EEF to ETE, June 26, 1888, FP, Carton 3.
105 ETE to EEF, June 24, 1888, ETE Correspondence.
106 ETE to EEF, April 2, 1888, ETE Correspondence.
107 EEF to ETE, Aug. 26, 1888, FP, Carton 3.
108 ETE to Sally Emerson, Aug. 28, 1888, ETE Correspondence; EEF to ETE, Aug. 23, 1888, FP, Carton 3.
109 ETE to Sally Emerson, Aug. 28, 1888, ETE Correspondence.
110 ETE to Caroline Cheney, Oct. 2, 1888, ETE Correspondence.
111 ETE to Caroline Cheney, Oct. 2, 1888. ETE Correspondence.
112 ETE to Sally Emerson, Aug. 28, 1888, ETE Correspondence.
113 ETE to Caroline Cheney, Oct. 2, 1888, ETE Correspondence.
114 EEF to ETE, Aug. 26, 1888, FP, Carton 3.
115 EEF to ETE, Oct. 19, 1888, FP, Carton 3.
116 EEF to LJE, Sept. 20, 1888, FP, Carton 3.

117 EEF to LJE, Sept. 20, 1888, FP, Carton 3.
118 EEF to ETE, Oct. 5, 1888, FP, Carton 3.
119 Daniel Chester French to EWE, Oct. 2, 1888, FP, Carton 3.
120 EEF to ETE, Oct. 5, 1888, FP, Carton 3.
121 EEF to ETE, March 24, 1889, FP, Carton 3. Mary Stroud, "Original Camera, Serial No. 540," *National Museum of American History, Smithsonian,* https://www.si.edu/object/original-kodak-camera-serial-no-54.
122 EEF to ETE, March 3, 1889, FP, Carton 3.
123 EWE to EEF, Oct. 15, 1889, EWE Papers, Box 2.
124 EWE to EEF, Oct. 16, 1889, EWE Papers, Box 2.
125 Tom Foran Clark, *The Significance of Being Frank: The Life and Times of Being Franklin Benjamin Sanborn* (Xlibris, 2015), chap. 23.
126 ETE to EEF, March 4, 1889, ETE to EEF, March 15, 1889, and ETE to [EEF?], June 1889, fragment, ETE Correspondence.
127 ETE to EEF, July, n.d.–Aug. 25, 1890, ETE Correspondence.
128 ETE to EEF, Sept. 7, 1887, ETE Correspondence.
129 ETE to EEF, Sept. 29, 1890, ETE Correspondence. Miss Leavitt was a nurse, not Louisa Sanborn's sister Caroline.
130 Anna McClure to ETE, Nov. 14, 1890, EF Correspondence (3810); Constance Emery McClure to ETE, Nov. 18, 1890, EF Correspondence (3351).
131 Constance Emery to ETE, Nov. 18, 1890, EF Correspondence (3351).
132 EEF to ETE, Dec. 7, 1890, FP, Carton 3.
133 Constance Emery Ellis to ETE, Dec. 1890, EF Correspondence (3357).
134 Edward McClure to ETE. Dec. 7, 1890, EF Correspondence, (3823); EEF to ETE, Dec. 9, 1890, EF Correspondence (3515).
135 Sarah Ripley [Haskins] Ansley to ETE, Jan. 22, 1891, EF Correspondence, (3103).
136 ETE to EEF, Dec. 9, 1890, ETE Correspondence.
137 Constance Emery Ellis to ETE, Dec. 10, 1890, EF Correspondence (3362).
138 EEF to ETE, Feb. 24, 1890, FP, Carton 3.
139 EEF to ETE, March 3, 1890, FP, Carton 3.
140 EEF to ETE, Aug. 30, 1890, FP, Carton 3.
141 EEF to ETE, Sept. 7, 1890, FP, Carton 3.
142 EEF to ETE, March 22, 1891, FP, Carton 3.
143 EEF to ETE, May 15, 1891, FP, Carton 3. The "peppermint" wrapper may have been dyed green; green dyes often contained arsenic. Jennifer Lunden, *American Breakdown* (New York: Harper Wave, 2023), 114.
144 EEF to ETE, July 30, 1891, FP, Carton 3.
145 EEF to ETE, July 15, 1891, FP, Carton 3.
146 EEF to ETE, Sept. 20, 1891, FP, Carton 3.
147 ETE to EEF, May 29, 1891, ETE Correspondence.
148 ETE to EEF, July 8, 1891, ETE Correspondence.
149 EEF to LJE, Sept. 18, 1891, FP, Carton 3.
150 ETE to EEF, Sept. 18, 1891, copy in Ellen's hand, Samuel Gray Ward and Anna Hazard Barker Ward papers, 1823–1934, Houghton, Ms AM 1456 (288).
151 The letters sent by the Forbes on this trip are not in the Emerson or Forbes collections at the Houghton or the Massachusetts Historical Society.

152 ETE to EEF, Jan. 11, 1892, ETE Correspondence.
153 ETE to EEF, March 17–March 24, 1892, ETE Correspondence.
154 Edith's side of the story is unclear; if she made her complaint in a letter, it is not one held her correspondence at the Massachusetts Historical Society or the Houghton.
155 ETE to EEF, April 27, 1892, ETE Correspondence.
156 ETE to EEF, April 27, 1892, ETE Correspondence.
157 Hanlon, *Emerson's Memory Loss*, 23.
158 Phyllis Cole, with Jana Argersinger, "Introduction," *Toward a Female Genealogy of Transcendentalism*, ed. Jana Argersinger and Phyllis Cole (Athens: University of Georgia Press, 2014), 10
159 EEF to ETE, May 20, 1892, FP, Carton 3; ETE to Sally Emerson, May 31, 1892, ETE Correspondence.
160 ETE to EEF, Sept. 20, 1892, ETE Correspondence.
161 ETE to Alice [Arthur], Sept. 20, 1892, ETE Correspondence.
162 ETE to EEF, Nov. 8, 1892, ETE Correspondence.
163 ETE to EEF, Nov. 13, 1892, ETE Correspondence. See also ETE to Clara Dabney, Dec. 7, 1892, ETE Correspondence.
164 ETE to Clara Dabney, Dec. 7, 1892. ETE Correspondence.
165 EEF to ETE, Nov. 26, 1892, FP, Carton 3.
166 "Funeral of Mrs. Emerson," *Boston Transcript*, Nov. 17, 1892.

Chapter Eight

1 Will Forbes to ETE, Nov. 29, 1892, FP, Carton 3.
2 EEF to ETE, Nov. 29, 1892, FP, Carton 3.
3 ETE to Mary [Blake], Dec. 7, 1892, ETE Correspondence.
4 ETE to Clara Dabney, Dec. 7. 1892, ETE Correspondence.
5 ETE to EEF, Jan. 6, 1893, ETE Correspondence.
6 Arthur Pier, *Forbes: Telephone Pioneer* (New York: Dodd, Mead, and Company, 1953), 205–6.
7 EEF to ETE, Jan. 17, 1893, FP, Carton 3.
8 EEF to ETE, Feb. 1, 1893, FP, Carton 3.
9 ETE to Haven Emerson, March 27, 1893, ETE Correspondence.
10 ETE to [Susan Haskins Ansley?], April 19, 1893, and ETE to EEF and Annie Emerson, April 19, 1894, ETE Correspondence.
11 ETE to Annie Emerson, June 2, 1893, ETE Correspondence.
12 ETE to Annie Emerson, June 2, 1893, ETE Correspondence.
13 ETE to Cousin Sarah [Haskins Ansley], April 11, 1893, and ETE to Cousin Sarah [Haskins Ansley], May 17, 1893, ETE Correspondence.
14 ETE to Annie Emerson, July 17, 1893, and ETE to EEF, July 20, 1893, ETE Correspondence.
15 ETE to EEF, July 20, 1893, ETE Correspondence.
16 EEF to ETE, Aug. 30, 1893, FP, Carton 3.
17 ETE to EEF, Sept. 6, 1893, ETE Correspondence.
18 ETE to Violet Forbes, Sept. 6, 1893, ETE Correspondence.

19 ETE to Sally Emerson, Sept. 19, 1893, ETE Correspondence.
20 ETE to EWE, July 25, 1893, ETE Correspondence.
21 Franklin Sanborn, *A. Bronson Alcott: His Life and Philosophy* (Boston: Roberts Brothers, 1893), 1:271
22 ETE to EWE, July 25, 1893, ETE Correspondence.
23 ETE to EEF, Oct. 11, 1893, ETE Correspondence.
24 ETE to Edith, Dec. 1, 1893, ETE Correspondence.
25 EEF to ETE, Oct. 1, 1893, FP, Carton 3.
26 EEF to ETE, Oct. 20, 1893, FP, Carton 3.
27 *The Annual American Catalogue* (New York: Publisher's Weekly, 1893), 69.
28 EEF to ETE, Nov. 21, 1893, FP, Carton 3; EEF Diary, January 30, 1893, FP, Box 24
29 EEF Diary, April 10, 1893, FP, Box 24; ETE to Roberts Brothers, April 10, 1883, EF Papers (669).
30 EEF to ETE, Oct. 5, 1893, FP, Carton 3.
31 EEF to ETE, Nov. 17, 1893, FP, Carton 3.
32 "New Books," *Boston Evening Transcript*, Oct. 19, 1893.
33 EEF to ETE, Nov. 17, 1893, FP, Carton 3.
34 EEF to ETE, Oct. 5, 1893, FP, Carton 3.
35 EEF to ETE Oct. 13, 1893, FP, Carton 3.
36 EEF to ETE, Nov. 21, 1893, FP, Carton 2. The volume was actually titled *The Natural History of Intellect*.
37 Nancy Simmons, "Arranging the Sibylline Leaves: James Elliot Cabot's Work as Emerson's Literary Executor," *Studies in the American Renaissance* (1983): 374.
38 ETE to EEF, Feb. 19, 1894, ETE Correspondence; Simmons, "Arranging," 374. For more on the collaborative nature of "Natural History of Intellect," see Christopher Hanlon, *Emerson's Memory Loss: Originality, Communality, and the Late Style* (New York: Oxford University Press, 2018), 18–45.
39 EEF to ETE, Oct. 3, 1893, FP, Carton 3.
40 ETE to EEF, Dec. 9, 1893, ETE Correspondence.
41 ETE to EEF, Dec. 1, 1893, ETE Correspondence.
42 ETE to EEF, Dec. 9, 1893, ETE Correspondence.
43 ETE to Addy Manning, Oct. 8, 1860, ETE Correspondence.
44 Stuart Marriot, *The Keystone to the Arch: Hudson Shaw and the Oxford University Extension Movement* (Printed for the author, 2018), 19–20, 41.
45 ETE to Lizzy [Simmons?], July 25, 1894, and ETE to Violet Forbes Feb. 8, 1894, ETE Correspondence.
46 ETE to Cameron Forbes, May 21, 1894, ETE Correspondence.
47 ETE to Violet Forbes, July 27, 1894, ETE Correspondence.
48 ETE to EEF, July 20, 1894, ETE Correspondence.
49 ETE to EEF, Aug. 1, 1894, ETE Correspondence.
50 ETE to EEF, Aug. 1, 1894, ETE Correspondence.
51 ETE to EEF, Aug. 27, 1894, ETE Correspondence.
52 ETE to EEF, Aug. 1, 1894, ETE Correspondence.
53 ETE to EEF, Aug. 27, 1894, ETE Correspondence.
54 ETE to EEF, May 22, 1894, ETE Correspondence.
55 ETE to EEF, July 27, 1894, ETE Correspondence.

56 EEF to ETE, Sept. 5, 1894, Forbes Paper, Carton 4.
57 EEF to ETE, Aug. 13, 1894, FP, Carton 4.
58 EEF to ETE, Aug. 13, 1894, ETE Correspondence.
59 EEF to ETE, Jan. 8, 1894, and EEF to ETE, June 20, 1894, FP, Carton 4.
60 EEF to ETE, Sept. 15, 1894, FP, Carton 4.
61 EEF to ETE, Sept. 15, 1894, Carton 4.
62 EEF to ETE, May 4, 1894, FP, Carton 4.
63 ETE to EEF, May 22–23, 1894, ETE Correspondence.
64 ETE to EEF?, Oct. 1894, and ETE to William Emerson, on the back of letter from ETE to Raymond Emerson, Nov. 13, 1894, ETE Correspondence.
65 ETE to Sally Gibbons Emerson, [Nov. and Dec. 1894], ETE Correspondence.
66 ETE to EWE, Dec. 11, 1894, ETE Correspondence.
67 Women's Parish Association President's Books, First Parish Records, Box V.1 (3), Concord Free Public Library, Concord, MA; ETE to EEF, Feb. 21, 1895, ETE Correspondence.
68 ETE to EEF, March 12, 1895, ETE Correspondence.
69 ETE to EEF and EWE, Aug. 1895, ETE Correspondence.
70 ETE to EEF, June 1, 1895, ETE Correspondence.
71 EEF to ETE, [Aug.?] 1895, FP, Carton 4.
72 ETE to EWE and Annie Emerson, Aug. 29, 1895, and ETE to EEF, Sept. 9, 1895, ETE Correspondence.
73 ETE to EEF, Sept. 9, 1895, ETE Correspondence.
74 ETE to EEF, July 16, 1896, ETE Correspondence.
75 EEF to ETE, Jan. 28, 1897, FP, Carton 4.
76 EEF to ETE, Jan. 28, 1897, FP, Carton 4.
77 ETE to EWE, April 20, 1897, and ETE to Ellen Emerson Jr., April 22, 1897, ETE Correspondence.
78 EEF to ETE, May 12, 1897, FP, Carton 4.
79 EEF to ETE, May 4, 1897, FP, Carton 4.
80 EEF to ETE, May 16, 1897, FP, Carton 4.
81 EEF to ETE, May 26, 1897, FP, Carton 4.
82 Order of the City Council of Boston, *Exercises of the Dedication of the Monument to Colonel Robert Gould Shaw* (Boston: Municipal Printing Office, 1897): 16, 19, 23.
83 EEF to ETE, June 18, 1897, FP, Carton 4.
84 EEF to ETE, Aug. 9, 1897, FP, Carton 4.
85 EEF to ETE, Aug. 27, 1897, FP, Carton 4; Michael Bliss, *William Osler: A Life in Medicine* (New York: Oxford University Press), 1999.
86 EEF to ETE, Aug. 27, 1897, FP, Carton 4.
87 EEF to ETE, Aug. 22, 1897, FP, Carton 4.
88 EEF to ETE, May 26, 1897, FP, Carton 4.
89 EEF to ETE, Aug. 22, 1897, FP, Carton 4.
90 EEF to ETE, Sept. 12, 1897, and EEF to EWE, Sept. 18, 1897, FP, Carton 4.
91 EEF to ETE, Oct. 4, 1897, FP, Carton 4.
92 "William Hathaway Forbes," *Boston Evening Transcript*, Oct. 12, 1897; "Personal Paragraphs," Spokane *Chronicle*, Oct. 27, 1897.

Chapter Nine

1. Life writing which examines women's later lives contributes to "counterbalancing the mainly one-sided, negative representations of ageing as perpetuated by dominant cultural discourse." Margaret O'Neill and Michaela Schrage-Früh, "Women and Aging: Private Meaning, Social Lives," *Life Writing* 16, no. 1 (2019): 1.
2. EEF to ETE, Dec. 2, 1897, FP, Carton 4.
3. EEF to ETE, Dec. 2, 1897, FP, Carton 4.
4. EEF to ETE, Jan. 13, 1898, and EEF to ETE, Feb. 22, 1898, FP, Carton 4.
5. ETE to EEF, March 15, 1898, FP, Carton 4.
6. Toby Anita Appel, "Arnold Carl Klebs, 1870–1943: Tuberculosis Specialist, Historical Bibliophile, and a Founder of the Medical History Library," *Yale University Library Online Exhibitions*, 2008, https://onlineexhibits.library.yale.edu/s/arnold-carl-klebs/.
7. EEF to ETE, April 3, 1898, FP, Carton 4.
8. ETE to EEF, Concord, Jan. 18, 1898, ETE Correspondence.
9. EEF to ETE, April 14, 1898, FP, Carton 4.
10. ETE to EEF, Concord, April 16, 1898, ETE Correspondence.
11. ETE to EEF, Concord, March 23, 1898, ETE Correspondence.
12. EEF to ETE, April 27, 1898, FP, Carton 4.
13. William Hixson, *Moorfield Storey and the Abolitionist Tradition* (New York: Oxford University Press, 1972), 49–51; Mario Rizzo, "The Antipaternalist Psychology of William James," *Behavioral Public Policy* (2023), 4.
14. Moorfield Storey, "Speech of Moorfield Storey," *Centenary of the Birth of Ralph Waldo Emerson* (Boston: Riverside Press, 1903), 105–6.
15. ETE to EEF, Aug. 22, 1900, ETE Correspondence.
16. George Boutwell, *Bryan or Imperialism: An Address by The Hon. George Boutwell Delivered at the National Liberty Conference of Anti-Imperialists* (Boston: New England Anti-Imperialist League, 1900), 20.
17. EWE to EEF, Sept. 10, 1893, EWE Papers, Carton 2.
18. ETE to EEF, Feb. 5, 1898, ETE Correspondence.
19. ETE to EEF, Aug. 31, 1898, ETE Correspondence.
20. Lidian Emerson, grave marker, Sleep Hollow Cemetery, Concord, Middlesex Count, MA.
21. EEF to ETE, April, 25, 1899, FP, Carton 4.
22. ETE to EEF, March 7, 1898, ETE Correspondence.
23. *LLJE*, 68.
24. *LLJE*, 129.
25. Meha Priyadarshini, "Gender and Material Culture History," *A Companion to Global Gender History*, ed. Teresa A. Meade and Merry E. Wiesner-Hanks (Newark: John Wiley & Sons, 2020), 113, 115.
26. *LLJE*, 81–83.
27. *LLJE*, 84, 167–68.
28. Randall Fuller, "Lydia Jackson Fuller," in *The Handbook of Ralph Waldo Emerson*, ed. Christopher Hanlon (New York: Oxford University Press, 2024), 490. Delores Bird Carpenter's editions of *The Life of Lydian Jackson Emerson* and *The Selected Letters of Lydian Jackson Emerson* helped jumpstart the scholarship on LJE in the 1980s.

29 *LLJE*, 84; EEF, "A Protest," in Ellen Tucker Emerson, "Life of Lidian Jackson Emerson," manuscript, EF Papers (358). See also Delores Bird Carpenter, "Lidian Emerson's 'Transcendental Bible,'" *Studies in the American Renaissance* (1980), 91–95.
30 EEF, "A Protest." She wrote another protest to counter Ellen's claim that Lidian insisted the kitchen doors be left open at night. Edith might not have written her protests until 1902, when Ellen wrote to Edith, "About Mother's life, you and Edward must keep in mind that I have no intention of holding on to anything you or he wish removed." It is unclear why they were discussing it then, as Ellen seems to have largely finished working on it earlier. ETE to EEF, June 7, 1902, ETE Correspondence.
31 *LLJE*, 239–43n272.
32 ETE to EEF, Aug. 6, 1896, ETE Correspondence.
33 ETE to EEF, Feb. 18, 1898, ETE Correspondence.
34 ETE to Violet Forbes Webster, Oct. 5, 1898, ETE Correspondence.
35 EEF to ETE, July 29, 1898, FP, Carton 4.
36 EEF to ETE, Aug. 29, 1898, FP, Carton 4.
37 EEF to ETE, Sept. 8, 1898, FP, Carton 4.
38 William Hathaway Forbes, *The Poems of William Hathaway Forbes* (Privately Printed, 1898).
39 ETE to Mary Miller Engel, Jan. 9, 1899, ETE Correspondence.
40 ETE to EEF, March 1, 1899, ETE Correspondence.
41 ETE to EEF, March 3, 1899, ETE Correspondence; EEF to ETE, Feb. 23, 1899, FP, Carton 4.
42 EEF to ETE, Jan. 25, 1899, EF Papers; David Hudson, Marvin Bergman, and Loren Horton, "Perkins, Charles Elliott," *The Biographical Dictionary of Iowa* (Iowa City: University of Iowa Press, 2008), 403–5.
43 EEF to ETE, Feb. 6, 1899 FP, Carton 4.
44 EEF to ETE, Feb. 6, 1899, FP, Carton 4.
45 EEF to ETE, Feb. 11, 1899, FP, Carton 4.
46 EEF to ETE, [March?] 1899, FP, Carton 4.
47 Ellen Emerson, Jr. to EEF, June 1, 1899, EEF to ETE, July 7, 1899, FP, Carton 4.
48 EEF to EWE, July 18, 1899, FP, Carton 4.
49 EEF to ETE, July 25, 1899, FP, Carton 4.
50 EEF to ETE, Aug. 11, 1899, FP, Carton 4.
51 EEF to EWE, July 18, 1899, EEF to ETE, Sept. 6, 1899, FP, Carton.
52 ETE to ETE, Aug. 28, 1899, ETE Correspondence.
53 EEF to ETE, July 25, 1899, and EEF to ETE, Aug. 11, 1899
54 EEF to ETE, Aug. 11, 1899, FP, Carton 4.
55 EEF to ETE, Sept. 24, 1899, FP, Carton 4.
56 EEF to ETE, Sept. 6, 1899, FP, Carton 4; ETE to RWE, Oct. 19, 1869, and ETE to Haven Emerson, Nov. 21, 1870, ETE Correspondence.
57 EEF to ETE, March 16, 1902, FP, Carton 4. See also Kathleen Weiler, *Maria Baldwin's Worlds: A Story of Black New England and the Fight for Racial Justice* (Amherst: University of Massachusetts Press, 2019).
58 "Charities Subscribed to by Mrs. W.H. Forbes, 1922." FP, Carton 23.
59 Kerri Greenidge, *The Grimkes: The Legacy of Slavery in an American Family* (New York: Liveright Publishing, 2023), 168. See also *Black Women Abolitionists: A Study in Activism, 1828–1860* (Knoxville: University of Tennessee Press, 1992).

60 Kyla Schuller, *The Trouble with White Women: A Counterhistory of Feminism* (New York: Bold Type Books, 2021).
61 Erica Hirshler, *A Studio of Her Own: Women Artists in Boston, 1870–1940* (Boston: Museum of Fine Arts Boston, 2001), 33.
62 ETE to EEF, Aug. 5–12, 1899, ETE Correspondence.
63 Margaret Bacon Hope, *Abby Hopper Gibbons: Prison Reformer and Social Activist* (Albany, NY: SUNY Press, 2000), 87–112; Sally Hopper Emerson, *The Life of Abby Hopper Gibbons, Told Chiefly Through Her Correspondence*, 2 vols., ed. Sarah Hopper Gibbons (New York: G.P. Putnam and Sons, 1897).
64 ETE to Sally [Gibbons Emerson], Dec. 26, 1899, ETE Correspondence.
65 ETE to Sally [Gibbons Emerson], March 3, 1899, ETE Correspondence.
66 ETE to Mary [Miller Engel], Dec. 28, 1899.
67 EEF to ETE, April 3, 1900, FP, Carton 4.
68 ETE to Mary [Miller Engel], Jan. 8, 1900, ETE Correspondence.
69 ETE to Mary [Miller Engel], April 7, 1890, ETE Correspondence.
70 William F. Emerson to ETE, April 18, 1900, FP, Carton 4.
71 EEF to ETE, May 10, 1900, FP, Carton 4.
72 ETE to EEF, April 24, 1900, ETE Correspondence.
73 ETE to EEF, April 24, 1900, ETE Correspondence.
74 EEF to ETE, May 31, 1900, FP, Carton 4.
75 EEF to ETE, June 14, 1900, and EEF to ETE, Aug. 26, 1900, FP, Carton 4.
76 EEF to ETE, July 27, 1900, FP, Carton 4.
77 EEF to ETE, July 27, 1900, FP, Carton 4.
78 EEF to ETE, Oct. 1, 1900, and EEF to ETE, July 27, 1900, Carton 4.
79 EEF to ETE, Sept. 21, 1900, FP, Carton 4.
80 EEF to ETE, Oct. 1, 1900, FP, Carton 4.
81 EEF to ETE Aug. 14, 1900, Forbes Correspondence, Carton 4.
82 EEF to ETE, Oct. 22, 1900, Forbes Correspondence, Carton 4.
83 EEF to ETE, Oct. 9, 1900, Forbes Correspondence, Carton 4.
84 EEF to ETE, Oct. 22, 1900, and EEF to ETE, Oct. 30, 1900, FP, Carton 4.
85 EEF to ETE, Oct. 22, 1900, FP, Carton 4.
86 ETE to Sally [Gibbons Emerson], Aug. 1, 1900, ETE Correspondence.
87 "Rev. Dr. Haskins Dies After Brief Illness," *Brooklyn Daily Eagle*, March 8, 1900: 2; Benjamin Kendall Emerson, *The Ipswich Emersons, A.D. 1636–1900* (Boston: David Clapp & Son, 1900), 180–81. The Haskins were Waldo's "double cousins": their mother was Waldo's father's sister and their father was Waldo's mother's brother.
88 ETE to Haven Emerson, May 8, 1900, ETE Correspondence.
89 ETE to Edward Forbes, Nov. 13, 1900, ETE Correspondence.
90 Benjamin Emerson, *The Ipswich Emersons*, 369
91 "Wedded at Brookline," *Boston Evening Transcript*, Jan. 16, 1901.
92 EEF to ETE, Feb. 10, 1901, FP, Carton 4.
93 EEF to ETE, July 25, 1901, FP, Carton 4.
94 Ellen Tucker, Jr. to EEF, May 13, 1901, FP, Carton 4; Beverly Wilson Palmer, *Selected Letters of Lucretia Coffin Mott* (Chicago: University of Illinois Press, 2002), l.
95 "Church Rebuilt," *Boston Globe*, Oct. 4, 1901, 5.
96 EEF to ETE, April 22, 1901, and EEF to ETE, Nov. 13, 1901, FP, Carton 4.

97 EEF to ETE, April 22, 1901, and EEF to ETE, Nov. 13, 1901, FP, Carton 4.
98 EEF to ETE, Feb. 21, 1902, FP, Carton 4.
99 EEF to ETE March 16, 1902, FP, Carton 4.
100 EEF to ETE, Feb. 21, 1902, FP, Carton 4.
101 EEF to ETE, Sept. 15, 1902, FP, Carton 4.
102 EEF to ETE, Oct. 19, 1901; Ruth Emerson Fletcher to EEF, March 7, 1902; and EEF to ETE, Sept. 15, 1902, FP, Carton 4; ETE to Sally [Gibbons Emerson], Sept. 23, 1902, ETE Correspondence.
103 EEF to Edward Forbes, Feb. 2, 1902, typescript, FP, Carton 19.
104 EEF to [ETE?], Aug. 1902, FP, Carton 4.
105 EEF to ETE, July 31, 1902, and EEF to ETE, Aug. 11, 1902, FP, Carton 4.
106 EEF to ETE, July 31, 1902, EEF to ETE, Aug. 11, 1902, FP, Carton 4.
107 ETE, "What I Can Remember About Father," manuscript, Houghton Library, Harvard University, MS Am 1280.227.
108 EEF Diary, Feb. 28, 1903, FP, Carton 24.
109 "Kenneth Webster," *Boston Globe*, Nov. 2, 1942: 10; "Kenneth Grant Tremayne Webster," *Class of 1893 Harvard College* (Cambridge, MA: Crimson Printing, 1918), 302.
110 Haven Emerson to EEF, April 9, 1903, and Susan Emerson to EEF, April 19, 1903, FP, Carton 4.
111 EEF to ETE, April 28, 1903, FP, Carton 4.
112 Len Gougeon, "Looking Backwards: Emerson in 1903," *Nineteenth-Century Prose*, 30, no. 1/2 (2003): 50.
113 "Pulpit Tribute to Emerson," *St. Joseph News*, April 23, 1903: 10.
114 Quoted in Gougeon, "Looking Backwards: Emerson in 1903," 67.
115 "Emerson Centennial," *Boston Evening Transcript*, May 23, 1903: 4.
116 William James, "Address of William James," *The Centenary of the Birth of Ralph Waldo Emerson* (Boston: Riverside Press, 1903), 76; Moorfield Storey, "Speech of Moorfield Storey" *Centenary of the Birth*, 105–6. See also Stephen Bush, "Sovereignty of the Living Individual: Emerson and James on Politics and Religion," *Religions* 8, no. 9 (2017): 164.
117 EEF to ETE, Milton April 28, 1903, FP, Carton 4.
118 "The Evening," *The Centenary of the Birth*, 97.
119 ETE to Haven Emerson, May 27–June 4, 1903, ETE Correspondence.
120 EWE, "Preface," in *Nature; Addresses and Lectures* (Boston: Houghton and Mifflin, 1903), vi.
121 EWE, "Preface," vii.
122 ETE to Annie Emerson, July 4, 1902, ETE Correspondence.
123 Storey, "Speech of Moorfield Storey," 104. The Emersons gave Moorfield access to Waldo's journals as he prepared, a sign of their friendship; Emerson scholars thought it lost for decades until it turned in in Moorfield's papers at the Library of Congress in the 1960s. John Broderick, "Emerson and Moorfield Storey: A Lost Journal Found," *American Literature* 38, no. 2 (1966): 177–86.
124 EEF to ETE, June 29, 1903, FP, Carton 4.
125 EEF to ETE, June 29, 1903, FP, Carton 4.
126 EEF to ETE, June 29, 1903, FP, Carton 4.
127 ETE to Haven Emerson, Concord, Sept. 1, 1903, ETE Correspondence.

128 ETE to EEF, June 17, 1903, ETE Correspondence.
129 ETE to Haven Emerson, Sept. 1, 1903, ETE Correspondence.
130 ETE to Sarah Haskins Ansley, Aug. 15, 1903, ETE Correspondence, and Ruth Emerson Fletcher to EEF, Oct. [5th?], 1903, FP, Carton 4.

Chapter Ten

1 ETE to Edith, June 1904, ETE Correspondence.
2 EEF to ETE, July 8, 1904, FP, Carton 5.
3 ETE to EWE, March 3, 1904, ETE Correspondence.
4 Ralph Waldo Emerson, *Poems*, ed. Edward Waldo Emerson (Cambridge, MA: Houghton Mifflin, 1904), 467.
5 ETE to EWE, March 5, 1904, ETE Correspondence.
6 ETE to Haven Emerson, Feb. 19, 1904, ETE Correspondence.
7 ETE to Haven Emerson, Feb. 19, 1904, ETE Correspondence.
8 EEF to Annie Emerson, Feb. 19, 1904, FP, Carton 5.
9 Camillus Gott, "William Cameron Forbes and the Philippines, 1904–1946," PhD diss (Bloomington: Indiana University, 1974), 25.
10 ETE to Mary [Miller Engel], Feb. 26, 1904, ETE Correspondence.
11 "Glad Hands." *Boston Globe*, June 21, 1904.
12 "Forbes-Emerson," *Boston Globe*, June 18, 1904.
13 ETE to EEF, May 13, 1904, ETE Correspondence.
14 Florence Emerson Forbes to EEF, Feb. 26, 1904, FP, Carton 5.
15 EEF to ETE, July 31, 1904, FP, Carton 5.
16 EEF to ETE, July 8, 1904, FP, Carton 5.
17 EEF to ETE, Aug. 15, 1904, FP, Carton 5.
18 EWE to EEF, Jan. 18, 1905, EWE Papers, Carton 3; Helena Emerson to EEF, Nov. 1, 1905 and Waldo E. Forbes to ETE, Nov. 15, 1905, FP, Carton 5.
19 EEF to ETE, Aug. 26, 1905, FP, Carton 3.
20 EEF to ETE, Nov. 12, 1905, FP, Carton 5.
21 ETE to Sally [Gibbons Emerson], Oct. 5, 1905, ETE Correspondence.
22 ETE to EWE, April 4, 1905, ETE Correspondence.
23 ETE to Sally [Gibbons Emerson], Oct. 5, 1905, and ETE to EEF, 1905, ETE Correspondence.
24 Ruth Emerson to EEF, Jan. 26, 1906, FP, Carton 4; William Emerson to EEF Oct. 3, 1902, and Ellen Emerson Jr. to EEF, Jan. 10, 1901, FP, Carton 4.
25 Annie Emerson to Rose Dabney Forbes, March 20, 1904, FP, Carton 5.
26 EEF to ETE, Aug. 13, 1906, Carton 5.
27 EEF to ETE, Sept. 28, 1906, and EEF to ETE, Sept, 17, 1904, FP, Carton 5.
28 EEF to ETE, May 25, 1906, FP, Carton 5.
29 EEF to ETE, Oct. 3, 1906, FP, Carton 5.
30 Manifest, SS *Arabic*, April 26, 1907, Edith Emerson Forbes, Ellen Forbes, and Susan Hallowell, *Ancestry.com*, accessed Jan. 5, 2024.
31 Haven Emerson to EEF, Dec. 9, 1906, FP, Carton 5.
32 EEF to "My Dear Children, Nov. 2, 1906, FP, Carton 25.
33 EEF to Forbes children, Nov. 8–Nov. 9, 1906, FP, Carton 5; "Mrs. Galt Dies," *Honolulu*

Star-Bulletin, Nov. 14, 1927, 1; John William Siddall, ed., *Men of Hawaii: A Biographical Reference Library*, rev. ed. (Honolulu: Honolulu Star-Bulletin, Limited, 1921) 2:165.
34. EEF to "My Dear Family," Nov 18–19, 1906, FP, Carton 25.
35. EEF to Forbes children, Nov. 21–22, 1906, FP, Carton 25.
36. EEF to Forbes children, Jan. 27, 1907, FP, Carton 25.
37. EEF to Forbes children, Nov. 26-Nov. 28, 1906, FP, Carton 25.
38. EEF to Forbes children, Dec. 6, 1906, FP, Carton 25.
39. EEF to Forbes children, Dec. 6, 1906, FP, Carton 25.
40. EEF to Forbes children, Jan. 4, 1907, FP, Carton 5.
41. Quoted in Daniel Immerwahr, *How to Hide an Empire* (New York: Farrar, Straus and Giroux, 2019), 125.
42. Peter W. Stanley, "William Cameron Forbes: Proconsul in the Philippines," *Pacific Historical Review* 35, no. 3 (1966): 286; Immerwahr, *How to Hide an Empire*, 125.
43. Kim Wagner, *Massacre in the Clouds: An American Atrocity and the Erasure of History* (New York: PublicAffairs, 2024), 4.
44. Lidian Jackson Emerson to her children, 1863, *SLLJE*, 219.
45. For an extensive discussion of the development of Baguio and Cameron Forbes' involvement, see: Immerwahr, *How to Hide an Empire*, 122–36.
46. Immerwahr, *How to Hide an Empire*, 130.
47. Immerwahr, *How to Hide an Empire*, 131.
48. ETE to Mary [Miller Engel], Dec. 31, 1906, ETE Correspondence.
49. ETE to EEF, Feb. 12, 1907, ETE Correspondence.
50. EEF to Forbes children, Jan. 27, 1907, FP, Carton 25.
51. EEF to ETE, Jan. 22, 1907, FP, Carton 5.
52. EEF to Forbes children, Feb. 10, 1907, FP, Carton 25.
53. EEF to Forbes children, Feb. 1, 1907 FP, Carton 25.
54. ETE to EEF, Feb. 12, 1907, ETE Correspondence.
55. ETE to EEF, Feb. 12–March 4, 1907, ETE Correspondence.
56. Ellen Emerson Jr. to EEF, March 20, 1907, FP, Carton 5.
57. EEF to ETE, April 5, 1907, FP, Carton 5.
58. EEF to Forbes children, Feb. 26–March 17, 1907, FP, Carton 25.
59. EEF to Forbes children, Feb. 26–March 17, 1907, FP, Carton 25.
60. EEF to Forbes children, March 19–March 22, 1907, FP, Carton 25.
61. EEF to Forbes children, March 23, 1907, FP, Carton 25.
62. EEF to Forbes children, April 16–April 17, 1907, FP, Carton 25.
63. EEF to Forbes children, April 23, 1907, FP, Carton 25.
64. EEF to Forbes children, April 2–April 5, 1907, April 23, 1907, FP, Carton 25.
65. Haven Emerson to EEF, May 8, 1907, FP, Carton 5.
66. EEF to ETE, Milton, Nov. 10, 1907 and John Haven Emerson Jr. to EEF, Dec. 23, 1907, FP, Carton 5.
67. EEF to ETE, Nov. 10, 1907, FP, Carton 5.
68. EEF to ETE, Nov. 10, 1907, FP, Carton 5.
69. EEF to ETE, Dec. 9, 1907, FP, Carton 5.
70. EEF to ETE, March 4, 1908, EF Correspondence, 3520.
71. ETE to Haven Emerson, March 14, 1908, typescript, EF Papers, 703.
72. ETE to Mary [Miller Engel], April 16, 1908, ETE Correspondence.
73. ETE to EEF, May 5, 1908, ETE Correspondence.

74 ETE to Anne Whitney, June 5, 1908, Anne Whitney Papers, Wellesley College Digital Repository, https://repository.wellesley.edu/object/wellesley12230.
75 ETE to EEF, Sept. 21, 1908, and ETE to Annie Emerson, Oct. 20, 1908, ETE Correspondence.
76 ETE to Edward and Annie Emerson, July 3, 1908, ETE Correspondence.
77 EEF to [?], Oct. 20, 1908, FP, Carton 5.
78 EWE to Anne Whitney, Nov. 6, 1908, Anne Whitney Papers, Wellesley College Digital Repository, https://repository.wellesley.edu/object/wellesley12224.
79 EWE to Anne Whitney, Dec. 5, 1908, Anne Whitney Papers, Wellesley College Digital Repository, https://repository.wellesley.edu/object/wellesley12223; EEF to Anne Whitney, Dec. 16, 1908, Anne Whitney Papers, Wellesley College Digital Repository, https://repository.wellesley.edu/object/wellesley12234; Violet Forbes Webster to Cameron Forbes, Jan. 25, 1909, ETE Correspondence.
80 Ellen Tucker Emerson, death certificate, Jan. 14, 1909, file 283, available in Massachusetts, U.S. Death Records, 1841–1915, *Ancestry.com*.
81 Haven Emerson to EEF, Dec. 11, 1908, FP, Carton 5.
82 Violet Forbes Webster to Cameron Forbes, Jan. 25, 1909, ETE Correspondence.
83 EEF, Jan. 12, 1909, diary, FP, Carton 25.
84 EEF to Cameron Forbes, Jan. 22, 1909, ETE Correspondence.
85 EEF to Cameron Forbes, Jan. 22, 1909, ETE Correspondence.
86 EEF to Cameron Forbes, Jan. 22, 1909, ETE Correspondence.
87 EEF to Cameron Forbes, Jan. 22, 1909, ETE Correspondence.
88 EEF diary, Jan. 17, 1909, FP, Carton 25.
89 "Bell Tolls Her Death: Miss Ellen Emerson of Concord, Mass." *Boston Globe*, Jan. 14, 1909: 4.
90 "Boston Days," *Times-Democrat* (New Orleans, LA): Jan. 31, 1909: 6.
91 *Fitchburg Weekly Sentinel* (Fitchburg, MA), Jan. 15, 1909: 4.
92 Elizabeth Powell Bond, "Ellen Tucker Emerson," *Friends' Intelligencer*, Feb. 6, 1909, 81–82; A.W. Jackson, "Ellen Tucker Emerson," *The Christian Register*, Jan. 28, 1909, 104–105; Loren McDonald, "Memorial Sermon," in *In Memoriam, Ellen Tucker Emerson*, ETE Correspondence; James Herbert Morse, "Ellen Tucker Emerson," typescript, ETE Correspondence.
93 Ellen Tucker Emerson, grave marker, Sleepy Hollow Cemetery, Concord, Middlesex County, MA.
94 The Women's Parish Association also printed their own version of the booklet to distribute to their members, with the same material in a different order; the members felt strongly the minister's remarks should be put first. Women's Parish Association Executive Committee Meeting Minutes, First Parish in Concord Records, Box V.1 (9), Concord.
95 EWE to EEF, March 14, 1909, EWE Papers, Box 3.
96 Elizabeth Hoar Storer, "Ellen Tucker Emerson," *Ellen Tucker Emerson, In Memories* (privately printed, 1909), ETE Correspondence.
97 "Emerson's Way," *The News* (Chattanooga, TN), Feb. 10, 1909: 3.
98 ETE to the Committee on Domestic Charities, April 28, 1902, First Parish in Concord Records, Box IV.8 (9), Concord Free Public Library, Concord, MA; "Self-Effacing Women," *Lexington Leader* (Kentucky), April 4, 1909: 2.

Chapter Eleven

1. EWE to EEF, April 6, 1909, EWE Papers, Box 3.
2. EEF, Jan. 25, 1909, diary, FP, Carton 25.
3. EEF Diary, Feb. 1, 1909, FP, Carton 25.
4. EEF Diary, Feb. 20, 1909, FP, Carton 25.
5. Susan Emerson to EEF, Nov. 4, 1909, FP, Box 5.
6. EEF Diary, Feb. 14, 1909, FP, Carton 25; United States 1920 Census, Milton, Norfolk County, Massachusetts, digital image, s.v. "Margaret Neill," *Ancestry.com*.
7. ETE to EEF, April 20, 1882, typescript, EF Papers, 703.
8. For example, see ETE to Clara Dabney, March 29, 1872, typescript, EF Papers, 703.
9. ETE to EEF, Jan. 1878, ETE Correspondence.
10. ETE to EEF, Jan. 1878, typescript, EF Papers, 703.
11. EWE to EEF, April 6, 1909, EWE Papers, Box 3.
12. "1906," *The Harvard Graduates Magazine* 18 (1909–1910): 342.
13. EEF Diary, June 25, 1909, FP, Carton 25.
14. EWE to EEF, July 30, 1909, EWE Papers, Box 3.
15. EEF Diary, Nov. 24, 1909, FP, Carton 25.
16. Susan Emerson to EEF, Nov. 28, 1909, FP, Box 5.
17. EEF Diary, Nov. 24, 1909, FP, Carton 25.
18. EEF Diary, Nov. 25, 1909, FP, Carton 25.
19. EEF Diary, Nov. 1, 1909, FP, Carton 25.
20. "Forbes-Forbes Wedding," *Boston Evening Transcript*, Jan. 22, 1910, 3.
21. "Forbes-Grinnell Wedding," *Boston Evening Transcript*, June 9, 1910, 10.
22. Ellen Emerson Jr. to EEF, July 19, 1910, FP, Carton 5.
23. Ellen Emerson Jr. to EEF, March 12, 1910, FP, Box 5.
24. EEF Travel Diary, 1910–1911, Aug. 27, 1910, typescript, FP, Carton 26.
25. EEF Travel Diary, 1910–1911, Sept. 17, 1910, typescript, FP, Carton 26.
26. "Alexander Whiteside," *Boston Evening Transcript*, Feb. 2, 1903, 3.
27. EEF to "Dear Family," Oct. 16, 1910, FP, Carton 26.
28. "Canton," *Boston Globe*, Oct. 27, 1910: 9.
29. EWE to EEF, Jan. 21, 1911, EWE Papers, Box 3.
30. "Warwick Greene Dies," *New York Times*, Nov. 20, 1929, 29.
31. EEF to "Dear Family, Oct. 16, 1910, EEF to "Dear Children" Oct. 16–19, 1910, FP, Carton 26.
32. EEF to "My Dear Sons and Daughters," Nov. 6–7, 1910, FP, Carton 26.
33. EEF to "Dear Children," Nov. 11, 1910, FP, Carton 26.
34. EEF to "My Very Dear Family," Oct. 31, 1910, FP, Carton 26.
35. EEF to "Dear Children," Oct. 24, 1910, FP, Carton 26.
36. EEF to "Dear Children," Oct. 24, 1910, FP, Carton 26.
37. EWE to EEF, July 14, 1910, EWE Papers, Box 3.
38. EEF Travel Diary, 1910–1911, Sept. 17, 1910, typescript, FP, Carton 26.
39. EEF to "My Very Dear Family," Oct. 31–Nov. 10, 1910, FP, Carton 26.
40. EEF to Dear Family, Travel Diary, 1910–1911, Nov. 25, 1910, typescript, FP, Carton 26.
41. EEF to "My Dears," Nov. 13–16, 1910, FP, Carton 26.
42. EEF to "My Dears," Nov. 13–16, 1910, FP, Carton 26.
43. EEF to "My Dears," Nov. 13–16, 1910, FP, Carton 26.

44 EEF to "My Dears," Nov. 13–16, 1910, EEF to "My Dear Sons and Daughters," Nov. 20, 1910, FP, Carton 26.
45 My Dear Sons and Daughters," Nov. 20, 1910, FP, Carton 26.
46 EEF to "Dear Family," Nov. 25, 1910, FP, Carton 26.
47 EEF to "Dear Family," Nov. 25, 1910, FP, Carton 26.
48 EEF to "Dear Family," Nov. 25, 1910, FP, Carton 26.
49 EEF to "My Sons and Daughters," Dec. 3–6, 1910, FP, Carton 26.
50 EEF to "My Dear Sons and Daughters," Nov. 20, 1910, FP, Carton 26.
51 EEF to ETE, April 27, 1898, FP, Box 4.
52 EEF to "My Dear Children," Jan. 12, 1911, FP, Carton 26.
53 EEF to "My Sons and Daughters," Dec. 3–6, 1910, FP, Carton 26. C.H. Hayes and E. M. Sait, "The Dependencies," *Political Science Quarterly* 25, no. 4 (1910): 745.
54 EEF to "Dear Children," March 7–10, 1909, FP, Carton 26; Gordon Campbell, "Aglipay, Gregorio," *The Oxford Dictionary of the Catholic Church*, ed. Andrew Louth (New York: Oxford University Press, 2022); Resil Mojares, *The War Against the Americans: Resistance and Collaboration in Cebu, 1899–1906* (Ateneo de Manila University Press, 1999), 140, 167.
55 EEF to "Dear Sons and Daughters," Dec. 20, 1910, typescript, FP, Carton 26.
56 EEF to "Dear Children," March 7–10, 1911, typescript, FP, Carton 26.
57 EEF to "Dear Children," Jan. 21, 1911, FP, Carton 26.
58 EEF to "Dear Children," Jan. 21, 1911, FP, Carton 26.
59 EEF to "Dear Children," March 7–10, 1911, FP, Carton 26.
60 EEF to "Dear Children," March 7–10, 1911, FP, Carton 26.
61 EEF to Forbes children, Feb. 4–13, 1911, FP, Carton 26.
62 EEF to Forbes children, March 24, 1911, FP, Carton 26.
63 EEF to Forbes children, March 27, 1911, FP, Carton 26.
64 EEF to Forbes children, March 30–April 2, 1911, FP, Carton 26.
65 EEF Diary, April 13, 1911, FP, Carton 25.
66 ETE Diary, 1912, "Memoranda," FP, Carton 25.
67 EEF Diary, April 17, 1918, FP, Carton 25.
68 EEF Diary, May 25, 1911, FP, Carton 25. "Massachusetts, US, Death Records, 1841–1915," digital image s.v. "Helen Forbes, 1905–1911," Ancestry.com.
69 EEF Diary, Sept. 3, 1911, FP, Carton 25.
70 EEF Diary, March 22–March 23, 1912, FP, Carton 25. "Alice Bache Gould Papers, Guide to the Collection," Jan. 2005, *Massachusetts Historical Society*, https://www.masshist.org/collection-guides/view/fa0207.
71 EEF Diary, March 30–April 28, 1912, FP, Carton 25.
72 EEF Diary, May 3–May 4, 1912, FP, Carton 25.
73 EEF Diary, Jan. 20, 1913, FP, Carton 25.
74 EEF Diary, March 6, 1913, FP, Carton 5; Ralph Forbes to EEF, March 15, 1913, FP, Carton 15.
75 "Obituary Notes," *Brooklyn Daily Eagle*, May 5, 1913, 3.
76 Peter Stanley, "William Cameron Forbes: Proconsul in the Philippines," *Pacific Historical Review* 35, no. 3 (1966): 299–301.
77 Eleanor Whiteside to EEF, Feb. 19, 1913, FP, Box 15.
78 "Leaves Labrador to Wed: Amelia Forbes, Society Girl Nurse, to Marry Raymond Emerson," *New York Times*, Aug. 6, 1912, 1.

79 Raymond Emerson to EEF, Jan. 19, 1913, FP, Carton 5.
80 "Emerson Statue Assured," *Boston Evening Transcript*, May 17, 1910, 12; Leslie Perrin Wilson, "Anniversary Celebration, Centennial of Unveiling of Daniel Chester French's Seated Emerson in the Concord Free Library," May 16, 2014, Concord Free Library, https://concordlibrary.org/special-collections/emerson-statue-celebration/.
81 Harold Holzer, *Monument Man: The Life and Art of Daniel Chester French* (Princeton, NJ: Princeton Architectural Press, 2019): 94.
82 A. Lawrence Lowell to EEF, Dec. 11, 1916, and Herbert Langfeld to EEF, June 26, 1917, FP, Carton 16; "B44: Ralph Waldo Emerson (Sculpture)", *Harvard Art Museums*, https://hvrd.art/o/304688.
83 Rose Hawthorne Lathrop to EEF, April. 5, 1902; Rose Hawthorne Lathrop to EEF, April 15, 1902; Newton M[ackintosh] to EWE, Aug. 21, 1902; Rose Hawthorne Lathrop to EEF, July 12, 1903; EEF to Director of Kensal Green Cemetery, after Aug. 26, 1914; Kenneth Havers to EEF, Sept. 17, 1914; Rose Hawthorne Lathrop to EEF, Nov. 24, 1914, FP, Carton 19.
84 Mother Mary Lathrop (Rose Hawthorne) to EEF, April 6, 1918, FP, Carton 17.
85 Lucia Bartlett to Alice Whitney, [June 8, 1914], Anne Whitney Papers, Wellesley College Digital Archives, https://repository.wellesley.edu/object/wellesley12071.
86 Edward Forbes to EEF, July 12, 1914, and Edward Forbes to EEF, July 29, 1914, FP, Carton 15.
87 Edward Forbes to Violet Forbes Webster, Aug. 29, 1914, typescript, FP, Carton 15.
88 Margaret Forbes to EEF, Sept. 15, 1914, FP, Box 16.
89 "Says Allies Will Fight Until the End," *Boston Globe*, Sept. 24, 1914.
90 Mary Miller Engel, *I Remember the Emersons* (Los Angeles: Times-Mirror, 1941), 161–62.
91 Engel, *I Remember the Emersons*, 162–63.
92 Amelia Forbes Emerson to EEF, March 13, 1917 and Amelia Forbes to EEF, April 1917, FP, Carton 5.
93 "Cardinal Mercer Fund," *Boston Globe*, May 30, 1916, 4; "Milton," *Boston Globe*, May 11, 1918: 3; "Notable Record in War Work Made by the Women of the Ever Ready Bible Class," *Boston Globe*, March 1, 1918: 8; "Sends $10,00 at Once for Belgians," *Boston Globe*, Oct. 22, 1914: 10; "Table Gossip," *Boston Sunday Globe*, Jan. 30, 1916, 55.
94 EEF to Mary Miller Engel, Dec. 9, 1916, FP, Box 16.
95 "A Nonsense Verse of Eighty Years Ago," in *Favorites of a Nursery of Seventy Years Ago: And Some Others of a Later Date*, ed. Edith Emerson Forbes (Boston: Houghton Mifflin, 1916), 154–55.
96 EEF, Reminiscences written for JEC, 1886, EF Correspondence (3502).
97 Heinrich Hoffman, *Slovenly Peter*, trans. Annis Lee Furnis, ed. Edith Emerson Forbes (New York: Houghton Mifflin, 1917).
98 EEF Diary 1922, "Cash Accounts," FP, Carton 25.
99 Concord Free Public Library, "Acknowledgement of Donation," Nov. 24, 1916, FP, Carton 16.
100 EEF to Mary Miller Engel, Dec. 9, 1916, FP, Carton 16.
101 "Cycles of Personal Belief," *Boston Globe*, May 13, 1917, 57.
102 "Table Gossip," *Boston Sunday Globe*, Oct. 26, 1919, 62.
103 M. M. H., *Memorial Sketches: Mary Bell Lewis Ellen Emerson Davenport*, (Privately Printed, 1922), 34–35; Charlotte Forbes to EEF, Aug. 13, 1921, FP, Carton 18.

104 Cameron Forbes to EEF, Aug. 16, 1921, FP, Carton 18
105 Untitled typescript, EWE Papers, Box 4.
106 EEF Diary, Aug. 7. 1922, FP, Carton 25.
107 EEF Diary, Aug. 29–Sept. 12, 1922, FP, Carton 25.
108 EEF Diary, July 20–July 25, 1924, FP, Carton 25; Mary Miller Engel to EEF, June 29, 1924, FP, Carton 18.
109 Quoted in Edith Emerson Webster Gregg, "Emerson and His Children: Their Childhood Memories," *Harvard Library Bulletin* 28, no. 4 (1980): 417. When Gregg published the article, she noted that the manuscript was "in possession of the author of this article." I have not located the manuscript in the Emerson or Forbes collections.
110 Gregg, "Emerson and His Children": 413.
111 Edith Stebbins to EEF, Feb. 1923, FP, Carton 18.
112 EEF Diary, Nov. 20–Nov. 23, 1922, FP, Carton 25.
113 Gregg, "Emerson and His Children," 416.
114 Gregg, "Emerson and His Children," 417.
115 Gregg, "Emerson and His Children," 422; EEF to Elizabeth Cabot, 1886, EF Correspondence, 3502.
116 W. Barksdale Maynard, *Walden Pond: A History* (New York: Oxford University Press, 2004), 228.
117 Maynard, *Walden Pond*, 229.
118 Donna deFabio Curtis, *Plymouth* (Charleston, SC; Arcadia Publishing, 2011), 23–24.
119 Helen Pierce to EEF, April 27, 1924, FP, Carton 18.
120 George Nutting, *Massachusetts: A Guide to its People and Places* (Cambridge, MA: Riverside Press, 1937), 325; Zachary Lamothe, *A History Lover's Guide to the South Shore* (Charleston, SC: History Press, 2020), 24.
121 "Charities Subscribed to by Mrs. W. H. Forbes During 1922," typescript, and Frederick Stone to EEF, Nov. 2, 1921, FP, Carton 23; Pauline Shaw Fenno to EEF, Feb. 26, 1926, FP, Carton 18.
122 EEF to Mary Miller Engel, June 3, 1926, FP, Carton 18.
123 "Wife of Asst. Prof Webster is Dead," *Boston Globe*, April 29, 1926, 2.
124 EEF to Mary Miller Engel, June 3, 1926, FP, Carton 18.
125 EEF to Mary Miller Engel, June 3, 1926, FP, Carton 18.
126 EEF to Mary Miller Engel, Feb. 20, 1924, FP, Carton 18.
127 EEF to Mary Miller Engel, June 3, 1926, FP, Box 18.
128 *Edith Emerson Forbes, 1841–1929* (Privately Printed, 1929), FP, Box 8.

FREQUENTLY CITED SOURCES

Archival Sources

Emerson Family Correspondence (hereafter EF Correspondence), Houghton Library, Harvard University, Cambridge, MA. MS Am 1280.226

Emerson Family Papers (hereafter EF Papers), Houghton Library, Harvard University, Cambridge, MA. MS Am 1280.235

Ellen Tucker Emerson Correspondence (hereafter ETE Correspondence), Harvard University, Cambridge, MA, 2003M-13

Edith Emerson Forbes and William Hathaway Forbes Papers and Additions (hereafter FP), Massachusetts Historical Society, Boston, MA.

Archives and Libraries

William Monroe Special Collections, Concord Free Public Library, Concord, MA.

Houghton Library, Harvard University, Cambridge, MA.

Published Sources

Ellen Tucker Emerson Letters, 1863–1865 (hereafter *ETE Letters*). Alexandria, VA: Alexander Street Press, 2010.

Emerson, Ellen Tucker. *The Letters of Ellen Tucker Emerson* (hereafter *LETE*), 2 vols. Edited by Edith E.W. Gregg. Kent, OH: Kent State Press, 1983.

Emerson, Ellen. *The Life of Lidian Jackson Emerson* (hereafter *LLJE*). Edited by Delores Bird Carpenter. East Lansing: Michigan State University Press, 1992.

Emerson, Ralph Waldo. *The Letters of Ralph Waldo Emerson* (hereafter *LRWE*), 10 vols. Edited by Ralph Rusk and Eleanor Tilton. New York: Columbia University Press, 1939–1995.

Emerson, Lidian Jackson. *The Selected Letters of Lidian Jackson Emerson* (hereafter *SLLJE*), 2 vols. Edited by Delores Bird Carpenter. Columbia: University of Missouri Press, 1987.

INDEX

abolition, 12, 14, 34, 39, 50, 178. *See also* Concord Female Anti-Slavery Society
Adams, Abel, 15, 26
Adams, Clover Hooper, 35, 95
Agassiz, Elizabeth, 30
Agassiz, Ida. *See* Higginson, Ida Agassiz
Agassiz, Louis, 30, 36, 215
Agassiz School for Young Ladies, 29, 30–33, 35, 39, 204
aging, ETE and 170, 176, 179, 184, 189, 201–2; LJE and, 142, 146–47; EEF and, 170–71, 180, 189, 199, 206, 215; Haskins cousins and, 192–93, 198. *See also* aphasia
Aglipay, Gregorio, 212
Alcott, Abby May, 15
Alcott, Anna, 13–15, 34, 54–55
Alcott, Bronson, 2, 14, 29, 34, 45, 54–55, 117; 127, 140, 160. *See also* Concord School of Philosophy
Alcott, Louisa May, 13, 29, 48, 54–55, 72, 83, 86, 103–4, 140
Alcott, May, 15, 54–56, 103
Anglicanism, 90, 97, 119, 198
Ansley, Sarah Haskins, 127, 142–43, 145, 166, 182–83, 187, 193, 198, 200
Anthony, Annie, 122, 211
anti-imperialism, 171–72, 187, 191, 196, 202. *See also* the Philippines; Spanish-American War
aphasia, 75–77, 87, 105, 110–11, 113–14, 116–17, 124–25, 136, 204; first signs of, 69; public speaking and, 71, 85–86, 90, 99, 103, 108–9, 117

aunthood, 19; ETE and, xv, 64, 67, 77, 79, 98–99, 104, 116, 120, 124, 133, 159, 189, 191, 201–3, 219–20; EEF and, 180, 184, 193, 208–9, 216, 220. *See also* Emerson, Mary Moody
the Azores, 70–73. *See also* travel to Europe

Bartlett, Josiah, 103
Bartlett, Lucia, 182, 217
Beecher, Henry Ward, 24, 69
Bersier, Eugène, 93
Bond, Elizabeth Powell, 203–4
Boreham, Mary, 209, 213
"Brahma," 190
Brown, Annie, 38–39
Brown, John, 39
Brown, Lucy Jackson, 2, 15, 68, 101
Brown, Sarah, 39
Brook Farm, 14, 19, 22
Bulkeley, Peter, 4
Burnham, Daniel, 197. *See also* the Philippines
Bush, 4–7, 10–11, 14, 143, 158, 171, 176–77, 187–88; fire in, 86–87, 125; pilgrimages to, 83, 189, 203; rental of, 151, 160–61, 166, 206, 223; restoration of, 87–88, 90, 97–99, 166; study, 36, 222. *See also* housekeeping; Thanksgiving

Cabot, Elizabeth Dwight, 105, 113, 120, 124, 133, 135, 172, 188
Cabot, James Elliot, 2, 83, 87, 125, 187–88; family of, 109, 111, 133, 136, 183;

277

Cabot, James Elliot (*continued*)
collaboration with Emersons, 105, 107, 110–11, 113–15, 117, 119–20, 128, 130, 136, 219, 221; friendship with Forbes family, 124, 135, 183. *See also* Carlyle, Thomas, correspondence of; *A Memoir of Ralph Waldo Emerson*
Cabot, Richard, 185
caregiving: ETE and, xiv, 72–73, 76, 83, 95, 110–11, 128, 182–83, 192–93, 111, 116–17, 125, 132, 138, 141–42, 144–45, 147, 169, 173, 180, 190; EEF and, xiv, 71, 73–74, 125, 177, 202
Carlyle, Thomas, xv, 2, 19, 130, 137, 146–47; correspondence of, 75–76, 85, 91, 127–28
Cary, Alice Forbes, 78, 194
Catholicism, 49, 68, 70, 93, 216, 133
Centennial Exposition, 108
Channing, Ellen Fuller, 12, 37
Channing, Ellery, 11, 23, 53, 56; children of, 14
Channing, William H., 111, 128
charities, 205, 218–19, 223
The Children's Yearbook, 161–62
Cheney, Birdy, 32
Cheney, Ednah Dow, 117, 119
Civil War, 40–43, 46–47, 49, 50, 53, 59–60
"Civilization at a Pinch," 42
Clarke, James Freeman, 7, 127
Clarke, Lillian, 45
Clarke, Sarah Freeman, 7, 45
Cleveland, Charlotte Haskins, 28, 119, 132, 142, 166, 174, 182–83, 187
Collected Works of Ralph Waldo Emerson, 131
Complete Works of Ralph Waldo Emerson, Centenary Edition, 187, 190–91
Complete Works of Ralph Waldo Emerson, Riverside Edition, 129–32, 137, 162, 187
Concord Female Anti-Slavery Society, 12
Concord Free Public Library, xviii, 99, 216, 207, 220
"Concord Hymn," 7, 83, 103
Concord, MA, 2, 4–5, 12, 97–98, 117, 140, 187; anniversaries of, 103, 134; Battle of, 5, 83, 159, 180–81; Civil War and, 41, 47, 53, 59–61; homesickness for, 98; Saturday Club and, 30; school examinations and, 47; Social Club and, 137; suffragists and, 83; walking in, 5, 13, 222. *See also* Concord Free Public Library; Concord School of Philosophy; First Parish, Concord; Walden Pond
Concord School Committee, 75, 77, 82, 133
Concord School of Philosophy, 117–19, 138, 174
"Concord Hymn," 2, 5, 83, 103
Conway, Moncure D., 77, 127–28
correspondence: in archival collections, xvi, xvii–xviii, 207, 214, 224; burning of, 48, 86; as creative work, xiv; condolence notes, 141, 143; editing and organizing of, 71, 73, 141, 168, 171, 190, 206–7, 210, 214, 224; Emerson family and, 1, 11, 16–17, 19–20, 62–63, 66, 72, 73, 80, 85, 94–95, 104, 140, 160, 169, 192, 197; expansion of in nineteenth-century, 16–17; EEF to WHF, 59–60; as family documentation, 43, 65, 67, 111, 167, 173, 184, 193; journal letters, xiv, 66, 144, 192, 212; reading aloud, 16, 161, 175, 184, 203, 206, 210; telephone and, 143–44; transcendentalism and, 17; triplicate block and, 192; travel and, 72, 95, 140, 146, 161, 165, 177–78, 192, 195–96, 199, 212–14. *See also* Carlyle, Thomas
Corson, Juliet, 123
Cotton, Sarah, 2

Dabney, Charles, 70
Dabney, Clara, 70, 72, 77, 84–85, 110, 126, 135, 147, 158, 207
Dabney, Roxanne, 72
Dall, Caroline Healey, 20
Davenport, Ellen Tucker Emerson, 122–23, 183, 185, 194, 197–98, 208–9, 211, 220–21
Davidson, Edith (Edie), 47–49, 64, 72–73, 98, 100, 109, 111
Davidson, Francis, 47
Davidson, Isabella Hale, 47–48
"Demonology," 113
The Dial, 7, 11–12
"Domestic Life," 222

editing: ETE and, xiv, 104–8, 113–15, 117–20, 128, 130, 200–201, 205; EEF and, xiv, 174, 200–203, 207, 210, 219, 224.

See also Cabot, James Elliot; Complete Works of Ralph Waldo Emerson, Riverside Edition; correspondence; Emerson Factory; Emerson, Ralph Waldo, journals of; *Letters and Social Aims*; *Parnassus*
education, 13–14, 28; of women, 21–22, 164. *See also* Agassiz School; Concord School Committee; Milton Academy; Sanborn, Franklin; Sedgwick School
"Education," 130
Emerson, Amelia Forbes, 216, 218
Emerson, Annie Keys, 112, 122, 201, 224; children of, 104, 112, 116, 120, 125, 197, 208, 221; marriage of, 81, 89, 94, 103, 107; relationship with in-laws, 81, 86–87, 99, 103–4, 112, 184, 193, 206
Emerson, Bulkeley, 6, 173
Emerson, Charles Chauncy (1808–1836), 2, 5
Emerson, Charles (1841–1916), 19, 91, 125, 127, 183; and Civil War, 41, 48, 51
Emerson, Charles Lowell (1876–1880), 109, 120
Emerson, Edward Bliss (1805–1834), 2, 24–25
Emerson, Edward Waldo, 11, 45, 54, 103, 160, 224; as author and editor, 128–29, 137, 146–47, 176, 181, 187–88, 190–91, 200, 202; anti-imperialism and, 172, 202; career of, 64, 103, 112, 120, 125, 129, 219; children of, 104, 112, 116, 120, 125, 197, 208–9, 221; desire to enlist, 42, 47, 53–55; education of, 29, 38–39, 42, 47, 51, 54, 64, 68, 81, 91, 94, 98; health of, 39, 42, 44, 66, 80, 85, 109, 193; marriage of, 81, 89, 94, 103, 107; relationship with sisters, 35, 64, 66, 160, 165, 200, 201, 206–7, 213, 222; relationship with WHF, 57, 81, 84–85, 122; travel and, 64, 81, 89–91, 93, 215; as uncle, 64, 98, 140, 145, 220. *See also* Complete Works of Ralph Waldo Emerson, Riverside Edition; Emerson factory; *Emerson in Concord: A Memoir*; sibling relationships
Emerson, Ellen Tucker (1811–1831) 1, 19
Emerson, Ellen Tucker (1839–1909): birth of, 1; death of, 202–3; as family historian, xv, 42–43, 49, 70, 166, 172–75, 185–86, 203; finances of, 100, 158, 171, 179; health of, 33, 65, 68, 70–71, 74–76, 83, 168, 191–92, 201–2; intellectual curiosity of, 75, 160, 164–65, 175, 189, 201; obituaries of, 203–4; will of, 205
Emerson, Ellen Tucker (1880–1921). *See* Davenport, Ellen Tucker
Emerson factory, xvi, 107, 113, 114–15, 117–20, 125, 128; Emerson canon and, xvi, 131–32; hiding of ETE's efforts for, 106–7; 130–31. *See also* Cabot, James Elliot; Complete Works of Ralph Waldo Emerson, Riverside Edition; *A Memoir of Ralph Waldo Emerson*
Emerson, Haven (1840–1913), 19, 34, 46, 51, 54, 66, 87, 120, 127, 145, 166, 182, 199, 215; children of, 120, 124, 145, 165, 183–84, 190, 192–94, 199, 209
Emerson in Concord: A Memoir, 137, 185, 200
Emerson, John, 112, 116
Emerson, Lidian Jackson: abolition and, 12, 34, 46, 172, 196; animal rights and, 119; Civil War and, 42; death, 147–48; 161; EEF's marriage and, 58–59, 63; finances, 5–6, 101, 115; gravestone, 172; health of, 10–11, 17–18, 20, 25–28, 32, 59, 68, 75, 79, 142, 147, 174; marriage of, 3–10, 18, 134, 126, 167, 173; legacy, 172, 200, 219, 221; name change, 4, 6; parents, 2; religion and, 3, 8, 12–13, 24, 65, 122; Thoreau, Henry David and, 17–18. *See also* grandmotherhood, motherhood; "Transcendental Bible"; widowhood
Emerson, Mary Moody, 5, 8, 42, 48–49, 130–31, 172
Emerson Memorial School, 189
Emerson, Raymond, xvii, 135, 216, 218
Emerson, Ralph Waldo: abolition and, 12, 38; Civil War and, 42, 60–61; death, 125; as father, 10, 12–13, 19, 22–25, 28, 30–31, 34, 36, 52, 63, 74, 76, 100, 120, 186, 219, 222–23; funeral, 126–27; grave, 134, 141, 172, 187, 189; marriage of, 3–10, 18, 134, 126, 167, 173; finances, 5–6, 9, 15, 34–35, 49, 81, 87, 91–92, 101, 135;

Emerson, Ralph Waldo (*continued*):
as grandfather, 64, 67, 76, 77, 85; health of, 10, 52, 119, 125–26; journals of, 188, 190, 200–201, 208; lecturing, 6, 9, 32, 42, 51, 66, 69, 71, 76, 80, 85, 105, 108, 114, 117; religion and, 12–13, 65, 134; will of, 128–30. *See also* aphasia; Emerson Factory; servants; travel to Europe; *entries for individual works*

Emerson, Ralph Waldo, legacy of, 124, 127, 132, 200, 219; centennial of, 186–87; canon and, xvi, 131–32; ETE and, 169, 185–87, 189; and EEF, 135–36, 161, 178, 187, 221–22. *See also* Collected Works of Ralph Waldo Emerson; Complete Works of Ralph Waldo Emerson, Centenary Edition; Complete Works of Ralph Waldo Emerson, Riverside Edition; *Emerson in Concord: A Memoir*; Emerson Factory; *A Memoir of Ralph Waldo Emerson*

Emerson, Ruth Haskins, 2, 5, 7, 11, 15, 24, 43, 120, 170, 172

Emerson, Sally Gibbons, 23, 49–50, 52, 104, 178, 192, 200, 204–5; marriage of, 34, 51, 54

Emerson, Susan, 19, 47–48, 51, 54, 68, 69

Emerson, Theresia Keveschi (Therci), 91, 125, 183

Emerson, Waldo, 1, 6, 104; death of, 8–11, 83, 207, 224

Emerson, William (1743–1776), 4, 104

Emerson, William (1769–1811), 2

Emerson, William (1801–1868), 19, 48, 51, 54, 69

Emerson, William (1835–1864), 19, 34, 48, 51, 54

Emerson, William (1875–1875), 104

Emerson, William Forbes (1884–1909), 133, 197, 180, 185, 207–8

Emery, Constance, 142–43

Engel, Mary Miller, 142, 169, 179, 201, 205, 218–19, 223

Farquahr, Miss, 94–96

Favorites of a Nursey of Seventy Years Ago, 219–20

First Parish, Concord, 4, 12, 34, 65–66, 125–26, 203; Committee on Domestic Charities, 205; 125, 128, 203; fire, 180–81; Sunday School, 47, 51, 60, 65–67, 110; Women's Parish Association, 123–24, 166, 221

Foord, Sophie, 14

Forbes, Alexander, 133, 145, 166, 168, 175, 177, 192, 180–81, 183, 194, 200, 213, 215; birth, 127; children, 214–15; health of, 157, 184, 200, 215; marriage of, 208

Forbes, Edward Waldo, 102, 111–12, 115, 122, 124, 141, 145, 159, 165, 168, 175–76, 194, birth, 98; children, 213, 217; family documents and, xvii; Fogg Art Museum, 209, 223; health, 121, 185; marriage of, 194, 197–99; travel and, 177, 180, 182, 209, 217–18

Forbes, Charlotte Grinnell, 208, 215

Forbes, Edith Emerson: birth, 6; death, 224; finances, 91–92, 98, 159, 170, 176, 185, 218–19, 220, 223; health, 49, 51–52, 65, 67, 102, 111–12, 116, 168, 176, 181, 192, 199, 223–23; memoir of father, 20, 221

Forbes, Ellen Randolph (1838–1860), 57, 58–59

Forbes, Ellen Randolph (Rosebud) (1880–1881), 120–22, 161

Forbes, Ellen Forbes (1886–1954), 194, 198, 208, 220

Forbes, Elise Cabot, 183–84, 193, 214

Forbes, Florence Emerson, 128, 184, 186, 188, 192–93, 197, 214

Forbes, Gerrit, 186, 188, 192–93, 197

Forbes, John Murray (1813–1898), 37–38, 55, 57, 59–60, 62, 70, 85, 87, 114, 168; death of, 176; grandchildren and, 116, 212; travel and, 78–79, 123

Forbes, John Murray (Don) (1871–1888), 111, 122, 124; birth, 81; death, 140–41, 143, 161, 175, 183; health, 115, 121;

Forbes, Malcom, 60, 87, 144, 147, 167, 186, 191, 208
Forbes, Margaret Leighton, 194, 197–99, 201, 208, 218
Forbes, Rose Dabney, 147, 167, 170, 193
Forbes, Ralph, 65, 67, 73, 76, 79–80, 81, 111, 115, 122, 124; 134, 145, 147, 159, 165, 168, 180–81, 194, 201, 215; birth, 64; children, 184, 214; 190, 193, 201; ETE and, 179, 207; health, 112, 121, 185, 200; marriage, 183
Forbes, Sarah Swain Hathaway (1813–1900), 57–58, 62, 85, 87, 115, 170, 180, 184; death of, 182
Forbes, Waldo Emerson, 124, 133, 141, 159, 168, 175, 176; birth, 116; health, 121–22, 166, 185, 215; travel and, 181, 192; as editor, 185, 200; marriage, 208; children, 213–15, 220; death, 220
Forbes, William Cameron (Cam) (1870–1959), 79–80, 111, 115, 122, 124, 133, 140, 145, 147, 159, 164, 168, 176, 180–81, 185, 218, 220; birth, 76; ETE and, 145, 179; in the Philippines, 191, 195–98, 201–2, 208, 211–13, 215; in Wyoming, 177, 185, 188
Forbes, William Hathaway (1840–1897), Civil War and, 42, 56, 57, 59; death, 169; ETE and, 57–58, 100, 115, 158–59; RWE and, 71, 88, 101, 102, 110–11; engagement of, 56–57; fatherhood and, 64, 73, 122, 124, 212; Harvard and, 57, 78; health, 64–65, 112, 167–169; marriage, xiii, 62–63, 73, 81, 116, 143–44, 162, 167, 198; National Bell Telephone, 116, 144; poems of, 175–76
"Forerunners," 191
"Fortune of the Republic," 114–15, 117
French, Daniel Chester, 103, 118, 141, 211, 216
Fuller, Margaret, 2, 7, 9–10, 14, 33, 45, 89

Galt, Anges, 195
Galt, John, 195, 213
Gardens and gardening: in Bath, 139; at Bush, 19, 146; in Japan, 195; in Milton, 67, 99–100, 111, 133, 190, 223; on Naushon, 138, 215; gardening catalogs, 171; in Penang, 210; in Plymouth, 222–23; in Shanghai, 213
Gibbons, Abigail Hopper, 23, 49–50
Gibbons, Sally. See Emerson, Sally Gibbons
Grant, Ulysses, 69, 103
Grandmotherhood: LJE and, 77, 140, 147; EEF and, 184, 187, 193, 201, 208, 213–15, 218
Gravestones, 49, 70, 199, 213, 217; of ETE, 204; of LJE, 172, 175, 200; of RWE, 134, 141, 166, 172. See also Sleepy Hollow Cemetery
Greene, Eleanor, 209, 213
Grief: ETE and, 9, 111, 140, 143, 147–48; EWE and, 197–98, 208, 214, 220–21, 223–24,; LJE and, 8–10, 122; RWE and, 8–10; Forbes family and, 121–22, 124, 140, 143, 148, 161, 175, 203, 206, 213–14, 216, 220
Grimm, Herman, 98
Grimm, Gisela, 98
Gould, Alice, 215

Hallowell, Susan, 194, 198
Haskins, Samuel, 132, 166, 182
Hastings, Sarah Forbes, 78
Hatheway, Conrad, 195, 211, 213
Hatheway, Mabel, 195
Hathorne, Julian, 15, 55
Hawthorne, Nathaniel, 15, 55, 99
Hawthorne, Rose, 15, 216–17
Hawthorne, Sophia, 15, 53, 68, 216–17
Hawthorne, Una, 15, 47, 49, 54–55, 57, 59, 63, 91, 146, 216–17
Heard, Grace, 166, 206
Hemenway, Charlotte, 209
Higginson, Henry Lee, 50–51
Higginson, Ida Agassiz, 35, 38, 223; marriage, 50–51; *Parnassus* and, 101; relationship with ETE 31–33, 36, 73, 86, 97, 103, 131
Higginson, Mary, 50

Higginson, Thomas Wentworth, 117, 178, 187
Hoar, Caroline, 92, 123
Hoar, Ebenezer, 39, 88, 98, 125
Hoar, Elizabeth, xv, 1, 5, 7, 11, 54, 62, 71, 99, 107, 111, 113, 173; death, 112–13; travel and, 92, 94, 97, 137
Hoar, Samuel, 187
Hotton, James Camden, 77, 88, 104
housekeeping, ETE and, 25–28, 32–34, 37, 48, 73, 83, 86, 145, 161, 163, 166, 201; LJE and, 3, 5, 7, 11, 25–28; EEF and, 37–38, 63, 77, 91, 99, 161, 163, 185, 193, 197, 211; Webster, Violet Forbes and, 144
Howe, Julia Ward, 119, 189
Hughes, Thomas, 92, 97

illness: arsenic poisoning, 144–45; cancer, 202, 216, 223; cerebral embolism, 220; diphtheria, 121; flu (grippe), 192, 194, 197, 215, 220; measles, 121; neurasthenia, 26; heart disease, 182; rest cure, 27; pneumonia, 121, 125, 197, 214; rheumatism, 102, 168, 176, 182, 190, 192, 201; scarlet fever, 8, 26, 112, 115–16, 124–25, 159, 207; smallpox, 80; tuberculosis, 1, 48, 51, 54, 109, 167–69, 192, 209; typhoid fever, 39, 48, 185; whooping cough, 64, 75. *See also* aphasia; caregiving; water cure
Ireland, Alexander, 180

Jackson, Abraham, 101
Jackson, Alice, 36, 145
Jackson, Charles (1770–1818), 2
Jackson, Charles (1805–1880), 2–3, 101, 222; children, 36, 80, 145, 161, 166
Jackson, Lidian, 145, 161, 166
Jackson, Lucy Cotton, 2
James, Alice, 46
James, Henry Jr., 46, 91, 96
James, Henry Sr., 46
James, Robertson, 46–47, 49
James, Wilkie, 46, 50, 53, 78
James, William, 46, 171, 187, 189, 196. *See also* anti-imperialism

Keyes, Alicia (Lily), 63–64, 81, 100, 114
Keyes, John, 54
Keyes, Martha Prescott, 64
Klebs, Margaret Forbes, 144, 167, 176

Lazarus, Emma, 109–10
Leavitt, Caroline, 84, 98
Legate, Helen, 112, 158, 166, 183, 190, 206, 223
Letters and Social Aims, 106, 128. *See also* Emerson factory
Lewis, Edmonia, 73, 178
Life of Lidian Jackson Emerson, xv, 7, 9, 55, 167, 172–76, 200
Lincoln, Abraham, 40, 43, 46, 51, 60–61
Lowell, Anna Cabot, 35, 91
Lowell, Charles Russell, 35, 56, 91, 147
Lowell, Frank, 87
Lowell, Josephine Shaw (Effie), 50, 56
Lowell, Nina, 77, 124, 167, 172

Mackintosh, Newton, 172
Mandac, Simeon, 212
Mann, Mary Peabody, 53, 118
Manning, Abigail (Addy), 23, 31, 178
Massachusetts Society for the Prevention of Cruelty to Animals, 119, 205
"May-Day," 107–8, 128
Maynard, Helen, 14, 28
McClure, Anna, 137, 142–43, 147–48, 178
McKay, Mary, 194, 198, 208, 215
A Memoir of Ralph Waldo Emerson, xv, xvi, 127–29, 185, 200; Emerson siblings contributions to, 133–37. *See also* Cabot, James Elliot; Emerson factory
"Memory," 117
Milton Academy, 116, 132–33, 175, 190
Milton, MA: First Parish, 221, 224; Forbes homes in, 63–67, 99, 183; kindergarten in, 111; vineyard in, 67. *See also* Milton Academy
Motherhood: LJE and, 1, 10–13, 19–20, 23–25, 44–45, 48, 52, 63, 121–22, 126, 140, 205; EEF and, 73–74, 81, 84, 102, 111–13, 121, 124, 134, 159, 165, 177, 183–84, 191, 193, 195, 198, 200, 202, 209, 211, 214–15,

223–24; nursing, 64–65; Webster, Edith Forbes and, 208, 215

National Bell Telephone Company, 116, 144
"Natural History of Intellect": lectures, 76, 78; volume, 162
Naushon, 37–38, 50, 57, 63, 65, 69, 82, 88, 99, 101–2, 111, 115, 140, 144, 165, 168–69, 193, 200–201, 215, 217; births on, 81, 98; editing work on, 101, 105, 114, 200–201; Forbes, Don, death, 140–41; homes on, 78, 138–39; Webster, Violet Forbes marriage, 189,
Neill, Margaret (Miss Bessie), 207, 210, 215, 218
New England Women's Club, 200, 205
Niagara Falls, 81, 115
Noa, Jessie, 118
Norton, Charles, 91, 127–28, 187
nurses, 133–34, 138, 193, 202. *See also* caregiving

Osgood, James, 102, 105
Oxford University, 97, 159, 182, 194; Müller, Max, 97; Oxford Summer Meeting, 163–65, 175, 189; Ruskin, John, 97

Parnassus: Cabot, James Elliot and, 105; ETE and, 77, 101, 210; EEF and, xvi, 75, 77–79, 101–2, 125, 136; WHF and, 102; Lazarus, Emma and, 109–110; profits from 129
Parsons, Hannah Haskins, 42, 48–49, 182–83, 187, 193, 198
Patmore, Coventry, 30–32, 83, 146, 210
Peabody, Elizabeth, 6, 53, 75, 118–19, 223
Perkins, Charles Elliot, 64, 176
"Perpetual Forces," 113–14, 117
the Philippines, 191–92, 195–96, 209–212; American imperialism and, vxi, 191, 196, 197, 211–12; revolts in, 196
photographs, 141, 161, 195, 200, 211, 214
Plymouth, MA, 41, 221; Brewster Garden, 222–23; LJE and, 2–4, 11, 134, 167
Plutarch's Morals, introduction to, 76–77

Portsmouth Grove Hospital, 45–46
"The Preacher," 117
"The Problem," 134
pregnancy, 63, 67, 71, 75, 77, 93, 120, 124; scarlet fever and, 112, 115–16; travel and, 78, 80
publishers: 101; Chatto and Windus, 104; Fields & Osgood, 88, 102; Houghton Mifflin, 129, 130, 132, 137, 162, 188, 219; Roberts Brothers, 161–62; Ticknor and Fields, 62. *See also* Hotton, James Camden; Norton, Charles

racism and prejudice, xv-xvi, 94, 132–33, 178, 196
railroads: 101; Boston and Maine, 168; Chicago, Burlington, and Quincy, 64, 176; to Concord, 12, 224; in Egypt, 96; financial panic of 1873 and, 98; Forbes family and, 37, 176; funerals and, 48, 126; in Greece, 199; in the Philippines, 196; Pullman car, 78–79; travel in the United States, 79, 108, 115, 122, 144, 177, 180, 188, 194, 213; views from trains, 181
reading, 11, 16–17, 113; children and, 11, 16–17, 79, 113, 215, 219; LJE and, 3, 23, 27–28, 118; ETE and, 23, 40, 49, 68, 72, 75, 95, 146–47, 164, 175, 201; RWE on, 99; EEF and, 35, 40, 49, 123, 135, 146–47, 161, 168, 221; Hoar, Elizabeth and, xv, 54, 113
Ripley, Elizabeth, 3, 80
Roosevelt, Theodore, 96, 186, 191
Russell, Cabot Jackson, 44, 50
Russell, LeBaron, 87

Sanborn, Franklin, 29, 37, 38, 44, 107, 117, 125, 167, 189; Brown, John and, 38–39; death of son, 141–42; proposal to EEF 44–45; school of, 29, 32, 35–36, 38–39; "Transcendental Bible" and, 160–61, 173
Sanborn, Louise Leavitt, 36–37, 45, 47, 84, 171, 160–61, 166; death of son, 141–42
Sanborn, Thomas, 141–42
Sanborn, Sarah, 29, 38
Schieferdecker, Charles, 51–52, 54. *See also* water cure

Schuyler, Georgina, 78
Sedgwick, Catharine, 22–23
Sedgwick, Elizabeth, 22–25
Sedgwick School, 22–25, 178–79
Selected Poems, 107, 110
self-reliance: concept of, xix, 118–19, 147; 187; "Self-Reliance," 7
servants: in Bush, 11, 14, 37–38, 73, 80, 146; domestics vs. help, 27; ETE and, 63, 93, 123, 163; LJE and, 26–27; RWE and, 44; EEF and, 79, 84, 98, 112, 133, 194, 207, 210; racism towards, 133, 178; travel and, 92, 94, 97, 122, 141, 181–82. *See also* housekeeping; nurses
Sewall, Lucy, 112
Shaw, Francis, 50
Shaw, Pauline Agassiz, 102, 109, 223
Shaw, Robert Gould, 50, 73, 168
sibling relationships, 6, 35, 145, 223; changes after marriage, 57–58, 63, 65, 81; differing memories in, 174–76; maternal instincts in, 12, 24; support in, 64, 66–67, 70, 99, 133, 165, 167, 169–70, 176, 190, 202–3, 207; tensions in, 53, 55, 65, 68, 74–76, 80, 100, 130, 132, 146, 162–63, 180, 200; travel and, 158–61, 165, 201. *See also* caregiving; Emerson factory; sisterhood
sisterhood: as partnership, xii, xvii, 21, 37–38, 40, 54, 58, 63, 70, 133, 170, 190–91; correspondence and, xiv, xviii, 24, 63, 140, 143–44, 159, 167, 192, 203. *See also* sibling relationships, caregiving
Simmons, Lizzie, 56
Sleepy Hollow Cemetery, 127, 134, 141, 166, 172, 217
Slovenly Peter, 219, 220
"Sovereignty of Ethics," 113
Spanish-American War, 171–72, 212
Stinson, Emma, 29
Storer, Elizabeth Hoar, 204–5
Storey, Moorfield, 171, 187–89, 191, 196
Stowe, Harriet Beecher, 32
Sumner, Charles, 58
"The Superlative," 113

Tappan, Caroline Sturgis, 8, 18, 21–22, 27–28, 33, 58, 81
Taylor, Jane, 16
temperance, 68, 74, 123, 164–65
Thanksgiving, 161, 170, 179, 208; at Bush, 65, 70, 73, 120, 145, 166, 170, 179; as national holiday, 51
Thayer, James Bradley, 78–79
Thoreau, Henry David, 2, 4, 13, 29, 38, 99, 222; death, 43, 54; Emerson children and, 11, 15–18, 28, 43, 44; LJE and, 17–18; RWE and, 14, 43
"Threnody," 10, 224
"Transcendental Bible," 7–8, 160, 173
Transcendentalism, xvi–xvii, 17, 90, 95; female contributions to, xvi, xvii, 119, 174; Mount Monadnock and, 56; suffrage and, 83; Transcendental Club, 2, 6. *See also The Dial,* "Transcendental Bible"
travel, to Asia, 195, 198, 210–11, 213–14. *See also* the Philippines
travel, to California, 78–81, 122–23, 180, 194, 215. *See also* railroads
travel, to Caribbean, 145–46
travel, to Egypt, 94–96, 199
travel, to Europe, 15–19, 81, 84–85, 87–94, 96–97; 138–40, 158–60, 158–65, 180, 181, 192–94, 209, 215, 217. *See also* railroads; the Azores
travel, to Florida, 141, 206
travel, to Hawaii, 195, 213
Twain, Mark, 70, 93

Unitarian ministers: Bulkeley, Benjamin, 128; Jackson, A. W., 203–4; MacDonald, Loren, 203–4; Pomeroy, Vivian, 224; Stebbins, Horatio, 79
Unitarianism, 2, 70; American Unitarian Association, 186; ETE and, 13, 23–24, 65–66, 90, 93, 100, 117–18, 134, 162–63; Unitarian conferences, 100, 115; Unitarian Grove Meeting, 118
University of Virginia, 108–9

"Voluntaries," 50
von Hoffman, Lily Ward, 49, 92–93
von Hoffman, Richard, 92

Walden Pond, 5, 12–13, 44, 109, 222
Ward, Anna Barker (1813–1900), 32–33, 46, 49, 52, 95, 110
Ward, Anna (1841–1875), 32
Ward, Elizabeth (Bessie), 49
Ward, Samuel, 32–33, 46, 56, 95
Ward, Thomas, 47, 49, 55
Ware, Harriet, 116
Warner, Langdon, 195, 213
Waterman, Mary, 56
water cure, in Bath, 139–40, 182, 192, 194; in Citronelle, AL, 171; in Hot Springs, VA, 168, 201, 209, 215; in New York City, 51–52, 54, 67
Watson, Mary, 41, 70–71, 72, 75, 167
Webster, Edith Forbes (Violet), 73, 76, 79–81, 115, 120, 122, 124, 133, 141, 159, 168, 176, 183, 186, 206; assistance to EEF, 102, 111, 139, 144–45, 165, 176–77, 186; birth, 67; children, 208, 215; death, 223; ETE and, 164, 175, 202–3; finances, 185;, health, 121; marriage, 186, 189–90; travel and, 178, 180–82; 188
Webster, Kenneth, 186, 189, 202

"What I Can Remember about Father," xv, 185–86, 188, 191
"What I Can Remember of Stories of Our Ancestors Told Me by Aunt Mary Moody Emerson," xv, 43
Wheeler, Ida, 22–24
Whiteside, Eleanor, 209–10, 215–16
Whiting, Anne, 39
Whiting, Jane, 14
Whitney, Anne, 31, 39, 178, 201–2, 217
Whitwell Family, 94–96
widowhood, 2, 126, 128, 175, 170–71, 175–76, 180, 182, 189, 194, 221
Williams, Mary, 209, 213
Wilson, Woodrow, 215
Woman's Journal, 83, 103, 119
women: history of, xv, 43, 173–74, 200, 223; reading and, 27, 146; same-sex relationships, 31–32, 36–37, 77, 137–38, 142–42, 145, 178–79; single, 37, 145, 179, 205. *See also* aunthood, education, motherhood, widowhood
women's rights, antisuffragists, 82–83; ETE and, xvi, 75, 81, 84, 104, 119, 123–24, 200; RWE and, 30–31, 83; LJE and, 83; EEF and, 81–83, 124. See also *Woman's Journal*
World War I, 217–220
Wyoming, 177–178, 185, 188–89

KATE CULKIN, born in New York City and raised in Denver, earned a BA in English from Middlebury College and a PhD in History from New York University. She is a member of the faculty of the Bronx Community College History Department and the CUNY Graduate Center MA in Biography and Memoir. On the steering committee of the Women Writing Women's Lives Seminar, she was a visiting scholar at the Oxford Centre for Life-Writing in 2023 and 2024. She is the author of *Harriet Hosmer: A Cultural Biography* and was an associate editor of the *Harriet Jacobs Family Papers*. Kate lives in New York City, blocks from her first home.

www.ingramcontent.com/pod-product-compliance
Lightning Source LLC
Chambersburg PA
CBHW030524230426
43665CB00010B/762